Gerard:
Another book to read while watching!
Happy Birthday
Love Anna
23-1-1974.

KITTY HAWK TO CONCORDE

JANE'S

100 Significant Aircraft

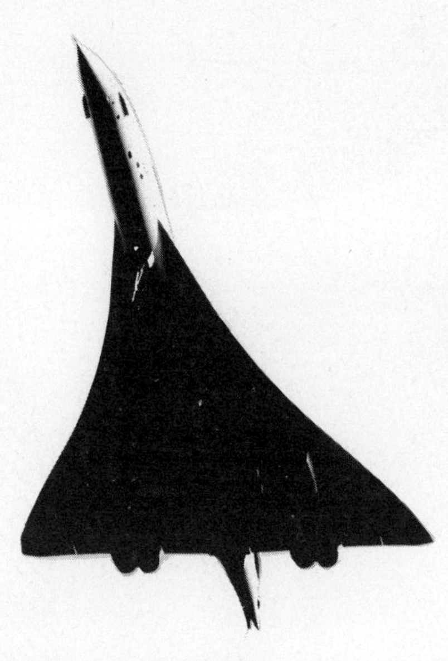

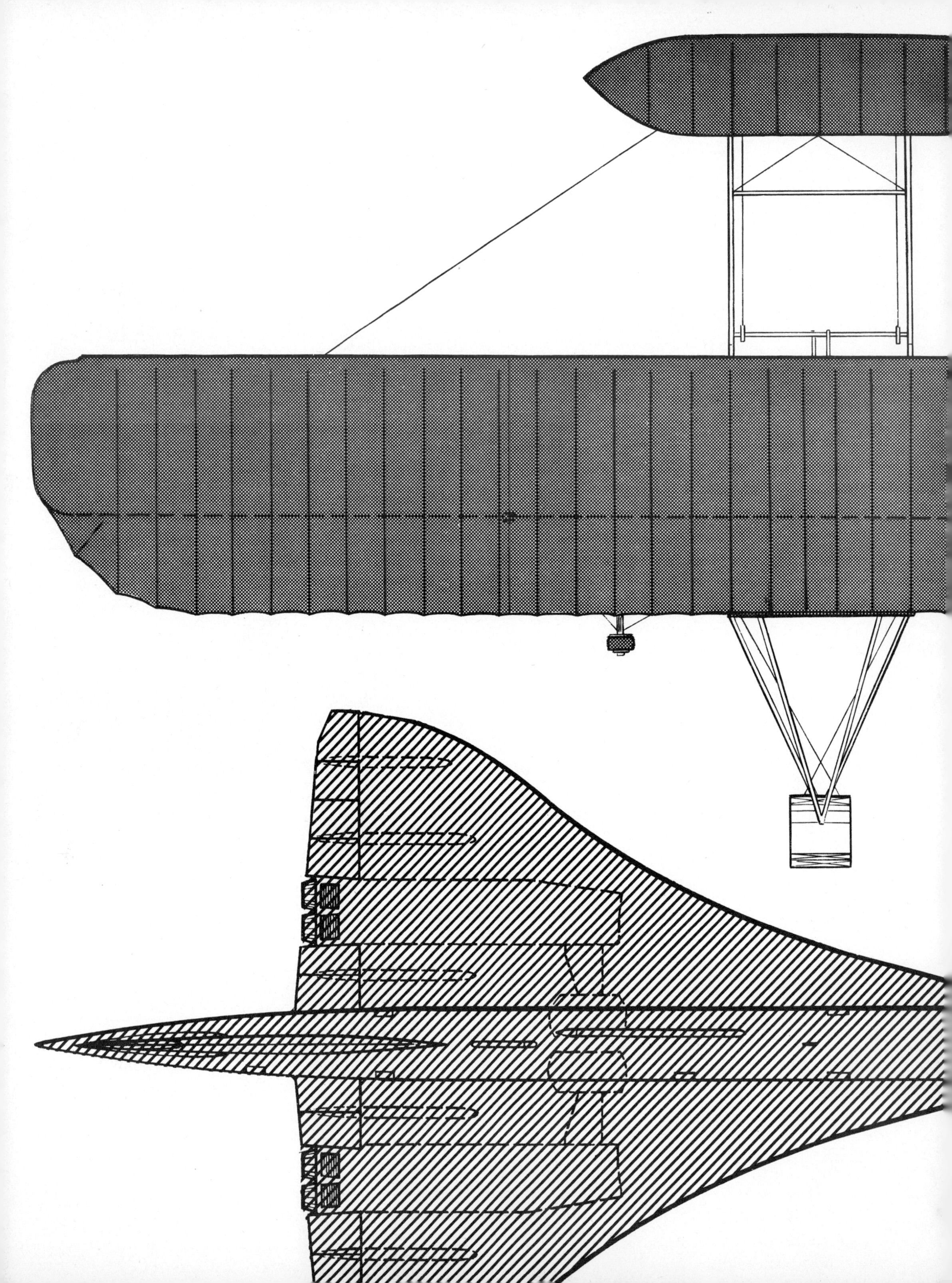

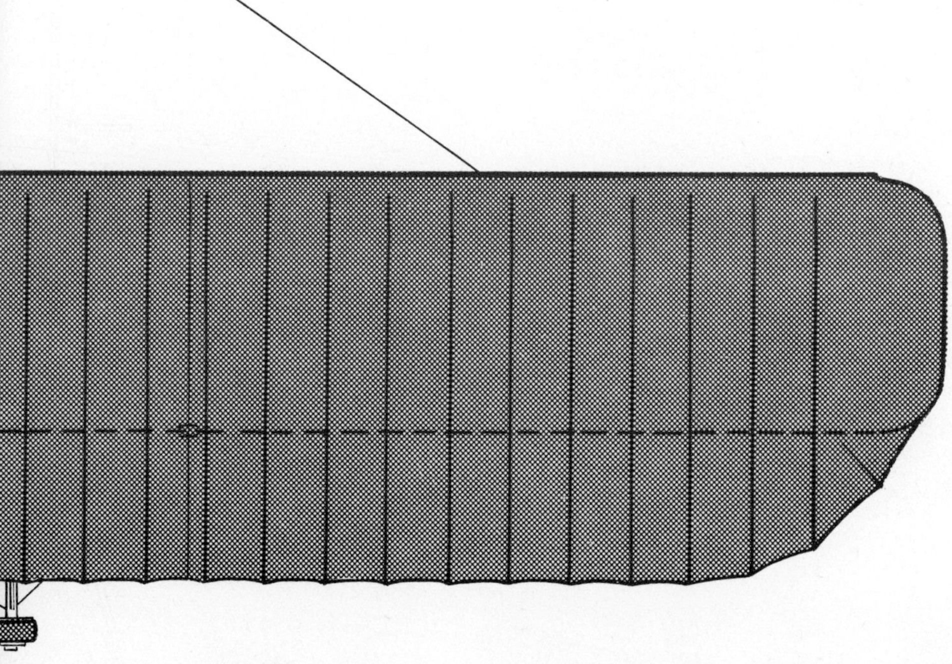

KITTY HAWK TO CONCORDE

JANE'S

100 Significant Aircraft

Compiled by H. F. KING, M.B.E.
Edited by JOHN W. R. TAYLOR, F.R.Hist.S., A.F.R.Ae.S., F.S.L.A.E.T.

SBN 354 000 802

First published in Great Britain for general circulation (with amendments) in 1970
by Jane's Yearbooks, Sampson Low Marston & Co. Ltd., 49/50 Poland Street, London W.1.
Previously published 1969 for limited circulation as *100 SIGNIFICANT AIRCRAFT*.

Printed and bound in Great Britain by Hazell Watson & Viney Ltd., Aylesbury, Bucks

KITTY HAWK TO CONCORDE

CONTENTS

One-hundred-year-old stereo pair of photographs, probably the oldest in existence showing a winged aircraft. Subject, Frederick Marriott's "Avitor" airship/aeroplane combination, flown in California in 1869. Marriott was associated with the British aeronautical pioneers Henson and Stringfellow and helped to found The Illustrated London News.

Mussel Manor, Shellbeach, Club House of the Aero Club of the United Kingdom, 4 May 1909; l to r, back row, J. D. F. Andrews, Oswald, Horace and Eustace Short, Frank McClean, Griffith Brewer, Frank Hedges Butler, Dr. W. J. S. Lockyer, Warwick Wright. Front row, J. T. C. Moore-Brabazon, Wilbur Wright, Orville Wright, the Hon. C. S. Rolls.

This historic photograph, showing the first men to fly a powered aeroplane in company with some of Britain's greatest pioneers, was taken during the Wright brothers' visit to the Aero Club's flying ground. They were able to see their biplane being produced under licence in the adjacent Short Brothers factory.

Charles Rolls, co-founder of the Rolls-Royce Company, made the first two-way crossing of the English Channel in a Wright biplane on 2 June 1910. Moore-Brabazon (later Lord Brabazon of Tara) made the first circular flight of one mile by a British aviator in an all-British machine on 30 October 1909, using one of the first aircraft of Short Brothers design.

FOREWORD

"Wouldn't it be interesting if all the great aircraft of history had been written up in *Jane's* style?" The chance remark set us thinking. . . . We were seeking some appropriate way in which to mark the Diamond Jubilee of *Jane's All the World's Aircraft*; what better than to choose one hundred of the most significant aircraft ever built and present them in a form as near as possible to that used for entries in the modern, highly-detailed *Jane's*?

First problem was to define what we meant by significant. For an aircraft to have been used for a single much-publicised flight, or to have achieved great success in war, was not enough. The "100 significant" types in this book had to represent milestones in the technical or operational development of the powered aircraft, introducing new design concepts or advancing performance to a spectacular degree.

Hurricane or Spitfire, B-10 or B-17, Concorde or Tu-144 . . . such choices were difficult to make and the end product will, inevitably, cause controversy. But the text explains why each particular type earned its place in our book, and we hope that the complete collection will give pleasure to our readers.

The text was written by H. F. King, former Editor of *Flight* magazine and one of aviation's most respected journalist/historians. His superbly detailed descriptions, resulting from years of research, are illustrated with hundreds of photographs and drawings which help to put the basic hundred aircraft into perspective *vis-à-vis* their contemporaries, many of which are also illustrated.

In its sixty years, *Jane's All the World's Aircraft* has recorded the whole development of the aeroplane from the time of Blériot's cross-Channel flight, in the year which witnessed the start of practical flying and the beginnings of the aircraft industry. It did the same for air cushion vehicles until they had progressed far enough to justify a *Jane's* of their own; and it has traced the whole history of rockets from V-2 to the first men on the Moon. In doing so, it has simply followed the pattern established by its Founder and first Editor, Fred T. Jane, who shared the faith of the early pioneers in the future of the flying machine and would have delighted in the stories of challenge, adventure and achievement recorded in these pages.

J. W. R. T.

WRIGHT FLYER

On 17 December 1903 the *Flyer*, a powered biplane designed and built by the brothers Wilbur and Orville Wright, of Dayton, Ohio, became the first heavier-than-air craft to make a sustained, controlled flight under its own power. The power plant, as well as the airframe, was of the brothers' own design and manufacture.

This most historic of all aeroplanes was not the first Wright aircraft to fly. In August 1899 the two men had built a biplane kite of 5 ft (1·52 m) span for tests with warping wings. Having established the possibilities of this control system they built and flew in 1900 a biplane glider of 17 ft (5·18 m) span, on which a few piloted flights were made in both kite and free-glider form. The tests of this No 1 glider were made at Kitty Hawk, North Carolina, and strengthened the brothers in their resolve to achieve powered flight once they had mastered the problems of control. In 1901 they built their No 2 glider, with a span of 22 ft (6·70 m). This had anhedral angle on the wings and a hip-cradle which could be swung right or left to operate the warping cables. Results were so unsatisfactory that the Wrights determined thenceforth to rely entirely upon their own investigations, instead of those of the German pioneer Otto Lilienthal. Their No 3 glider was built in August and September 1902, following the systematic testing of aerofoil sections in a wind tunnel and on a bicycle. The new glider had a span of 32 ft 1 in (9·78 m) and made nearly a thousand glides. A problem of "warp drag" arose, and was solved by replacing the two fixed fins by a single movable rudder, with its cables attached to the warp cradle. In March 1903 the brothers applied for a patent based on the latest form of their glider, and this was granted in 1906. Meanwhile, during the summer of 1903, they were building the *Flyer*. They also built their own four-cylinder water-cooled engine, and, after some remarkable and original research into blade design, the required propellers. Following an unsuccessful attempt by Wilbur on 14 December 1903, the first flights were achieved on the morning of 17 December. The location was Kill Devil Hill, Kitty Hawk, where the Wright Memorial Shaft now stands. The first flight of all was made by Orville. This was of twelve seconds duration and covered about 120 feet (36·60 m). Of the three flights which followed on that day the longest was 852 feet (259 m) lasting for 59 seconds.

Start of a glide, 10 October 1902, pilot Orville

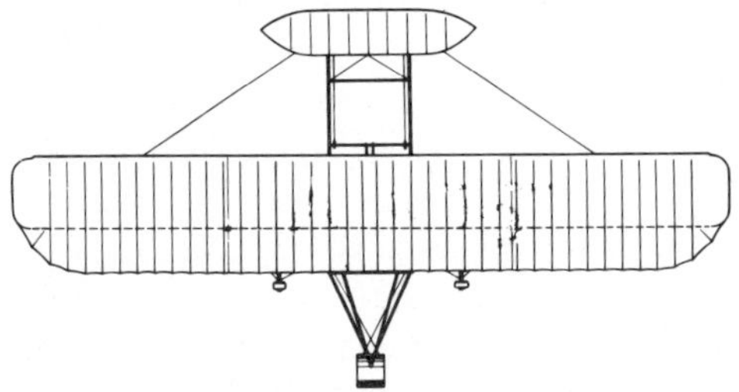

Balance for measuring lift

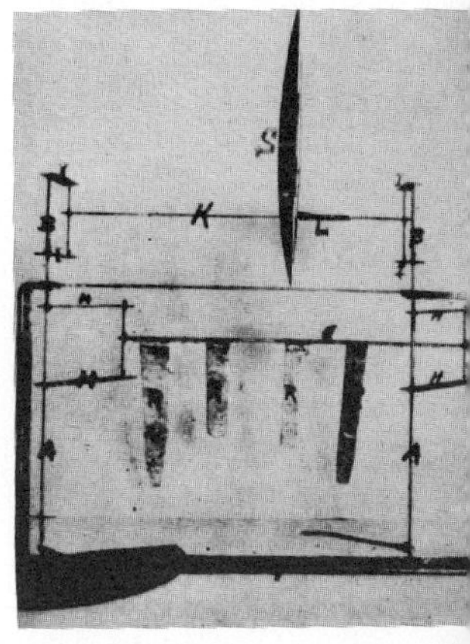

In 1928 the *Flyer* was sent to the Science Museum, South Kensington, London, where it remained until after Orville Wright's death in 1948. It was formally installed in the Smithsonian Institution, Washington, on 17 December 1948.

The "Flyer" making the first powered, sustained and controlled flight, on 17 December 1903. Orville Wright was piloting. He lived into the modern air age, dying in 1948. Wilbur Wright, seen on foot, made dramatic flights in Europe in 1908

With characteristic thoroughness the Wright brothers kept a careful record of their experiments and made numerous excellent photographs, among them this classic study of the "Flyer"

TYPE:

Single-engined experimental biplane.

WINGS:

Braced unstaggered biplane. Starboard wings 4 in (0·10 m) longer than port wings to provide additional lift for engine. Constant chord, but curving trailing-edge towards tips of warping sections. "Droop" about 10 in (0·25 m). Two spruce spars, 4 ft 1 in

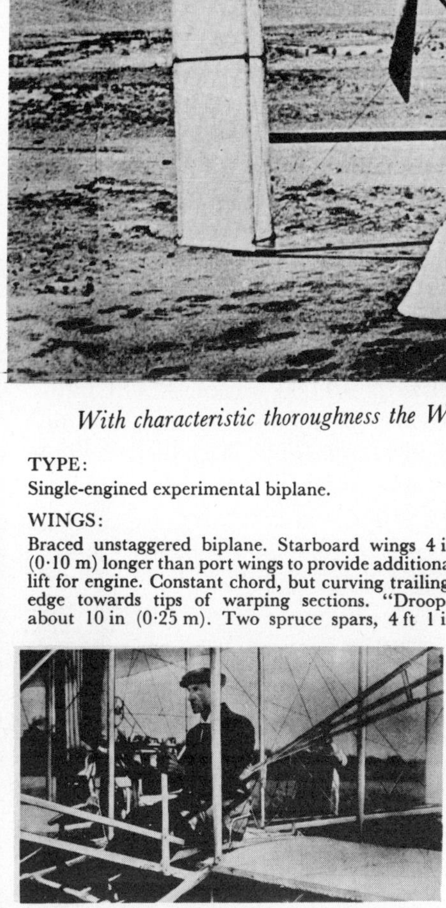

Wilbur Wright in developed "Flyer" (1908)

(1·24 m) apart, and two-piece reinforced ash ribs. Wings covered with unbleached muslin, cut on the bias and undoped. Nine pairs of interplane struts, forming eight wing bays, starboard inner bay carrying engine and corresponding port bay carrying pilot. Propeller mountings carried in bays immediately outboard. Warping sections for lateral control in two outermost bays. Metal eye at each end of each bracing strut slipped on to an open steel hook attached to spar. Lift and anti-lift wires attached to hook on one side and to strut end on other side. Front spars further strengthened by a spanwise horizontal wire attached to each intersection point of front bracing wires in each wing bay. Four rear inner bays similarly braced, but with additional wooden struts making up a strong four-bay truss outboard of which wings could be warped. No rear bracing in outboard bays. Outer portions of spars in these bays free to bend to allow helical warping.

CONTROL SECTIONS:

Braced biplane elevator structure carried on upturned tips of landing gear skids and braced to lower wing. Both surfaces warped by rotation of elevator control shaft running transversely between surfaces. Elevators actuated through this shaft by wooden lever forward of lower leading-edge, moved fore and aft by pilot's left hand. Double vertical rudder surfaces mounted on booms attached to upper wing and rear ends of skids. Wing warping and rudder control by sideways movement of pilot's torso.

LANDING GEAR:

Two skids, or runners, braced to upper and lower wings. Trolley for take-off, running on a 60-foot (18·29 m) monorail. Trolley made up of two adapted cycle wheel-hubs mounted fore-and-aft on wooden block. Skids rested on six-foot plank carried transversely by trolley. Third bicycle hub attached to forward cross-piece between skids to prevent nosing over on launching rail. Aircraft steadied when stationary by trestles under wing-tips. Trestles removed for take-off and wing steadied manually. Aircraft held in check for engine running by wire attached to monorail. Wire slipped by pilot for take-off.

The first public flight in a "Flyer" was made by Wilbur at Hunaudières

POWER PLANT:

Four-cylinder water-cooled engine of 12–16 hp. Ignition by low-tension magneto with make-and-break spark. Petrol fed to engine by gravity in constant stream and vapourised by running over large heated surface of water jacket. Engine mounted horizontally. Two pusher propellers behind wings, carried on shafts between wings. Shafts driven through cycle-chain transmission in tubes, one crossed for counter-rotation. Petrol tank under top wing. Vertical radiator. Weight of power plant, including magneto, radiator, tank, water, fuel, tubing and accessories, slightly over 200 lb (90·70 kg). Geared propellers of 8 ft 6 in (2·59 m) diameter. Sprocket ratio of transmission 23:8. Propellers made of three laminations of spruce.

ACCOMMODATION:

Pilot in prone face-down position in padded wooden cradle slightly above lower wing. Base of cradle moved on rubbing strip to protect wing fabric. Instruments: anemometer head and gauge, stop-watch.

DIMENSIONS:

Wing span 40 *ft* 4 *in* (12·29 *m*)
Chord 6 *ft* 6 *in* (1·98 *m*)
Gap 6 *ft* 2 *in* (1·88 *m*)
Length overall 21 *ft* 1 *in* (6·43 *m*)
Height overall 8 *ft* 0 *in* (2·44 *m*)

AREAS:

Wings, gross 510 *sq ft* (47·38 m^2)
Rudders, gross 21 *sq ft* (1·95 m^2)
Elevators, gross 48 *sq ft* (4·46 m^2)

WEIGHTS AND LOADINGS:

Weight empty 605 *lb* (274·42 *kg*)
Weight loaded 750 *lb* (340·20 *kg*)
Wing loading 1·47 *lb/sq ft* (7·17 *kg/m*²)

PERFORMANCE:

Writing in 1907 *Orville Wright declared: "In the flights of* 1903, *we carried* 63 *lbs per horsepower at a speed of* 30 *miles an hour". This statement is indicative not only of performance but of the actual engine power* (12 *hp approx.*). (63 *lb* = 28·6 *kg*; 30 *mph* = 48·30 *kmh.*)

Leon Bollée, with "Flyer" in tow

VOISIN BIPLANE

On the Voisin biplane in the upper picture Henri Farman flew the first closed-circuit kilometre (13 January 1908). The other machine was built for Leon Delagrange and is seen making its first flight (30 March 1907)

The Voisin brothers, Gabriel and Charles, established the classic type of pusher biplane, with forward elevator and rudder in the tail, at their factory at Billancourt, France, in 1907. The first example was completed by March. This was built for Henry Kapferer, and though it had a box-kite tail, it lacked the side-curtains on the wings as on the Voisin floatplane gliders built and tested in 1905. It never flew, and in June 1908 Orville Wright remarked: "From what Wilbur says in a letter just received, Kapferer is earnestly in favour of the formation of a company to take over our invention. From this I would infer that the French are not so sanguine of success as they were some months ago". The next example of the Voisin biplane was built for Leon Delagrange, and this made "hops" in March 1907. A similar machine was ordered by the French-domiciled Englishman Henri Farman in June 1907 and on 9 November of that year Farman covered a distance of 3,380 ft (1,030 m) in 1 min 14 sec. This was the first occasion on which an aeroplane other than the Wrights' remained airborne for more than a minute. The Farman machine was extensively modified during 1908/9 and achieved numerous flights of note, including a circuit of 1 km (actually about 1,500 m = 4,920 ft) in 1 min 28 sec on 13 January 1908. This gained for Farman the Deutsch-Archdeacon prize of 50,000 francs and, for the Voisins, medals testifying to the quality of their construction. A second aircraft of the same type was supplied to Delagrange in 1908, probably incorporating components of his first and also having modifications introduced by Farman (monoplane elevator, dihedral on wings, smaller tail). After a crash-landing, two side-curtains were fitted in the interests of lateral stability. Late in July 1908 these two side-curtains were removed and four were fitted to enclose the outer bay on each side. The gap was also increased.

In May 1908 Farman had installed two inner side-curtains, and on 6 July flew for 20 min 20 sec. This was the first occasion on which a European pilot had exceeded a ¼ hr flight duration, and Farman was awarded the Armengaud prize of 10,000 francs. About mid-August Farman fitted four side-curtains and in October incorporated ailerons, a notable departure, though anticipated in the USA by F. W. Baldwin's *White Wing*. With the machine in this form he accomplished the world's first true cross-country flight (27 km = 16·78 miles, Bouy to Rheims in 20 min).

TYPE:

Single-seat pusher biplane.

WINGS:

Box-kite type, with or without side-curtains. Single-surface wings with two spars, front spar forming leading-edge. Ash ribs. No lateral controls. Aircraft had to be turned in large circle to avoid stalling. By the end of 1907 Farman had given the wings dihedral angle for lateral stability. Later he covered the wings with Continental rubberised fabric instead of the original varnished silk, fitted four side-curtains and flap-type ailerons. Later still he added a third small wing above main cellule.

FUSELAGE:

Tail carried on twin booms. Ash construction with steel joints and several parts of steel tubing. Central chassis a single unit, carrying controls, engine, seat and frontal elevator at tip of fabric-covered nacelle. After first tests Farman exchanged original biplane elevators for monoplane surface.

TAIL UNIT:

Originally two-cell box-kite type with twin rudders hinged to outboard side-curtains. Farman installed single cell with central rudder. In November 1907 Farman reduced tailplane span from 19 ft 8 in (6·00 m) to 6 ft 11 in (2·10 m). Rudder controlled by wheel which also operated forward elevator. System comprised wheel on a sliding shaft. To operate elevator the wheel was pushed forward or pulled backward. The rudder was operated by rotating a cable-wound drum by turning the wheel.

LANDING GEAR:

Two-wheel main unit braced to nacelle. Coiled-spring shock-absorbers. One tail-wheel attached to each extremity of lower tailplane. Delagrange machine was at one stage fitted with floats for tests on the Lake d'Engien, the aircraft then being known as the Delagrange-Archdeacon. No flights were achieved in this form.

POWER PLANT:

Kapferer machine had 20–25 hp Buchet eight-cylinder engine. Delagrange machine had 50 hp Antoinette engine driving Voisin all-metal propeller of 6 ft 11 in (2·10 m) diameter at 1,000 rpm. In 1908 Farman installed 50 hp Renault in place of Antoinette, but restored Antoinette after one flight.

DIMENSIONS:

Wing span 33 *ft* 6 *in* (10·21 *m*)
Chord 6 *ft* 7 *in* (2·01 *m*)
Gap 5 *ft* 0 *in* (1·52 *m*)

WEIGHTS:

Original Farman machine was heavier than Delagrange and weighed about 1,145 *lb* (520 *kg*).

Taken in November 1907, this picture of Henri Farman's Voisin shows to advantage the leading-edge front spars, as retained on the later Voisin bombers (pages 30–31)

On this machine Paul Cornu made what is generally acknowledged as the first manned helicopter flight

CORNU HELICOPTER

Models of helicopters were constructed during the fifteenth century by Leonardo da Vinci in Italy and during the nineteenth century by Sir George Cayley in England, but not until the twentieth century did man-lifting aircraft of this type become a serious possibility by virtue of light petrol engines. There are two conflicting claims to the distinction of having achieved the first man-lifting flight of a rotary-winged aircraft, both concerning Frenchmen. The one now generally admitted is on behalf of Paul Cornu, whose twin-rotor helicopter of 1907 is contended to have been the first to make a "free" flight. This claim may not be strictly true, for the machine is said to have been tethered to prevent it rising to a dangerous height. The counter-claim advanced on behalf of Louis Breguet and Professor Richet is generally considered to be nullified by the fact that the craft was manually stabilised from the ground. Nevertheless, this latter flight has chronological priority, having been achieved on 29 September 1907, whereas the Cornu machine first lifted a man on 13 November in the same year.

The drawing of the Cornu helicopter below is from the classic book "The Helicopter Flying-Machine" by J. Robertson Porter (1911)

Reference to the experiments during 1909–10 by the Russian Igor Sikorsky will later be found under "Sikorsky VS-300", and it may be added that Breguet built a research helicopter of note in 1935. This, the Breguet-Dorand *Gyroplane Laboratoire*, had contra-rotating co-axial rotors. Other names which may be mentioned here in tribute to their work on helicopter development are those of Oehmichen, Isacco and Pescara in France, de Bothezat in the USA, Florine in Belgium, D'Ascanio in Italy and Asboth in Hungary.

Cornu's first working model (1906) used an old 2 hp Buchet engine, weighed 28 lb (12·70 kg) and easily lifted 35 lb (15·87 kg). The two rotors were driven by a single belt transmission, a scheme which was to prove disadvantageous in the full-size machine which was finished in August 1907.

TYPE:

Single-seat experimental helicopter.

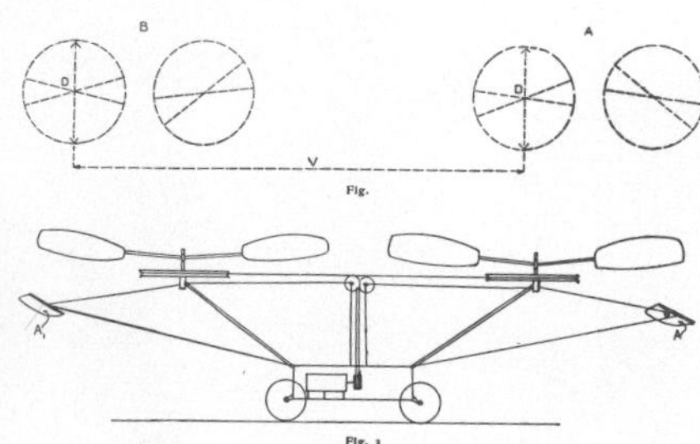

ROTOR SYSTEM:

Two rotors carried fore-and-aft on outriggers. Drive by endless belt, 66 ft 0 in (20·12 m) long and 4 in (102 mm) wide. Two-blade rotors, 19 ft 8 in (5·99 m) diameter. Ball bearings used throughout in driving mechanism. Rotors built up on steel pulleys, 5 ft 10 in (1·77 m) diameter, with aluminium hubs and tangential wire spokes. Pulleys carried driving belt and also formed a substantial anchorage for the rotor blades. Blades built of steel tubing and covered with rubber-proofed silk. Each blade 5 ft 10 in (1·77 m) long, tapering slightly towards tips. Max chord 35·4 in (90 cm). Angle of incidence adjustable. Each blade held in position by wire cables fixed to the sides of the pulleys and braced to the stem of the other blade by wires passing over a central support. Propulsion and steering effected by two planes, formed of flat tubing and covered with silk, placed immediately beneath the rotors. These planes were pivoted about a horizontal axis and were held in place by two supports fastened to a prolongation of the rotor shafts. Side-to-side movement of the planes and their angular setting controlled by two levers, placed to right and left of pilot. Horizontal propulsion was obtained by the reaction of the air thrown down by the rotors on to the planes, the angle of inclination of which, being controllable, could be made to alter the speed and direction of the helicopter. Direction also controlled by lateral movement of the planes.

FUSELAGE:

Main frame in the form of an open Vee, consisting of a single large-diameter steel tube, to which were brazed at intervals six "stars" of smaller tubing carrying the bracing wires. Whole frame braced by stranded wire cable, forming a girder of great strength. Pilot's seat and engine at centre of Vee.

LANDING GEAR:

Four wheels, independently mounted.

POWER PLANT:

Antoinette water-cooled engine of 24 hp. Water tank towards front of machine. Fuel tank, holding 1½ Imp gallons (6·82 litres) under pressure, behind pilot. Oil tank over engine. Accumulators and coil under pilot's seat.

PERFORMANCE:

Loaded with a sack of soot weighing 110 lb (50 kg), placed on the pilot's seat, the machine lifted clear of the ground on 27 September 1907, two days before the manned ascent of the Breguet-Richet. The total weight of the machine on this occasion was 518 lb (235 kg). On 13 November 1907 the machine lifted M. Cornu about 1 foot (0·30 m) from the ground, the total weight then being some 573 lb (260 kg). During this trial, which lasted for about 20 seconds, the rotors ran at 90 rpm and the engine at 900 rpm.

The Breguet-Richet helicopter (right) lifted a man on 29 September 1907 but was manually stabilised by four men, holding a pole under each rotor

BLERIOT XI

The first crossing of the English Channel by a heavier-than-air craft was made on 25 July 1909 by the French designer/constructor/pilot Louis Blériot, who thus won a prize of £1,000 offered by the *Daily Mail* newspaper. This courageous and historic crossing, which had an incalculable influence on public thought and opinion, had been preceded on 19 July by an unsuccessful attempt by Hubert Latham in an Antoinette.

Although research in recent times has indicated that the Blériot XI monoplane which accomplished the Channel flight was mainly designed by Raymond Saulnier, the contribution of Louis Blériot to the advancement of aeronautics was very great. Co-operating with Ernest Archdeacon and Gabriel Voisin in 1905 this maker of automobile lamps constructed a biplane glider on floats, but thereafter concentrated on machines of monoplane type. Having tried the tail-first and Langley-type tandem layouts he built his Type VII, the true ancestor of the modern tractor monoplane, and one of astonishingly clean aerodynamic design. In the aeronautical section of the *Salon d'Automobile* in December 1908 Blériot exhibited the monoplanes Types IX and XI and the biplane Type X. The first flight of the Type XI was in January 1909, the engine then being a 30 hp 7-cylinder R.E.P., driving an inefficient four-blade propeller. During April and May the aircraft was modified to take a 3-cylinder Anzani engine, driving a two-blade Chauvière propeller. A central fin, originally fitted, was removed, the rudder was enlarged and deepened, and the "elevons" at the ends of the tailplane were arranged to function solely as elevators, lateral control being achieved solely by wing warping.

The cross-Channel flight on 25 July 1909 began at 4.41 am at Les Baraques, near Calais, and ended in Northfall Meadow, by Dover Castle at 5.17½ am. The distance was about 23½ miles. The actual aircraft used is now preserved in the Paris *Conservatoire des Arts et Métiers*. Later versions were very numerous.

Louis Blériot greets his wife from the quay at Dover after making the first crossing of the English Channel in an aeroplane. A balloon had crossed in 1785

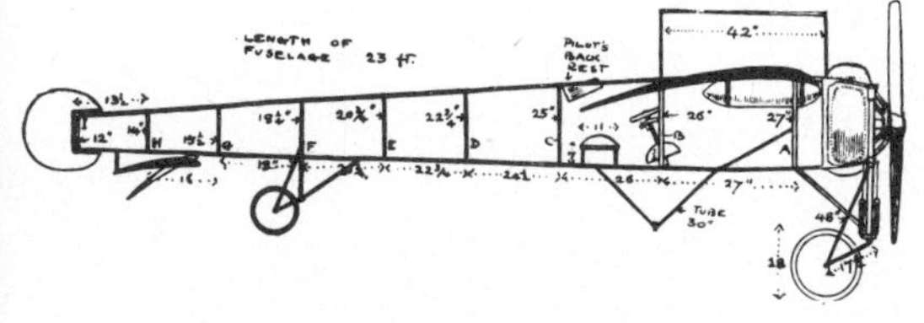

Contemporary dimensional sketch

TYPE:
Single-seat monoplane.

WINGS:
High-wing wire-braced monoplane. Constant chord, curved tips. Each panel readily detachable. Two ash spars. Some ribs of wood, others of aluminium strip, reinforced in front by a strip of wood. Main rib at root of each wing entirely of wood, having built-up channel section. Wings double-surfaced and covered with waterproof Continental fabric. Front spar projected from wing root and spigoted into socket formed in a rectangular aluminium member secured to fuselage. Joint secured by bolts. Rear spar bolted to aluminium brackets. One bracing cable above wing on each side from front spar to the foremost of two fore-and-aft braced tubular-steel inverted-Vee kingposts. Two bracing cables below wing on each side, anchored to front landing gear strut. Tubular-steel pylon for warping cables below

A castoring landing gear was fitted

fuselage. Warping accomplished by Blériot *cloche* system (Patent No 21497 of 1908). Vertical control column with fixed horizontal wheel at top and on universal joint at base. Column passed through inverted cup-shaped fitting (*cloche*) and was attached rigidly to this fitting. Four cables were also attached to the *cloche*, two running down over pulleys aft to elevators and two to a rocker arm, to the pivot of which were fixed a disc (forward) and a pulley (aft). Around the disc were attached the main positive-warping cables which pulled the outboard trailing-

The cross-channel Blériot on display after its historic flight in the Grand Palais, Paris, scene of many great aeronautical exhibitions in later years (see also pages 82–83). The stand was a special one. Blériot's own display is seen at right

The Blériot XI ("Channel Type" or "Type Onze") was a favourite sporting mount and was frequently modified

edge portions of the wings down on one side. Running free under the pulley was a continuous inner bracing wire, attached to each wing between the attachment of the warping cable and the fuselage. This wire adjusted itself to the degree of warp exerted by the pilot. To bank to port the column was rocked to port, thus pulling down the starboard trailing-edge and raising the port trailing-edge. The "passive" warping cable connecting the upper surfaces of the trailing-edge, and which automatically pulled up one wing when the other was lowered, passed over the second of the kingposts mentioned.

FUSELAGE:

Square section at front, tapering aft of cockpit to knife-edge at sternpost. Four ash longerons. Vertical and transverse struts lightly mortised into longerons. Diagonal wire bracing, with tensioners, in each bay. Cross-Channel machine had fabric covering over two bays aft of cockpit section. Otherwise uncovered.

TAIL UNIT:

Braced tailplane attached below bottom longerons by two channel-section aluminium clips bolted to longerons. Bracket extensions of clips carried single main spar, constituting a steel tube and allowing tailplane incidence to be adjusted on the ground. Lug at trailing-edge drilled with holes so that incidence could be set with some precision. Two bracing struts at each side, foremost from top longerons to tips of tailplane at spar, rearmost from vertical struts to outboard tips of trailing-edge. Two elevators outboard of tailplane tips, actuated from front and back of *cloche*. Vertical rudder with balance portion above fuselage, actuated from rudder bar.

LANDING GEAR:

Castoring type. Two main wheel assemblies on outriggers at front of fuselage. Assemblies attached to two tubular steel columns, braced together by two wooden beams, upon one of which the front of the fuselage rested. This beam was stayed to the heads of the steel column by a steel strap. The upper beam was merely a bracing strut between the columns. The columns themselves were braced to the longerons, but the forks which carried the wheels were hinged, as well as pivoted, to the lower ends of the columns and the wheel hubs were stayed independently to sliding collars. These collars rode on a portion of the upper ends of the columns, which were turned smooth to receive them. The collars were anchored to the lower ends of the columns by a pair of very strong elastic bands, these constituting the main suspension. Inside the columns were springs for returning the wheels to their normal positions after deflection to one side or another. The connection between the springs and the wheel brackets was by a single flexible wire, working over a swivelling pulley. A third, smaller, wheel was carried in an assembly forward of the tail.

POWER PLANT:

One Anzani 3-cylinder air-cooled "fan type" (semi-radial) piston engine of 22/25 hp. Bore and stroke 105 mm × 120 mm. Max rpm 1,400. Engine attached by four channel-section steel brackets bolted to face of crankcase and drilled for lightness. Chauvière two-blade walnut propeller, 6 ft 6 in (1·98 m) diameter. Throttle and ignition controls on pilot's control column.

EQUIPMENT:

Cross-Channel machine carried a cylindrical air-bag in the fuselage behind the cockpit in case of forced descent.

DIMENSIONS:

Wing span 25 *ft* 7 *in* (7·80 *m*)
Wing chord 6 *ft* 7 *in* (2·00 *m*)
Wing area 150 *sq ft* (13·93 m^2)
Overall length 26 *ft* 3 *in* (8·00 *m*)

WEIGHTS:

Weight empty 463 *lb* (210 *kg*)
Weight loaded 661 *lb* (300 *kg*)

PERFORMANCE:

Speed 36 *mph* (58 *kmh*)

The flotation bag was not required

GOUPY II

The French Goupy II biplane, first flown in March 1909, was the first notable example of the classic type of tractor biplane which, within a few years, established an ascendancy over the classic pusher type which developed from the 1907 Voisin. The Goupy II had a predecessor of 1908, a tractor triplane called Goupy I. This had a distinction of its own, being the first full-scale triplane to fly. It was built for Ambroise Goupy at the Voisin establishment and made four short flights between 5 September and 7 December 1908. This triplane weighed 1,100 lb (500 kg), had side curtains at the wing tips, a biplane box-kite tail and was powered by a 50 hp Renault engine.

The Goupy II biplane was built by Blériot, and exhibited a number of features bearing the Blériot stamp, notably the castoring undercarriage. It was not strictly the first tractor biplane, for in 1905 F. Ferber had made a "power glide" on a biplane glider in which he had fitted a 12 hp Peugeot engine driving a tractor propeller, and in 1907 a Monsieur de Pischoff had built a tractor biplane without the forward elevator as used by Ferber. Ferber was, in fact, experimenting with a tractor biplane as early as 1903, but this was slung on a whirling arm. The staggering of the biplane wings of the Goupy machine had been antedated in a striking manner by a glider built in England during 1908 by Lt. Porte and Lt. Pirie, both of the Royal Navy. This glider crashed during early trials.

Collaborating with Ambroise Goupy in his biplane venture was Mario Calderara, who was one of Wilbur Wright's first two Italian pupils. The first flight was on 9 March at Buc. After 1909 the tractor biplane type of aircraft was developed with particular success by Louis Breguet in France and A. V. Roe in England. In developed forms Goupy biplanes themselves achieved a measure of success, but this was not sustained.

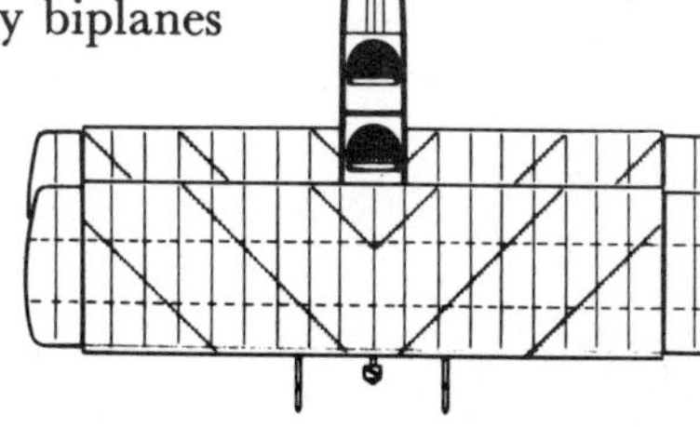

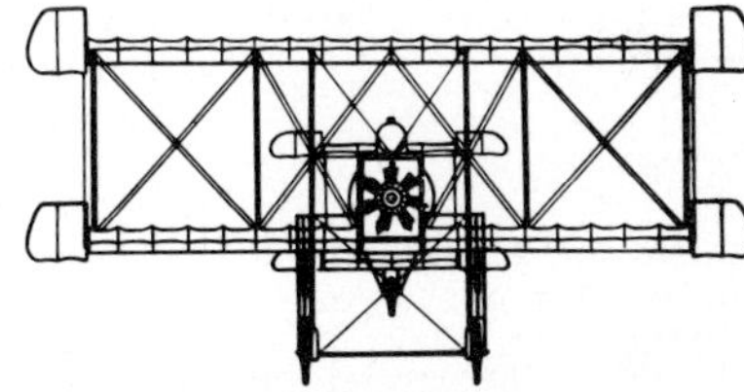

TYPE:
Single-seat biplane.

WINGS:
Three-bay biplane of very short span and having pronounced positive stagger. Wings double-surfaced. Lateral control at first by wing warping, but pivoted wing-tip ailerons were later fitted on all four wings.

FUSELAGE:
Open Blériot type.

TAIL UNIT:
Staggered biplane type, with elevators at tips of upper and lower planes, acting as on contemporary Blériot monoplanes. Original machine had two additional elevators forward of wings. Single rudder. Control by Blériot *cloche* system.

LANDING GEAR:
Blériot castoring type main gear, with third wheel under fuselage forward of tail.

POWER PLANT:
R.E.P. engine of 24 hp, driving two-blade tractor propeller.

DIMENSIONS:
Wing span 20 *ft* 0 *in* (6·09 *m*)
Length overall 23 *ft* 0 *in* (7·01 *m*)
Wing area 236·8 *sq ft* (22 *m*²)

WEIGHT:
Weight loaded 550–640 *lb* (250–290 *kg*)

The biplane wings and tractor propeller pioneered by the Goupy II were features exploited by Louis Breguet and A. V. Roe

SANTOS-DUMONT DEMOISELLE

The prototype above was known to its designer/pilot Alberto Santos-Dumont as "No 19"

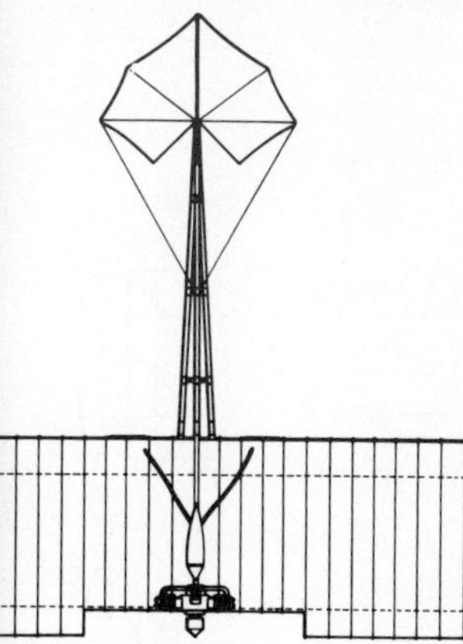

The name Demoiselle, meaning in this instance dragonfly, was conferred on a family of very small aeroplanes built in France by the Brazilian Alberto Santos-Dumont and generally considered to date from 1909, though having earlier origins. This type was the world's first "light aeroplane". The first of the Demoiselle family was called by Santos-Dumont (who had made the first officially observed powered flight in Europe on 12 November 1906) his *No 19*, and was built in 1907. Its wing span was 16 ft 5 in (5 m) and it weighed 242 lb (110 kg). A two-cylinder Dutheil-Chalmers horizontally-opposed engine of 20 hp was mounted on the wing and drove a two-blade metal propeller. The cruciform tail unit was carried on a bamboo pole. This unit comprised an elevator-cum-rudder with a separate elevator working in conjunction in front. The pilot sat beneath the wing and controlled the machine laterally by rocking himself from side to side. Late in 1907 *No 19* made three flights, of 623 ft (190 m), 656 ft (200 m) and 492 ft (150 m) respectively.

In 1908 a developed version called *No 19-bis*, was built, but apparently never flew. This had a 24 hp Antoinette engine mounted between the wheels and driving the two-blade propeller by means of a belt. The *No 20*, of more robust construction, and having the engine on the wing as in *No 19*, formed the basis for subsequent aircraft of the type and is now preserved in the Paris *Musée de l'Air*. This version made its first flight at Issy on 6 March 1909.

The Demoiselle may justifiably be regarded as the world's first "home-built" aircraft, in the sense that Santos-Dumont retained no rights to its design, giving it freely to anyone who chose to build a machine of the type. Examples were, in fact, acquired for sporting purposes, but the vogue was short-lived by reason of the Demoiselle's somewhat difficult flying characteristics and steep gliding angle.

The following description applies to the 1909 type.

TYPE:
Single-seat sporting monoplane.

WINGS:
Braced monoplane structure in two halves. Two ash spars of irregular section, deepest some distance outboard, where dihedral began to lessen. Front spar about 9 in (23 cm) behind leading-edge, rear spar about 12 in (33 cm) forward of trailing-edge. Bamboo ribs beneath spars. Wings double-surfaced and covered with silk. Light bamboo corner-stays at tips obviated heavy end-ribs. Internal wire bracing but external bracing below wing only. Outer trailing-edges free to warp for lateral control. Leading-edge cut back to accommodate propeller.

FUSELAGE:
Main frame formed by three bamboo poles, about 2 in (5 cm) diameter at thickest point, arranged two at lower level, one central above. Interconnecting steel struts of oval section. All knots in bamboo smoothed down and binding added between knots to prevent splitting. Diagonal wires with tighteners. Main frame divided aft of wing trailing-edges for dismantling. Brass sockets fitted at divisions.

TAIL UNIT:
Cruciform type, fitted at end of main frame on universal joint of ball-and-socket type. Tail surfaces movable up and down for elevating, sideways for steering. Control by steel wires carried over vertical member about 3 ft (0·91 m) forward of tail. This member curved at lower end to form skid, in conjunction with spring attached to lowest point of tail unit. Tail surfaces built up on bamboo ribs. No camber.

LANDING GEAR:
Two main wheels, with axle, braced to main frame and wings. Sprung tail-wheel.

POWER PLANT:
Two-cylinder horizontally opposed Darracq water-cooled engine of about 30 hp. Weight about 110 lb (49·89 kg). Engine mounted above wing on upper member of main frame, with additional supports between cylinder heads and front spars. Two-blade wooden tractor propeller, about 6 ft 6 in (2·00 m) diameter. Brass petrol tank above centre-line, carburettor below engine. Special type of radiator, in two sections. Each section fitted spanwise under inner wings, running full chord. About 100 very small copper tubes in each element.

ACCOMMODATION:
Pilot seated under wing on sheet of canvas stretched between two lower main bamboo members. Switch for ignition system on elevator lever. This lever lay close to the pilot's right hand. Small hand-wheel near pilot's left hand for directional steering. Third lever against pilot's back for wing warping. Leaning to one side caused rear edge on opposite side to flex down. Springs in all control wires to maintain them taut.

DIMENSIONS:
Wing span 18 *ft* 0 *in* (5·49 *m*)
Chord 6 *ft* 5 *in* (1·96 *m*)
Length overall 20 *ft* 0 *in* (6·09 *m*)

WEIGHT:
Weight loaded 242 *lb* (109·77 *kg*)

The adventurous Brazilian appears at right by the tail of a later model

DUNNE D.5

The remarkable tailless gliders and powered aeroplanes built by the Englishman J. W. Dunne (internationally known for his book *An Experiment with Time*) have seldom been accorded their rightful place in aeronautical history; for although tailless aircraft have never achieved general adoption their possibilities have long appeared attractive. The Westland-Hill Pterodactyl series of the 1920s and 1930s and the tailless Northrop and Armstrong Whitworth types of more recent years were notable, if unfruitful, technical achievements.

In his earliest experiments Dunne was preoccupied with the attainment of inherent stability, his inspiration being the winged seed of the Zanonia, a Javanese climbing plant. A tailless glider of Dunne's design was built for the War Office in 1907 and tested secretly in Scotland. Powered flight was attempted in 1908 and Dunne succeeded in becoming airborne. Development during 1909 led to the Dunne D.5, which was flying at Eastchurch in 1910, and in 1912 the D.8 made a notable flight from Eastchurch to Paris. The D.5 is the subject of the following description.

TYPE:
Tailless biplane.

WINGS:
Swept-back biplane wings. Parallel chord, no stagger. Narrowing gap along leading-edge towards tip. Varying camber throughout, but rear surfaces flat aft of a line drawn from rear wing-tips to front of apex formed by wings. Maximum camber towards tips, minimum inboard. Wings double-surfaced. Two main spars of wood and numerous ribs. Inter-plane struts attached by steel ferrule joints of type adopted by Short Brothers, who built the aircraft. Vertical side-curtains between wings at tips. Hinged tip portions for lateral control. Tip surfaces coupled by wires to two levers, one on each side of pilot, for independent or simultaneous use as rudders or elevators.

FUSELAGE:
Short nacelle on bottom wing housing pilot, controls and power plant. Nacelle very carefully designed and constructed as Dunne considered not only streamlining but the possible effect of disturbed flow on the lifting qualities and stability of the wings. Nacelle of lattice-work and strip-steel construction, knife-edged at bow and stern.

LANDING GEAR:
Main twin-wheel assembly attached to nacelle. Principal members in tension. Wheels capable of independent movement. Rear wheel and skid. Skids under wing-tips.

POWER PLANT:
One 50 hp Green four-cylinder water-cooled engine mounted in nacelle and driving two two-blade wooden propellers through transmissions carried on a lateral beam which also supported propellers at its extremities. Propeller diameter 7 ft 0 in (2·13 m). Two vertical outboard radiators.

ACCOMMODATION:
Pilot's seat at forward end of nacelle.

DIMENSIONS:
Wing span 46 *ft* 0 *in* (14·02 *m*)
Wing chord 6 *ft* 0 *in* (1·83 *m*)
Length of nacelle 18 *ft* 0 *in* (5·48 *m*)
Gross wing area 527 *sq ft* (48·96 m^2)

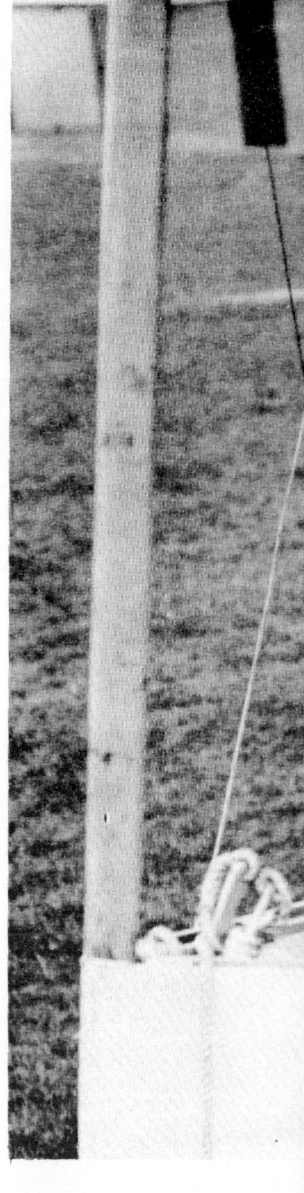

Water-cooled and air-cooled engines were fitted to the Dunne aircraft. The British Green four-cylinder water-cooled unit is seen in the D.5 behind the pilot and at right is the Dunne D.8 with French air-cooled Gnome rotary. Aircraft to Dunne's basic designs were built in the USA

A man of uncommon intellect, J. W. Dunne was experimenting, in conditions of great secrecy, with a glider in 1907 and a powered aircraft in 1908, but left testimony with the Science Museum authorities that the 1908 machine was "more of a hopper than a flier"

CURTISS HYDRO-AEROPLANE

The man best-known in aeronautical history as the designer, constructor and pilot of pioneer floatplanes and flying boats is the American Glenn Curtiss; but acknowledgement of his earliest work must be prefaced with some observations concerning even remoter experiments. A patent for an amphibious aircraft having retractable wheels was granted to the Frenchman Alphonse Pénaud in 1876, and during 1898/99 the Austrian Wilhelm Kress built what Octave Chanute who saw the machine in 1903, described to Wilbur Wright as a "flying boat". This remarkable aircraft was the first full-size aeroplane to have a petrol engine, but never succeeded in leaving the water. The Australian Lawrence Hargrave was among other early exponents of aeronautical experiments from water and the first manned flight from that element was made by Gabriel Voisin on 6 June 1905, using a Voisin-Archdeacon float glider of box-kite type, towed from the River Seine by a motor boat. The first powered flight from water was made by Voisin's friend Henri Fabre on 28 March 1910, using a remarkable machine having three "lifting" floats of patented form, and of a type later used by Voisin on the first successful amphibious aircraft.

Glenn Curtiss was experimenting with a floatplane version of his *June Bug* at the end of 1908, but this was over two years before he finally succeeded in taking off from water, using the aircraft later described. The date was 26 January 1911. After the initial flight the machine was frequently and extensively altered, at one stage having a third wing and at another retractable wheels. (For later instances of Curtiss' work and influence see Curtiss NC-4 and Felixstowe-Porte F.2A.)

TYPE:
Experimental floatplane.

WINGS:
Braced biplane structure. Wooden construction, using ash and spruce. Bracing by cables and wires. Baldwin rubber-silk covering, tacked to ribs and laced. Two bays on each side, outboard of centre bay. Outermost pair of struts at extreme tips of wings. Interplane ailerons carried on two rear struts.

FUSELAGE:
Wooden boom structure, supported at front by top and bottom wings, carrying tailplane with rear elevator attached. Booms parallel in plan, converging to point in side elevation. Bracing by struts and wires. Forward elevator (biplane and monoplane types both tried) carried on similar structure and working in concert with rear elevator. Vertical triangular surface above front elevator attached to long bamboo pole for fore-and-aft control.

LANDING GEAR:
Single main float under wing. Width 6 ft 1 in (1·85 m), length 7 ft 1 in (2·16 m), depth 1 ft 4 in (0·41 m). Float set at slight angle of incidence and braced to pick-up points of inner pair of interplane struts. Sides of float extended below bottom to act as runners for protection of float when coming into contact with ground before or after launching. Sheet-steel construction over wooden framework. When aircraft was at rest about 3 in (7·60 cm) of main float remained above surface. Main float supported aircraft on water above a speed of about 30 mph (48 kmh). Smaller forward float, approximating in shape to main float. Width 4 ft 4 in (1·32 m), length 1 ft 6 in (0·46 m) max depth 1 ft 4 in (0·41 m). Above the level of this float, and a little forward, was a canvas "water shield", 6 ft (1·83 m) wide and 2 ft (0·61 m) deep, set at an angle of 45° to protect the pilot and power plant from spray and to serve as an additional safeguard against inadvertent diving. Wooden hydrofoil, to aid in lifting forward part of aircraft at take-off, under extreme forward end of front framework, about 1 ft (0·30 m) below level of forward float. Hydrofoil dimensions: width 6 ft (1·83 m), chord 8 in (0·20 m), max thickness 1½ in (3·80 cm), incidence about 25°. Air bags under wing-tips for lateral stability. In February 1911 a single scow-shaped float was fitted centrally in place of the elaborate gear described. This float at one stage carried the elevator at its forward end.

POWER PLANT:
Curtiss water-cooled engine mounted between wings and driving two-blade wooden propeller.

ACCOMMODATION:
Pilot seated over leading-edge of lower wing, with wheel control.

DIMENSIONS:
Wing span 26 *ft* 0 *in* (7·92 *m*)
Chord 4 *ft* 9 *in* (1·45 *m*)

PERFORMANCE:
Max speed 50–55 *mph* (80–88 *kmh*)

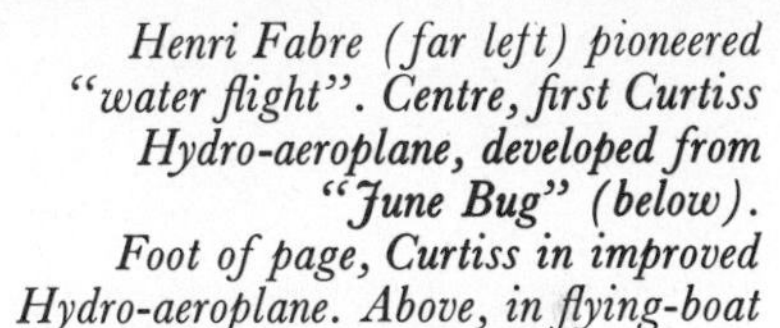

Henri Fabre (far left) pioneered "water flight". Centre, first Curtiss Hydro-aeroplane, developed from "June Bug" (below). Foot of page, Curtiss in improved Hydro-aeroplane. Above, in flying-boat

SHORT TRIPLE TWIN

Although it is sometimes claimed that the Short brothers Oswald, Horace and Eustace established the world's first aircraft company the distinction appears to belong more rightfully to the Voisin brothers (1905). Nevertheless, the Short company dates from 1908, and in the following year it received the first true "production" contract, to build Wright biplanes. To the Shorts, moreover, credit is due for numerous technical advances, and not the least of these followed the granting to the brothers in 1911 of patents covering the installation in aircraft of multiple engines. The first practical expression of the ideas propounded was the Triple Twin biplane, constructed towards the end of 1911. Although this was not the first multi-engined aircraft, having been preceded by the twin-engined machines of Maxim and Ader, among others, it was the first to exploit the twin-engine formula in the interests of safety, for it was able to maintain height with either of its two Gnome engines throttled back. The first flight was on 18 September 1911, when Frank McLean, for whom the machine was built, made a solo trip. This was followed by eight circuits of Eastchurch airfield with Commander C. R. Samson as passenger, and during the course of these circuits each engine in turn was throttled back.

The Triple Twin was followed in October 1911 by the Tandem Twin, a generally similar machine, but having the front engine directly coupled to a propeller.

The Tandem Twin, which followed a few weeks after the Triple Twin, was another essay in power plant arrangement

The Triple Twin originally had wings of equal span, but upper extensions were later added

TYPE:

Twin-engined biplane.

WINGS:

Braced biplane wings of parallel chord and equal span. Top wing later extended to 50 ft (15·24 m). Central bay with elevator attachments (frontal), then outboard on each side, one narrow bay, picking up landing gear attachments, one broad bay, with tractor propeller carried at outer struts, and one shorter bay, with outermost struts at extreme tip. Ailerons on all four wings. Wings of great strength and double-surfaced. At each rib station, picking up vertical bracing struts, there was a special horizontal strut joining the front and rear spars and visual externally. This form of construction had been used on previous Short machines and was adopted in the interests of tautness, there being no tighteners in the wire bracing. Rear spar passed over ribs and enclosed in fabric pockets. Front spar attached to ribs with metal plates at top and bottom. Interplane struts attached by U-bolts, passed through two small side plates, bolted in turn to the ferrule of the strut. Side plates made erection and dismantling easier and prevented the possibility of a strut "jumping".

A propeller mounted forward of its engine was a feature of the Triple Twin

FUSELAGE:

Nacelle on lower wing, seating pilot and passenger side-by-side, following racing-car practice. Dual control. The outriggers for the forward elevator, instead of being attached at the outboard struts of the second wing-bracing bay, in line with the tail booms (as was common at the period), were attached to the narrowly separated struts of the centre bay. The outriggers were thus only 3 ft 6 in (1·07 m) apart, necessitating slotting of the elevator, as the outriggers could not be attached to the ends of the elevator as usual.

TAIL UNIT:

Monoplane type, with tailplane on top rear pair of outriggers and triple rudders beneath.

LANDING GEAR:

Of exceptional strength. Two wheels and two skids. Wheels carried at ends of long "dead" axle, triangulated with kingposts at each end. End of one kingpost connected by distance piece to rear vertical strut carrying skid, and axle further anchored by two wires acting as radius rods from front portion of skid. Wheels thus allowed vertical motion, and stress largely removed from axle itself. Each skid strengthened by wire bracing and kingpost. Two sprung tail-skids.

POWER PLANT:

Two 50 hp Gnome rotary air-cooled engines mounted in tandem in nacelle, one forward of cockpit and one behind, and rotating in opposite directions. Forward engine driving two tractor propellers carried on outboard interplane struts. Two-chain pinions attached in place of ordinary airscrew on pilot's side of aluminium shield fitted over engine, the chaincases emerging from the sides of the nacelle. Chains of Renold type. Port chain crossed to obtain counter-rotation. Front propellers driven through gear reduction of 2:1. Rear propeller driven direct by second engine. Diameter of propellers 8 ft 6 in (2·59 m). Pitch of tractor propellers 8 ft 6 in (2·59 m), pitch of rear propeller 4 ft 8 in (1·42 m). Two fuel tanks between interplane struts.

ACCOMMODATION:

Pilot and passenger side-by-side, with two complete sets of controls. Control columns rocked backwards and forwards for elevator control, wheel at top of each column for aileron control, foot-bars for rudder control. Instrument panel in front of pilot's seat, with engine cut-out switches and rpm indicators.

DIMENSIONS:

Wing span 34 *ft* 0 *in* (10·36 *m*)
Wing chord 6 *ft* 6 *in* (1·98 *m*)
Wing gap 6 *ft* 4 *in* (1·93 *m*)
Length overall 45 *ft* 0 *in* (13·71 *m*)

WEIGHTS:

Weight empty 1,800 *lb* (816 *kg*)
Weight loaded 2,100 *lb* (953 *kg*)

PERFORMANCE:

Estimated speed 35–55 *mph* (56–88 *kmh*)

SIKORSKY GRAND

The Sikorsky biplane built in Russia during 1912/13 was officially named *Russian Knight* but became generally known as the *Grand* by reason of its great size. With its wing span of 92 ft (28·00 m) it was by far the largest heavier-than-air craft built up to that time. It was the first four-engined aircraft to fly and the first to have a passenger cabin.

The idea of such an aircraft occurred to the designer Igor Sikorsky towards the end of 1911 and financial support was secured in September 1912. By November of that year construction was well advanced. Numerous difficulties were encountered. For example, there were no suitable aircraft wheels, and a landing gear had to be devised using sixteen wheels of a type available. Sikorsky was warned that no aircraft could be flown from an enclosed cabin because the pilot would not be able to recognise fully and quickly any change from normal flying attitude. In an open cockpit this could be judged from the intensity and direction of the airstream.

The first flight, of less than ten minutes duration, took place on 13 May 1913. A mechanic stood on the open "bridge", or balcony, ahead of the cabin, Sikorsky was at the controls, and there was a third crew-man in the cabin who was to move forward or aft if the aircraft proved nose- or tail-heavy. On 2 August 1913, after rearrangement of the engines, a flight of 1 hr 54 min was made with eight persons aboard. After being damaged on the ground by an engine falling from a crashing aircraft the *Grand* was dismantled. Fifty-three flights had been made with no serious trouble.

In January 1914 an improved type, named *Ilia Mourometz*, was flown. This was the first of about seventy very large aircraft of the same general type.

Igor Sikorsky ranks as one of the few great designers who not only schemed their aircraft but tested them also. He is seen in the "Grand" (figure at right) with his crew

TYPE:

Four-engined passenger-carrying biplane with enclosed cabin.

WINGS:

Biplane wings of constant chord and high aspect ratio, unstaggered. Wooden construction, with fabric covering and wire bracing. Five sets of parallel interplane struts on each side, the innermost pairs very close to the fuselage. Upper-wing extensions, carrying ailerons, braced by additional pairs of outward-sloping struts.

FUSELAGE:

Main fuselage a shallow structure of rectangular section. Cabin superstructure built up from a point ahead of wings to vicinity of rear interplane struts.

TAIL UNIT:

Braced monoplane tail with two vertical surfaces (later reduced to one) at about mid-span on each side. Rudders effective enough for pilot to hold course with two engines stopped on one side.

LANDING GEAR:

Main gear comprising sixteen wheels in four pairs on each side, carried on braced structure together with two main fore-and-aft skids and two auxiliary skids outboard of wheel groups. Additional skid under tail.

POWER PLANT:

Four 100 hp four-cylinder Argus water-cooled engines mounted on lower wings. Engines originally arranged in two tandem pairs, close inboard, to mitigate effects of assymetric thrust in event of power failure. Tests disclosed large margin of directional control, but propeller efficiency was low, especially on take-off. Accordingly, in June 1913, two rear engines mounted outboard in same manner as other pair. Engines uncowled, with radiators on sides. Cylindrical petrol tanks above engines. Two-blade wooden propellers.

ACCOMMODATION:

Open-topped nose section of fuselage constituted a balcony, accessible through a door in the front of the large enclosed cabin. Searchlight mounted in gimbals at the bow. Pilots' compartment in forward part of cabin, with two seats and dual control. Wheel control for ailerons. Entire front and side sections of cabin formed of continuous windows. Cabin luxuriously decorated and furnished. Four seats, sofa and table. Washroom and wardrobe at rear.

EQUIPMENT:

Four tachometers for engines. Two altimeters. Glass U-tube containing alcohol connected to a form of pressure receiver to indicate flying speed. Ball in curved glass tube to act as bank indicator. Long streamline tube mounted ahead of cabin window to indicate incidence.

DIMENSIONS:

Wing span 91 *ft* 11 *in* (28·00 *m*)
Length overall 65 *ft* 8 *in* (20·00 *m*)
Wing area 1,292 *sq ft* (120 *m*²)

WEIGHTS:

Weight empty 5,950 *lb* (2,700 *kg*)
Weight loaded 9,000 *lb approx.* (4,080 *kg*)

PERFORMANCE:

Cruising speed 55 *mph approx.* (88 *kmh*)

In his biography Igor Sikorsky cites as the most important factor in the pioneering period of aviation the creation of large four-engined aircraft. His "Grand" was the first

The Emperor Nicholas II and Igor Sikorsky on the balcony of the "Grand" The searchlight is seen

Р.Б.В.З.
1120

AVRO TYPE F

The idea of enclosing the pilot and/or passengers within the body of an aeroplane to afford them protection from the elements and to lessen air resistance was by no means new when the Avro Type F single-seat cabin monoplane appeared in April 1912. In his proposed amphibious tractor monoplane of 1876, Alphonse Pénaud arranged for the pilot to be enclosed, and at the Olympia Aero Show held in London in 1911 was a Piggot monoplane wherein the pilot was entirely within the highly streamlined contours of the fuselage. Later this aircraft was modified so that the pilot's head was outside the body. The Blériot *Berline* built, like the Avro Type F, in 1912, had a cabin for the passengers but an open cockpit for the pilot, and a Rumpler shown in Berlin at about the time the Avro appeared had a hood over the tandem cockpits and even a writing desk for the passenger. The Avro Type F, however, must be acknowledged as the first aeroplane to fly (1 May 1912) with totally enclosed accommodation as an integral part of the design. Although it was predicted that oil thrown back by the engine would obscure the pilot's view this was not the case. Also in 1912 A. V. Roe produced the Type G cabin biplane, in which his brother, H. V. Roe became the first man to type a letter in flight.

The engine of the Avro Type F is in the Science Museum, London, and the rudder is preserved by the Royal Aero Club.

In the Avro Type G enclosed biplane A. V. Roe's brother typed a letter in flight

The Type F was significant not only in having enclosed accommodation but because its Viale engine was one of the first of the classic air-cooled radial type

The early Avro illustration below shows the disposition of the windows in the upper surface

AVRO MONOPLANE. 1912 TYPE.
The First Totally Enclosed Aeroplane to fly in the World.

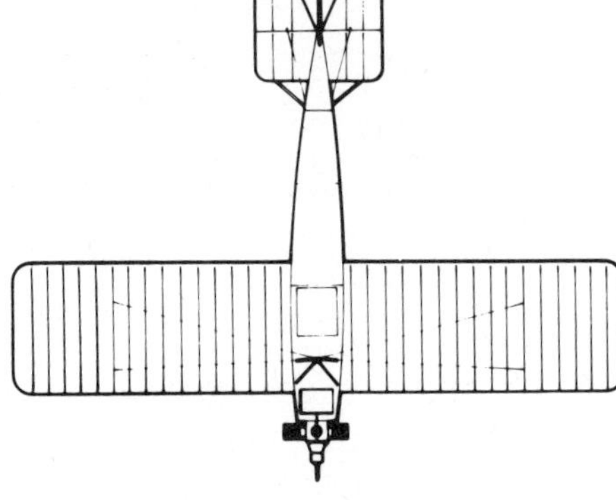

TYPE:
Single-seat cabin **monoplane.**

WINGS:
Mid-wing braced monoplane. Constructed in two halves round built-up front spar and rear spar which allowed wings to warp for lateral control. Front spar of I section. Rear spar "rocked" in concert with a single vertical strut carrying the warping wires above and below the wing.

FUSELAGE:
Box-girder structure with four ash longerons reinforced by triangular plywood stiffeners in each bay. Fuselage symmetrical about horizontal axis, rectangular in section. Longerons curved down very steeply towards nose and embraced by steel cap which formed engine mounting. Further support for the engine provided by two ash bearers, one each side, extending horizontally from the front of the fuselage. Half-way along rear fuselage the fabric covering could be unlaced to expose steel jointing plates, enabling the fuselage to be dismantled.

TAIL UNIT:
Braced monoplane type, with balanced rudder above and below fuselage.

LANDING GEAR:
Central skid attached to fuselage by two sets of Vee struts in tandem, both sloping forward to take landing loads. Laminated axle of spring steel clipped to skid and carrying two wheels. Rubber inserts between skid and supporting steel struts. Sprung tail-skid attached to fuselage and bottom of rudder.

POWER PLANT:
One 35 hp Viale 5-cylinder air-cooled radial engine driving two-blade wooden tractor propeller.

ACCOMMODATION:
Enclosed cockpit entered through sheet-aluminium trapdoor in roof. Non-inflammable celluloid windows in front of fuselage, in sides, and in floor. Circular holes in sides for pilot's head to be thrust out in emergency. Central control column and rudder bar. Engine switch, throttle and spark-advance lever grouped together in line.

DIMENSIONS:
Wing span 28 *ft* 0 *in* (8·53 *m*)
Length overall 23 *ft* 0 *in* (7·01 *m*)
Wing area 158 *sq ft* (14·68 m^2)

WEIGHTS:
Weight empty 550 *lb* (250 *kg*)
Weight loaded 800 *lb* (363 *kg*)

PERFORMANCE:
Max speed 65 *mph* (104 *kmh*)
Initial rate of climb 300 *ft/min* (91 *m/min*)

Alliott Verdon Roe, who later changed his name to Verdon-Roe, was a dogged experimenter with tractor aircraft of triplane, biplane and monoplane type and his early work found its full expression in the 500/504 series of biplanes (pages 42–43). He wrote before his death in 1958: "I kept paper and pencil by my bedside (and still do) to sketch and write ideas before forgetting them"

DEPERDUSSIN MONOCOQUE RACER

Ingenuity of construction and extremely high speed were the salient characteristics of the French Deperdussin monoplanes of 1912/13. Armand Deperdussin had established his aircraft factory in 1910 and specialised in monoplanes of basically Blériot type. During 1910 the highest recorded speed was 106·51 kmh (66 mph) achieved by Leon Morane on a Blériot. In 1911 Edouard Nieuport attained 130·06 kmh (81 mph) on a Nieuport monoplane and in 1912 Jules Vedrines was timed at 174·10 kmh (108 mph) on a Deperdussin of extremely clean aerodynamic design. In 1913 Prevost won the first Schneider Trophy contest by finishing the course alone in a Deperdussin racing monoplane mounted on floats at an average speed of 45·75 mph (74 kmh) and during the same year Prevost broke the world's speed record three times at Reims, the highest figure being 126·67 mph (203 kmh).

The sporting aviatrix demonstrates that not all the Deperdussin monoplanes offered the snug accommodation of the monocoque racing type with its close-fitting fuselage and streamlined headrest for the pilot. Note also faired landing gear

The word "streamlining" assumed a new significance with the coming of the Deperdussin racers

The performance of the Deperdussin racers was attributable to clean aerodynamic design, high power, high wing loading with low aspect ratio and excellence of finish. It has sometimes been assumed that the sleek fuselage which characterised all these machines was always a monocoque structure, but this is disproved by a description of the "100-hp Deperdussin Racing Monoplane" published in February 1912 which observed: "The growing trend of opinion in favour of the torpedo type of body has gained another adherent, for in the machine at present under review this feature has been incorporated for the first time in the Deperdussin design. The main body proper consists of a lattice girder which tapers towards the rear, of exactly the same type as, but of more generous dimensions than, that employed on the ordinary type of machine. Throughout its whole length this girder is encased by a shell of three-ply wood, enough being cut away on a level with the back of the wings, in order to accommodate the pilot". This description may be compared with that of the 1913 racing machine which follows. The fuselage in this instance is of the true monocoque type, as pioneered by Deperdussin from techniques developed by Ruchonnet and Béchereau.

TYPE:

Single-seat racing monoplane.

WINGS:

Braced monoplane type, of parallel chord, and set in "shoulder" position. Small camber and very thin section. Spars of hickory and ash, ribs of pine, the whole covered with strong linen cloth doped with Emaillite. Upper and lower bracing wires secured to pylons above fuselage and to front legs of landing gear respectively. Lateral control by warping. Upper warping wires passed round pulleys in the pylons and lower ones taken to a drum on a transverse rocking lever on the rear cross-member of the landing gear.

FUSELAGE:

Of true monocoque type; construction as follows: Three thin layers of tulip wood were glued together over a detachable form or jig, tulip wood being particularly suitable. When the glue had set, the underlying form was removed, thus leaving a shell composed of a large number of strips running across one another and affording great strength. Thickness of shell about 4 mm ($\frac{1}{8}$ in). Shell then covered inside and out with fabric, glued on and varnished. To the shell were then attached engine bearers, attachments for landing gear, tail, etc.

TAIL UNIT:

Monoplane type. Triangular fin carrying rudder, elevator behind mid-set tailplane.

LANDING GEAR:

Very carefully faired, consisting of two U-shaped members of three-ply wood attached to fuselage with fore-and-aft fairing between upper extremities and carrying at their lower ends a tubular axle for two wheels, sprung by rubber shock-absorbers.

ACCOMMODATION:

Cockpit over trailing-edge with streamlined headrest for pilot. Inverted U-shaped member in cockpit carried handwheel, movable backwards and forwards for elevator operation and rotated to actuate warping wires. Foot-bar for rudder.

POWER PLANT:

One 160 hp Gnome 14-cylinder rotary engine driving two-blade wooden propeller the hub of which was in a spinner of large diameter. Propeller diameter 7 ft 7 in (2·31 m). Entire installation of unprecedented neatness. Engine mounted on steel bearers. Engine enclosed in circular aluminium cowling, small space being left between cowling and spinner for cooling air. Circular holes in cowling some distance aft of leading edge.

DIMENSIONS:

Wing span 21 *ft* 10 *in* (6·65 *m*) (*span varied*)
Length overall 20 *ft* 0 *in* (6·09 *m*)
Wing area 104 *sq ft* (9·66 *m²*)

WEIGHT:

Weight loaded 1,350 *lb* (612 *kg*)

PERFORMANCE:

Max speed 130 *mph* (209 *kmh*) *approx.*

BRISTOL SCOUT

Military Bristol Scouts carried improvised armament. Sometimes a Lewis gun was fixed to the fuselage

A class of aircraft developed to a very high pitch in Great Britain before the war of 1914 was the very small and light single-seat biplane, suitable for sporting use in peacetime or "scouting" in war. No provision was made for armament. The first of this class was designed specifically for military purposes at the Royal Aircraft Factory, Farnborough, and was designated B.S.1. This little biplane of 1912 was mainly the work of Geoffrey de Havilland and is the true progenitor of all "scouts" and "fighters", although itself unarmed. Cleanness of design gave it a speed of 92 mph (148 kmh). The S.E. 4 development of 1914 had wing flaps and a cockpit canopy. The better-known Sopwith Tabloid did not appear until many months after the B.S.1 and the Bristol Scout dated from early 1914. In April 1914 the 22-ft (6·70 m) wings initially fitted were replaced by a set of 24 ft 7 in (7·49 m) span and other alterations were made. In this form the Scout was lost in the English Channel during a London-Paris-London air race. Sometimes called the Bristol Bullet (although the name Scout was used early in 1914) the type was eventually produced for scouting and fighting purposes as the Scout B, C and D.

The original Bristol Scout was used as a sporting mount by Lord Carbery and subsequent to the slight embarrassment above was lost in the English Channel

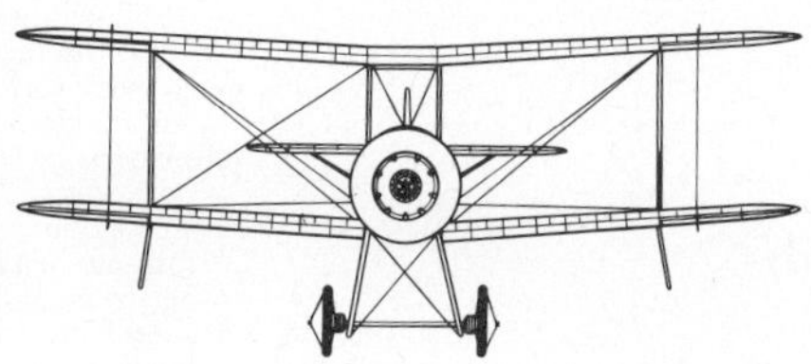

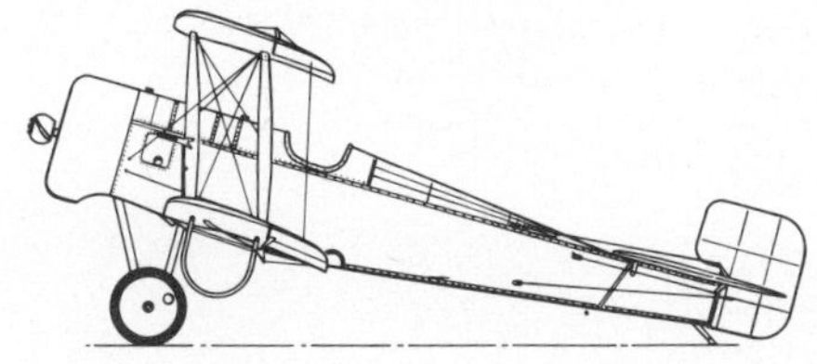

Pistols and rifles formed the earliest armament; then followed Lewis guns, mounted either to fire at an angle to clear the propeller arc or fired deliberately through the arc, the resulting holes being bound with sticky tape. The first operational installation of a fixed Vickers gun was made on a Bristol Scout (the mechanical fire-control gear was of Vickers design) and some machines had the later Scarff-Dibovsky mechanism. Rifle grenades and Ranken darts were also carried as offensive weapons. On 17 May 1916, a Scout was successfully launched from the top wing of a Porte Baby flying-boat in flight.

The following description applies to the Scout as originally constructed in 1914.

TYPE:

Single-seat scouting or sporting biplane.

WINGS:

Braced biplane type. Constant chord, raked tips. Special Coanda section. Two wooden spars. Internal bracing by piano wire. External diagonal bracing by stranded cables. Ailerons on all four wings. One set of spruce interplane struts on each side.

FUSELAGE:

Rectangular section, with four ash longerons in forward portion, spruce being used for the rear longerons. Vertical and transverse spruce struts. Bracing by high-tension steel piano wires attached to steel-plate joints. Front portion of fuselage, to a point behind pilot's seat, covered with aluminium. Rear portion fabric-covered.

TAIL UNIT:

Braced monoplane type. Tailplane on top of fuselage. Balanced rudder pivoted round extension of sternpost. All control cables duplicated.

LANDING GEAR:

Simple Vee type. Tubular axle resting in angle between struts and sprung by rubber cord. Short tail skid sprung inside fuselage by rubber cord.

POWER PLANT:

One 80 hp Gnome air-cooled rotary engine driving a Bristol two-blade wooden propeller of 8 ft (2·44 m) diameter. Hemispherical nose cowling cut away at bottom. Fuel carried behind engine.

ACCOMMODATION:

Pilot's seat slung from fuselage structure on piano wires. Wire strainers incorporated in suspension enabling seat position to be adjusted to suit pilot. Engine switch on control column.

DIMENSIONS:

Wing span 22 *ft* 0 *in* (6·70 *m*)
Length overall 19 *ft* 9 *in* (6·02 *m*)
Wing area 156 *sq ft* (14·49 *m*²)

WEIGHTS:

Weight empty 616 *lb* (279 *kg*)
Weight loaded 956 *lb* (434 *kg*)

PERFORMANCE:

Max speed 95 *mph* (153 *kmh*)
Min speed 47 *mph* (75·60 *kmh*)
Endurance 3 *hr*

VICKERS F.B.5 GUNBUS

Rounded wing-tips and a new gun mounting were features of the developed Gunbus

When war came in 1914 none of the Powers engaged was able to put into the field a type of aircraft designed or developed specifically for combat, although a firearm had been discharged from an aeroplane as early as August 1910 (Curtiss pusher biplane; pilot Glenn Curtiss; marksman 2nd Lt. Jacob E. Fickel; weapon Springfield rifle). A Lewis drum-fed machine gun, a type of weapon admirably adaptable for aerial use, had been fired from a Wright biplane on 7 June 1912, and a belt-fed Maxim had been mounted on the F.E.2 pusher of the Royal Aircraft Factory, Farnborough, in the summer of the same year. At the Olympia show during 1913 appeared the first of several Vickers fighting biplanes (of the type later generically classed as "gunbus") known as the E.F.B.1 Destroyer, which led to the Vickers F.B.5 (Fighting Biplane No 5). The Destroyer had staggered wings and mounted a Maxim gun, with limited arcs of fire, in the nose of the nacelle. A Vickers gun (Maxim development, belt-fed) was later installed in the E.F.B.2 and 3, but only the adoption of the Lewis gun in 1914 provided the light, self-contained weapon that was really needed for aircraft of this class.

A parallel may be drawn between the laying down by Vickers of a batch of fifty F.B.5s in expectation of official orders with the similar act of faith by the Hawker company respecting the eight-gun Hurricane of the Second World War. The first F.B.5 Gunbus reached France in February 1915, and before a specific squadron was equipped aircraft of the type were used for the escort of reconnaissance machines.

The following description relates to the aircraft in the form in which it appeared in the summer of 1914, after much development, but before being further improved under the designation F.B.9. On the F.B.9 a new gun-mounting of wind-balanced type and of Vickers design made its appearance.

Of classic pusher layout, the F.B.5 was often confused by German pilots with the later F.E.2b

TYPE:
Two-seat fighter.

WINGS:
Unstaggered biplane of equal span. Square-cut tips. Fabric-covered wooden construction. Ailerons on all four wings.

FUSELAGE:
Tail unit carried on steel-tube booms attached to wings and converging in plan. Booms forming forward bay specially strengthened with inner liner to give protection against flying fragments of broken propeller. Booms braced by vertical struts and vertical and horizontal wires. Covered nacelle on lower wing, carrying uncowled engine at rear and gunner in cutaway nose section. Pilot in line with leading-edges. Nacelle of welded steel-tube construction. Duralumin covering forward, fabric at rear. Cable bracing to upper and lower wings.

TAIL UNIT:
Cable-braced monoplane type, with tailplane carried on upper booms. Tailplane of very deep chord, elevator with cut-out for rudder.

LANDING GEAR:
Two main wheels and two "toothpick" skids carried beneath nacelle on four struts. Wire bracing between struts and from forward skid-attachments to bottom wings. Tail-skid attached to rear of lower booms. Flexible under-wing skids beneath outer pairs of interplane struts. Side area of nacelle kept to mini-

One of the early experimental Gunbus prototypes seen below may be compared with the production version above. Note in particular the different vertical tail surfaces

A pre-eminent consideration in the Gunbus design was a wide field of fire

mum to avoid excessive fin effect ahead of wings and benefit gunner's field of fire.

POWER PLANT:

One 100 hp Gnome Monosoupape air-cooled rotary engine driving two-blade wooden pusher propeller. Clerget and Smith static engines fitted experimentally.

ARMAMENT:

Gun mounting of pillar type in extreme nose of nacelle carrying a single Lewis gun of 0·303 in (7·7 mm) calibre. Spare ammunition magazines in cockpit. Twin Lewis guns mounted experimentally.

DIMENSIONS:

Wing span 36 *ft* 6 *in* (11·05 *m*)
Wing chord 5 *ft* 6 *in* (1·67 *m*)
Wing gap 6 *ft* 6 *in* (1·98 *m*)
Length overall 27 *ft* 2 *in* (8·28 *m*)
Wing area 392 *sq ft* (36·42 *m*)

WEIGHTS:

Weight empty 1,220 *lb* (553 *kg*)
Weight loaded 2,050 *lb* (930 *kg*)

PERFORMANCE:

Max speed at 5,000 *ft* (1,525 *m*) 70 *mph* (112·50 *kmh*)
Time of climb to 5,000 *ft* (1,525 *m*) 16 *min*
Service ceiling 9,000 *ft* (2,740 *m*)
Endurance 4½ *hr*

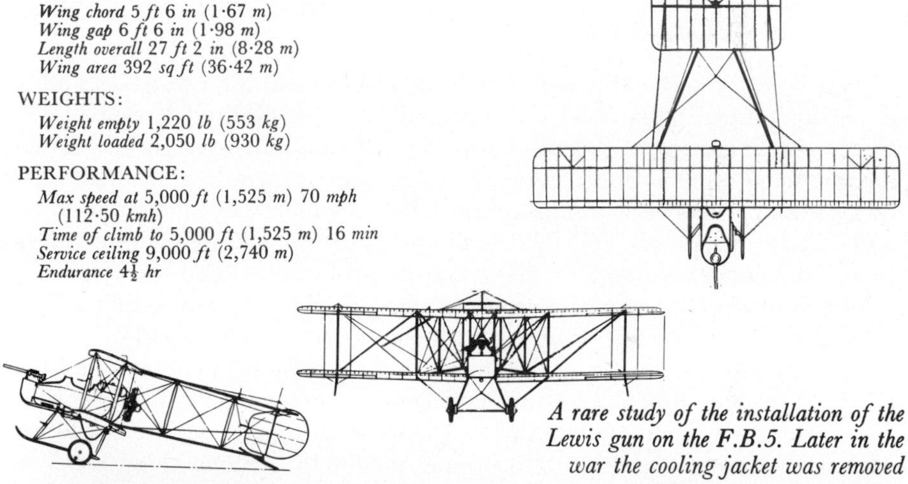

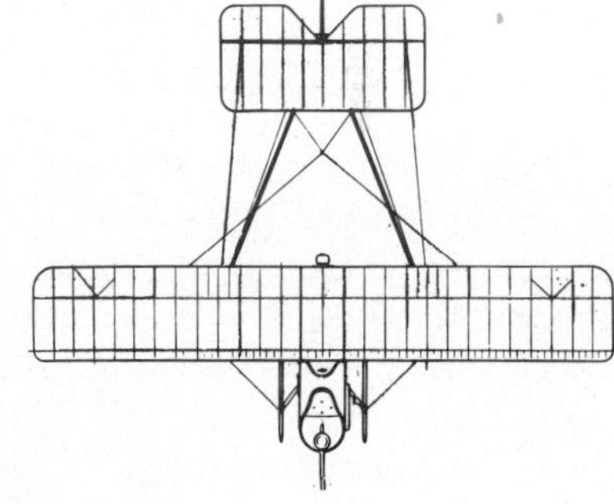

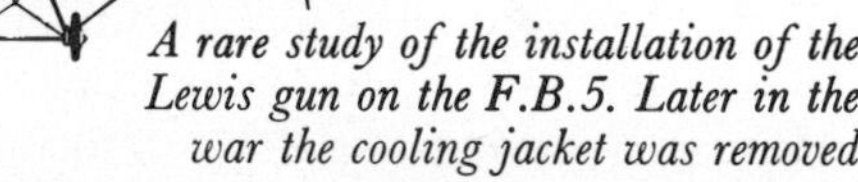

A rare study of the installation of the Lewis gun on the F.B.5. Later in the war the cooling jacket was removed

What it lacked in aesthetic appeal the Voisin Bomber made good in terms of robustness and adaptability. Band-brakes were fitted on the rear wheels

VOISIN BOMBER

Robustness, reserve of power and adaptability were the essential qualities of a new type of Voisin pusher biplane which appeared in 1914. Gabriel Voisin has recounted: "The Voisin '13·50 metres' of July 1914 was the only machine with a metal structure. It was also the first to be fitted with an engine which was both powerful and simple. The Canton-Unne that we had chosen was a nine-cylinder radial which was safely able to give one hundred and thirty horsepower at 1,200 revolutions a minute". (The historic Gnome air-cooled rotary engines of considerably lower power had hitherto been favoured.)

The remarkable engine referred to was of water-cooled radial type, and the name "Canton" has sometimes led to the erroneous assertion that it had its origins in Switzerland. It was, in fact, made by the Salmson company in France according to the designs of G. H. M. Canton and P. G. Unné. A licence was acquired by the Dudbridge Iron Works in Gloucestershire, England, and the excellence of the engine led to its adoption for a number of early bombing and torpedo-dropping machines. Among these the Voisin biplane was pre-eminent. One of the earliest examples was fitted with a 37 mm gun and the Voisins had, in fact, installed a heavy gun on one of their machines as early as 1910, though this was never fired. Great structural strength was necessary for absorbing the recoil of such heavy ordnance, and this strength was further evident in at least two incidents (one involving Gabriel Voisin himself) of collisions between Voisin biplanes and other aircraft, with the Voisins landing safely on both occasions. Another feature of the Voisin which gave it a superiority over other comparable types was its four-wheeled undercarriage, which allowed it to be operated from rough surfaces. On 1 August 1914, the Voisin was ordered into production, and sustained the greater part of France's bombing effort until 1916. A number of other manufacturers, including Breguet, built bombers of this type in great quantity, the Breguet 14, which was itself to achieve an unusual measure of success not appearing until 1917. Armed with a Hotchkiss rifle-calibre machine gun a Voisin biplane scored the first victory over an enemy aircraft in combat (5 October 1914).

Tapering ailerons added to the distinctive appearance of early versions of the Voisin Bomber, a type directly descended from the Voisin biplane of 1907 (see page 10)

After the autumn of 1915 the Voisin bombers flew mostly at night, a mission suggested by this squadron marking

A heavy gun was installed on a Voisin biplane as early as 1910 and Hotchkiss guns of 37 mm or 47 mm calibre were mounted on the "avion canon" versions of the bomber

Such were the qualities of the steel-framed Voisin that it continued in service throughout the war. The later developments were of greater span and higher power, the engine generally fitted being the 220 hp Peugeot, and a prominent recognition feature of these machines was the pair of streamlined fuel tanks mounted beneath the upper wings. A feature of particular technical interest was the fitting of wheel-brakes. The ultimate version to go into service was fitted with a 300 hp Renault engine.

The following description relates in general to the class of aircraft known as "Voisin Bomber", though other experimental bombers were built by the same constructor.

TYPE:
Single-engined bomber.

WINGS:
Braced biplane of unequal span (upper wings slightly longer). Steel construction with front spar at leading-edge, where interplane struts were attached (compare Voisin biplane of 1907). Ailerons on all four wings, of greater chord than wings on earlier versions. Three pairs of interplane struts on each side, with reduced wire bracing on later models. Slight stagger on earlier models, eliminated later.

FUSELAGE:
Tail carried on four steel booms attached to wings, converging in plan. Nacelle for crew of two and power plant mounted on lower wings and braced to top wings.

TAIL UNIT:
Monoplane type, with tailplane mounted on upper booms and very deep, narrow-chord rudder working within a trailing-edge cut-out.

LANDING GEAR:
Very sturdy four-wheel type with coiled-spring shock-absorbers. Rear pair of wheels in line with engine; forward pair, of narrower track, carried forward of nacelle. Band-brakes on rear wheels. Safety skid under rudder.

POWER PLANT:
Typically one Canton-Unné (Salmson), Peugeot or Renault water-cooled engine driving two-blade wooden pusher propeller. Overhung support for Canton-Unné. Two laterally disposed radiator blocks in inverted-Vee arrangement. Fuel tanks in nacelle and also under wings in later versions.

ACCOMMODATION AND ARMAMENT:
Crew of two in "bathtub" nacelle. In the aircraft manned by Frantz and Quenault, which gained the first air-to-air victory in history, as already mentioned, the gunner had a strip-fed Hotchkiss gun, one of a number procured by the direct action of Gabriel Voisin, and having a mounting of Voisin's devising. This was in the form of a steel-tube pyramid, with its apex over the pilot's head. The gun malfunctioned and could fire only single shots. Bomb load on that occasion was six 90 mm artillery shells. Later aircraft had a variety of armament, notably a single Hotchkiss gun of 37 mm or 47 mm calibre. Standard bombers carried bombs vertically on the sides of the nacelle and also under the wings. Maximum bomb load of the highest-powered long-span version was about 600 lb (270 kg). The components of a field-hospital could be carried in under-wing containers.

The following particulars relate to a typical aircraft of early pattern.

DIMENSIONS:
Wing span 48 *ft* 4 *in* (14·73 *m*)
Length overall 31 *ft* 2 *in* (9·50 *m*)
Height overall 12 *ft* 6 *in* (3·81 *m*)

WEIGHTS:
Weight empty 2,140 *lb* (971 *kg*)
Weight loaded 3,025 *lb* (1,372 *kg*)

PERFORMANCE:
Max speed 74 *mph* (119 *kmh*)
Typical range 300 *miles* (483 *km*)

SOPWITH 1½ STRUTTER

Above, an early British example. Below, a late French specimen

The curious name of this aircraft derived from the fact that, instead of having two pairs of interplane struts on each side (which was common practice in 1916, when the type went into service with the Royal Flying Corps and Royal Naval Air Service) it had one pair in addition to a pair of diagonal struts running from the fuselage to a point on the top wing where the conventional pair might otherwise have been located. The type was first produced as a two-seat fighter, but was also used as a single-seat bomber, with internal stowage, and as a "ships' aeroplane". As a fighter this aircraft had a double distinction: it was the first British aircraft to be produced with a synchronised Vickers gun as standard armament and the first to have the Scarff ring mounting for the rear Lewis gun. This mounting was devised by Warrant Officer F. W. Scarff of the British Admiralty's Air Department and was very extensively employed until the Second World War, not only by the British flying services, but by very numerous air forces throughout the world.

Large numbers of 1½ Strutters were built in France.

TYPE:
Two-seat fighter.

WINGS:
Braced biplane with one pair of interplane struts on each side. No centre-section. Two halves of upper wing met on centre line, at which point they were attached to the fuselage top longerons by two pairs of inverted-vee struts. From the lower ends of these struts two long struts ran outboard to the upper wing. Wooden construction. Two main spars. Double flying wires in single-bay truss. Struts bracing top wing to fuselage of steel tubing, elliptical in section. Dihedral on main wing panels but not on centre-section of lower wing. Some aircraft had large areas of upper wing covered with transparent material. Air-brakes behind rear spar on lower centre-section. Braking surfaces pivoted about spanwise axis and moved upwards through 90°. Portions projecting below centre-section formed aerodynamic balances.

FUSELAGE:
Fabric-covered wooden structure with wire cross-bracing. Plywood decking in cockpit areas. Bay behind engine braced by wooden diagonal members and covered with aluminium panels. Fuselage section rounded forward, flat-sided aft.

TAIL UNIT:
Braced fabric-covered structure. Fin and rudder of steel-tube construction. Adjustable tailplane with two wooden spars. Incidence varied by handwheel in cockpit.

LANDING GEAR:
Two main wheels on Vee structure of steel tubes. Each wheel on half-axle, pivoted at inner end about a point near the centre of a spreader bar. Half-axle had limited vertical movement in slot at apex of its Vee strut assembly, restrained by rubber cord in tension.

POWER PLANT:
One nine-cylinder air-cooled rotary engine of Clerget or Le Rhône type (110 to 145 hp) driving two-blade wooden propeller. Overhung mounting, circular cowling. Main fuel tank behind pilot's seat. Service tank above and behind engine. Fuel delivered to tank by wind-driven pump. Hand pump in pilot's cockpit.

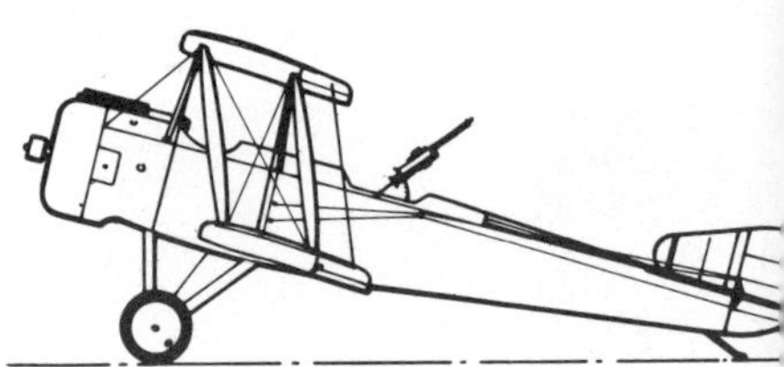

With the Tabloid, a precursor of the 1½ Strutter, are T. O. M. Sopwith (left) and pilot Harry Hawker

Albert
6 July 1917

The famous Scarff ring gun-mounting can have encircled few more illustrious personages than King Albert of Belgium. In the view below the Lewis gun is stripped of its cooling jacket

ACCOMMODATION:

Tandem open cockpits for pilot and gunner. Pilot under wing and separated from gunner by fuel tank.

ARMAMENT:

One fixed synchronised Vickers 0·303 in (7·7 mm) belt-fed machine-gun on fuselage centre-line ahead of pilot. Sopwith patented padded windscreen over rear of gun. One Lewis 0·303 in drum-fed gun on Scarff ring mounting over rear cockpit. (Some early machines had pillar-type or Nieuport mounting.) Several non-standard armament schemes, notably two Lewis guns for upward firing. Specialised single-seat bomber version had internal bomb bay in place of rear cockpit.

DIMENSIONS:

Wing span 33 *ft* 6 *in* (10·21 *m*)
Length overall 25 *ft* 3 *in* (7·69 *m*)
Height overall 10 *ft* 3 *in* (3·12 *m*)

WEIGHTS:

Weight empty 1,305 *lb* (592 *kg*)
Weight loaded 2,250 *lb* (1,120 *kg*)

PERFORMANCE:

Max speed at 10,000 *ft* (3,050 *m*) 98·5 *mph* (158 *kmh*)
Time of climb to 10,000 *ft* (3,050 *m*) 24 *min* 36 *sec*
Service ceiling 15,500 *ft* (4,699 *m*)
Endurance 3¾ *hr*

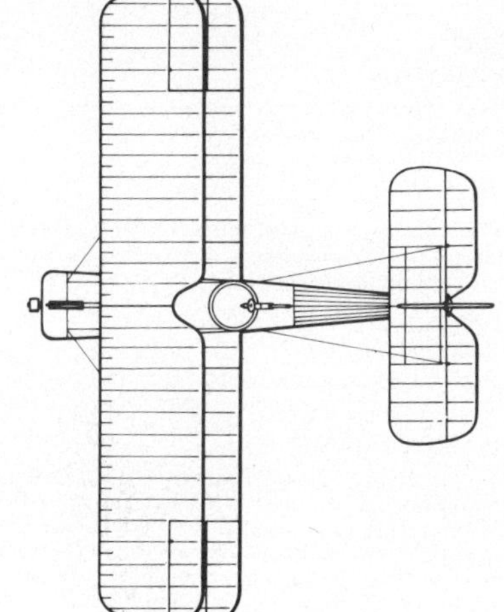

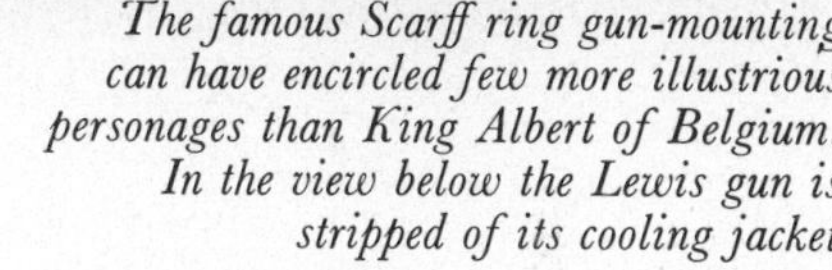

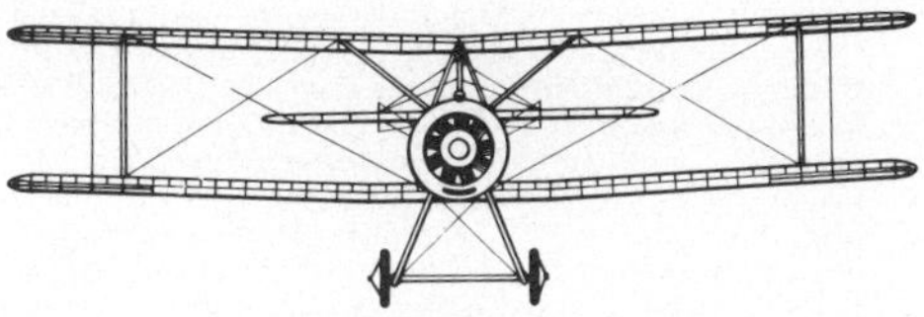

CAPRONI BOMBER

Generally known as the "450 hp Caproni", the Ca.33 (150 hp Isotta-Fraschini engines)

An American specimen

The Italian constructor Gianni Caproni built his first aeroplane in 1912. By this time Italy had made the first bombing attacks from aeroplanes in the history of warfare, these having occurred in the Libya War of 1911–12. When the war ended Italy possessed nine airships and fifty aeroplanes. After Italy declared war on Austria on 25 May 1915 the Italian bombing effort quickly mounted. On 20 August two 300 hp Caproni bombers raided Aisovizza from Pordenone. By early 1916 the Caproni squadrons in service numbered nine, an impressive figure for the period, and by the spring of 1917, fourteen.

The first large Caproni aeroplane (Ca.30) was built in 1913; this had the central nacelle and twin fuselages which were the salient characteristic of bombers to follow and was itself remarkable in having three Gnome engines installed in the nacelle. One of these drove a pusher propeller and the others drove two tractor propellers indirectly. Thereafter designs and designations proliferated. Thus the Ca.31 received the military designation Ca.1. This model had two engines in the noses of the twin fuselages and set the pattern for its successors. The Ca.32 had three engines (100 hp Fiat), and the Ca.33 the same number of 150 hp Isotta-Fraschinis. This version was built in quantity and was generally known as the "450hp Caproni". It was operated not only by the home-based Army Air Service but served with the Italian Navy in Albania as a torpedo bomber. (Italy's pioneering of torpedo-dropping by aircraft will later be mentioned in connection with the Sopwith Cuckoo). Refined versions were the Ca.34 and Ca.35, and the Ca.36 was a Ca.33 with detachable wings for ease of storage.

The name Caproni is closely identified with giant triplanes, a series of which followed the Ca.40 of late 1917. This had a wing span of nearly 100 ft and its three Isotta-Fraschini engines developed a total of 600 hp. It was over 20 ft tall. The Ca.41 was a more powerful, and somewhat rearranged version; the Ca.42 was used by Britain's Royal Naval Air Service; and the Ca.43 was a seaplane. There were other developments of the type, the whole family being known generically as Ca.4s.

The following description applies to the widely used Ca.33 biplane, which took part in many heroic operations; and it remains to record that succeeding biplanes were the considerably refined and more powerful Ca.44 (three Fiat engines), the Ca.45 with redesigned nacelle and radiators, and the Liberty-engined Ca.46.

TYPE:
Three-engined bomber.

WINGS:
Braced biplane type of equal span and unstaggered. Three bays of bracing outboard of engines. Wooden construction with fabric covering. Inversely-tapered ailerons on all four wings. Wings cable-braced to front of nacelle, as well as having the usual inter-plane bracing. Top wing stayed to nacelle by two struts.

FUSELAGE:
Two fuselages of rectangular section, carrying engines at front and tail at rear. Wooden structure with fabric covering.

TAIL UNIT:
Monoplane type, with tailplane mounted on ends of fuselages. Three rudders, with centre rudder stayed to tailplane by two struts.

LANDING GEAR:
Twin double-wheel assemblies under outboard engines. Two nose-wheels beneath front of nacelle Two tail-skids under fuselages. Wing-tip skids.

POWER PLANT:
Three 150 hp Isotta-Fraschini six-cylinder in-line water-cooled engines. Two engines in nacelles on lower wings with two-blade wooden propellers only slightly forward of leading-edges. Third engine at rear of nacelle driving two-blade wooden pusher propeller. Radiators above engines. Fuel tanks in fuselage behind pilot's cockpit.

ACCOMMODATION AND ARMAMENT:
Gunner in nose of nacelle with one Revelli 6·5 mm (0·25 in) machine-gun or (occasionally) large-bore shell-firing gun. Two pilots side-by-side forward of leading-edges. Gunner above tail of nacelle with one, two or three Revelli machine-guns. Gunner's position was a platform carried above the third engine on an open-work structure with a gun ring at its upper extremity, level with the trailing-edge of the top wing. Bombs carried externally, up to a weight of about 1,000 lb (453 kg). Torpedo alternative load beneath fuselage.

DIMENSIONS:
Wing span 72 *ft* 10 *in* (22·20 *m*)
Length overall 35 *ft* 9 *in* (10·89 *m*)

WEIGHTS:
Weight empty 5,080 *lb* (2,304 *kg*)
Weight loaded 8,400 *lb* (3,810 *kg*)

PERFORMANCE:
Max speed 70–75 *mph* (112–120 *kmh*)
Time of climb to 3,280 *ft* (1,000 *m*) 8 *min*
Ceiling 13,400 *ft* (4,084 *m*)

Powered by American Liberty engines the Ca.46 was a late development in the series of bombers for which Italy is renowned. The field of fire commanded from the rear gun position is apparent

The Italians were using aeroplanes for bombing in the Libya War of 1911–12. This contemporary drawing was captioned: "The Italian Army Aeroplanes Dropping Bombs on an Arab Encampment"

DE HAVILLAND D.H.4

Notwithstanding its high performance, the D.H. 4 carried heavy armament. The pilot had one or two Vickers guns and the gunner a ring-mounted Lewis gun

The D.H.4 was the most notable high-performance day bomber of the First World War and the type most closely comparable with the D.H. Mosquito of the 1939 war. Unlike the Mosquito it carried heavy defensive armament. Although designed for the then-new B.H.P. (Beardmore-Halford-Pullinger) six-cylinder engine the type achieved its greatest fame with the twelve-cylinder Rolls-Royce Eagle. Using this engine the first D.H.4 Squadron went to France in March 1917. With the Liberty engine the type served with US squadrons during 1918.

TYPE:
Two-seat day bomber.

WINGS:
Two-bay braced biplane. Two spruce spars, spindled out between ribs. Ailerons on all four wings, attached to rear spars. Compensating or balance cables carried externally along leading-edges.

FUSELAGE:
Wooden box girder type with fabric covering, but forward portion, running as far aft as gunner's cockpit, covered with plywood. No internal wire bracing in forward portion. Two portions attached by fishplates. Rearmost of four bays in rear portion plywood-covered. Spruce longerons, ash engine-bearers.

TAIL UNIT:
Braced monoplane type. Incidence of tailplane controllable over range +2 deg to +5 deg.

LANDING GEAR:
Vee structure, with rubber cord shock-absorbers at apices of Vees. Later aircraft had taller undercarriage.

POWER PLANT:
Alternative engines 200 hp R.A.F. 3A, 230 hp B.H.P., 250 hp Rolls-Royce Falcon, 375 hp Rolls-Royce Eagle VIII and earlier marks, 260 hp Fiat A.V.5000. Frontal radiator. Main fuel tanks between cockpits. (US machines had Liberty engine).

ACCOMMODATION:
Pilot's cockpit under top wing, widely separated from gunner's cockpit. Gunner's cockpit had full dual control, with detachable control column, throttle control, airspeed indicator and altimeter.

ARMAMENT:
Fixed synchronised 0·303 in Vickers gun for pilot, mounted on port side of cowling. Ammunition supply 600 rounds. A few aircraft had two fixed Vickers guns. Aldis optical sight. Rear gun mounting originally of pillar type, and some aircraft had two pillar mountings. Standard installation was Scarff ring mounting, carrying one or two 0·303 in Lewis guns. Bomb carriers under wings and fuselage. Typical loads: 8 × 20 lb (9·07 kg) or 4 × 112 lb (50·8 kg) or 2 × 230 lb (104 kg). Bombs released by pilot. Bomb sight of Negative Lens type.

DIMENSIONS:
Wing span 42 *ft* 4½ *in* (12·90 *m*)
Length overall 30 *ft* 2 *in* (9·19 *m*)
Height overall 10 *ft* 1¾ *in* (3·09 *m*)

WEIGHTS:
Weight empty 2,387 *lb* (1,083 *kg*)
Weight loaded 3,472 *lb* (1,575 *kg*)

PERFORMANCE (Rolls-Royce Eagle VIII engine):
Max speed at S/L 143 *mph* (230 *kmh*)
Max speed at 15,000 *ft* (4,570 *m*) 126 *mph* (202 *kmh*)
Landing speed 52 *mph* (83 *kmh*)
Climb to 10,000 *ft* (3,050 *m*) 9 *min*
Absolute ceiling 23,500 *ft* (7,160 *m*)
Normal endurance 3¾ *hr*

One fault in the D.H.4 was that the pilot and gunner were too widely separated for ready intercommunication in combat

FOKKER E.I, II and III

Significant fighter

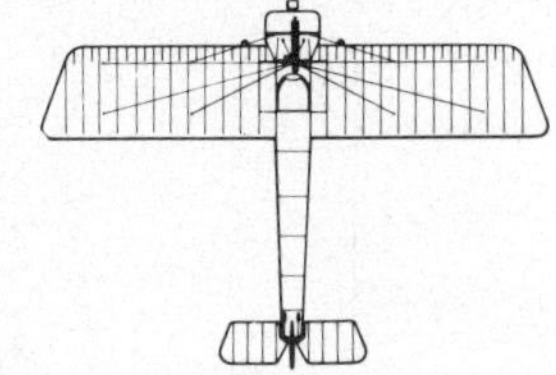

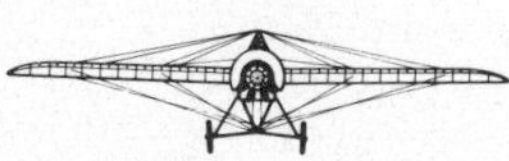

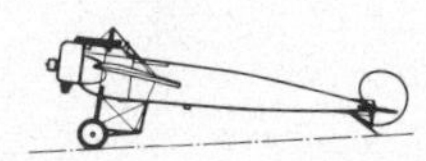

The Fokker E.I single-seat monoplane (Eindecker No 1) was first built in 1915 and was a fighting aircraft of the highest significance, not in respect of design or performance but because of its fixed machine-gun firing through the propeller arc, enabling the pilot to aim the aircraft bodily at the target. This armament, the effectiveness of which became acutely apparent in the winter of 1915–16, was occasioned by, but not copied from, a Morane monoplane flown by Lt. Roland Garros which fell into German hands on 19 April 1915. This aircraft was fitted with a Hotchkiss machine-gun and Saulnier armoured propeller. Tests in Germany with a similar propeller gave poor results and the Dutch aircraft designer Anthony Fokker, whose factory was at Schwerin, in Mecklenburg, was asked to study the problem. To this end he was given a Parabellum M.G.14 machine-gun and ammunition. The outcome was a mechanical synchronising gear, the main credit for which is probably due not to Fokker but to his collaborator Heinrich Luebbe. A similar device had been patented before the war by Franz Schneider. The gun received by Fokker, together with its associated gear, was installed on a Fokker M.5K monoplane, which thereupon became known as the M.5K/MG. The aircraft itself was based on the design of a pre-war Morane-Saulnier monoplane, but had a welded steel-tube fuselage, deeper rear spars and other improvements. The E.I was a "productionised" development mounting the LMG.08 Maxim-type gun (commonly known as "Spandau"). The E.II differed in having an Oberursel engine of 100 (instead of 80) hp, reduced wing span and other alterations, but the E.III, the most common variant, reverted to wings of longer span. The E.IV was fitted with a 100 hp or 160 hp engine and, experimentally, with three guns.

The following details apply in general to all variants, but in particular to the E.III.

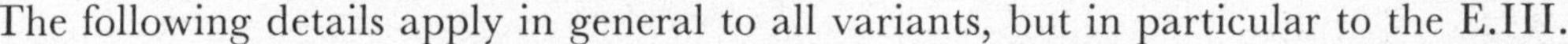

At the front of the cooling jacket of the LMG.08 machine-gun on this captured E.III is the rectangular frame-type sight

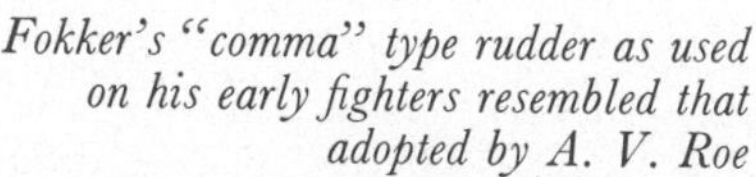

Fokker's "comma" type rudder as used on his early fighters resembled that adopted by A. V. Roe

TYPE:
Single-seater fighter.

WINGS:
Mid-wing wire-braced monoplane. Constant chord, raked tips. Two I-section ash or pine spars, spindled out on router. Poplar ribs, steel-tube compression struts attached to spars by ball-and-socket fittings to allow wing to warp for lateral control. Piano-wire internal bracing. Wing attached to fuselage by chordwise bolts. Four external bracing cables and four warping cables on each side, above and below wing. Upper bracing cables anchored to pylon above fuselage, lower wires to undercarriage. Pulleys for warping cables at apices of pylons.

FUSELAGE:
Welded steel-tube structure of rectangular section tapered to horizontal knife-edge at rear.

TAIL UNIT:
All-moving monoplane type. No fixed tailplane or fin. "Comma" type rudder.

LANDING GEAR:
Wide-track split-axle type of steel-tube construction.

POWER PLANT:
Oberursel rotary air-cooled engine of 80 or 100 hp driving two-blade wooden propeller. Petrol in gravity tank behind engine and rear tank behind cockpit. Automatic petrol feed between rear and gravity tanks by means of windmill-driven pump on starboard front landing gear strut. Petrol capacity 15·40 Imp gallons (70 litres), oil capacity 3·52 Imp gallons (16 litres). Aluminium-sheet cowling.

ACCOMMODATION:
Bench-type seat, enabling passenger to be carried behind pilot. Engine revolution-counter also indicated oil flow. Petrol cocks, altimeter and fuel contents gauge in cockpit, compass in wing.

ARMAMENT:
One LMG.08 Maxim-type belt-fed machine-gun of 7·9 mm (0·311 in) calibre on top of fuselage forward of cockpit. Two guns occasionally fitted. Fokker *Stangensteuerung* (push-rod control) synchronising gear, comprising a system of cams and push-rods between the engine oil-pump drive and the gun trigger. Tripod head-rest to assist in aiming. Alternatively ring-and-bead or rectangular frame-type sight.

Specimens of the Fokker E.III are preserved in Germany and England.

DIMENSIONS:
Wing span 29 ft 4 in (8·95 m)
Length overall 23 ft 4 in (7·11 m)

PERFORMANCE:
Max speed with 80 hp engine 80 mph (128 kmh) approx. (An E.III, captured in April 1916, was tested with the engine not running full-out. Max speed near the ground was 86–88 mph (138–142 kmh), and at 11,000 ft (3,350 m) 78 mph (125·60 kmh). Rate of climb at 1,000 ft (305 m) was 700 ft/min (213 m/min)).

FELIXSTOWE/PORTE F.2A

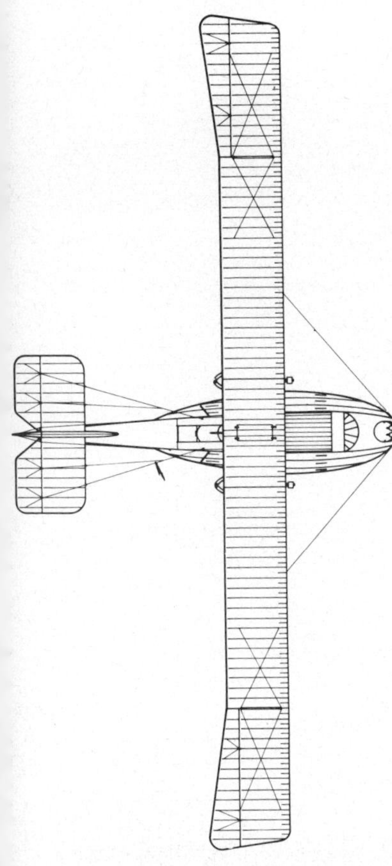

Allusion was made under "Goupy II" to an early glider built by two British naval lieutenants, one of whom was Lt. J. C. Porte. This officer was to have a very distinguished, though unhappily brief, career as designer and pilot of flying-boats, largely in association with Glenn Curtiss. The Curtiss floatplane, or "hydro-aeroplane", earlier described was succeeded by the classic type of flying-boat, with full-length central hull carrying the tail. With this class of aircraft the name of Curtiss is particularly associated, although, as already mentioned, Wilhelm Kress was experimenting with an indubitable flying-boat at the turn of the century. In any case, the credit for the classic type of central-hull flying-boat is more properly due to the French designer Denhaut who, in 1912, ante-dated the Curtiss flying-boat with his Donnet-Lévêque pusher.

Lieutenant Porte was brought into contact with Curtiss through the acquisition by the White and Thompson Co., Ltd. of the British agency for the Curtiss flying-boat. Previously he had flown for the British Deperdussin company. In 1914 Porte went to the USA to join Curtiss who had been commissioned by Rodman Wanamaker to design and build a flying-boat (*America*) capable of crossing the Atlantic. This aircraft, a pusher type with two 90 hp Curtiss OX engines, was completed in June 1914. In August 1914 Porte returned to England, which was then at war, and was accepted into the Royal Naval Air Service. Intensive development of Curtiss-type flying-boats for use by that Service followed under Porte's direction and a series of craft was developed at the RNAS station at Felixstowe. The first to have a Porte hull was accordingly designated F.1. The F.2 had a Porte hull, the wings of a Curtiss H.12 and a new tail. This proved generally superior to the Service-type H.12 and was ordered into production during 1917. In developed form as the F.2A this was not only an extremely fine example of flying-boat construction but of high significance as a weapons platform, carrying not only bombs for anti-submarine work but a very heavy armament of Lewis guns for engaging Zeppelins or other enemy aircraft. Many valiant and successful actions were fought by these flying-boats.

Open-cockpit F.2A with bow gunner at the ready

As a Squadron Commander, J. C. Porte initiated a scheme for extending the radius of action of F.2As by towing them on special lighters

TYPE:

Twin-engined flying-boat.

WINGS:

Braced biplane type of unequal span. Fabric-covered wooden two-spar construction. Unbalanced ailerons, tapering inboard, on "extension" sections of upper wing, outboard of fixed wire-braced stabilising fins on top of wing. Three parallel pairs of bracing struts outboard of engines. Stabilising floats under outermost pair of struts. Main bays and upper-wing extensions wire-braced.

HULL:

Two-step type with four wooden longerons and spacers forming box girder. Forward of rear spar the side frames were in the form of "N" girders. Behind rear spar frames braced with wires or tie-rods. Spars of centre-section of bottom wing integral parts of hull. Bottom longerons spaced by transverse mahogany "floors", Vee-shaped and forming central planing bottom. Floors notched out for two-thirds of depth to fit over solid keelson, this being correspondingly notched for one-third of its depth. Keelson a continuous member from stem to stern. Very broad lateral extension "fins" built out from sides of hull. Form of construction of planing bottom modified very considerably as result of experience with wrenched steps and seepage. Three-ply planking used extensively throughout hull. Early fabric top to rear hull later changed for plywood. Two bracing struts from each side of hull, one to outboard end of centre-section of bottom wing, in way of engine-mounting attachments, the second to the root of the bottom wing.

TAIL UNIT:

Braced monoplane type. Tailplane mounted on fin and braced by four struts on each side. Control wires for tail surfaces running from point on top of hull.

POWER PLANT:

Two Rolls-Royce Eagle 12-cylinder water-cooled engines supported on Vee-strut assemblies and further braced by struts to hull. Frontal radiators. Four-blade wooden propellers. Main fuel tank holding 409 Imp gallons (1,859 litres) in hull. Gravity tank (26 Imp gallons = 118 litres) in top centre-section. Fuel delivery by wind-driven pumps.

ACCOMMODATION:

Gunner in bows with table extending from his seat to the nose. Stowage for ammunition drums under table. Pilot and assistant pilot in enclosed cockpit (enclosure sometimes deleted). Seats with kapok cushions to serve as lifebuoys. Assistant-pilot's seat hinged to afford clear passage fore-and-aft. Some feet aft was a wireless cabinet, with operator's seat, and to port of this a ration box was fitted. Engineer accommodated aft.

ARMAMENT:

Typically, a Scarff ring mounting in the bows for a Lewis gun (sometimes twin guns), a single Lewis

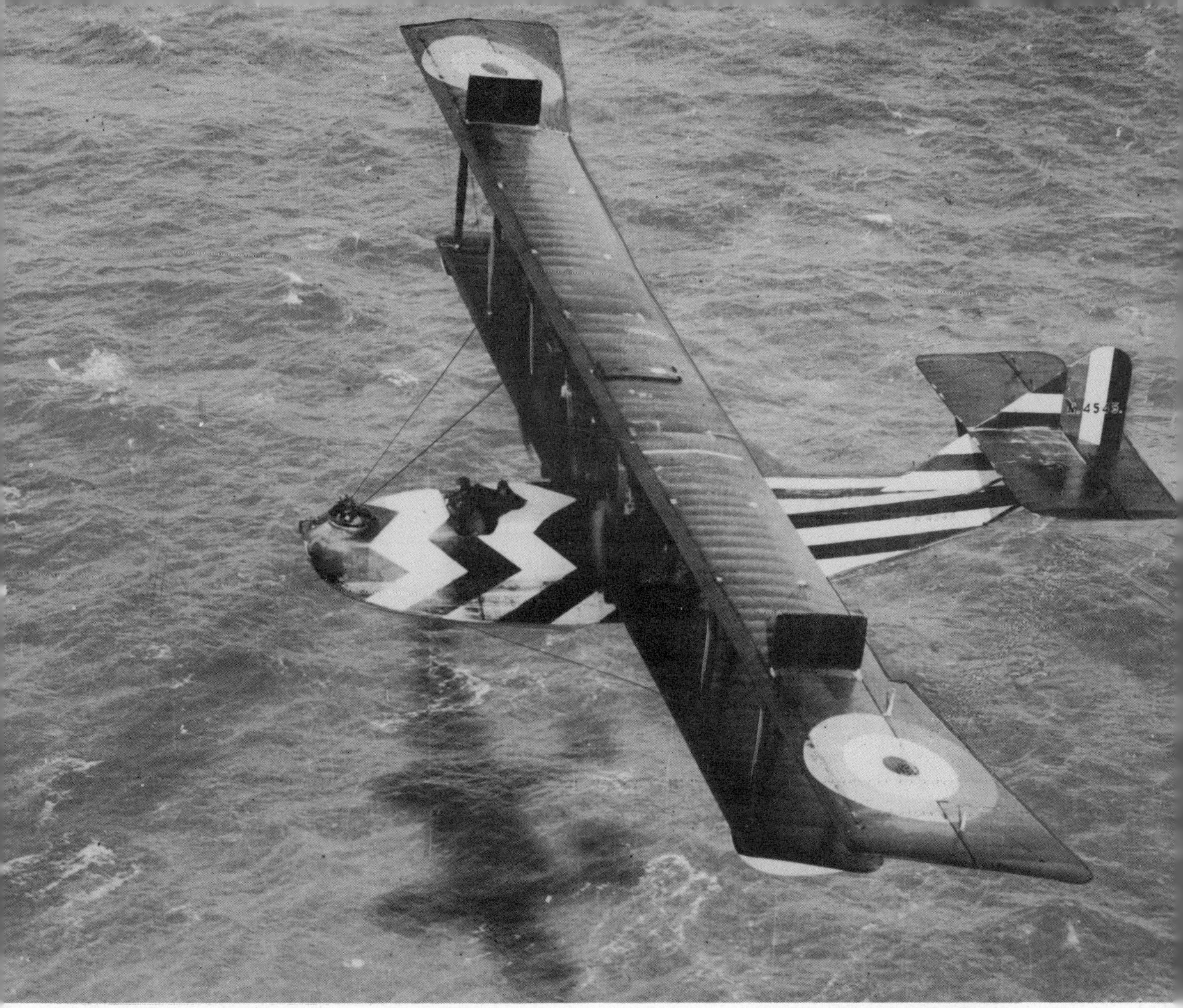

Another F.2A without cockpit enclosure for the pilots. Bizarre paint schemes of the kind displayed were adopted as a means of identification

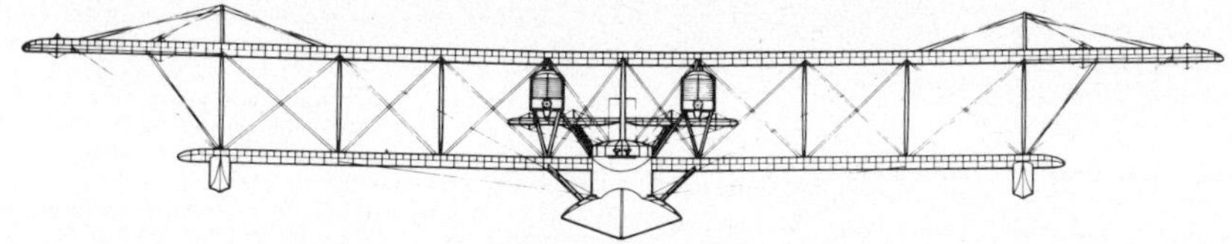

gun on a pillar mounting at each of two waist hatches abaft of wings, and one or two Lewis guns on mounting above hull in this same area. An experimental installation of twin "fighting tops" on the upper wings was made for two Scarff ring mountings, each with twin Lewis guns. Under-wing provision for two 230 lb (104 kg) bombs.

DIMENSIONS:

Wing span 95 *ft* 7½ *in* (29·13 *m*)
Length overall 46 *ft* 3 *in* (14·09 *m*)
Height overall 17 *ft* 6 *in* (5·33 *m*)
Wing area 1,133 *sq ft* (105 *m*²)

WEIGHTS:

Weight empty 7,549 *lb* (3,424 *kg*)
Weight loaded 10,978 *lb* (4,536 *kg*) .

PERFORMANCE:

Max speed at 2,000 *ft* (610 *m*) 95·5 *mph* (153 *kmh*)
Max speed at 10,000 *ft* (3,050 *m*) 80·5 *mph* (129 *kmh*)
Time of climb to 6,500 *ft* (1,980 *m*) 16 *min* 40 *sec*
Service ceiling 9,600 *ft* (2,925 *m*)
Endurance 6 *hr*

F.2A with enclosed pilot's cockpit

The Gotha high-altitude bombers were outstanding among 1914–18 aircraft

GOTHA G IV and G V

Together with Zeppelin dirigibles, twin-engined bombers of Gotha type were responsible for the heaviest and longest-ranging bombing attacks mounted by Germany in the 1914–18 war. The legend grew, indeed, that all German airships were Zeppelins and all large bombers were Gothas, which was not the case.

The initial success of the Gotha bombers can be largely attributed to their high-altitude capability; yet this was reconciled with an effective bomb load and ingenious armament. Although an efficient aeroplane in both the technical and military senses, these machines had their weaknesses. So light was the structure built, with the object of procuring a high operational altitude, that specially prepared airfields were found to be necessary. The sturdy all-steel Voisin bombers, as already noted, were capable of operating from rough surfaces; but it must also be remarked that the Gothas were of a class which would rank today as "strategic" bombers, and all aircraft of this class which operated during the 1939–45 war had specially prepared bases.

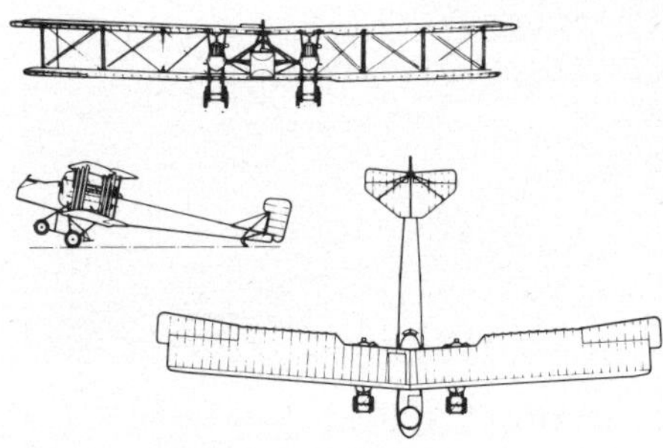

Additional wheels were a boon for night flying

Gothas are especially remembered for the severity of their raids on London, and among these that of 13 June 1917 is historic. Fourteen new Gothas then attacked in daylight, inflicting more casualties than all the Zeppelin raids previously. This led not only to a public clamour for more effective defences but also, indirectly, to the establishment of Britain's own Independent Force of the RAF, which developed the technique of "strategic" bombing to the highest pitch attained in World War I.

Although sizable aircraft, the Gothas were small compared with the Zeppelin (Staaken) R-type bombers which, with Gotha escort, also raided London. Wing span of these bombers was over 137 ft (62·14 m).

The following description applies in general to the Gotha G IV and G V, which were the principal production versions.

TYPE:

Twin-engined bomber.

WINGS:

Braced biplane type, with sweepback from centre line. Equal span, except for overhanging balance portions of top ailerons. Three bays of bracing outboard of engine nacelles. Two-piece upper wings, centre-section for lower wings. Two main spars of spruce I-section, walled with birch ply and wrapped with fabric. Plywood ribs, extensively lightened, tacked to spars. Fabric covering. Interplane struts of steel tube, with plywood fairing. Ailerons of welded steel tubes, fabric-covered and interconnected. Trailing-edge of top wings cut away to clear pusher propellers.

FUSELAGE:

Rectangular-section one-piece structure with spruce longerons and spacers. Bracing by stranded steel cables. Plywood skinning.

TAIL UNIT:

Braced monoplane type, with balanced rudder and unbalanced elevator. Steel-tube construction, with fabric covering. Bracing by steel-tube struts.

LANDING GEAR:

Two main twin-wheel units, one below each engine nacelle. Shock-absorption by tension springs in main legs.

POWER PLANT:

Two 260 hp Mercedes D IVa six-cylinder in-line water-cooled high-compression engines in pusher installations on the lower wings. Smaller nacelles, clear of wing, on G V. Radiators at front of nacelles. Two-blade wooden propellers. Fuel tanks aft of pilot's cockpit.

ACCOMMODATION AND ARMAMENT:

Gunner's cockpit in nose with ring mounting for Parabellum machine-gun. Pilot on port side to rear, with folding seat for second crew-member. Rear-gunner's position immediately aft of trailing-edges, in association with a special plywood-lined "tunnel" and a Vee-shaped opening in the top decking, allowing the Parabellum gun to be sighted and fired backwards and downwards through the fuselage. Wire-mesh propeller-guards at this position. Bombs carried externally under centre-section. Load varied, but typical complement for a raid on London was six bombs of 110 lb (50 kg).

DIMENSIONS:

Wing span 77 *ft* 10 *in* (23·72 *m*)
Length overall 40 *ft* 7 *in* (12·37 *m*)
Height overall 14 *ft* 1 *in* (4·29 *m*)

WEIGHTS (G V):

Weight empty 5,700 *lb* (2,585 *kg*)
Weight loaded 8,600 *lb* (3,900 *kg*)

PERFORMANCE (G V):

Max speed at 12,000 *ft* (3,657 *m*) 72 *mph* (114 *kmh*)
Time of climb to 12,000 *ft* (3,657 *m*) 35 *min*
Ceiling 20,500 *ft* (6,250 *m*)

JUNKERS J1

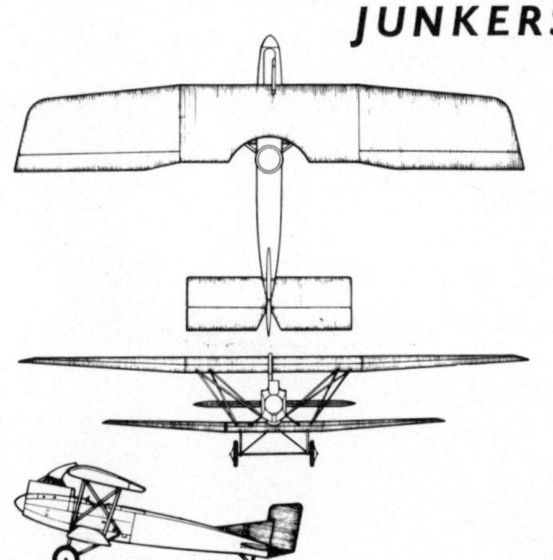

The J 1 was a notable aircraft not only by reason of its metal construction but because it was the first specialised armoured ground-attack aircraft

Before 1910 the name of Hugo Junkers had been associated mainly with engines, but in the course of that year he was granted a patent, reading, in abstract, "In order to make the ratio between the supporting capacity of an aeroplane and the resistance to forward motion as large as possible, the non-supporting parts of the machine are arranged in casings having their upper and lower surfaces shaped so as to act as supporting-planes while reducing the head resistance to a minimum". Reference was further made to "a supporting plane formed with an enlarged central part adapted to carry the aviators &c., the front part being composed of glass or other transparent material". Here was the germ of the cantilever monoplane idea, and an astonishing forecast of the Junkers G.38 airliner of 1931. Junkers built his first all-metal monoplane (smooth-skinned) in 1915, using tinplate. This was not the first all-metal aeroplane to fly, the distinction having been gained by the French *Tubavion* monoplane of Ponche and Primard (1912).

The following description relates not to a Junkers monoplane but to the J 1 cantilever biplane of 1917 which had a particular interest not only in point of structure but in being the first specialised (as distinct from adapted) ground-attack aircraft. The designation "J 1" is that under which the aircraft was operated by the German Air Force. The factory designation was J 4.

TYPE:

Two-seat ground-attack aircraft.

WINGS:

Cantilever biplane type. Lower wing much smaller than upper. Top wing with large centre-section, braced to fuselage by steel-tube struts in the form of a cross. Smaller bottom centre-section built in one unit with landing gear and braced to extremities of upper centre-section by two struts on each side. All wings with swept-back leading-edges. Whole of wings outboard of centre-sections pure cantilever structures, without bracing, and tapering in thickness. Construction entirely metal, including covering. Ten tubular duralumin spars in upper wings, six in lower, braced by smaller duralumin tubes. Junctions between spar tubes and bracing tubes effected by steel collars, with welded lugs pinned to spars. Bracing tubes flattened, slipped over lugs and riveted. Towards wing-tips bracing tubes replaced by corrugated duralumin strips, riveted directly to tubes and steel collars no longer employed. Wing spars joined to centre-section spars by screwed steel collar fitting, carried by sleeves slipped into, and riveted to, the spars. Sheet duralumin covering 0·015 in (0·38 mm) thick, corrugated to a pitch of 1¾ in (44·45 mm) and a depth of ⅓ in (7·6 mm). Sheets riveted together and to spars. Ailerons of balanced type, fitted to top wings only.

FUSELAGE:

Built in two distinct portions. Front portion an armoured steel box of 5 mm (0·19 in) steel plate riveted together and housing engine, fuel tanks and crew. This portion stiffened by internal bracing and formers of duralumin. Aft of observer's seat fuselage of duralumin tube construction, with longerons, struts and diagonal bracing. Steel joints between bracing tubes and longerons, in form of sleeves fitting tightly round longerons and pinned to them. Lugs welded to sleeves, and flattened ends of bracing tubes slipped over, and riveted to, these lugs. In two rearmost bays vertical tubes replaced by strong duralumin bulkheads carrying four duralumin cross-tubes for tailplane spar connections. Another pair of tubes fixed to stern-post. Junction between two portions of fuselage at point where four longerons butted against the rear plate of the forward armoured box portion, forming a bulkhead behind the observer. A steel stud, 12 mm (0·47 in) diameter, with a head fitting inside each longeron, passed through the bulkhead and was secured by a nut and split pin.

TAIL UNIT:

General construction similar to that of wings. Front spar not connected to fuselage. Fin and rudder dependent for their strength solely on their duralumin covering.

LANDING GEAR:

Built in one unit with lower centre-section. Two steel-tube Vees, each with a stiffening tube running from top of front tube to point about half-way down rear tube. Vees vertical in front view and having their bases braced by steel tubes to the middle of the lower centre-section. Steel-tube axle with rubber shock absorbers. Three steel-tube struts to fuselage from attachment points of Vees to lower centre-section. Ash tail-skid on steel-tube pyramid and having a spiral spring, fitted below tail.

POWER PLANT:

One 200 hp Benz Bz. IV six-cylinder water-cooled in-line engine in armoured cowling (sides and front). Two-blade wooden propeller. Exhaust discharging over top wing. Engine-bearers of ash, carried on sheet-steel supports braced by duralumin tubes. Fuel tank of brass sheet made in form of armchair to seat pilot. Capacity 26 Imp gallons (118 litres). Radiator on lower surface of upper wing, consisting of broad, flat, horizontal water-tubes with corrugated-strip distance pieces. Cooling surface 110 sq ft (10·22 m^2).

ARMAMENT AND EQUIPMENT:

Two fixed machine-guns for pilot, one machine gun on ring mounting for observer. Two fixed downward-firing guns tried, but not standardised. Radio in observer's cockpit.

DIMENSIONS:

Wing span 55 *ft* 0 *in* (16·76 *m*)
Length overall 29 *ft* 8 *in* (9·04 *m*)

WEIGHTS AND LOADINGS:

Weight empty 3,724 *lb* (1,690 *kg*)
Weight loaded 4,569 *lb* (2,073 *kg*)
Wing loading 8·5 *lb/sq ft* (0·79 m^2)
Power loading 19·9 *lb/hp* (9 *kg/hp*)

PERFORMANCE:

Max speed at S/L 96 *mph* (154 *kmh*)
Endurance 2 *hr*

AVRO 504K

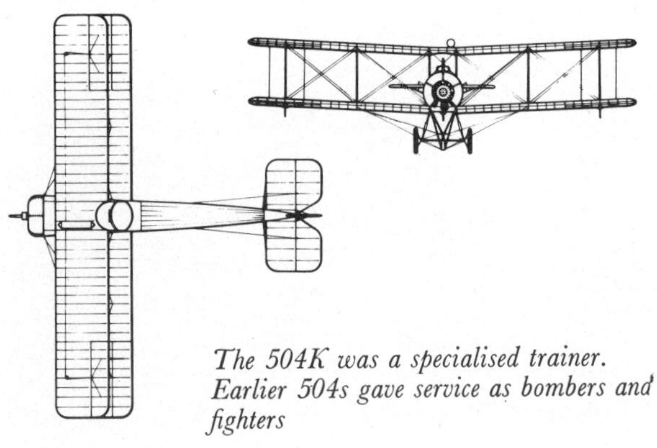

The 504K was a specialised trainer. Earlier 504s gave service as bombers and fighters

The Avro 504K stands pre-eminent among training aircraft not only for its intrinsic merit but for its association (together with its predecessor the 504J) with the School of Special Flying formed at Gosport, England, in July 1917 by Major R. R. Smith-Barry. The 504 series of tractor biplanes was derived from A. V. Roe's biplane of 1908 by way of his four types of triplane, the Type D biplane of 1911 (one example of which became the first British seaplane to fly) and the Avro 500 (Type E) of 1912. The apparent influence of the Goupy II biplane has already been mentioned. The prototype 504 appeared in 1913 and quickly established its all-round excellence in performance and handling. Numerous derivatives were supplied to the Royal Flying Corps and the Royal Naval Air Service and were used for fighting and bombing. The most historic operation conducted with the type was the raid on the Zeppelin sheds at Friedrichshafen on 21 November 1914. Each machine carried four 20 lb (9·07 kg) bombs and a violent explosion was caused in the gas plant. The

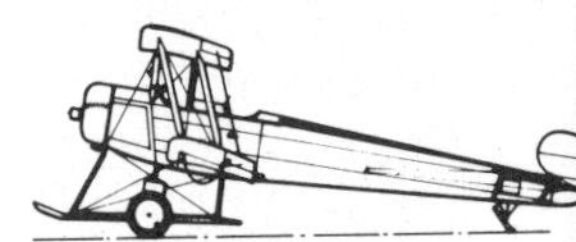

Peaceful years: The entry for this aircraft in "Lloyd's Aviation Record" read: Type, Avro 504K biplane. Owners, Messrs. Thomas and Griffiths. No. of passengers, including pilot and crew, 3. Airworthiness Certificate issued, 29/7/27.

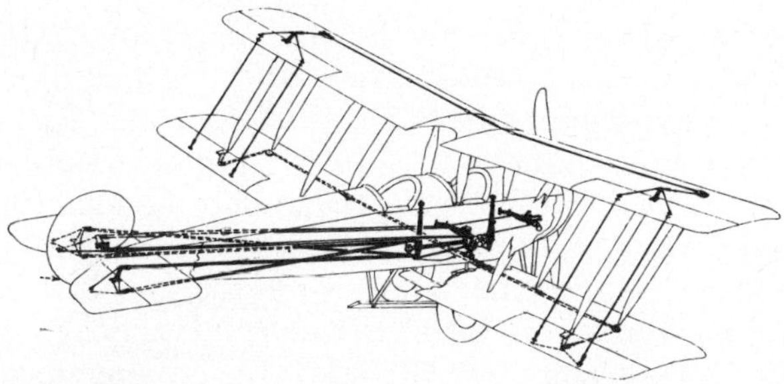

Drawing from "Schedule for the Avro 504K" showing the run of the flying controls

The Avro publication below was inscribed by Roy Chadwick, designer-to-be of the Lancaster bomber (page 105)

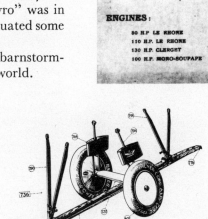

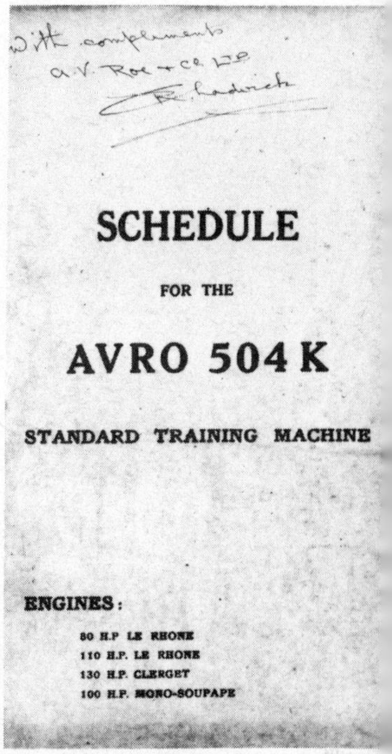

With complements
A.V. Roe & Co Ltd
R. Chadwick

SCHEDULE

FOR THE

AVRO 504 K

STANDARD TRAINING MACHINE

ENGINES:

80 H.P LE RHONE
110 H.P. LE RHONE
130 H.P. CLERGET
100 H.P. MONO-SOUPAPE

fitting of the 100 hp Gnome Monosoupape engine in the autumn of 1916 brought into being the sub-type 504J, or "Mono Avro" as it became known, and among the first units to receive this version was the Gosport flying school already mentioned. One reason for the success of the type as a trainer was the readiness with which it gave notice of faulty handling. The incorporation of a new engine mounting to permit the installation of any of several types of rotary engine brought into being the 504K, or "Standard Avro", which was to continue in Royal Air Force service until the late 1920s, when it was succeeded by the 504N, with Armstrong Siddeley Lynx stationary radial engine. The "Lynx Avro" was in turn succeeded by the Avro Tutor, which, although of entirely new design, perpetuated some of the distinctive features of the 504 series.

In post-war years numerous Avro 504s were converted for "joyriding", or "barnstorming", and trainer variants were widely employed by air forces throughout the world.

TYPE:
Two-seat trainer.

WINGS:
Staggered biplane structure, with two wooden spars, wooden ribs and fabric covering. Woods used, spruce, ash, walnut. Centre-section carried above fuselage on four struts. Ailerons on all four wings. Top and bottom wings and ailerons interchangeable.

FUSELAGE:
Four rectangular-section channeled ash longerons, strengthened by flanges of three-ply wood. Struts of ash. Fabric covering.

TAIL UNIT:
Monoplane type, with braced tailplane. No fin. Balanced rudder.

LANDING GEAR:
Two wheels and central ash skid on steel-tube structure. Rubber cord shock absorbers.

POWER PLANT:
One 80 hp Le Rhône, 110 hp Le Rhône, 130 hp Clerget or 100 hp Gnome Monosoupape rotary engines in standard aircraft. Numerous non-standard installations for civil use. Main fuel tank capacity 20 Imp gallons (90·9 litres). Gravity petrol tank capacity 4 Imp gallons (18·18 litres). Oil tank capacity 6½ Imp gallons (29·54 litres). Two-blade wooden tractor propeller. Engine supported on two steel-plate bearers.

ACCOMMODATION:
Instructor and pupil in tandem cockpits with dual controls and safety belts. Both seats on a single assembly. Instruments: compass, air-pressure gauge, cross level, air-speed indicator, watch, altimeter, pulsometer, rpm indicator. Also on instrument panel were two plates: one engine-speed warning plate and one reading: "Instructions to Pupils to Turn to the Left. I. Left rudder, left warp. Together. II. Centralise rudder. Pull stick towards right elbow. Together. III. Right rudder. Right warp. Together."

DIMENSIONS:
Wing span 36 *ft* 0 *in* (10·97 *m*)
Length overall 28 *ft* 11 *in* (8·81 *m*)
Height 10 *ft* 5 *in* (3·17 *m*)
Wing area 330 *sq ft* (30·66 m^2)

WEIGHTS (110 hp Le Rhône engine):
Weight empty 1,230 *lb* (558 *kg*)
Weight loaded 1,823 *lb* (827 *kg*)

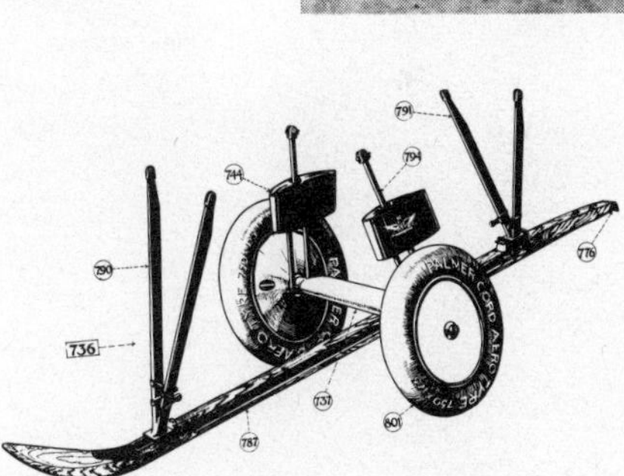

The "toothpick" landing gear as shown in the "Schedule"

PERFORMANCE (110 hp Le Rhône engine):
Max speed 90 *mph* (145 *kmh*)
Cruising speed 78 *mph* (125 *kmh*)
Climb to 8,000 *ft* (2,440 *m*) 6·5 *min*
Service ceiling 16,000 *ft* (4,875 *m*)
Endurance 3 *hr*
Range 250 *miles* (402 *km*)

VICKERS VIMY

This sculpture of Capt J. Alcock and Lt A. Whitten Brown is at London Heathrow Airport

Although the Atlantic Ocean had been crossed indirectly by the American Curtiss NC-4 flying boat commanded by Lt.-Cdr. A. C. Read (16–27 May 1919), the first direct crossing was made by a British Vickers Vimy, manned by Capt. J. Alcock and Lt. A. Whitten Brown. The Vimy took off from a meadow near St. John's, Newfoundland, on 14 June 1919 and crash-landed in a bog near Clifden, Galway, Ireland on the following day. The distance of 1,890 miles had been covered in 15 hr 57 min, at an average speed of 118 mph. Fuel remained for another 800 miles. A similar Vimy made the first Britain-Australia flight, manned by Captain Ross Smith, his brother Keith (navigator) and Sergeants Bennett and Shiers (mechanics). This Vimy left Hounslow, near London, on 12 November 1919 and reached Port Darwin, over 11,000 miles away, on 10 December. A third Vimy was used during 1920 for a less successful flight from Brooklands to Cape Town (W/C. H. A. van Ryneveld and F/L. C. J. Quintin Brand, with two mechanics).

The Vimys used for these flights were converted bombers, of a type designed by R. K. Pierson. The prototype was first flown on 30 November 1917, and though Vimys were never used operationally during the First World War one example did reach France. After the war the type was used by the RAF as a bomber, mail-carrier and trainer, and was developed into the Vimy Commercial, which was closely related to the RAF's Vernon bomber-transport.

The Transatlantic Vimy is now in the Science Museum, South Kensington, London.

The Transatlantic Vimy was erected and test-flown at a field in Newfoundland sportingly offered by Raynham, one of a number of pilots competing for the "Daily Mail" prize of £10,000

A turtle deck covered the gunner's cockpit

TYPE:

Twin-engined bomber.

WINGS:

Unstaggered biplane wings in three assemblies: centre section extending to outer edges of engine nacelles and two outer sections of two bays each. Dihedral (3°) on outer sections only. Wooden construction with fabric covering. Spars of box section, built up from spruce and three-ply and bound with fabric. Interplane struts (except those carrying engines) of hollow spruce. Engine nacelles supported on four vertical steel struts of circular section with wooden fairings. Horn-balanced ailerons on all four wings.

FUSELAGE:

Rectangular-section composite structure in two parts. Portion ahead of rear wing spars of steel tubing. Rear section with longerons of McGruer's patent wooden tubing, braced with swaged steel tie-rods.

TAIL UNIT:

Biplane type of wood and fabric construction with two fins of "K" shape and two balanced rudders.

LANDING GEAR:

Main gear consisting of two two-wheel units attached beneath engine bays. Palmer cord tyres, 900 mm × 200 mm. Elastic shock absorbers on axles. Large wooden skid under forward fuselage as precaution against nosing over, replaced on Atlantic machine by wheel. Wheel removed before Atlantic crossing. Wooden tail skid and two protective skids under tailplane.

Alcock and Brown acclaimed by Royal Aero Club secretary Harold Perrin

The Transatlantic Vimy climbs away, burdened with its extra petrol. One tank was shaped to serve as a buoyancy raft, recalling Blériot's air bag

POWER PLANT:

Atlantic aircraft had two Rolls-Royce Eagle VIII twelve-cylinder vee-type water-cooled engines of 360 hp each, cowled in faired nacelles with frontal radiators. Adjustable louvres for temperature regulation. Four-blade wooden propellers, diameter 10 ft 5 in (3·17 m). Form of engine nacelle determined in Vickers' private wind tunnel to secure minimum resistance from a body having a flat front face. Other engines fitted were 200 hp Hispano-Suiza, 260 hp Sunbeam Maori, 260 hp Fiat A-12, 300 hp Fiat A-12bis, 230 hp B.H.P., 260 hp Salmson, 375 hp Lorraine and 400 hp Liberty. A few RAF trainers had Bristol Jupiter or Armstrong Siddeley Jaguar engines.

ACCOMMODATION:

Vimy bomber had a Scarff gun ring with Lewis gun in nose and aft of wings, and provision for a gun firing through floor. Bombs carried under fuselage and centre section. Atlantic aircraft stripped of military equipment. Alcock (pilot) sat on right. Flying instruments: air-speed indicator, altimeter, rate-of-climb indicator, bank indicator. Revolution counters and fuel-flow indicators in sides of engine nacelles. Brown (navigator) sat on left. Sextant of

standard naval pattern with deep-cut scale. Six-inch drift bearing-plate. Appleyard course and distance calculator. Standard aircraft compass on left side of cockpit in addition to two other compasses for pilot. Navigator responsible for radio transmitter and receiver. One of extra petrol tanks shaped to serve as a buoyancy raft (buoyancy 600 lb = 272 kg). Extra fuel tanks fitted in fuselage in place of bombs and gear and rear gunner. Gunner's cockpit covered by turtle deck. Fuel capacity increased from 470 Imp gallons (2,137 litres) to 865 Imp gallons (3,932 litres). Even at higher weight Atlantic machine was capable of maintaining flight on one engine at 70 mph (112·5 kmh). Alcock and Brown had Gieve life-saving jackets.

DIMENSIONS:

Wing span 67 *ft* 0 *in* (20·42 *m*)
Length overall 42 *ft* 8 *in* (13·00 *m*)
Height overall 15 *ft* 3 *in* (4·65 *m*)
Tailplane span 16 *ft* (4·87 *m*)
Wing area 1,330 *sq ft* (123·56 *m*²)

WEIGHTS AND LOADINGS:

Weight empty 6,700 *lb* (3,039 *kg*)
Weight loaded (*bomber*) 12,500 *lb* (5,669 *kg*)
Weight loaded (*Atlantic machine*) 13,300 *lb* (6,033 *kg*)
Wing loading (*Atlantic machine*) 10 *lb/sq ft* (48·82 *kg/m*²)

PERFORMANCE:

Max speed with bombs at 10,000 *ft* (3,050 *m*) 100 *mph* (161 *kmh*)
Climb to 10,000 *ft* (3,050 *m*) *with bombs* 50 *min*
Range (*bomber*) 835 *miles* (1,344 *km*)
Range (*Atlantic machine*) 2,440 *miles* (3,927 *km*)

The nose wheel, which had been substituted for the skid of the standard bomber, was removed in Newfoundland and the Vimy tipped over on landing in an Irish bog

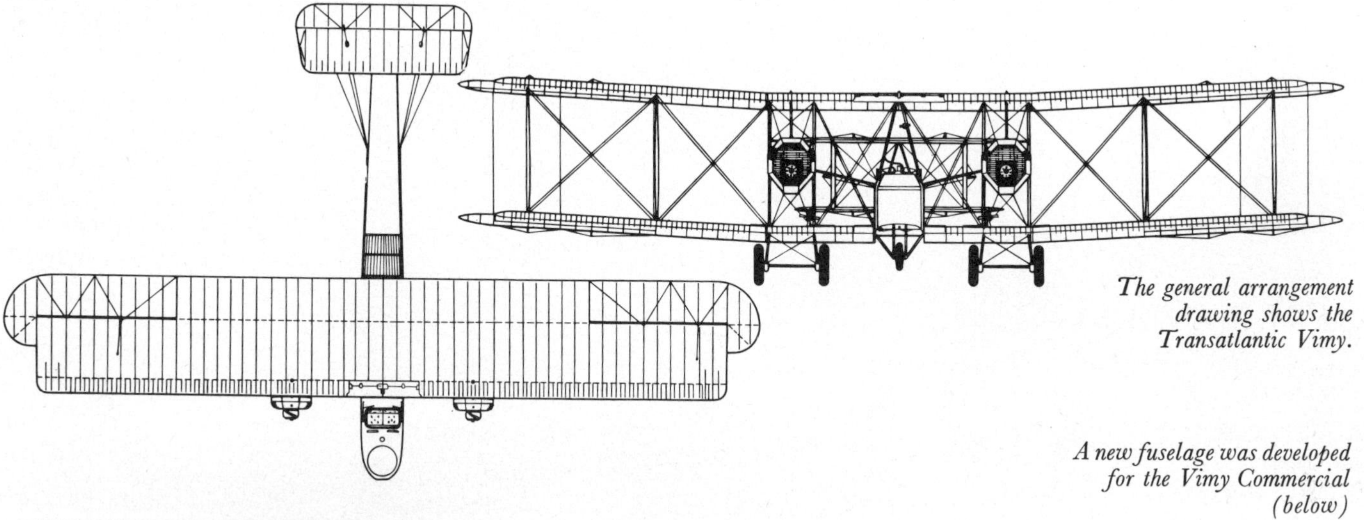

The general arrangement drawing shows the Transatlantic Vimy.

A new fuselage was developed for the Vimy Commercial (below)

FARMAN GOLIATH

Goliaths were a familar sight on European air routes

Like the Vickers Vimy, the Farman Goliath was designed as a bomber and developed during 1918/19 as an airliner. But whereas an entirely new fuselage, of very large cross-section, was built for the Vimy Commercial (placing it high on the list of claimants to the title of the "world's first real airliner") the French machine retained its original bomber fuselage, with adaptations. The furnishings in the first machine were Spartan and the bleakness of the passengers' surroundings was accentuated by diagonal cross-bracing members inherited from the bomber. These were removed in succeeding machines, and some striking schemes of décor were apparent in accordance with the tastes of operators. Although the Goliath itself had a severity of appearance by reason of its blunt-nosed fuselage and "clipped-off" wing-tips it was a design of high efficiency, for which the high aspect ratio of the wings, and the thickness of their section, were in large degree responsible.

This efficiency was demonstrated on 1 April 1919, when Lieutenant Lucien Bossoutrot took a Goliath carrying four passengers to a height of 20,670 ft (6,300 m). Three days later the Goliath climbed to 20,340 ft (6,200 m) carrying fourteen passengers, the time of climb being 1 hr 5 min as on the previous occasion; and on 5 May, with 25 passengers, a height of 16,730 ft (5,100 m) was attained in 1 hr 15 min. During August of the same year, with Bossoutrot and Coupet as pilots, and with a crew of six, a non-stop flight of 1,274 miles (2,050 km), from Paris to Casablanca, was completed in 18 hr 23 min. The Goliath entered commercial service on the London–Paris service of Cie des Grands Express Aériens on 29 March 1920.

TYPE:

Twin-engined airliner.

WINGS:

Equal-span unstaggered biplane. Wings of very deep section and high aspect ratio. Ailerons on all four wings. Early machines had balanced ailerons extending beyond wing-tips, but these were later shortened to wing-tips. Two-spar wooden construction, with fabric covering. Wing carried above fuselage on two pairs of struts. One pair of struts each side in line with engines. Two pairs each side outboard.

FUSELAGE:

Wooden fabric-covered structure of rectangular section. Width 4 ft 4 in (1·32 m). Nose of airliner longer than that of bomber to provide for forward passenger cabin. First machine had diagonal structural members interfering with passenger accommodation, but these were eliminated later. Early-production aircraft had pronounced turtle-deck fairing on top of fuselage, but this was later reduced in height.

TAIL UNIT:

Braced monoplane type, with triangular fin and tall rectangular rudder.

LANDING GEAR:

Two main assemblies, one under each engine nacelle. Each unit carried two wheels, one on each side of a central faired "trouser" structure. Lower members of this structure wire-braced to lower wing outboard and upper and lower members cross-braced inboard. Tail-skid under rear fuselage.

POWER PLANT:

Earliest aircraft of the type were powered with two 230 hp Salmson Z.9 nine-cylinder water-cooled radial engines, with exhaust-collector forming radiator frame. Nacelles of rectangular section on lower wing. Four-blade wooden propellers. Most of early aircraft re-engined with 260 hp Salmson CM.9 engines, and engines of several makes and types subsequently installed, including Gnome-Rhône Jupiter (Bristol licence) and Armstrong Siddeley Jaguar air-cooled radials. One machine had four engines in tandem pairs; another had three engines.

ACCOMMODATION:

Varied considerably according to period and operator. Typically two passenger cabins, separated by raised open cockpit for crew of two, located under leading-edge of top wing. Four wicker-work seats in forward cabin, eight in rear. Racks for light luggage. Continuous line of windows extending round nose of fuselage to end of rear cabin. Large passenger-access door at rear of cabin on starboard side. Night-flying equipment.

DIMENSIONS:

Wing span 86 *ft* 10 *in* (26·5 *m*)
Length overall 47 *ft* 0 *in* (14·33 *m*)
Wing area 1,733 *sq ft* (161 m^2)

WEIGHTS:

Weight empty 5,510 *lb* (2,500 *kg*)
Weight loaded 10,516 *lb* (4,770 *kg*)

PERFORMANCE:

Cruising speed at 6,560 *ft* (2,000 *m*) 74·6 *mph* (120 *kmh*)
Ceiling 13,120 *ft* (4,000 *m*)
Range 248 *miles* (400 *km*)

A Goliath at Croydon, which served as London's airport between the wars

SOPWITH CUCKOO

Proposals for dropping torpedoes from aircraft date back to 1912, but the first actual release occurred in February 1914. The leading figure connected with this event was the Italian General A. Guidoni, who, in 1912 had been ordered to help a Mr. Pateras Pescara in developing a torpedo-carrying aircraft. Using a Farman biplane, General Guidoni succeeded in dropping a weight of 170 lb (77 kg) and concluded that with a machine of 6,000 lb (2,720 kg) gross weight he could carry and release a torpedo. He thereupon built a large monoplane with floats and hydrofoils and having two Gnome engines in tandem. With this machine he succeeded, in February 1914 as stated, in dropping a torpedo of 750 lb (340 kg). He repeated the operation several times before the first drop was made in England a few days before the outbreak of war. These early experiments were all made with seaplanes, and the first torpedo-carrying aircraft with a wheeled landing gear was an adapted German Albatros B. II of 1915. In the winter of 1916 Commander (later Rear Admiral Sir) Murray Sueter of the Royal Navy, who had instigated the early British torpedo-dropping experiments, had the idea of operating torpedo-carrying aircraft from aircraft carriers. His early notions included the use of catapults. As in the earlier experiments, he enlisted the aid of Mr. (later Sir Thomas) Sopwith, and construction of the Cuckoo was put in hand. After some delay, through lapsing of official interest during Commander Sueter's absence, the Cuckoo was completed.

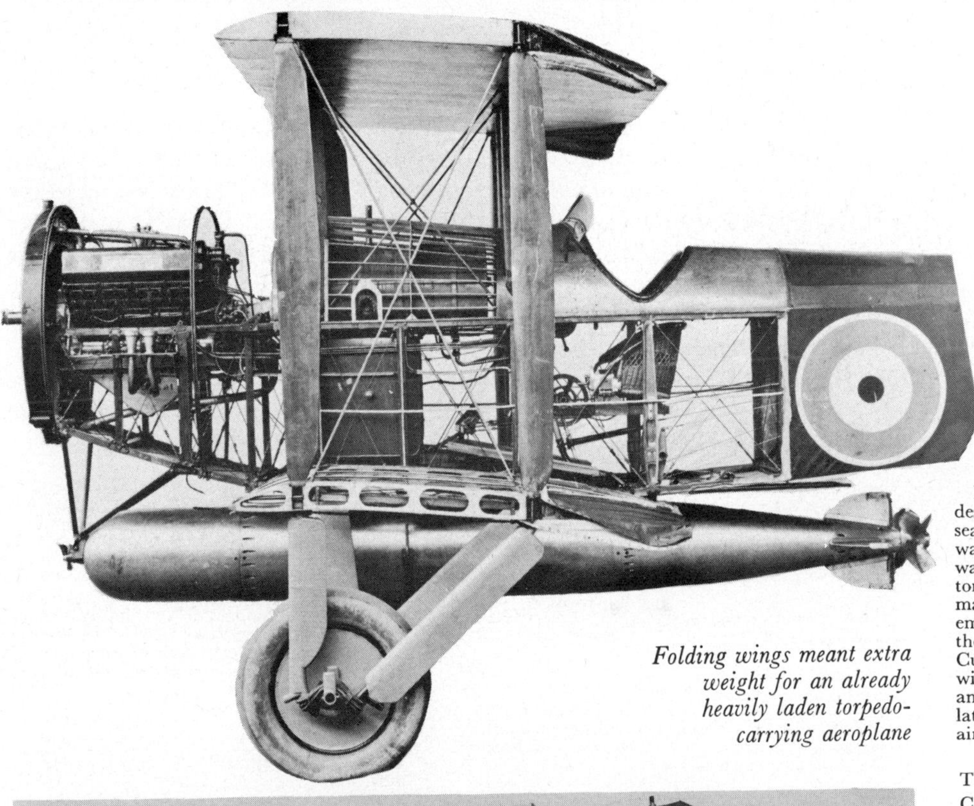

Folding wings meant extra weight for an already heavily laden torpedo-carrying aeroplane

It was an adaptation of a large single-seat bombe designated B.1, but not to be confused with the single seat version of the 1½ Strutter already mentioned, anc was itself designated T.1. The Cuckoo, as the typ was named, was thus the world's first carrier-born torpedo-dropper with wheel landing gear. Afte many exigencies, the first squadron of Cuckoos wa embarked in HMS *Argus* on 19 October 1918, bu these aircraft were never used on operations. Th Cuckoo was one of the earliest aircraft to be fitte with deck-landing arrester gear. It was produced by and developed by, the Blackburn company, whic later produced a unique succession of naval strik aircraft culminating in the Buccaneer.

TYPE:
Carrier-borne single-seat torpedo dropper.

WINGS:
Three-bay unstaggered biplane wings with jointe spars for folding at attachment point of innermo struts. Two-spar wooden fabric-covered constructio Three bays of decreasing width from outboard ba Ailerons on all four wings. Wide top centre-sectic with four vertical struts to fuselage and four lower centre-section.

FUSELAGE:
Wooden construction with cross bracing. Fabı covering except for area round cockpit.

TAIL UNIT:
Monoplane type with adjustable tailplane on top fuselage.

The Cuckoo was the first torpedo-carrying aeroplane to be designed to operate from the deck of an aircraft carrier. This slightly damaged specimen is seen on board H.M.S. "Furious"

LANDING GEAR:

Special split type to permit carrying of torpedo. Two main assemblies, each formed of steel tubes welded and pinned together and each in two portions. One Vee-shaped portion placed parallel to fuselage, the end lugs being bolted to the front and rear spars of the lower centre-section. Other portion with one end lug bolted to bottom longeron of fuselage and bent to form axle for one wheel, the other end resting in the apex of the Vee. Shock absorbers formed by 28 ft (8·53 m) of 15 mm (0·59 in) diameter elastic, given ten complete turns round axle and apex of Vee. Steel struts streamlined by wooden fairings, attached by metal clips, the whole being wrapped with fabric and then doped. Production Cuckoos had higher tail skid than prototype to allow ample clearance for torpedo.

POWER PLANT:

One Hispano-Suiza, Sunbeam Arab or Wolseley Viper 8-cylinder water-cooled engine with circular frontal radiator. Two-blade wooden tractor propeller.

ARMAMENT:

No guns carried. 18 in (45 cm) Mk. IX torpedo of 1,000 lb (453 kg) and of adapted Naval Whitehead type carried in steel crutches under fuselage. Provision for torpedo depth-setting and heating, the latter by exhaust tail pipes of special mats. Mechanical torpedo release.

DIMENSIONS:

Wing span 46 *ft* 9 *in* (14·22 *m*)
Wing chord 6 *ft* 3 *in* (1·90 *m*)
Wing gap 6 *ft* 0 *in* (1·83 *m*)
Length overall 28 *ft* 6 *in* (8·69 *m*)

WEIGHTS (Arab engine):

Weight empty 2,199 *lb* (998 *kg*)
Military load 1,099 *lb* (499 *kg*)
Pilot 180 *lb* (81 *kg*)
Fuel and oil 405 *lb* (183 *kg*)
Flying weight 3,883 *lb* (1,761 *kg*)

PERFORMANCE (Arab engine, with torpedo):

Max speed at 2,000 *ft* (610 *m*) 103·5 *mph* (166·5 *kmh*)
Climb to 6,500 *ft* (1,980 *m*) 15 *min* 40 *sec*
Service ceiling 12,100 *ft* (3,680 *m*)
Endurance 4 *hr*

The Cuckoo made a significant contribution to the technique of torpedo dropping, initiated by the great Italian designer/constructor Guidoni in February 1914. Float landing gear had previously handicapped aircraft in this class

NAVY-CURTISS NC-4

Airborne

The NC-4 was a triumphant example of collaboration between a Government department and a private constructor, the triumph being implicit in the first east-west crossing of the Atlantic, in May 1919.

Mention has already been made (Felixstowe/Porte F.2A) of the flying boat *America* constructed in 1914 to make the Atlantic crossing. Although never gaining any such distinction it was acquired by Britain's Royal Naval Air Service and was the true ancestor of all large British and American flying boats of 1914–18. In the USA, on 25 August 1917, Admiral Taylor, Chief Naval Constructor, formulated a plan for attacking U-boats from the air, remarking "The ideal solution would be big flying boats or the equivalent, that would be able to fly across the Atlantic to avoid the difficulties of delivery &c.". The Curtiss Aeroplane and Motor Corporation had been building aircraft for Great Britain and Russia since 1915 and had also constructed in 1916 the Model T triplane flying boat which, with its wing span of 133 ft (40·54 m) was the largest aircraft ever constructed.

Waterborne: The Stars and Stripes hangs limply from the top wing of the NC-4 during preparations for the Atlantic crossing. Size is accentuated by the working party distributed on the hull, starboard engine nacelle and tailplane

The US Navy's "fleet" of NC flying-boats assembled before departure

As a result of Admiral Taylor's suggestion Glenn Curtiss was invited to Washington for talks with Navy representatives, and the "NC" (Navy-Curtiss) design emerged from a pooling of ideas. Technically the most interesting feature was the supporting of the tail unit not on the stern of a long hull but on outriggers. It was desired to avoid a lengthy hull, the consideration being that what did not exist could not be weak. Hull shape was decidedly a "Navy-Curtiss" product. The first machine (NC-1) was initially flown on 4 October 1918. NC-4 was launched at Far Rockaway on 30 April, 1919. It was planned to send all four craft (the only ones ordered) on an Atlantic flight, but NC-2 was dismantled to provide spares for the others. On 16 May the remaining three left Trepassy, Newfoundland. NC-1 and NC-3 both made forced alightings, and NC-1 eventually sank. NC-4 (Lt.-Cdr. A. C. Read) reached Horta, in the Azores, on 17 May, continued to Ponta Delgada on 20 May and on 27 May crossed to Lisbon. The voyage was completed on 31 May at Plymouth.

TYPE:
Four-engined flying boat.

WINGS:
Braced biplane structure with wings of unequal span. Dihedral on lower wings only. Three bays of bracing outboard of central engine bays. Balanced ailerons, extending beyond wing-tips, on upper wings only. Stabilising fins above outermost struts, stabilising floats below these struts. Main wing structure of Western spruce. Most of wing fittings of chrome-vanadium steel, with an ultimate strength of 150,000 lb/sq in (1,054 kg/cm^2). All flying, landing and control cables of normal stranded aircraft type. Doped fabric covering.

Commander of the NC-4: Lieutenant-Commander A. C. Read, United States Navy

Above, NC-4 entering Lisbon Harbour. Below left, early Curtiss pilot John H. Towers, later commander of NC-3 (seated left). Below right. Charles A. Lindbergh, lone Atlantic pilot (May 20–21 1927)

FUSELAGE:
Short broad-beamed wooden hull with step just forward of wing trailing-edge. Main keel members of oak or rock elm. Most of remaining structure of spruce, with spruce or cedar planking. Turtle deck of cedar or cottonwood-birch three-ply veneer. Tail carried on massive outrigger structure of box beams, attached to upper wings and stern of hull. Cross-bracing by one large Vee, stiffened by smaller diamond.

TAIL UNIT:
Braced biplane type of unequal span. Balanced elevators on both planes. Upper extension strut-braced outboard. Three rudders, centre rudder without fin.

POWER PLANT:
Four Liberty 12-cylinder water-cooled Vee-type engines, driving three tractor and one pusher propellers. Central nacelle, housing one tractor and the pusher installation, braced to upper and lower wings and to outboard nacelles. Rectangular radiator block above and ahead of each engine. Two-blade wooden propellers. Original Olmstead propellers replaced for Atlantic flight by propellers designed by Bureau of Steam Engineering. Fuel in 10 tanks, 9 in hull and 1 gravity-feed tank in upper wing. Total capacity 1,890 US gallons (7,150 litres). Fuel tanks of aluminium, piping partly of aluminium, partly of copper. Fuel pumps driven by small wooden propellers. Electrical generators also propeller-driven. Fuel pumps in duplicate, and hand-operated auxiliary pump also provided. Current from generator fed to storage batteries. Electrical system supplied radio, interior lighting system, navigation lights and landing lights.

ACCOMMODATION:
Crew consisting of five: 2 pilots, 1 navigator, 1 radio operator and 1 engineer. Two separated side-by-side cockpits in hull forward of wings for pilots. Complete sets of instruments, including compass, in each cockpit. Navigating station in forward hull section, navigator having use of bow hatch for taking sights. Navigator's equipment included compass, sextant, drift sight, W/T and R/T radio equipment and radio direction indicator. Transmitting radius about 300 miles (480 km) in air, 100–150 miles (160–240 km) on water.

DIMENSIONS:
Wing span (top) 126 *ft* 0 *in* (38·40 *m*)
Wing span (bottom) 114 *ft* 0 *in* (34·75 *m*)
Wing chord 12 *ft* 0 *in* (3·66 *m*)
Wing gap at centre 14 *ft* 0 *in* (4·27 *m*)
Length overall 68 *ft* 3·5 *in* (20·85 *m*)
Length of hull 44 *ft* 9 *in* (13·64 *m*)

WEIGHTS AND LOADING:
Weight equipped 15,100 *lb* (6,850 *kg*)
Weight loaded 28,500 *lb* (12,925 *kg*)
Wing loading 12 *lb/sq ft* (58·58 *kg/m*^{2})

PERFORMANCE:
Max speed (full load) 91 *mph* (146 *kmh*)
Max speed (light) 96·7 *mph* (115·7 *kmh*)

DAYTON-WRIGHT R.B. RACER

The Dayton-Wright Airplane Company was formed during the 1914–18 war for the production of aircraft in quantity. Orville Wright acted as consulting engineer. Although the principal products of the company were to the designs of other manufacturers (notably D.H.4) the post-war R.B. Racer, built in 1920 for the Gordon Bennett race of that year, was a machine of remarkably original, indeed prophetic, design. As early as May 1917 Orville Wright had remarked in a letter to Glenn L. Martin: "The company was organised by Messrs. Deeds and Kettering and H. E. Talbott, Senior and Junior. . . . They are going to carry out some of my ideas in creating a sport in aeronautics". An even more sanguine outlook was expressed in a Dayton-Wright advertisement of 1920 announcing the construction of the R.B. Racer. This declared that the machine represented "some recent departures in airplane construction which will be developed in building planes for commercial purposes. Chief among these are the retractable landing chassis and variable camber wings". This declared policy was never carried out as planned, for in 1923 the parent company, General Motors Corporation, dissolved the Dayton-Wright organisation as it stood. From it, however, grew the Consolidated Aircraft Corporation, for which the future was golden. It was stated at the time of the completion of the R.B. Racer: "The two-fold purpose in designing this racer was: first, to bring the Gordon Bennett cup back to America, and, second, to offer to the aviation world something new in airplane construction and performance". The first objective was never achieved, for the aircraft retired from the race when trouble was experienced with the variable-camber gear. But the second objective was assuredly attained.

Although itself unsuccessful, as was the somewhat similar XPS-1 open-cockpit fighter, the Dayton-Wright R.B. Racer truly represented what its builders claimed as "some recent departures in airplane construction"

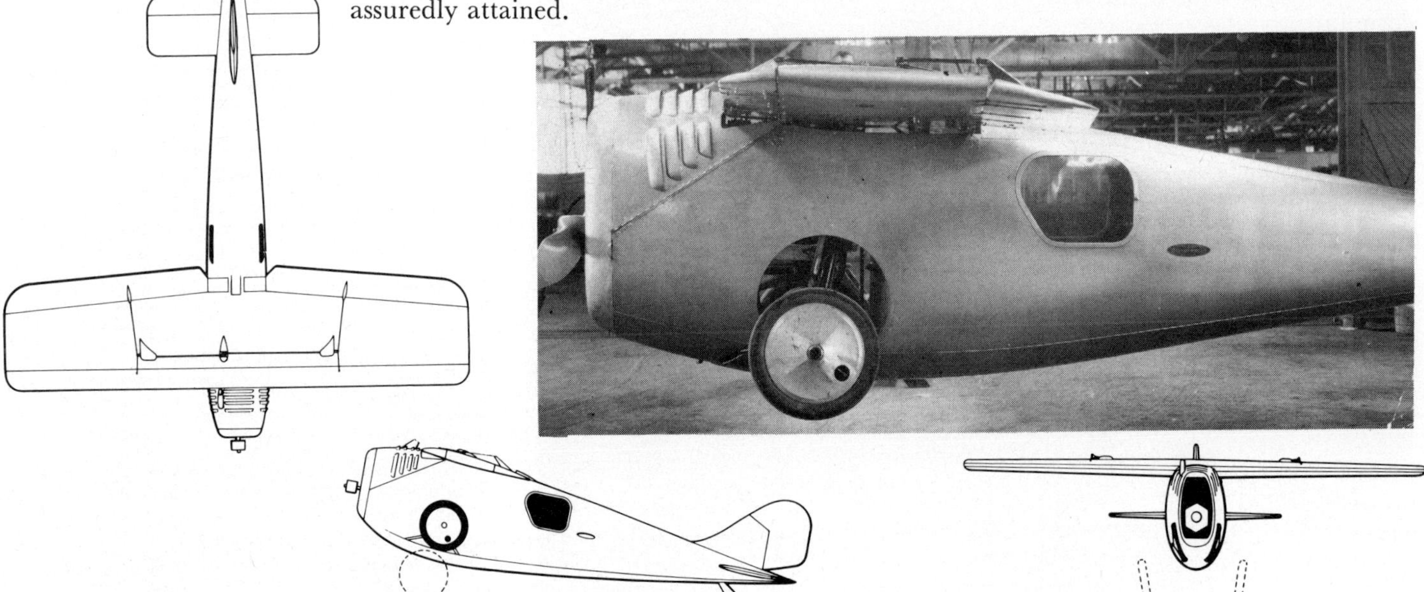

TYPE:
Single-seat racer.

WINGS:
High-wing cantilever monoplane. Thin wing, tapering in plan and thickness. Square tips with rounded corners. Wooden two-spar construction. Variable-camber gear with operating mechanism largely external above wing surface, taken from a point slightly to port of centre-line. Variable camber achieved by raising or depressing both leading- and trailing-edges.

FUSELAGE:
Wooden semi-monocoque structure, with veneer covering, supplied by National Veneer Products Co. Valspar varnish made by the Valentine Co. Four large cut-outs in sides, two to serve as wheel-wells, two for pilot's windows.

TAIL UNIT:
Cantilever monoplane type. Balanced rudder.

LANDING GEAR:
Retractable type. Wheels on independent assemblies, drawn up entirely within fuselage contour. Wheels by Dayton Wire Wheel Co., tyres by Goodyear Tire and Rubber Co., shock-absorber cord by J. C. Wood Elastic Co.

POWER PLANT:
One Hall-Scott Liberty Six 6-cylinder water-cooled engine delivering 250 hp at 2,200 rpm. Delco ignition system. AC spark plugs. Two Miller carburettors. Deep frontal radiator made by Dayton-Wright Co., using tubes manufactured by US Cartridge Co. Aluminium for cowling supplied by Aluminium Co. of America. Two-blade wooden propeller by Hartzell Propeller Co. Single exhaust outlet above cowling. Louvres in sides.

ACCOMMODATION AND EQUIPMENT:
Pilot entirely within contour of fuselage. Sliding cockpit roof. Large window in each side made of celluloid supplied by E. I. Dupont de Nemours Co. Fair downward vision but very limited vision forward. Instruments by Sperry, Foxboro and N.C.R.

DIMENSIONS:
Wing span 21 *ft* 2 *in* (6·45 *m*)
Wing chord at fuselage 6 *ft* 6 *in* (1·98 *m*)
Wing chord at tip 4 *ft* 0 *in* (1·22 *m*)
Angle of incidence 1°
Length overall 22 *ft* 8 *in* (6·91 *m*)
Height overall (*in line of flight* 8 *ft* 0 *in* (2·44 *m*)

AREAS:
Wings (*including ailerons*) 102·74 *sq ft* (503 *kg/m*²
Ailerons 23 *sq ft* (112 *kg/m*²)

WEIGHTS AND LOADING:
Weight empty 1,400 *lb* (635 *kg*)
Weight loaded 1,850 *lb* (839 *kg*)
Wing loading 18 *lb/sq ft* (87·90 *kg/m*²)
Power loading 7·4 *lb hp* (3·36 *kg/hp*)

PERFORMANCE:
Max speed 200 *mph* (320 *kmh*) *approx.*
Landing speed 64 *mph* (103 *kmh*)
Endurance 1½ *hr*
Ceiling 15,000 *ft* (4,570 *m*)

JUNKERS F13

The F13 in its original form (above) may be compared with the later British-registered example in the larger picture. Aircraft of this type were successfully operated on floats and skis and the F13 in its numerous versions played a leading part in the development of commercial flying

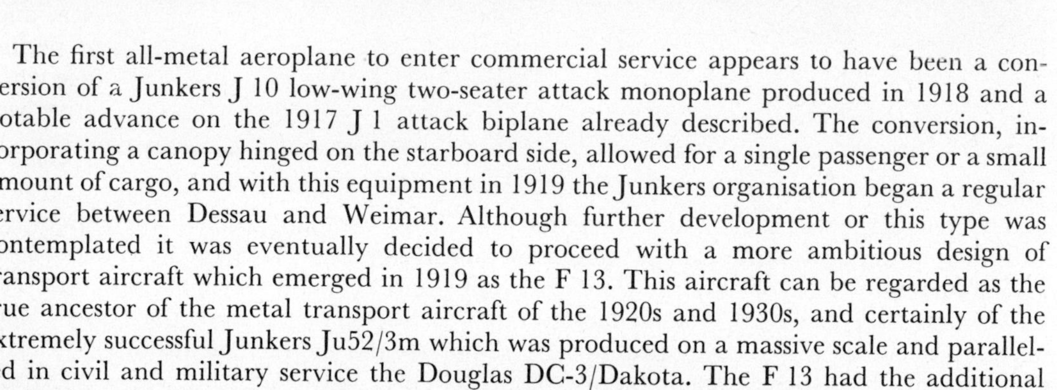

The first all-metal aeroplane to enter commercial service appears to have been a conversion of a Junkers J 10 low-wing two-seater attack monoplane produced in 1918 and a notable advance on the 1917 J 1 attack biplane already described. The conversion, incorporating a canopy hinged on the starboard side, allowed for a single passenger or a small amount of cargo, and with this equipment in 1919 the Junkers organisation began a regular service between Dessau and Weimar. Although further development or this type was contemplated it was eventually decided to proceed with a more ambitious design of transport aircraft which emerged in 1919 as the F 13. This aircraft can be regarded as the true ancestor of the metal transport aircraft of the 1920s and 1930s, and certainly of the extremely successful Junkers Ju52/3m which was produced on a massive scale and paralleled in civil and military service the Douglas DC-3/Dakota. The F 13 had the additional distinction of being the first transport aeroplane equipped with seat belts.

The first F 13 ever constructed (1919) was still giving service in 1939. In much-modified form it was being used for joy-riding in Berlin. Production continued until 1932, and of 322 machines built six were supplied to the USA.

The following is a general description of the F 13 as a type, of which there were some 60–70 variants.

The F 13 was the first transport aeroplane to be equipped with seat belts and these are visible in the view of the cabin interior. Entry via the characteristically shaped door is demonstrated in the lower picture

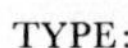

TYPE:
Four-passenger transport.

WINGS:
Low-wing cantilever monoplane. Wing of thick section and moderate taper. Centre-section built integral with fuselage. Nine tubular duralumin spars, braced by duralumin tubes to form a metal girder of great strength. Corrugated duralumin skin. Mating ferrules at edge of centre-section, allowing outer wing panels to be drawn together and held by substantial through-bolts.

FUSELAGE:
Substantially of rectangular section, but with domed top, especially over cabin section. Structure built up on series of metal frames, with corrugated duralumin skin.

TAIL UNIT:
Cantilever monoplane type, of metal construction with corrugated skin. Original machines had triangular fin and pointed rudder, but this arrangement was later replaced by a squatter assembly. Under-fin fitted when floats installed. Movable surfaces not at first balanced, but balanced later.

LANDING GEAR:
Main gear of fixed, divided-axle type, with two laterally disposed and one transverse Vee members. Tail skid or wheel. Aircraft operated successfully on floats and skis. Skis of plain or streamlined type.

POWER PLANT:
Prototype aircraft had 160/170 hp Mercedes D.IIIa. First production machines had 185 hp B.M.W. IIIa. Airframe progressively strengthened to accept increasingly powerful engines, notably 280/310 hp Junkers-L5. Armstrong Siddeley Jaguar and Pratt & Whitney Wasp radial air-cooled engines also fitted.

ACCOMMODATION:
Early aircraft had divided open cockpit for crew of two, side-by-side. Cockpit later enclosed. Cockpit over forward part of wing, with passenger cabin immediately behind. Cabin with three windows on each side, second window on each side being let in to access door. Door narrowed sharply below sill line. Four passenger seats, two separate seats forward, bench-type double seat at rear. Seat belts and racks for light luggage.

DIMENSIONS:
Wing span 58 *ft* 2¾ *in* (17·75 *m*)
Length overall 31 *ft* 6 *in* (9·60 *m*)
Wing area 473·61 *sq ft* (44 m^2)

WEIGHTS:
Weight empty 2,535 *lb* (1,150 *kg*)
Weight loaded 3,814 *lb* (1,730 *kg*)

PERFORMANCE:
Cruising speed 87 *mph* (140 *kmh*)
Landing speed 59 *mph* (95 *kmh*)
Ceiling 13,120 *ft* (4,000 *m*)
Endurance 5 *hr*

CURTISS R-2C1 NAVY RACER

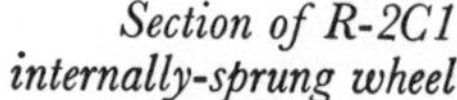

Section of R-2C1 internally-sprung wheel

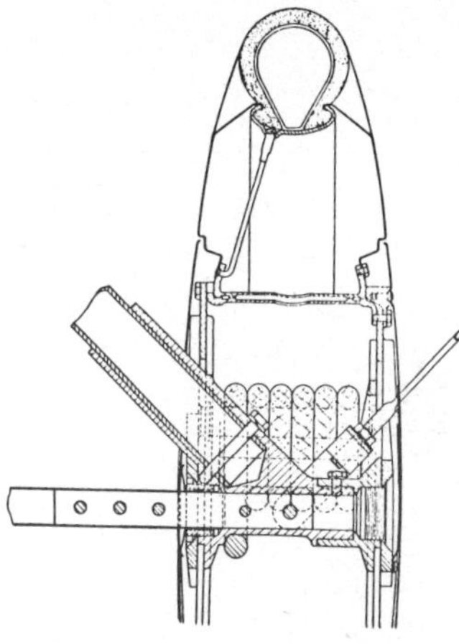

Although the Curtiss-Reed propeller is not fitted here the special wheels and radiators are seen

Curtiss racing seaplanes, closely related to the R-2C1 landplane, achieved notable successes. The Curtiss-Reed propeller is in evidence here

The year 1923 was a momentous one for the Curtiss company, which was reorganised in that year under the title Curtiss Aeroplane and Motor Company, Inc., for machines of its manufacture won not only the Pulitzer Trophy and Schneider Trophy races but set a new world's speed record. Salient factors in these achievements were the Curtiss-Reed metal propeller, Curtiss-developed surface radiators and improvements in the Curtiss D-12 engine. These developments were exploited not only in the USA but in Great Britain, the rights to their use having been acquired by the Fairey company for application to the Fox day bomber of 1925, which set a new standard of performance in its class, and Firefly fighter. In the Curtiss R-2C1 Navy Racer of 1923 the fullest advantage was taken of the new developments to augment performance. In an R-2C1 Lt. Alford J. Williams, USN, won the Pulitzer Trophy race over 200 km (321·86 miles) at an average speed of 243·67 mph (392 kmh) and in a machine of the same type Lt. H. J. Brow, USN, finished second at 241·78 mph (388 kmh). In November of the same year these two officers engaged in a dramatic duel in raising the world's speed record, the figure ultimately recorded by Lt. Williams being 266·6 mph (429 kmh). Structurally the R-2C1 differed little from the 1922 Curtiss Army Racer, but incorporated the features already mentioned. The Curtiss D-12 engine was redesigned with $\frac{1}{8}$ in (3·17 mm) greater bore and thus delivered an extra 50 hp. Speed was augmented a further 10 mph by the Curtiss-Reed two-blade metal propeller, essentially a metal sheet twisted to suitable shape. The wing radiators had proved themselves the previous year. Other changes were a slightly increased wing area and the lowering of the upper wing to the top of the fuselage.

TYPE:

Single-seat racer.

WINGS:

Braced biplane wings of unequal span and chord. Top wing attached directly to fuselage. One single, thick faired strut on each side. Wings built on Curtiss multi-spar system, with plywood covering, giving great rigidity and contour stiffness. Main lift wires attached to undercarriage, as on Curtiss Army Racer. Fabric-covered ailerons, with steel and duralumin frames, on all four wings.

FUSELAGE:

Wooden structure of very small cross-section, built of "Curtiss-Ply", a two-ply veneer of spruce $\frac{3}{32}$ in (2·38 mm) thick. Weight of fuselage 127 lb (57·60 kg)

TAIL UNIT:

Unbraced cantilever type with fabric-covered surfaces over steel and duralumin frames. Rudder and elevator not balanced.

LANDING GEAR:

Cross-axle single-strut type with shock-absorbers inside special wheels. Wheels faired with aluminium shields, and groove between wheel and tyre fabric-covered to achieve smooth oval section. Supporting legs meeting on centre-line.

POWER PLANT:

One special Curtiss D-12 twelve-cylinder water-cooled engine driving two-blade wooden or Curtiss-Reed metal propeller. Wing radiators of corrugated sheet-brass, developed by Curtiss circa 1921, over large areas of all four wings.

DIMENSIONS:

Wing span (top) 22 *ft* 0 *in* (6·71 *m*)
Wing span (bottom) 19 *ft* 3 *in* (5·87 *m*)
Wing chord (top) 4 *ft* 8 *in* (1·42 *m*)
Wing chord (bottom) 3 *ft* 4 *in* (1·01 *m*)
Length overall 19 *ft* 8½ *in* (6·0 *m*)
Height overall 6 *ft* 10 *in* (2·08 *m*)
Wing area 148 *sq ft* (13·8 *m²*)

WEIGHTS AND LOADING:

Weight loaded 2,071 *lb* (942 *kg*)
Wing loading 14 *lb/sq ft* (68·2 *kg/hp*)
Power loading 4·17 *lb/hp* (1·88 *kg/hp*)
Max speed 266·6 *mph* (429 *kmh*)
Min speed 74 *mph* (119 *kmh*)

Photographed in its native Spanish setting is the C.6A, a revolutionary aircraft embodying components of the prosaic Avro 504K

CIERVA AUTOGIRO

A very significant improvement in the safety of aircraft, and a wide extension of their fields of usefulness, were signalled by the experiments of the Spaniard Don Juan de la Cierva which began in Madrid during 1920. The name "autogiro" was coined by this inventor to signify that the rotor of his craft was revolved by "autorotation", occasioned by the forward passage through the air. To obviate the rolling motion resulting from unbalanced lift between the advancing and retreating rotor blades he utilised a "flapping" hinge. By this means the advancing blade rose automatically as its increased airspeed gave it more lift, but the movement of the air in relation to the blade was changed, the angle of attack reduced and lift accordingly decreased. An opposite process worked on the retreating blade, thus balancing the lift forces and rendering the system stable.

Don Juan de la Cierva

The first experiments of 1920 were made with a converted Deperdussin monoplane (Cierva C.1) which did not fly. The problem of unbalanced lift led to failure with the two succeeding machines, but the C.4 and C.5 showed greater promise during 1922–23. Financed by the Spanish Government, Cierva was able to build his C.6A, consisting of an Avro 504K fuselage with the wings removed, a four-blade articulated rotor mounted on a steel-tube pylon, and a special undercarriage. A horn-balanced elevator was fitted and Bristol Fighter ailerons were fixed on outriggers. Later an Avro oleo undercarriage was procured. The C.6A was first flown, by a Spanish military pilot, in May 1924, and results were greatly encouraging. On 12 December 1924 another pilot made a cross-country flight of $7\frac{1}{2}$ miles. The historic C.6A was brought to England and was demonstrated at Farnborough on 15 October, 1925. Reduction of take-off run was achieved by pre-spinning the rotor with ropes.

Left, early experimental Avro-built autogiros. Below, the C.19, which achieved distinct success in the early 1930s

TYPE:
Experimental autogiro.

WINGS:
No wings originally fitted, but ailerons carried on outriggers in positions of lower wings of normal Avro 504K. Short wings, carrying ailerons, added during development trials to relieve rotors of part of load in forward flight. Four-blade rotor on pylon above fuselage. Rotor speed 140 rpm.

FUSELAGE:
Standard Avro 504K type, adapted to take rotor pylon and outriggers for ailerons.

TAIL UNIT:
Avro 504K type.

LANDING GEAR:
Avro 504K type.

POWER PLANT:
One 130 hp Clerget nine-cylinder rotary air-cooled engine, installed as in Avro 504K. Two-blade wooden propeller.

ACCOMMODATION:
One cockpit only, behind rotor pylon.

DIMENSIONS:
Rotor diameter 36 *ft* 0 *in* (10·97 *m*)
Length overall 34 *ft* $4\frac{1}{8}$ *in* (10·46 *m*)

WEIGHT:
Weight empty 1,490 *lb* (676 *kg*)

An early C.6

SAVOIA-MARCHETTI S-55

Although the S-55 achieved its greatest fame as a military type it served also as an airliner

The most historic formation flight ever made in peacetime was undertaken in 1933, when General Balbo led twenty-four Savoia-Marchetti flying boats from Orbetello, Italy, via Iceland, Greenland and Labrador to the Century of Progress Exposition in Chicago. The return trip was by way of New York, the Azores and Lisbon. The fine performance of the Italian flying boats on this occasion was the more remarkable because their basic design was already about ten years old. The first S-55 was flown in 1924, and although the type was intended primarily as a torpedo bomber a civil variant was operating a Brindisi-Constantinople service in 1925. Some notable long-distance flights followed, and in particular a cruise round the Atlantic Ocean by Colonel the Marchese de Pinedo in 1927. In 1930 twelve S-55s, led by General Balbo, flew from Rome to Rio de Janeiro, across the South Atlantic.

The S-55s used for the North American flight of 1933 represented a considerable improvement on the original model. Designated S-55X, they were powered by two 800 hp Isotta-Fraschini Asso engines. The tops of the twin hulls merged with the wings and the lower surfaces of the wings merged with the hulls. The ends of the tail booms were faired together and into the tailplane, and a single radiator block served both engines. Adjustable-pitch metal propellers were fitted.

The following description relates to the S-55 in its standard military form.

The Scarff gun mountings in the bows of the S-55 above distinguish it as a military type and the torpedo slings under the centre-section proclaim its function. General Balbo, whose name is most closely connected with the S-55, is seen below in conversation with the Italian pilot Donati on the occasion of a successful Italian attempt on the world's duration record for light aircraft

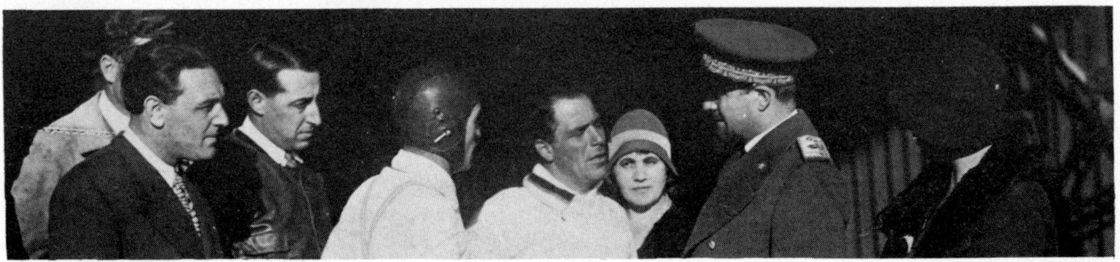

General Italo Balbo

Even today the term "Balbo" is used by English-speaking pilots to connote a large formation, but seldom has the grandeur of massed aircraft been the equal of that which is typified in the picture above. The distinctive twin hulls of the S-55 made their own contribution to the impression of massive strength conveyed by this veritable aerial armada

TYPE:

Twin-engined, twin-hulled torpedo bomber flying boat.

WINGS:

Thick-wing cantilever monoplane. Wing in three sections, the centre-section having a hull attached at each extremity. Two outer panels tapering in chord and thickness and having coarse dihedral. Wing constructed round three main spars and plywood ribs and covered with plywood. Eighteen watertight compartments. Balanced ailerons.

FUSELAGE:

Two short, single-step hulls under extremities of centre-section. Structure of ash, spruce and plywood, with plywood covering. Skin doubled below flotation line, with doped fabric between the two skins.

TAIL UNIT:

Monoplane type, with two fins and three rudders mounted above it. Tailplane mounted on outriggers running from heels of hulls and wing. Balanced one-piece elevator. Adjustable tailplane.

POWER PLANT:

Two 700 hp Fiat A-24R twelve-cylinder Vee, or 800 hp Isotta-Fraschini Asso eighteen-cylinder W-type, water-cooled engines in tandem above centre-line. Nacelles on "N" struts. Main fuel tanks in hulls. Oil tank between engines. One large frontal radiator block. Entire engine installation detachable from wing.

ACCOMMODATION AND ARMAMENT:

Pilots' cockpit, seating two side-by-side, in centre of wing leading-edge. Dual controls. Scarff ring mountings for machine-guns in nose and tail of each hull. Torpedo or bombs slung under centre-section, between hulls.

DIMENSIONS:

Wing span 79 *ft* 11 *in* (24·36 *m*)
Length overall 54 *ft* 2 *in* (16·51 *m*)
Height overall 16 *ft* 5 *in* (5·00 *m*)
Wing area 990 *sq ft* (92 m^2)

WEIGHTS AND LOADING:

Weight empty 11,460 *lb* (5,200 *kg*)
Normal loaded weight 16,975 *lb* (7,700 *kg*)

PERFORMANCE:

Max speed 146·5 *mph* (236 *kmh*)
Time of climb to 9,840 *ft* (3,000 *m*) 23 *min*
Ceiling 13,776 *ft* (4,200 *m*)
Normal range 1,242 *miles* (2,000 *km*)
Max range 2,174 *miles* (3,500 *km*)

The roomier hulls of the commercial version of the S-55 are in evidence here. One machine of this type was operated in America

The ill-fated, but nevertheless historic, S.4 under construction. The Napier Lion engine is installed and awaits its aluminium cowling, portions of which are seen. The aircraft was otherwise mainly of wooden construction

The Schneider Trophy

Below and upper right, the completed S.4

SUPERMARINE S.4

Generally known during the brief period of its existence as the Supermarine-Napier S.4, this racing floatplane of 1925 was of extremely refined design and was the true ancestor of the Spitfire fighter of the Second World War. Even the wing somewhat resembled that of the fighter which was to follow some ten years later. This employed a high-speed section developed at the Royal Aircraft Establishment, Farnborough, and a trial wing was constructed for testing to destruction at that Establishment before adoption of the wing-form for the racer.

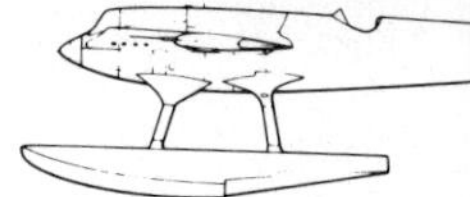

Instructions to proceed with the building of the S.4 were issued by the Air Ministry on 18 March 1925, and the first flight was made on 25 August of that year. Having regard to the several novel features embodied in the design this was a remarkable achievement. On 13 September the makers' test pilot Capt. Henri Biard set up a world's speed record for seaplanes, covering a 3-km course at 226·6 mph (364·6 kmh). Performance was later improved by engine tuning and fitting a propeller of higher efficiency, but the S.4 met with an accident before participating, as intended, in the 1925 Schneider Trophy race at Baltimore. This was won by Lt. Doolittle in an Curtiss Army biplane with a speed of 232·57 mph (374 kmh).

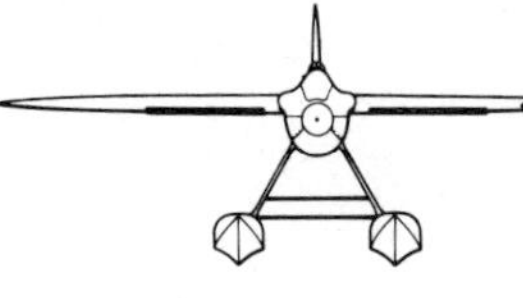

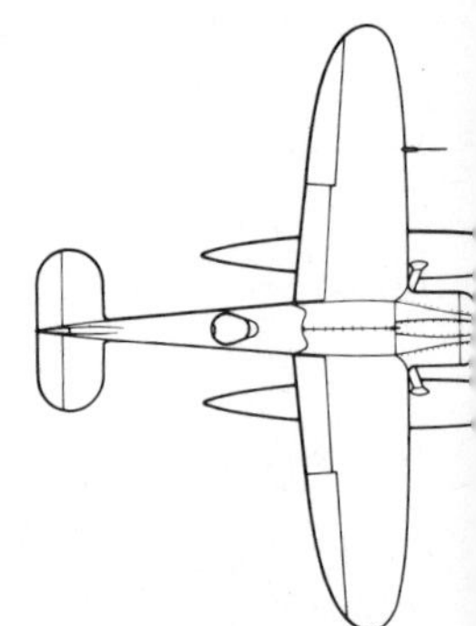

An S.5 being prepared for launching. The figure in meditation on the left is the designer R. J. Mitchell

TYPE:
Single-seat racing floatplane.

WINGS:
Mid-wing cantilever monoplane type, slightly tapered in plan and thickness. Plan form suggestive of Spitfire but leading- and trailing-edges straight. Entire wing in one piece. Three-ply covering throughout, taking share of loads. Plain trailing-edge flaps inboard of ailerons. Ailerons geared in with flap mechanism, so that entire trailing-edge could be drooped. Ailerons not balanced.

FUSELAGE:
Aft of rear float-strut attachments fuselage of wooden monocoque construction, but forward portion covered entirely with aluminium cowling, giving access to engine bay and fuel-tank bay from above and below. Two sections bolted together. Lateral cylinder-banks of engine faired into wing roots, allowing exhaust stubs of lateral cylinder banks to discharge below wing.

TAIL UNIT:
Cantilever monoplane type with all controls internal. Tailplane and fin built in to form single unit.

LANDING GEAR:
Two wooden single-step floats on four cross-braced splayed-out high-tensile steel tubes with fore-and-aft auxiliary bracing struts in prominent triangular fairings. Main support tubes braced together within fuselage, thus forming complete structure on which remainder of aircraft was erected.

POWER PLANT:
One Napier Lion "W"-type 12-cylinder water-cooled engine of special racing type. Two-blade Fairey-Reed duralumin propeller. Two Lamblin radiators, one under each wing, following wing contour but not of "surface" type.

ACCOMMODATION:
Open cockpit well aft of wing with small windscreen and cut-away sides.

DIMENSIONS:
Wing span 30 *ft* 6 *in* (9·30 *m*)
Length overall 27 *ft* 0 *in* (8·23 *m*)
Wing area 136 *sq ft* (12·63 *m*²)

WEIGHTS AND LOADING:
Weight loaded 3,150 *lb* (1,429 *kg*)
Wing loading 23·1 *lb/sq ft* (117 *kg/m*²)

PERFORMANCE:
Max speed at S/L 239 *mph* (385 *kmh*)
Landing speed 90 *mph* (145 *kmh*)
Range at full power 320 *miles* (515 *km*)

Whether in action or at rest the Supermarine racing seaplanes were objects of beauty. The S.6 (above) was the first to have a Rolls-Royce engine

In action above, and waterborne below, is the S.4's Lion-engined successor the S.5

FOKKER FVII-3m

"Josephine Ford", first (transpolar) FVII-3m

Richard E. Byrd, polar navigator

The first aircraft of this type ever constructed was the first aeroplane to fly over the North Pole. Bearing the name *Josephine Ford* and manned by Floyd Bennett and Richard E. Byrd, it made the round trip from Spitzbergen on 9 May 1926 and rests today in the Ford Museum. Byrd was navigator on the Polar flight and used a specially developed sun compass. Numerous flights of great historical significance were later accomplished by aircraft of the same type, notably the *Southern Cross* of Charles Kingsford-Smith.

The first FVII-3m (the type-number was sometimes written as FVIIa-3m) was initially flown on 4 September 1925. It was a three- engined development of the FVIIa and differed from it in having three Wright Whirlwind engines instead of the single Packard Liberty installed in its predecessor. Engines of several other types were fitted to production examples, including the Armstrong Siddeley Lynx. The later FVIIb-3m had a larger wing, with a straight inner trailing-edge, and operated at a higher weight.

TYPE:

Three-engined transport.

WING:

Cantilever monoplane type of wooden construction, attached directly to fuselage by four bolts. Plywood covering. Sharp taper in thickness, moderate taper in plan. Inset ailerons. Ailerons made as integral part of wing and sawn out before covering.

FUSELAGE:

Welded tubular-steel structure of rectangular section, fabric-covered.

LANDING GEAR:

Split type. Main members two vertical struts, with rubber shock-absorber rings, attached to outboard engine-mountings. Two steel-tube Vees hinged to bottom longerons, the apices being attached to the bases of the vertical struts. Tension of shock-absorbers adjustable by adding or removing rubber rings. Mudguards over wheels. Steerable tail-skid.

POWER PLANT:

Three Wright Whirlwind, Armstrong Siddeley Lynx or similar radial engines. Nose engine-mounting attached to fuselage by four bolts. Outboard engines suspended under wing and attached by three bolts. Nacelles behind outboard engines, containing oil tanks. Fuel tanks in wing, supplying engines entirely by gravity. Capacity 158 Imp gallons (720 litres). Two-blade wooden propellers.

ACCOMMODATION:

Cockpit under wing leading-edge with provision for W/T and night-flying equipment. Door at rear giving access to passenger cabin, seating eight in armchairs. Lavatory behind cabin. Luggage compartment behind lavatory, a second compartment under pilot's cockpit.

DIMENSIONS:

Wing span 63 *ft* 4 *in* (19·30 *m*)
Length overall 47 *ft* 7 *in* (14·50 *m*)
Height overall 13 *ft* 10 *in* (3·90 *m*)
Wing area 630 *sq ft* (58·5 *m*²)

WEIGHTS AND LOADING (Armstrong Siddeley Lynx engines):

Weight empty 5,180 *lb* (2,350 *kg*)
Weight loaded 1,860 *lb* (4,100 *kg*)
Wing loading 14·35 *lb/sq ft* (70 *kg/m*²)
Power loading 14·33 *lb/hp* (6·5 *kg/hp*)

PERFORMANCE:

Max speed 118 *mph* (190 *kmh*)
Cruising speed 102 *mph* (164 *kmh*)
Minimum speed 61 *mph* (98 *kmh*)
Time to climb to 3,280 *ft* (1,000 *m*) 7 *min* 42 *sec*
Time to climb to 6,560 *ft* (2,000 *m*) 19 *min* 00 *sec*
Service ceiling 10,825 *ft* (3,300 *m*)

The Fokker commercial monoplanes of the 1920s and 1930s, of which the FVII-3m was the most famous, had a welded steel-tube fuselage and wooden cantilever wing. The "landing gear" seen is temporary

The Tri-motor (left) was created by "Bill" Stout ("Simplicate and add more lightness"). Below, Whirlwind engine

FORD TRI-MOTOR

Although embodying the most appealing features of Fokker and Junkers practice, the family of Ford-built three-engined transport aircraft that went by the generic name of Tri-motor stemmed largely from the work of William B. Stout. The story is best taken up with a quotation from *Jane's All the World's Aircraft* of 1933, thus: "The original Stout Metal Airplane Company was purchased in August 1925 by Mr. Henry Ford, and was incorporated as a division of the Ford Motor Company. During 1929 the factory space was considerably enlarged and a production of four complete three-engined monoplanes per week was reached, but since 1930 the output of the Ford works has steadily declined until, today, they are virtually closed down. The famous Ford tri-motor monoplane has been amply described in previous issues of this Annual. The large numbers which were in use on American air lines have gradually disappeared, with the result that today Ford is but a name in the pre-depression history of American air transport."

This, however, was by no means the end of the story, for although the Tri-motor disappeared from the trunk routes it continued to render exemplary service in secondary fields, and a number are still airworthy today. More than this, the Tri-motor is perpetuated in the current edition of *All the World's Aircraft* under the heading of Aircraft Hydro-Forming Inc., whose Bushmaster 2000 is a modernised reincarnation of the Tri-motor according to the ideas of Mr. Stout, the originator.

The original Tri-motor of 1925 was a development of the single-engined Stout Air Pullman of 1924. In 1931 the Ford company produced a single-engined (Hispano-Suiza) specialised freight-carrying development, but this never achieved popularity. At that time the Tri-motor was being built in three models. These were the 4-AT-E, with Wright J-6 or Pratt & Whitney Wasp Junior engines; the 5-D, with Pratt & Whitney Wasps; and the 7-AT with a Wasp in the nose and a Wright J-6 under each wing. These three models carried, respectively, 11, 14 and 13 passengers.

TYPE:
Three-engined transport.

WINGS:
High-wing cantilever all-metal monoplane, tapering in chord and thickness, attached to top of fuselage. Structure consisting of three cantilever spars united by fore-and-aft intermediate trussing, and the whole skeleton frame covered with duralumin sheet 12/1,000 in (0·3 mm) thick, with corrugations parallel to chord.

FUSELAGE:
All-metal structure with flat sides and bottom, domed top and upswept under-line, comprising a series of transverse duralumin bulkheads covered with corrugated metal skin, the corrugations running lengthwise.

TAIL UNIT:
Monoplane type. Construction as for wing. Balanced rudder. Adjustable tailplane.

LANDING GEAR:
Divided type, comprising two vertical telescopic legs with rubber-in-compression shock-absorbers. Upper ends of legs attached to outboard engine-mountings, lower ends hinged to bottom members of fuselage by two steel-tube Vees. Internal expanding servo-hydraulic brakes. Steerable tailwheel.

POWER PLANT:
Three radial air-cooled engines, as stated in introductory notes. One engine in fuselage nose, two underslung from wing on struts. Small streamline nacelles for wing engines. Fuel tanks in wing. Standard Steel metal propellers.

ACCOMMODATION:
Pilots' enclosed cockpit with side-by-side dual control ahead of leading-edge. Passenger cabin under wing, seating 11 to 14 passengers in wicker chairs. Openable windows of unsplinterable glass. Electric dome lights, ventilating system and cabin exhaust heater.

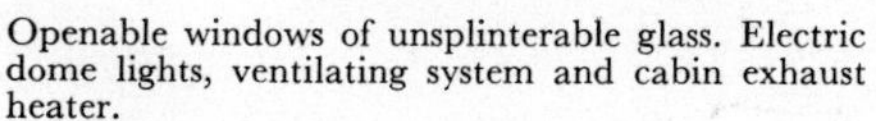

DIMENSIONS (4-AT-E):
Wing span 74 *ft* 0 *in* (22·56 *m*)
Length overall 49 *ft* 10 *in* (15·19 *m*)
Height overall 11 *ft* 9 *in* (3·58 *m*)
Wing area 765 *sq ft* (71·00 *m²*)

WEIGHTS AND LOADING (4-AT-E):
Weight empty 6,500 *lb* (2,948 *kg*)
Weight loaded 10,130 *lb* (4,598 *kg*)
Wing loading 12·9 *lb/hp* (63 *kg/m²*)
Power loading 11·3 *lb/hp* (5·11 *kg/hp*)

PERFORMANCE (4-AT-E):
Max speed 132 *mph* (212 *kmh*)
Cruising speed 107 *mph* (172 *kmh*)
Landing speed 57 *mph* (92 *kmh*)
Ceiling 16,500 *ft* (5,030 *m*)
Normal range 570 *miles* (917*km*)

Forerunner of the Ford Tri-motor was the single-engined Stout Air Pullman, developed jointly by George H. Prudden and William B. Stout

LOCKHEED VEGA

The Vega above is an early model, with Wright Whirlwind engine, equipped with ski landing gear. Below is one of several derivative types, the Altair, itself related to the Orion

Structurally and aerodynamically the Vega high-wing monoplane of 1927 links the Deperdussin Monocoque racer of 1913 with the de Havilland Mosquito of 1940. Production totalled 131 aircraft, and a number of these were record-breakers of one sort or another. This first Lockheed product established a company tradition of technical excellence which has continued unbroken, whether the class of aircraft concerned be transport or fighter. Most famous of all the Vegas was one acquired in 1930 by F. C. Hall, an oil magnate from Oklahoma City. This he named *Winnie Mae*, after his daughter. A pilot, Wiley Post, was hired to fly the machine on business trips for Mr. Hall, but fate held a higher calling for the Vega. Having achieved success in the National Air Races of 1930, Post, with navigator Harold Gatty, left New York in June, 1931 in an attempt on the round-the-world record. Eight days, fifteen hours, fifty-one minutes later they were back in New York, their purpose achieved. In July, 1933 Post set out again, this time alone, but with new navigational aids. The Vega now circled the world in 7 days 18 hr 49 min.

Over the years the Vega underwent considerable development, and was one of the first aircraft to take advantage of the newly developed NACA long-chord cowling. With Pratt & Whitney Wasp SC1 engine the late-model Vega had a maximum speed of 195 mph (314 kmh) and cruised at 170 mph (273 kmh). Dimensions remained unchanged, but weight rose sharply. The empty weight of 2,725 lb (1,233 kg) and loaded weight of 4,750 lb (2,154 kg) may be compared with the figures for the original Vega, which is the subject of the following description.

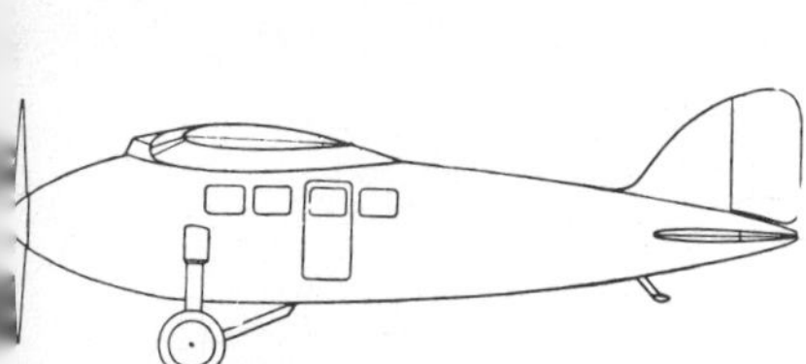

Early concept of Vega

The Vega in early form. Vegas made history with Wiley Post, James Mattern, Art Goebel, Amelia Earhart and Sir Hubert Wilkins

Late-model Vega, with NACA cowling, owned by Paul Mantz

The Sirius was Lockheed's first low-wing model and owed much to its Vega parentage. Built especially for Colonel Charles Lindbergh, it was powered by a Wright Cyclone engine and was flown by Lindbergh on a 29,000-mile survey trip to Labrador, Greenland, Iceland, Europe, the Azores, Africa and back to the USA

Wiley Post with the most famous of all Vegas. Post began his flying career in the "barnstorming" days and included wing-walking and parachuting in his repertoire.

Wiley Post and the Vega were pioneers in pressure-suit development, and Lockheed followed up their work with the pressure-cabin XC-35

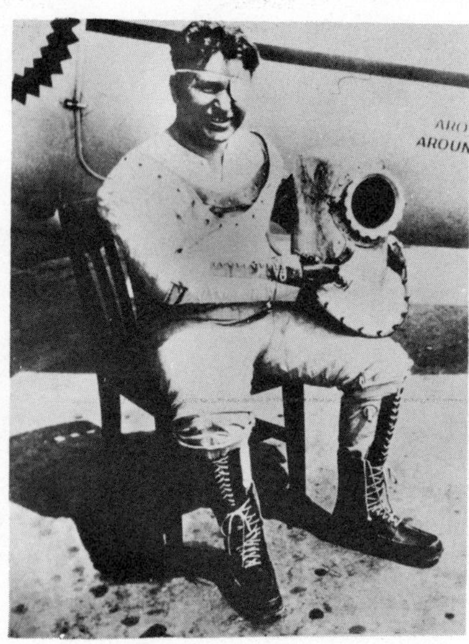

TYPE:

Single-engined passenger-carrying monoplane.

WINGS:

High-wing cantilever monoplane. Wing in one piece, tapering in chord and thickness. Two spruce box spars with spruce girder ribs and covering of three-ply $\frac{3}{32}$ in (2·38 mm) thick.

FUSELAGE:

Spruce veneer shell, having external appearance of monocoque type, but actually a "bivalve", the two halves being glued together with casein glue and pressed to shape in a mould under 150 tons (152·40 tonnes) pressure. The two halves of the shell thus produced were then assembled on a series of laminated-spruce formers.

TAIL UNIT:

Cantilever monoplane type, constructed in same manner as wings. All surfaces roughly elliptical in outline. Movable surfaces unbalanced.

LANDING GEAR:

Split-axle type. Each half-axle supported a telescopic leg with rubber cord and hydraulic shock-absorbers. Junction of axle and telescopic leg braced by thrust tube running back to centre-line of fuselage. Lockheed hydraulic wheel-brakes.

POWER PLANT:

One Wright Whirlwind J-5 seven-cylinder radial air-cooled engine of 220 hp. Engine mounting of steel, attached to forward frame of fuselage, with intervening fireproof bulkhead. No wood in engine bay. Two 50 US gallon (189 litres) fuel tanks in wing, giving gravity feed. Jettison valves fitted.

ACCOMMODATION:

Pilot in cockpit with sliding cover in leading-edge cut-out. Cabin of 100 cu ft (2·8 m^3) capacity below wing. Entrance door on port side and four glazed portholes on each side. Four or six seats.

DIMENSIONS:

Wing span 41 *ft* 0 *in* (12·49 *m*)
Overall length 27 *ft* 6 *in* (8·38 *m*)
Wing area 275 *sq ft* (25·50 m^2)

WEIGHTS AND LOADING:

Weight empty 1,650 *lb* (750 *kg*)
Normal loaded weight 2,918 *lb* (1,330 *kg*)
Permissible overload weight 3,200 *lb* (1,370 *kg*)
Wing loading (normal) 10·5 *lb/sq ft* (52 kgm^2)
Power loading (normal) 13·2 *lb/hp* (6 *kg/hp*)

PERFORMANCE:

Max speed 135 *mph* (217 *kmh*)
Landing speed 50 *mph* (80 *kmh*)
Initial rate of climb 925 *ft/min* (281 *m/min*)
Service ceiling 15,900 *ft* (4,580 *m*)
Range with normal fuel at 110 *mph* (172 *kmh*) 550 *miles* (890 *km*)

HAWKER HART

Entering a diving attack at left are Demon two-seat fighters. This type was one of many Hart derivatives and was eventually fitted with a power-operated turre

The high-performance day bomber had its origins in the D.H.4 and the idea was perpetuated in the Fairey Fox of 1925. Though a metal development of the original Fox was put forward as a possible replacement for the earlier machine in Royal Air Force service a production contract was awarded instead to the H. G. Hawker Engineering Co. Ltd. respecting the Hart. In numerous versions, and with several different names, this basic type achieved an exceptional measure of success in several air forces. A companion type no less successful was the Fury single-seat fighter, embodying the same system of construction. It was, in fact, this form of construction, allied with all-round excellence of performance and handling, which achieved for the Hart and Fury, and their variants, the success already noted. While credit for the design of both types must go to Sir Sydney Camm (see also Hawker Siddeley Harrier) the system of metal construction utilised was evolved from the ideas of F. Sigrist. This involved the extensive use of steel and/or duralumin tubing, fuselage construction, for instance, being based on the use of steel longerons and steel or duralumin struts. Durability, accessibility and ease of maintenance and replacement were virtues strongly apparent.

The Hart day bomber was first flown in 1928 and was quickly adapted as a two-seat fighter, which entered service as the Demon. This type had two fixed guns for the pilot and one free gun, initially on a Hawker ring mounting, later in a Frazer-Nash powered turret. The deck-landing fleet fighter-reconnaissance version of the Hart was the Osprey, the army co-operation variant the Audax, and there was a version without military equipment known as the Hart Trainer. The Hardy was developed for general-purpose duties and the Hector was a later army co-operation development with 24-cylinder Napier Dagger air-cooled engine in place of the liquid-cooled Rolls-Royce 12-cylinder engines standardised by the RAF.

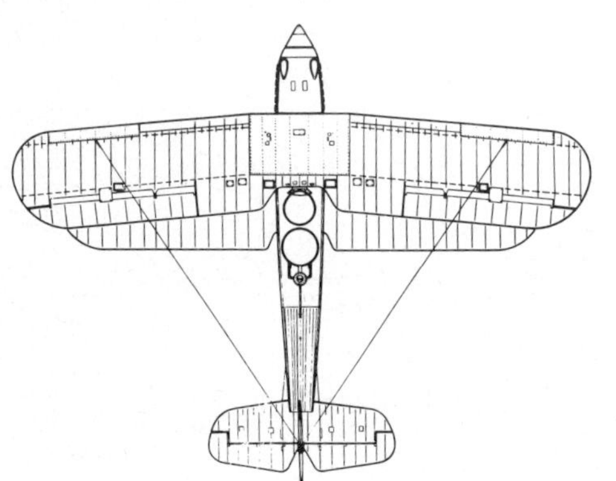

The Hind was an improved Hart day bomber. For export many types of engines were installed, ranging from the Lorraine Algol to the Hispano-Suiza 12Y series. The Fury single-seater was also exported with various types of engine, and had a naval carrier-borne counterpart in the Nimrod. Although a new design, the famous Hurricane of 1935 was originally called the Fury Monoplane.

The following description relates to the original Hart day bomber.

TYPE:

Two-seat day bomber.

WINGS:

Unequal-span, single-bay, staggered biplane. Centre-section carried above fuselage on splayed-out struts. Top outer sections swept back and fitted with Frise ailerons and Handley Page leading-edge slots. Bottom sections with dihedral and strong-points for bomb-carrier attachments. Metal construction, with fabric covering. Spars built up of two many-sided booms and a longitudinally-corrugated web, the whole riveted together. All wiring-plates and other wing fittings assembled on to flat bearing surfaces, sides and top of spars always presenting a flat surface.

Harts equipped not only regular RAF squadrons but Auxiliary units also. This machine belonged to the City of Edinburgh squadron

Installation of Rolls-Royce Kestrel engine

Hart prototype on test at Brooklands

The Audax was an army co-operation variant

FUSELAGE:

Rectangular metal structure, fabric covered. Flat bottom, domed top. Structure in four sections of mixed steel and duralumin, the longerons and more highly stressed parts being of steel. All tubes round, but flattened at joints, the whole being assembled by flat plate fittings, steel ferrules and hollow rivets.

TAIL UNIT:

Braced monoplane type, covered with fabric. Balanced rudder and elevators. Adjustable tailplane.

LANDING GEAR:

Cross-axle Vee type, with front legs of Vees incorporating oleo springing.

POWER PLANT:

One Rolls-Royce Kestrel IB unsupercharged 12-cylinder water-cooled engine of 480 hp. Underslung retractable radiator. Vickers-Potts oil cooler. Two-blade wooden propeller.

ARMAMENT:

One fixed Vickers belt-fed gun for pilot, mounted in port side of cockpit and firing along trough in cowling by means of Constantinesco synchronising gear. Ammunition supply 500 rounds. Ring-and-bead sights on tube ahead of windscreen. One free Lewis drum-fed gun for observer/bomb aimer on Hawker wind-balanced ring mounting. Ammunition supply eight drums of 96 rounds. Prone bomb-aiming position in rear fuselage. Wimperis course-setting bomb sight at sliding hatch below pilot. Bombs carried under wings. Possible loadings 4 × 112 lb (50·8 kg) or 2 × 230/250 lb (104/113 kg), with 4 × 20 lb (9·07 kg) sighter bombs.

DIMENSIONS:

Wing span (top) 37 *ft* 3 *in* (11·35 *m*)
Wing span (bottom) 31 *ft* 4 *in* (9·55 *m*)
Length overall 29 *ft* 4 *in* (8·94 *m*)
Height overall 10 *ft* 5 *in* (3·17 *m*)
Wing area 348 *sq ft* (32·33 m^2)

WEIGHTS:

Weight empty 2,530 *lb* (1,147 *kg*)
Weight loaded 4,554 *lb* (2,066 *kg*)

PERFORMANCE:

Max speed at 10,000 *ft* (3,050 *m*) 172 *mph* (277 *kmh*)
Time of climb to 10,000 *ft* (3,050 *m*) 8·6 *min*
Ceiling 21,320 *ft* (6,560 *m*)

The first squadron of Britain's Royal Air Force to be equipped with Hawker Hart day bombers was No 33, stationed at the historic airfield at Eastchurch

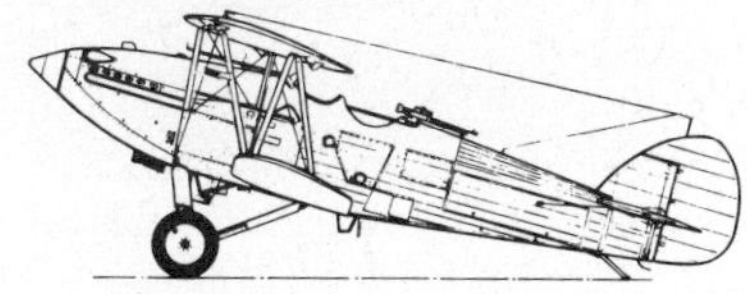

DORNIER Do X

When the Do X accomplished its maiden flight on 25 July 1929 it was incomparably the largest aeroplane in the world. On 21 October the implications of its bulk became apparent when it lifted 150 passengers, a crew of 10 – and 9 stowaways. Engine troubles beset the great machine from the beginning, and the original twelve Siemens-built Bristol Jupiter air-cooled radial engines were replaced by water-cooled Curtiss Conquerors. With the original installation severe cooling difficulties were encountered. Each engine nacelle, or "power egg", housed two engines in tandem, the forward engine driving a wooden four-blade tractor propeller and the rear one a two-blade pusher propeller, rotating in opposite directions. Most cylinder temperatures of the rear engines were too high and oil temperatures excessive. When the Conqueror engines were substituted their greater weight was partly balanced by some structural alterations and power output was unrestricted. Formerly the service ceiling was 420 m (1,377 ft). Another alteration was the deletion of the small auxiliary "over-wing" connecting the engine nacelles. This had affected flow over the main wing.

The most notable flight of the Do X began at Friedrichshafen on 2 November 1930. The destination was America. By way of Amsterdam and Calshot (England) the flying-boat reached Lisbon, where fire damaged one wing. The craft was beached in the River Tagus, and the damage repaired. Then began the crossing of the Atlantic by way of the Canary Islands, where the hull was damaged. Again repairs were completed in the open and another successful take-off made. The crossing of the South Atlantic was made from Bolama, Portuguese Guinea, by way of the Cape Verde Islands and Fernando Noronha, to Natal, Brazil. Thence the craft flew down the South American coast to Rio de Janeiro and after a stay of some weeks she left for New York, by way of the West Indies. The arrival at New York was on 27 August 1931, nearly ten months after leaving Germany.

Two other Do Xs were built and delivered to Italy. These had Fiat engines.

Although the Do X achieved no commercial success her construction was a notable event in aeronautical history. As Charles Lindberg had done on his Atlantic crossing the Do X flew occasionally at an extremely low level to take advantage of "ground effect", or "surface effect". Thus she may have foreshadowed massive surface-skimming craft of the future.

Difficulties experienced with the Siemens-built Bristol Jupiter air-cooled engines of the Do X, installed above, led to the substitution of water-cooled Curtiss Conquerors, in vigorous action at right

DO-X
LUFT HANSA
D-1929

The sponsons, or stub wings, which gave the Do X lateral stability on the water, were a Dornier characteristic

TYPE:

Twelve-engined passenger-carrying flying-boat.

WINGS:

High-wing braced monoplane. Aspect ratio 5. Three parallel struts on each side from hull sponsons to wing. Three smaller struts on each side bracing sponsons to hull. Three spars and ribs of light alloy. Leading-edge and walkway beneath engines of corrugated light-alloy sheeting. Rest of wing fabric covered. Fabric-covered narrow-chord ailerons with small auxiliary metal-covered balancing planes set ahead and above.

HULL:

Two-step type. Sharp bows. Bottom concavely curved to first step; thence Vee-shaped, with lessening included angle, to rear step, where water-rudder fitted. Sponsons for lateral stability on water beneath wings, serving also as part of wing-bracing structure. Construction of flat plate and open angles of light metal.

TAIL UNIT:

Sesquiplane type. Small plane on top of hull, with plane of much greater span above, passing through fin. Both planes braced to each other and to hull. Elevators on top plane, balanced with servo-planes above tailplane. Narrow-chord rudder, balanced by one auxiliary surface on each side. Fin, balancing rudders and tailplanes covered with light-alloy sheet. Elevators and main rudder fabric-covered.

POWER PLANT:

Twelve 600 hp Curtiss Conqueror water-cooled engines (see also introductory notes) in tandem pairs above wing. Nacelles mounted on steel-tube struts and cross-braced by additional struts. Normal fuel capacity 16,000 litres (3,500 Imp gallons). Oil capacity 1,900 litres (418 Imp gallons).

ACCOMMODATION:

Cabin for two pilots side-by-side forward of wing, with captain's cabin and navigating room behind, then engineer's compartment with engine-controls and instruments. Passenger accommodation on deck below. Fuel tanks and stores below passenger deck.

DIMENSIONS:

Wing span 157 *ft* 5 *in* (48·00 *m*)
Length overall 131 *ft* 4 *in* (40·05 *m*)
Wing area 4,887 *sq ft* (454 m^2)

WEIGHTS:

Weight empty 65,040 *lb* (29,500 *kg*)
Normal flying weight 114,640 *lb* (52,000 *kg*)
Max flying weight 123,460 *lb* (56,000 *kg*)

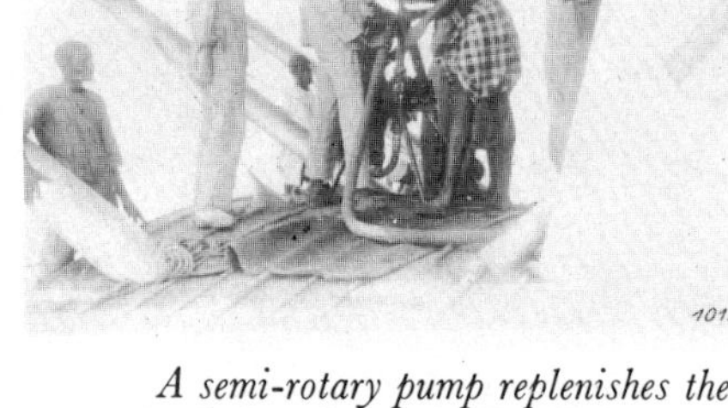

A semi-rotary pump replenishes the fuel tanks of the Do X from one of the sponsons while the massive wing gives shade

PERFORMANCE:

Max speed 134 *mph* (216 *kmh*)
Cruising speed 118 *mph* (190 *kmh*)
Service ceiling 1,640 *ft* (500 *m*)

Set ahead and above the ailerons were metal-covered balancing planes

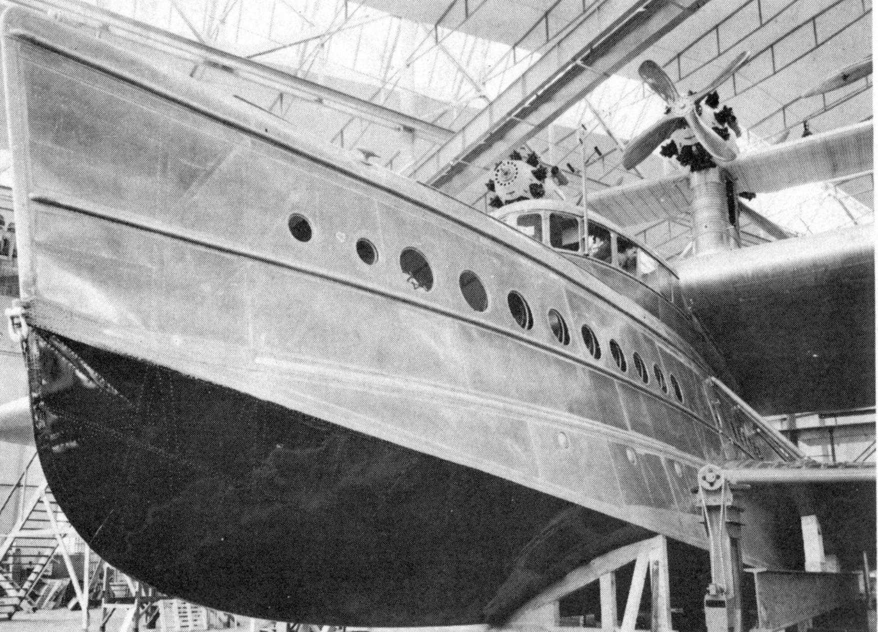

A shipbuilder's yard, rather than an aircraft factory, is suggested by this view of the Jupiter-engined Do X dated June 1929—the month of the first flight. The Conqueror-powered version (left) displays appropriate registration

DE HAVILLAND MOTH

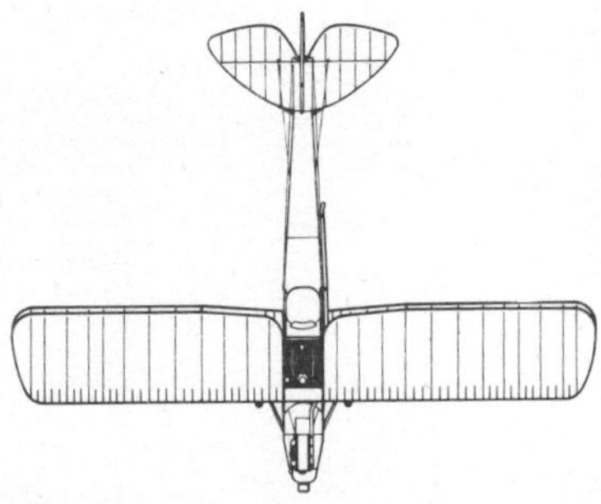

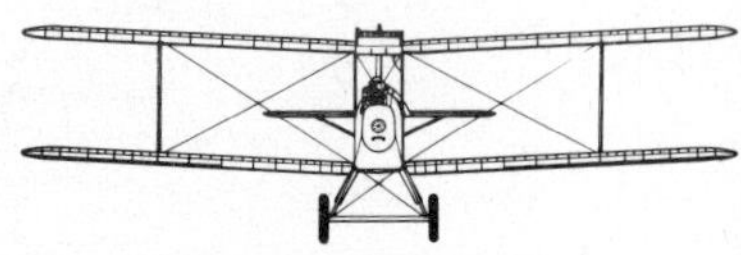

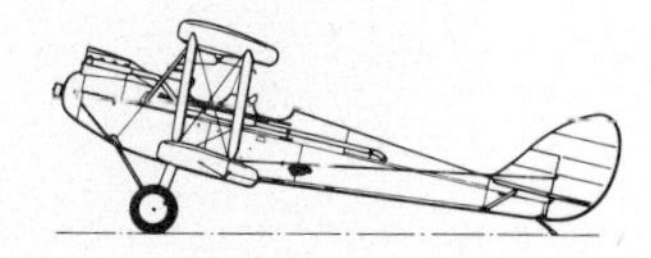

Although a notable attempt at producing an economical and useful two-seater light aircraft for private ownership had been made in England after the Armistice (Sopwith Dove, 1919) no commercial success was achieved, and it remained for the de Havilland company to meet the need with the Moth. This aircraft grew from a realisation by its designer, Captain (later Sir Geoffrey) de Havilland that the D.H.51 type was too large and the D.H.53 too small. He therefore suggested to Major Frank Halford, who had been associated with the engine originally intended for the D.H.4, that he should, in effect, cut in half an air-cooled Renault engine of the war-surplus type then available, and adapt and improve the result, no other suitable engine being on the market. This was done, and the first Moth, with 60 hp Cirrus engine, was initially flown in 1925. The same year also saw a boom in the flying club movement in Great Britain, and the Moth quickly established its popularity not in Great Britain alone, but, in several developed forms, throughout the world. The first Moth ever built was flown by Sir Alan Cobham (famed for his flight from England to Cape Town and back in a D.H.50J) from London to Zurich and back in a day. In 1927 a Moth accomplished the London–Cape Town and return flight, another gained the height record for light aeroplanes and yet another the first prize for aerobatics at the Copenhagen International meeting. In the following year Captain de Havilland himself raised the height record mentioned to 19,980 ft (6,089 m). In 1928 de Havilland produced their own engine for the Moth – the Gipsy – and this became standard. Tremendous success attended the Moth with its new power plant. In 1930 Francis Chichester and Amy Johnson flew Moths to Australia and there were further triumphs in 1931, including a new England–Australia record by C. W. A. Scott of 9 days 4 hours.

Development was unceasing, and the complete nose of the Gipsy III Moth was standard also on the Fox Moth, Tiger Moth and Puss Moth, all of which were types of high achievement in their own right. *Jane's All the World's Aircraft* declared in 1931: "The Gipsy Moth is without doubt the predominant light aeroplane in the world, and is the outcome of nearly seven years' and more than thirty million flying miles of experience."

The following description applies to the original Cirrus Moth.

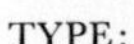

TYPE:

Two-seat light aircraft.

WINGS:

Braced biplane type. Equal span and chord. Slight stagger. Uniform dihedral. Fabric-covered wooden two-spar construction. Centre-section, containing fuel tank, supported at front spar by a pair of inverted Vees of oval-section steel tube, rendering cross-bracing unnecessary in the side panels and allowing free entrance to front cockpit. Wings hinged to fold at inner ends of front spars. Rear spar of bottom wing dropped below fuselage so that when wings were folded trailing-edge passed under fuselage. Maximum folded width 9 ft 8 in (2·95 m). One pair of spruce interplane struts on each side. Main and incidence bracing of streamline wire. Ailerons on bottom wings only.

FUSELAGE:

Standard de Havilland three-ply covered type, with domed top.

TAIL UNIT:

Braced monoplane type, of "butterfly" plan form. Rudder and elevator unbalanced.

LANDING GEAR:

Axle carrying two wheels supported by pair of hinged struts raked backwards from below engine bay and supported by nearly-vertical telescopic members housing rubber-in-compression shock absorbers.

POWER PLANT:

One 60 hp Cirrus 4-cylinder in-line air-cooled engine supported directly by top longerons and isolated from cockpits by inclined fireproof bulkhead. Long exhaust pipes enabling two occupants to communicate without speaking tube if necessary. Two-blade wooden propeller.

ACCOMMODATION:

Two tandem cockpits. Front cockpit under centre-section, rear one under cut-out in trailing-edge. Dual controls. When front control column removed hinged aluminium trapdoor covered socket and all moving parts so that a careless passenger could not jam mechanism with feet. Adjustable rudder pedals. Adjustable windscreens. Speaking tube for inter-communication.

DIMENSIONS:

Wing span 29 *ft* 0 *in* (8·84 *m*)
Length overall 23 *ft* 6 *in* (7·17 *m*)
Height overall 8 *ft* 7 *in* (2·60 *m*)
Wing area 225 *sq ft* (21 *m*)

WEIGHTS AND LOADING:

Weight empty 764 *lb* (347 *kg*)
Weight loaded 1,250 *lb* (567 *kg*)
Wing loading 5·5 *lb/hp* (27 *kg/m²*)
Power loading 20·8 *lb/hp* (9·5 *kg/hp*)
Max speed 90 *mph* (145 *kmh*)
Min speed 38 *mph* (61 *kmh*)

The aerobatic qualities of the original Moth, were developed to an uncommonly high pitch in in the later Tiger Moth, still a favourite for display work

A favourite among the ladies, the Moth put up many distinguished performances in their hands. Best remembered is Amy Johnson's flight from England to Australia in 19½ days (1930)

HANDLEY PAGE H.P.42

Disposition of the Bristol Jupiter engines

First Air Mail service to Cape Town

To the order of Imperial Airways the Handley Page company, which had previously constructed an eminently successful line of large bombers and airliners, produced in the early 1930s a class of aeroplane which the company itself described as "the world's first real airliner". Academically this claim would be difficult to substantiate, but the H.P. 42, which was the subject of the claim, was the first machine designed specifically for airline service in the layout of which passenger comfort was a dominant consideration. Not only were the seats very comfortable and the appointments generally of an extraordinarily high standard, but the basic arrangement of the entire aircraft was studied to the same end. Thus, no passengers were seated in line with the engines, the corresponding space being occupied by baggage, freight or mail. Another point was that passengers could step almost directly into the interior by virtue of the low-slung fuselage. This high standard of comfort, combined with questions of dependability and short take-off and landing runs, militated against performance, and it was of the H.P.42 that the historic declaration was made that it had "built-in headwinds". The makers could nevertheless console themselves that with the introduction of the type by Imperial Airways a standard of comfort was set that rivals could ignore only at their peril, and one which was perpetuated in the Short Empire flying boat (which see).

The H.P.42 was built in two forms, the "E" or Eastern type, for operation in semi-tropical conditions on the long mail routes between Karachi, Cairo and Kisumu, and the "W" (Western) for the London – Continental services.

The first H.P.42 was initially flown in November 1930.

The name "Handley Page" was for many years identified with very large aircraft, the first of which were the 0/100, 0/400 and V/1500 bombers of the 1914–18 war. Twin-engined Handley Page airliners were followed into the service of Britain's Imperial Airways by the majestic HP 42

A well-remembered scene from the 1930s: H.P.42 at Croydon

TYPE:
Four-engined airliner.

WINGS:
Braced biplane of unequal span. Lower wings with sharp anhedral angle as far as engine-mountings, then at dihedral angle as upper wings. Two spars of corrugated duralumin, with stainless-steel fittings at pick-up points. Duralumin tubular ribs. Interplane bracing mainly by struts in form of Warren girder. Outermost pair of struts on each side originally cross-braced by third strut, but wires later substituted. Handley Page slots and differential ailerons on top wing.

FUSELAGE:
In two distinct sections, roughly oval in cross-section, united by four pin-joints. Front section, comprising flight compartment and passenger cabins, of all-metal semi-monocoque construction, with built-up duralumin bulkheads at each end of both saloons to give torsional stiffness without need for struts across interior. Outer skin of front section of corrugated duralumin, with inner skin of wood, and, between the two, soundproofing material. Rear section a wire-braced four-sided structure of steel tubes, fabric covered.

TAIL UNIT:
Braced biplane type, with triple fins and rudders. Construction similar to that of wings. All control surfaces balanced.

LANDING GEAR:
Two Dunlop wheels with 60 × 21 in (1524 mm × 534 mm) tyres mounted on straight axles and sprung by oleo-pneumatic shock-absorbers. Internal-expanding brakes pneumatically operated through independent pedals by pilot. Tailwheel with oleo-pneumatic shock-absorber.

POWER PLANT:
Four Bristol Jupiter XFBM (42W) or XIF (42E) nine-cylinder air-cooled radial engines mounted two in top and two in bottom wings. Total horsepower 2,200. Four-blade wooden propellers. Four main fuel tanks with total capacity of 500 Imp gallons (2,273 litres) in top wings. Gas-starter in compartment between passenger cabins. Special device on throttle quadrant to prevent upper engines being opened up first.

ACCOMMODATION:
Western Type: Enclosed flight compartment in extreme nose. Dual controls. Wireless room immediately behind, and then forward passenger cabin, seating 20. Seats four abreast, with gangway between. Similar cabin aft, for 18 passengers. Compartment for mail and luggage (250 cu ft = 7·08 m³) between the two cabins, occupying whole of starboard side of central section of fuselage. Lavatories and buffet opposite this compartment. Second luggage and freight compartment behind rear cabin. Eastern Type: As foregoing, but passenger cabins arranged for 12 and 12 respectively. Mail and baggage capacity 500 cu ft (14·16 m³).

DIMENSIONS:
Wing span 130 *ft* 0 *in* (39·62 *m*)
Overall length 89 *ft* 9 *in* (27·36 *m*)
Overall height 27 *ft* 0 *in* (8·23 *m*)

WEIGHTS (Western Type):
Payload 8,500 *lb* (3,855 *kg*)
Weight loaded 29,500 *lb* (13,380 *kg*)

WEIGHTS (Eastern Type):
Payload 7,000 *lb* (3,175 *kg*)
Weight loaded 28,000 *lb* (12,700 *kg*)

PERFORMANCE (Western Type):
Max speed 127 *mph* (204 *kmh*)
Cruising speed 95–105 *mph* (153–169 *kmh*)
Landing speed 51·5 *mph* (83 *kmh*)
Initial rate of climb 670 *ft/min* (204 *m/min*)

PERFORMANCE (Eastern Type):
Max speed 120 *mph* (193 *kmh*)
Cruising speed 95–105 *mph* (153–169 *kmh*)
Landing speed 50 *mph* (81 *kmh*)
Initial rate of climb 845 *ft/min* (257 *m/min*)

TAYLOR CUB

In the 1931 edition of *Jane's All the World's Aircraft* the following entry appeared: "The Taylor Aircraft Company. Head Office and Works: Bradford, Pennsylvania. Incorporated: 1931. President: C. Gilbert Taylor. Secretary and Treasurer: W. T. Piper." It was further remarked: "The Taylor Aircraft Co. manufactures the Taylor Cub two-seat light monoplane, a description of which follows." The essence of that description is now reprinted, 38 years later, in tribute to the best-known light aeroplane of all time, and one which in progressively developed form, continued in production until 1950, the name Cub in later years having the familiar prefix "Piper". This came about as follows.

The secretary and treasurer named was William T. Piper, an oil producer who, having been invited to a business meeting of the Taylor company, developed not only an enthusiasm for flying but an entirely new career. When C. G. Taylor moved in 1936 to Ohio to build similar aircraft under the trade-name Taylorcraft the Bradford plant was bought by Mr. Piper, whose business was later centred on Lock Haven, Pennsylvania. The Piper J3 Cub, which was the first of the Cub series to be produced in really massive quantities, appeared in 1938, and since that year new Piper designs have achieved world-wide success. Current productions are the PA-18 Super Cub 150, Aztec, Turbo Aztec, Comanche, Pawnee, Cherokee, Twin Comanche, Navajo and Pocono.

Between 1931 and 1950 the total of Cubs built was 23,512, and several hundreds are still in use today.

TYPE:
Two-seat light aircraft.

WINGS:
High-wing braced monoplane. Wings supported above fuselage by system of steel-tube struts, forming framework of cockpit. Wings with spruce spars and aluminium-alloy ribs, the whole fabric-covered. Narrow-chord ailerons operated by rods and torque tubes.

FUSELAGE:
Rectangular structure of welded steel tubes, with fabric covering.

TAIL UNIT:
Monoplane type. Welded steel-tube framework, covered with fabric. All surfaces unbalanced.

LANDING GEAR:
Divided type, with two side Vees and two half-axles. Cast aluminium wheels on roller bearings.

POWER PLANT:
One 35 hp Continental A-40 four-cylinder horizontally-opposed air-cooled engine. Two fuel tanks in wings, total capacity 9 US gallons (34 litres).

ACCOMMODATION:
One cockpit, seating two in tandem, under wing. Dual control, with front control detachable.

DIMENSIONS:
Wing span 35 *ft* 2 *in* (10·72 *m*)
Length overall 22 *ft* 6 *in* (6·86 *m*)
Height 6 *ft* 6 *in* (1·98 *m*)
Wing area 184 *sq ft* (17·09 m^2)

WEIGHTS AND LOADINGS:
Weight empty 510 *lb* (231·30 *kg*)
Weight loaded 925 *lb* (420 *kg*)
Wing loading 6 *lb/sq ft* (29·28 kg/m^2)
Power loading 22 *lb/hp* (9·90 *kg/hp*)

PERFORMANCE:
Max speed 80 *mph* (128·75 *kmh*)
Cruising speed 70 *mph* (112·65 *kmh*)
Landing speed 26 *mph* (41·85 *kmh*)
Range 225 *miles* (362 *km*)

One of the original Taylor Cubs, displaying features which were to endear themselves to many thousands of private pilots

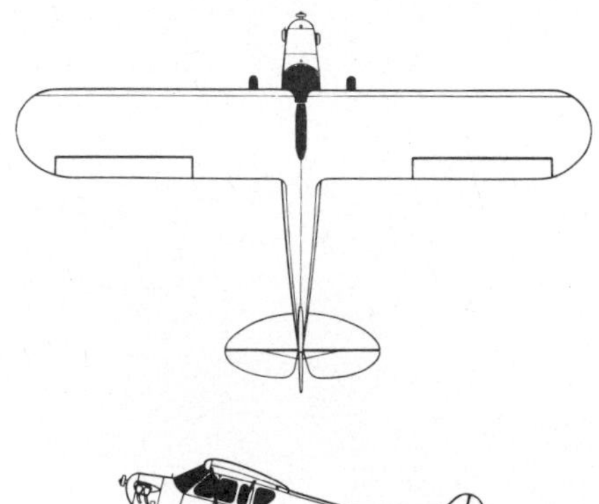

Another early Cub, displaying the beginnings of the "paint job" which was to become so distinctive a feature of American light aircraft. In all essentials the Cub remained a simple aeroplane throughout

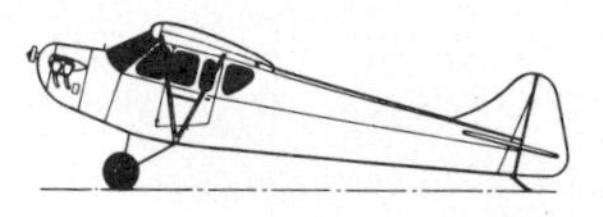

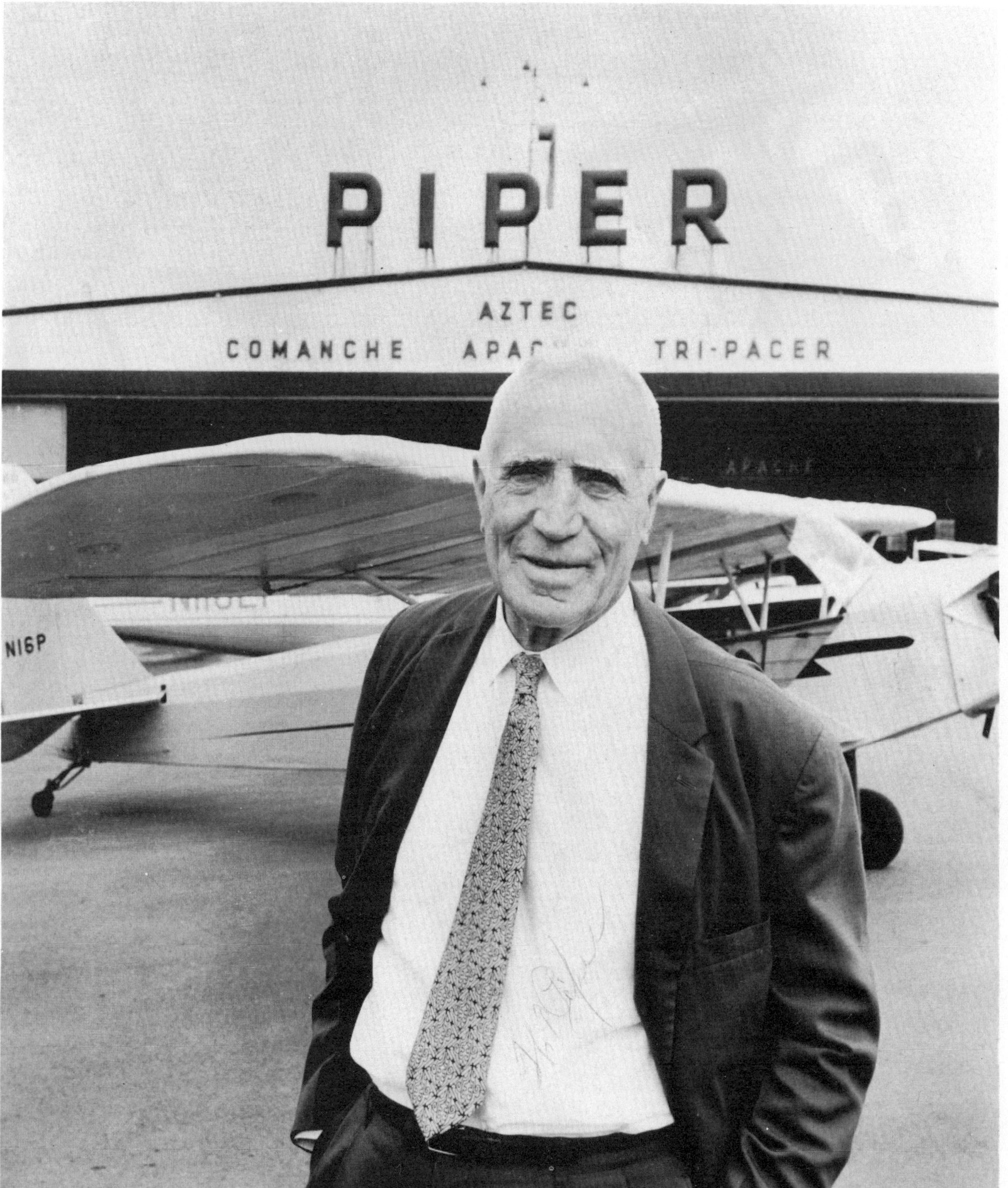

Symbolising the founding of the Piper fortune in the aeronautical field instead of the oil field, a Cub stands between the founder of that fortune, Mr William T. Piper, and a notice proclaiming a few of the Cub's successors. In the 1931 edition of "Jane's All the World's Aircraft" Mr Piper was named as Secretary and Treasurer of the Taylor Aircraft Company

GRUMMAN FF-1

The first FF-1 was faster than many contemporary single-seaters.

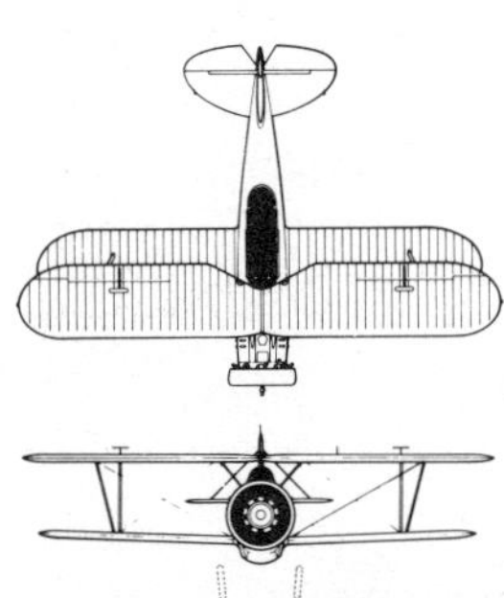

The retractable landing gear for which this biplane fighter of 1931 was remarkable had a triple significance. The first lay not in the use of such a gear to enhance performance but in its application to amphibious aircraft. In this connection it must be recorded that when Leroy R. Grumman left the US Navy in 1920 he became successively a design engineer and general manager for the Loening company. The founder of that company was one of America's most distinguished aircraft designers, who had built a remarkable flying boat before 1914, and who, during the 1920s, developed a form of amphibian which achieved a marked success. An example of this amphibian is preserved today in the National Air and Space Museum. The landing gear was made retractable into the hull. After Mr. Grumman went into business for himself in 1929 he continued to develop amphibious landing gears, especially for observation-type aircraft, and supplied a quantity of these to the US Navy. The Grumman gear consisted of a single large float of all-metal construction divided into five watertight compartments.

The retractable mechanism was made of welded steel tubes, and was so arranged that the wheels could be drawn into pockets in the sides of the float. The complete installation, as eventually developed, provided for catapulting and deck arresting. The second of the three significant associations mentioned concerned not amphibious operation but the attainment of high performance in a fighter aircraft. In 1931 Mr. Loening's company was successful in a US Navy competition for a two-seat fighter, and this materialised as the FF-1, as later described. The third association of the retractable landing gear is with the Dayton-Wright R.B. Racer of 1920, described on an earlier page.

The FF-1 and its scout counterpart the SF-1 were supplied in some quantity to the US Navy and aircraft of the same type were built in Canada by the Canadian Car & Foundry organisation. Bearing the name Goblin, a few of these aircraft were used by the Royal Canadian Air Force. Of greater historical interest is the fact that earlier aircraft of the type, built by the same organisation, were used in the Spanish Civil War by the Republicans. These had been supposedly intended for Turkey.

In US Navy service the FF-1 and SF-1 were followed by a succession of types, among which the Hellcat fighter and Avenger torpedo bomber of the Second World War achieved particular fame. In the Korean war the Grumman Panther became the first jet aircraft to be used in combat by the US Navy.

TYPE:

Two-seat fighter.

WINGS:

Braced biplane with sharply staggered wings of unequal span and equal chord. Top wing in two panels, meeting on centre-line, with small cut-out at leading-edge and large cut-out at trailing-edge. Balanced long-span ailerons, on top wings only, actuated by struts running diagonally from leading-edges of lower wings. Main interplane struts of N form. Top wings carried above fuselage on four splayed-out struts. Wire bracing in plane of front spars only. Wing construction embodying aluminium alloy spars and ribs, with fabric covering.

FUSELAGE:

Semi-monocoque structure of aluminium-alloy. Very deep forward part to accept retracted wheels, and relatively broad to provide adequate wheel track, the landing gear being attached to the fuselage.

TAIL UNIT:

Monoplane type, with metal-covered fin and tailplane and fabric-covered rudder and elevator. Rudder balanced, elevator not. Fin and tailplane braced to each other by single strut on each side.

LANDING GEAR:

Two wheels, each mounted on retractable triangulated assembly. Outer faces of wheels not covered when retracted, but faired accordingly. Small tailwheel.

POWER PLANT:

One Wright Cyclone E (later F) series nine-cylinder air-cooled radial engine with short-chord ring cowling. Two-blade adjustable-pitch metal propeller. Last SF-1 fitted experimentally with Pratt & Whitney R-1535-80 engine.

ACCOMMODATION AND ARMAMENT:

Pilot and navigator/gunner in tandem cockpits with telescoping sliding roofs. One or two fixed Browning machine-guns in fuselage for pilot, with optical and ring-and-bead-sights. Two free Browning machine guns on manually operated mounting in rear cockpit.

DIMENSIONS:

Wing span 34 *ft* 6 *in* (10·51 *m*)
Length overall 24 *ft* 6 *in* (7·47 *m*)
Height overall 9 *ft* 5 *in* (2·87 *m*)
Wing area 310 *sq ft* (28·8 m^2)

WEIGHTS AND LOADING:

Weight empty 3,221 *lb* (1,461 *kg*)
Weight loaded 4,800 *lb* (2,177 *kg*)
Wing loading 15·5 *lb/sq ft* (74·7 kg/m^2)
Power loading 6·22 *lb/hp* (2·8 *kg/hp*)

PERFORMANCE (with Wright Cyclone SR-1820-F engine, of later type than Cyclone originally fitted, which gave max speed of 197 mph (317 kmh) at 6,000 ft (1,830 m):

Max speed at 5,300 *ft* (1,615 *m*) 216 *mph* (347 *kmh*)
Landing speed 65 *mph* (105 *kmh*)
Initial rate of climb 1,600 *ft/min* (488 *m/min*)
Service ceiling 22,500 *ft* (6,858 *m*)
Range at cruising speed 647 *miles* (1,030 *km*)

P.Z.L. P.1

The P.1 was the first of a remarkable series of single-seat fighters with characteristic "gull" wings

A P.Z.L. P.11 in Polish markings

A P.Z.L. P.24G as used by Greece

From 1916 onwards repeated attempts were made to improve the field of vision that could be commanded by the pilot of a single-seat fighter, in the recognition that success in combat might often be dependent on this consideration. Numerous unconventional arrangements of pilot, engine and wings were tried, and there was a vogue for "gull-winged" monoplanes and biplanes of which the Polish P.Z.L. monoplane fighters of 1930 onwards afford the best examples. The first machine of the series was the P.1, which is the subject of the following description, but there were several developments along the same basic lines, incorporating more powerful engines and heavier armament. In the latter connection these Polish fighters have another historical interest, for they were among the first of those built during the inter-war years to have the resurgent armament of "cannon" as tentatively used in the 1914–18 war. These guns were of 20 mm bore and could be mounted to fire through the propeller hub of an Hispano-Suiza water-cooled engine or be installed in the wings outboard of the propeller arc. Notable among such fighters was the P.Z.L. P.24 (1933) which had two 20 mm Oerlikon FF guns in the wings and by virtue of good aerodynamic design and the fitting of a Gnome-Rhône engine of the 14K series was able to achieve well over 250 mph.

Fighters of this general type achieved considerable success in the export market and were operated against the German and Italian Air Forces.

TYPE:

Single-seat fighter.

WING:

High-wing braced monoplane. Greatest depth of each wing at bracing-strut attachment. Inner sections of each wing sloped down, with diminishing section, to point of attachment on fuselage. Two parallel bracing struts on each side. Wings built up of two I-section spars made from duralumin sheet, duralumin ribs, and corrugated duralumin covering. Less highly stressed parts of wings covered with electron. Ailerons of narrow chord, extending over practically whole of trailing-edge and used as flaps for landing. Each aileron a box-girder, built up from duralumin and electron and having inset ball-bearing hinges.

FUSELAGE:

Flat-sided structure with rounded, removable top and bottom. Main structure in two sections, with joints just aft of wing. Structure made up of rectangular duralumin bulkheads and outer duralumin skin.

TAIL UNIT:

Monoplane type, with cantilever fin and braced tailplane. Duralumin and electron construction, similar to wings. Adjustable tailplane, braced by single strut on each side. Unbalanced rudder, balanced elevators.

LANDING GEAR:

Divided type. Each wheel supported by faired cantilever leg and independently sprung by Vickers oleo-pneumatic shock-absorbers in the fuselage. Tail-skid similarly sprung.

POWER PLANT:

One Hispano-Suiza or Lorraine twelve-cylinder Vee water-cooled engine of 600 hp driving two-blade metal propeller. Cylinder blocks faired into sloping inner sections of wings. Removable cowling of electron. Two duralumin fuel tanks, of 88 Imp gallons (400 litres) capacity, in wings, with gravity feed to collector tank in fuselage, whence fuel pumped to engine. Oil tank (also forming oil cooler) above engine. Retractable Lamblin radiator beneath fuselage. Fireproof bulkhead and automatic fire-extinguisher.

ARMAMENT:

Two synchronised rifle-calibre machine-guns ahead of cockpit.

DIMENSIONS:

Wing span 35 *ft* 7 *in* (10·85 *m*)
Overall length 22 *ft* 11 *in* (6·98 *m*)
Overall height (*in flying attitude*) 10 *ft* 0 *in* (3·05 *m*)
Wing area 210 *sq ft* (19·5 m^2)

WEIGHTS AND LOADING:

Weight empty 2,350 *lb* (1,066 *kg*)
Weight loaded 3,440 *lb* (1,560 *kg*)
Wing loading 16·4 *lb/sq ft* (80 kg/m^2)
Power loading 5·75 *lb/hp* (2·6 *kg/hp*)

PERFORMANCE:

Max speed at S/L 190 *mph* (306 *kmh*)
Landing speed 62 *mph* (100 *kmh*)
Time of climb to 16,400 *ft* (5,000 *m*) 8 *min*
Service ceiling 26,240 *ft* (8,000 *m*)
Endurance at cruising speed 2 *hr*

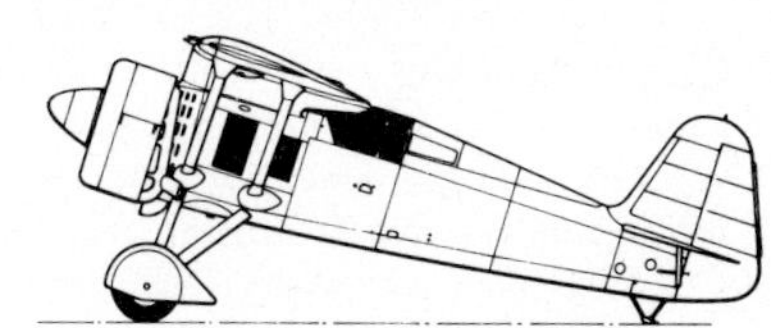

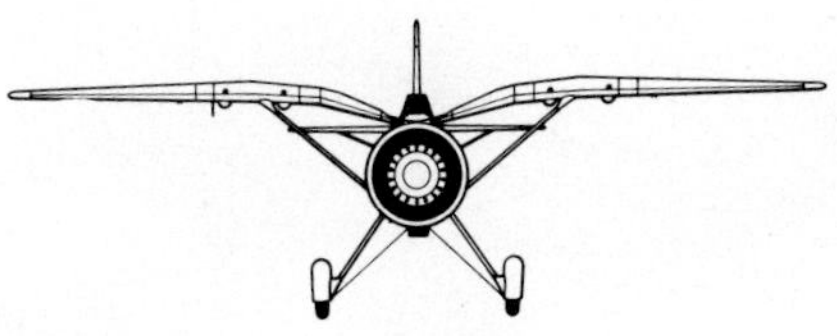

The purpose of the "inverted-gull" wing roots of the He 70 was elimination of tail-buffeting

HEINKEL He 70

Especially notable among the Lockheed single-engined types which succeeded the Vega, already described, was the low-wing Orion, and it was the outstanding performance of this aircraft which motivated Deutsche Lufthansa in 1932 to commission the Heinkel company to design a four-passenger machine with emphasis on speed. The result was a low-wing monoplane having extraordinary beauty of line and powered with a glycol-cooled B.M.W. VI engine. The first example was given its maiden flight on 1 December 1932. The second of the type was named *Blitz (Lightning)*, and this was unofficially adopted as a class name for the small fleet of He 70s operated by the sponsoring airline. One aircraft of the type was rebuilt as a military prototype and quantity-production of attack-bomber and reconnaissance variants was undertaken for the Luftwaffe. The same close relationship between a civil airliner and a bomber pertained in the case of the twin-engined He 111, which dated from 1935. This type was likewise initiated by Deutsche Lufthansa and, together with the Junkers Ju 88, constituted the standard equipment of Germany's twin-engined bomber force at the outbreak of war in 1939.

Evidence of the efficiency of the He 70 design was afforded in 1933, when one of the prototype aircraft set eight records for speed over distances of 100–2,000 km (62–1,243 miles) with loads of 500 and 1,000 kg (1,102 and 2,204 lb). With these loads over 100 km the recorded speed was 357 kmh (221·83 mph) and an absolute maximum speed of 377 kmh (234·26 mph) was established in the course of other tests. So advanced was the design of the He 70 that an example was acquired by Rolls-Royce in England for use on engine-development work. This had a Kestrel engine, and there was also a version for the Hungarian Air Force (He 170) with a Gnome-Rhône Mistral Major radial engine. The following description relates to the early-production version (He 70A).

"Blitz" (Lightning) was a fitting name for the He 70, a transport with fighter performance. It was among the first aircraft with retractable landing gear, and the B.M.W. VI engine gave low drag

TYPE:

Single-engined high-speed transport.

WINGS:

Cantilever low-wing monoplane with "inverted-gull" roots to eliminate possibility of tail-buffeting. Elliptical plan-form. Wing in one piece, built up of two spruce-and-plywood box spars, closely spaced ribs and plywood planking. Two cut-outs in fuselage to accept spars. Spars attached by bolts. Split trailing-edge flaps and narrow-chord ailerons.

FUSELAGE:

Semi-monocoque duralumin structure, built up of hollow frames and longitudinal members and covered with smooth sheet. Countersunk rivets used for covering.

TAIL UNIT:

Cantilever monoplane type. All surfaces elliptical and built up in similar manner to wing. Trim-tabs in elevator.

LANDING GEAR:

Retractable type. Each unit consisted of a tripod, one unit of which was an oleo leg. Top of leg, and top of a backwardly- and inwardly-inclined leg, hinged to front and rear spars respectively. Top of third leg slid inwardly on rail in wing, drawing wheel into wing by cable. Hydraulic retracting mechanism. Undercarriage normally worked by wireless-operator, but handle easily accessible to pilot. Wheel-brakes fitted. Oleo-sprung tail-skid retractable with main gear.

POWER PLANT:

One 630 hp B.M.W. VI 12-cylinder Vee engine on detachable welded steel-tube mounting. Ethylene-glycol cooling, with small retractable radiator under fuselage. Two fuel tanks, with total capacity of 95 Imp gallons (430 litres) in wings.

ACCOMMODATION:

Pilot's cockpit behind fireproof bulkhead offset to port, with sliding canopy. Seat adjustable vertically in flight, horizontally on ground. Full blind-flying equipment. Radio operator behind pilot at lower level. Additional folding seat for passenger behind pilot. Main cabin for four passengers behind rear bulkhead of pilot's compartment. Two cross-seats, with arm- and head-rests. Separate window, of curved non-shatterable glass, for each passenger. Two forward windows openable. Cabin heating and ventilation. Access door, with curved flush window and countersunk handle, on starboard side. Baggage compartment aft of cabin, with manhole in rear bulkhead permitting inspection of rear fuselage.

DIMENSIONS:

Wing span 48 *ft* 6 *in* (14·78 *m*)
Length overall 37 *ft* 8$\frac{1}{2}$ *in* (11·48 *m*)
Wing area 392·9 *sq ft* (36·5 m^2)

WEIGHTS AND LOADINGS:

Weight empty (*including cabin furnishing, radio and full blind-flying equipment*) 5,070 *lb* (2,300 *kg*)
Weight loaded 7,297 *lb* (3,310 *kg*)
Wing loading 18·4 *lb/sq ft* (90 *kg/*m^2)
Power loading 11·44 *lb/hp* (5·2 *kg/hp*)

PERFORMANCE:

Max speed 221 *mph* (355 *kmh*)
Cruising speed 193 *mph* (310 *kmh*)
Landing speed 62 *mph* (100 *kmh*)
Climb to 3,280 *ft* (1,000 *m*) 3 *min*
Service ceiling 19,680 *ft* (6,000 *m*)
Normal range 497 *miles* (800 *km*)

Glimpsed through the cabin windows of this Boeing 247D are additional fuel tanks for participation in the MacRobertson Race from England to Australia in 1934. The aircraft was otherwise standard

BOEING MODEL 247

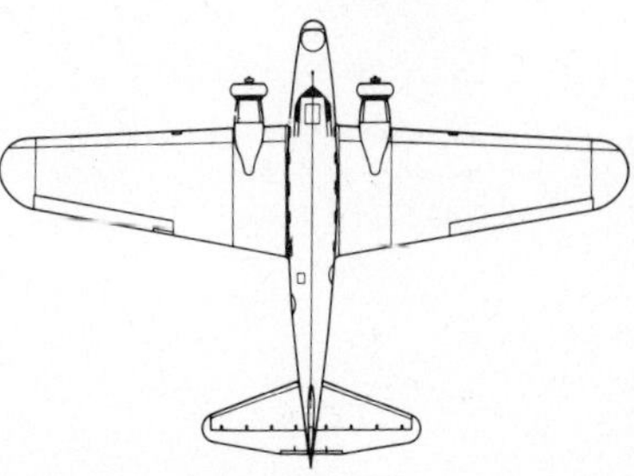

The 1920s and early 1930s witnessed a strong preference among airlines for three-engined aircraft, notwithstanding the relative inefficiency of the nose engine by reason of a bulky fuselage behind it. In Europe the principal types were built by Fokker, Junkers, Savoia-Marchetti, Fiat and Wibault; in Great Britain by Armstrong Whitworth and de Havilland; in the USA by Ford, Boeing and, again, by Fokker. Though aerodynamic efficiencies of a high order were achieved, in particular by the later types of Savoia-Marchetti, the class was destined to languish until the 1960s (de Havilland Trident, Boeing 727). The change of emphasis to a twin-engined type, in the interests of performance and economy, was marked by the introduction of the Boeing Model 247, the first example of which was first air-tested on 8 February 1933. A total of 70 machines of this general type was ordered in 1932 by the companies comprising United Air Lines. The final eleven were completed as Model 247Ds and all of the original type remaining in service with UAL were retrospectively modified to 247D standard. Of the total of 61 "plain" 247s built the last two went to Lufthansa in Germany. A single 247, redesignated 247A served as an executive transport and research-and-development aircraft with the Pratt & Whitney Division of United Aircraft Corporation. This was fitted with the then-new 14-cylinder Twin Wasp Junior engines.

This Model 247 is airworthy today

The most notable development of the basic type was, as already indicated, the Model 247D of much-improved performance. This had geared Wasp engines instead of the original direct-drive type, NACA cowlings in place of short-chord rings, three-blade controllable-pitch propellers, rearward-sloping windscreen and fabric-covered movable tail surfaces instead of metal. The 247 was the first airliner to have wing- and tail-deicing, by rubber "over-shoes".

One of the Model 247Ds originally ordered by UAL was specially prepared for Col. Roscoe Turner and Clyde Pangbourne to compete in the MacRobertson England–Australia air race of 1934. This was placed second in the transport division and third in overall speed. Victorious in the transport division was the Douglas DC-2, which, its historical eminence notwithstanding, was placed second in chronology to the Boeing Model 247 now described.

TYPE:

Twin-engined airliner.

WINGS:

Low-wing cantilever monoplane. All-metal wing in five sections: centre-section, two outboard panels, two wing-tips. Outboard sections bolted to stubs carrying engine nacelles. Spars of aluminium alloy and chrome-molybdenum steel tubes. Aluminium-alloy ribs and smooth aluminium-alloy skin. Trailing-edge of wing and leading-edge of stub detachable to facilitate repairs and shipment.

FUSELAGE:

Semi-monocoque structure of duralumin members and bulkheads, with aluminium-alloy skin, built in three sections. Tail-cone from rudder-post aft detachable.

TAIL UNIT:

Cantilever monoplane type. All surfaces of aluminium-alloy, including covering. Boeing patent trailing-edge flaps for trimming on rudder, elevators and port aileron.

LANDING GEAR:

Divided type, with Boeing oleo legs and hydraulic brakes operating simultaneously or individually. Gear electrically retracted into wing-stubs. Auxiliary manual control. Large low-pressure types. Swivelling tail-wheel with oleo-pneumatic shock-absorber.

POWER PLANT:

Two 550 hp Pratt & Whitney Wasp nine-cylinder radial supercharged engines, driving two-blade Hamilton Standard controllable-pitch propellers. Boeing short-chord ring cowlings. Fuel tanks in wing-stubs, carrying total of 275 US gallons (1,036 litres). Fuel fed by engine-driven pump with auxiliary hand pump. Engine-driven dynamo and storage battery for lighting. Pressure fire-extinguisher controlled by pilot and portable hand-extinguishers.

ACCOMMODATION:

Provision for ten passengers, two pilots, stewardess, baggage and cargo. Pilots' compartment considerably aft from nose, with inward-sloping Vee windscreen. Cargo space (60 cu ft = 1·70 m) in nose and additional 65 cu ft (1·84 m³) in rear of fuselage. Main cabin insulated against noise and temperature. Windows of non-splinterable plate glass. Thermostatically controlled heating-cooling system. Dome lights and individual reading lamps. Visual inter-communication system. Lavatory.

DIMENSIONS, EXTERNAL:

Wing span 74 *ft* 0 *in* (22·55 *m*)
Length overall 51 *ft* 4 *in* (15·65 *m*)
Height overall 16 *ft* 0 *in* (4·88 *m*)
Wing area 836·13 *sq ft* (77·6 *m*²)

DIMENSIONS, INTERNAL:

Cabin:
Length 20 *ft* 0 *in* (6·09 *m*)
Height 6 *ft* 0 *in* (1·83 *m*)

PERFORMANCE:

Max speed 182 *mph* (293 *kmh*)
Cruising speed 171 *mph* (275 *kmh*)
Landing speed 59 *mph* (96 *kmh*)
Initial rate of climb 1,320 *ft/min* (402 *m/min*)
Climb to 10,000 *ft* (3,050 *m*) 11 *min*
Service ceiling 18,000 *ft* (5,650 *m*)

Boeing 247, before first test

DOUGLAS DC-2

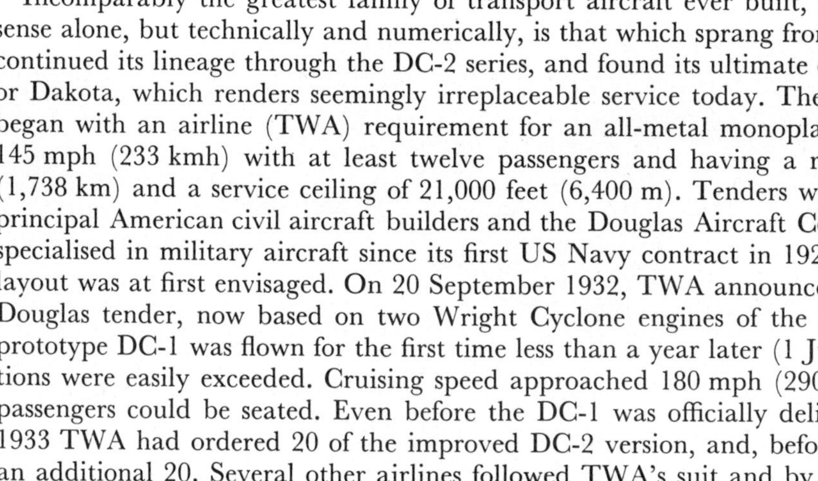

Incomparably the greatest family of transport aircraft ever built, not in the historical sense alone, but technically and numerically, is that which sprang from the DC-1 of 1933, continued its lineage through the DC-2 series, and found its ultimate destiny in the DC-3, or Dakota, which renders seemingly irreplaceable service today. The saga of the "DCs" began with an airline (TWA) requirement for an all-metal monoplane able to cruise at 145 mph (233 kmh) with at least twelve passengers and having a range of 1,080 miles (1,738 km) and a service ceiling of 21,000 feet (6,400 m). Tenders were invited from the principal American civil aircraft builders and the Douglas Aircraft Company (which had specialised in military aircraft since its first US Navy contract in 1921). A three-engined layout was at first envisaged. On 20 September 1932, TWA announced acceptance of the Douglas tender, now based on two Wright Cyclone engines of the latest type, and the prototype DC-1 was flown for the first time less than a year later (1 July 1933). Specifications were easily exceeded. Cruising speed approached 180 mph (290 kmh) and fourteen passengers could be seated. Even before the DC-1 was officially delivered in September 1933 TWA had ordered 20 of the improved DC-2 version, and, before the year was out, an additional 20. Several other airlines followed TWA's suit and by June 1934 (the first machine had flown in May) seventy-five DC-2s had been sold.

The DC-3 series had its origins in an American Airlines requirement for a larger version, the first example of which was initially flown on 17 December 1935. Success was world-wide, and in the coming war a total of over 10,000 military DC-3s (C-47 Skytrain, R4D and Dakota) were to be manufactured. For comparison with the following description of the DC-2 it may be noted that the DC-3 has a span of 95 ft (28·95 m), a length of 64 ft 5½ in (19·63 m) and a loaded weight of 26,900 lb (12,200 kg).

Bust of Donald W. Douglas. He founded the company bearing his name in 1920

TYPE:
Twin-engined airliner.

WINGS:
Cantilever low-wing monoplane of Douglas-Northrop cellular multi-web construction. Centre-section, parallel in chord and extending under fuselage, carrying an engine nacelle at each extremity. Outer wing panels sharply tapered and detachable by multi-bolted flange joints. Entire trailing-edge of wing between ailerons, including portion under fuselage, fitted with split flaps. Ailerons metal-framed and fabric-covered. Trim-tab in port aileron.

FUSELAGE:
Semi-monocoque all-metal structure, with transverse frames of formed sheet, longitudinal members of extruded bulb angles and smooth sheet covering.

TAIL UNIT:
Cantilever monoplane type. Tailplane and fin of multi-cellular construction, using same alloy as wing and fuselage. Rudder and elevator fabric-covered. Trim-tabs in rudder and elevator.

LANDING GEAR:
Two retractable units, each comprising two oleo shock-absorbers and a wheel fitted with hydraulic brakes. Brakes differentially controlled through rudder pedals. Wheels retracted upward and forward, small portion of each wheel protruding when raised to facilitate emergency landings.

POWER PLANT:
Two geared and supercharged Wright Cyclone SGR-1820 F-3 nine-cylinder radial air-cooled engines, each rated at 710 hp at 8,000 ft (2,438 m). Controllable-pitch three-blade metal propellers. Engine mountings interchangeable, complete with all accessories, forward of fireproof bulkhead. Two main fuel tanks, each of 180 US gallons (681·3 litres) capacity, and two auxiliary fuel tanks, each of 75 US gallons (283·9 litres) capacity in wing centre-section.

ACCOMMODATION:
Pilots' cockpit forward of wing, accessible through corridor from passenger cabin. Emergency exit in roof. Dual controls. Passenger cabin normally seating 14. Seats adjustable for reclining or facing backward and rubber-mounted to minimise vibration. Ventilating and steam-heating systems. Cargo and mail compartment in plane of engines and propellers and separated from rest of aircraft by sound-deadening bulkhead 2·5 in (6·35 cm) thick. Capacity 1,000 lb (454 Kg). Loading door in side of fuselage. Additional cargo and baggage compartment, with loading door, aft of passenger cabin. Passenger cabin entered by door on port side, with buffet aft of door. Lavatory at rear of cabin. Emergency exit opposite main entrance door.

DIMENSIONS, EXTERNAL:
Wing span 85 *ft* 0 *in* (25·91 *m*)
Overall length 61 *ft* 11¾ *in* (18·90 *m*)
Overall height 16 *ft* 3¼ *in* (4·96 *m*)

DIMENSIONS, INTERNAL:
Passenger cabin:
Length 26 *ft* 0 *in* (7·92 *m*)
Height 6 *ft* 3 *in* (1·91 *m*)
Width 5 *ft* 6 *in* (1·68 *m*)

WEIGHTS AND LOADING:
Weight empty 12,075 *lb* (5,477 *kg*)
Weight loaded 18,000 *lb* (8,165 *kg*)
Wing loading 19·2 *lb/sq ft* (97·3 *kg/m²*)
Power loading 12·7 *lb/hp* (5·76 *kg/hp*)

The DC-2 was a developed version of the TWA-inspired DC–1, first flown on 1 July 1933

PERFORMANCE:
Max speed (propeller pitch set for cruising) 213 *mph* (343 *kmh*)
Cruising speed at 8,000 *ft* (2,438 *m*) 191 *mph* (306 *kmh*)
Landing speed 58 *mph* (93·34 *kmh*)
Initial rate of climb 1,000 *ft/min* (305 *m/min*)
Service ceiling 23,700 *ft* (7,225 *m*)

DC-2 PH-AKT "Toekan" of KLM. Today this great international operator flies DC-8s. The prefix denoting "Douglas Commercial" dates from the DC-1 of 1933

Douglas C-47 (military DC-3 development) dropping supplies into the streets of Mandalay during the battle of 1945

The "DC-2½". It flew with one wing of a DC-2 and one of a DC-3

The DC-3 was the aircraft chosen for the famous Air France night-mail services

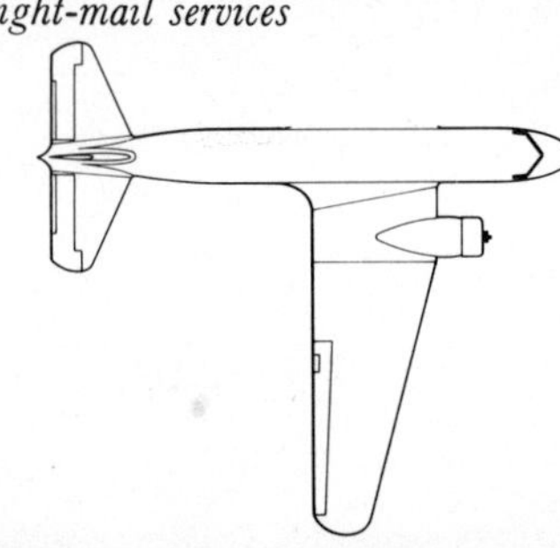

SIKORSKY S-42

Igor Sikorsky

The name *American Clipper* was conferred on 12 October 1931 by Mrs. Hoover, wife of the President of the United States, on a new type of large Sikorsky flying-boat designated S-40. Although impressive this craft was of conservative design in following the lines of the earlier and smaller S-38 twin-engined amphibian which had achieved success. The next large Sikorsky flying-boat, which was to perpetuate the name *Clipper*, was far from conservative. Not only was the hull of full-length tail-carrying type (the tail of the S-40 had been carried on outriggers in a manner reminiscent of the Navy-Curtiss NC-4) but the fullest advantage was taken of wing flaps and variable-pitch propellers. The first take-off was made on 29 March 1934, and within a short period of development and test flying the S-42 had established ten world records for payload to height. In June 1937 the last of an order for ten S-42s was delivered to Pan American Airways. This was, in fact, an S-42B, differing from the original version in having extra fuel tankage. Named *Pan American Clipper III* this craft made three round-trip survey flights over the North Atlantic during the summer of 1937, while the other S-42s continued in service in the Pacific, South American and Bermuda divisions of Pan American Airways. These machines themselves had accomplished trail-blazing flights, first flying (17 April 1935) from San Francisco to Hawaii and then opening up routes further across the Pacific to New Zealand.

The significance of the Sikorsky *Grand* of 1913 has already received recognition in these pages, and this may be related to the S-42 in the words of Igor Sikorsky himself. Thus: "The successful flights of the S-42 across both major oceans may be considered as concluding the pioneering period of aviation. The most important factor in this story is the creation of various types of large aircraft with four engines. This work actually began on September 17, 1912 and resulted, exactly twenty-five years later in the successful commercial crossing from shore to shore of both major oceans."

Static above is the S-38, another S-42 precursor. Active below is the S-42

TYPE:

Four-engined commercial flying-boat.

WINGS:

High-wing braced monoplane. Wing in one piece. Two spars, with compression struts and metal stressed-skin covering on both surfaces forward of rear spar. Aft of rear spar ribs and fabric covering. Spars, compression struts and ribs in form of trusses extruded duralumin shapes and bent sheet-duralumin sections, fastened with steel bolts and duralumin rivets. Wing joined to hull by faired superstructure and braced by two struts on each side. Outboard of struts differentially-controlled balanced ailerons fitted on tapered wing panels. Centre portion of wing untapered and carrying hydraulically-controlled split flap. All external metal surfaces flush-riveted.

HULL:

Two-step type with long stern. Nine watertight compartments. Structure composed of deep keel, widely spaced transverse frames and heavy stringers. Keel and frames of plate girder type. Duralumin shapes and sheet used throughout. All seams sealed with fabric and marine glue. Flush riveting all over.

TAIL UNIT:

Braced monoplane type. Twin fins and rudders. Elevator and rudder balanced. All surfaces of metal, with fabric covering. Patented unsymmetrical self-compensating rudders and fins to offset unsymmetrical engine thrust.

POWER PLANT:

Four Pratt & Whitney Hornet geared air-cooled radial engines, each giving 700 hp at 3,500 ft (1,070 m) in nacelles faired into wing leading-edge. Eight fuel tanks and four oil tanks in wing. Direct-drive electric starters and provision for hand cranking. Quickly removable NACA cowlings. Three-blade Hamilton-Standard controllable-pitch propellers.

ACCOMMODATION:

Anchor compartment in bow. Pilots' compartment next, with provision for mechanic and radio operator. Third compartment equipped for baggage and/or freight, but adaptable for passengers on short flights. Four main passenger cabins, each seating eight. Two toilets and water fountain aft of last compartment. Eighth compartment for main entrance and steward's accommodation. Tail compartment available for additional baggage or freight.

DIMENSIONS:

Wing span 114 *ft* 2 *in* (34·80 *m*)
Length overall 67 *ft* 8 *in* (20·62 *m*)
Height overall 17 *ft* 4 *in* (5·28 *m*)
Wing area 1,330 *sq ft* (123·56 m^2)

WEIGHTS AND LOADING:

Weight empty 19,764 *lb* (8,965 *kg*)
Weight loaded 38,000 *lb* (17,236 *kg*)
Wing loading 28·58 *lb/sq ft* (140 kg/m^2)

PERFORMANCE (at 36,000 lb = 16,330 kg):

Max speed at 5,000 *ft* (1,525 *m*) 182 *mph* (293 *kmh*)
Speed at 12,000 *ft* (3,650 *m*) *at* 70 *per cent hp* 170 *mph* (274 *kmh*)
Stalling speed 65 *mph* (105 *kmh*)
Initial rate of climb 1,000 *ft/min* (305 *m/min*)
Ceiling 16,000 *ft* (4,880 *m*)
Take-off run (*still air*) 30 *sec*
Range at cruising speed 1,200 *miles* (1,930 *km*)

The S-42, spanning the pages above, had a precursor in the S-40 below

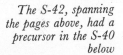

Boeing and Martin also made "Clippers". Above, Boeing 314, lower left, Martin 130

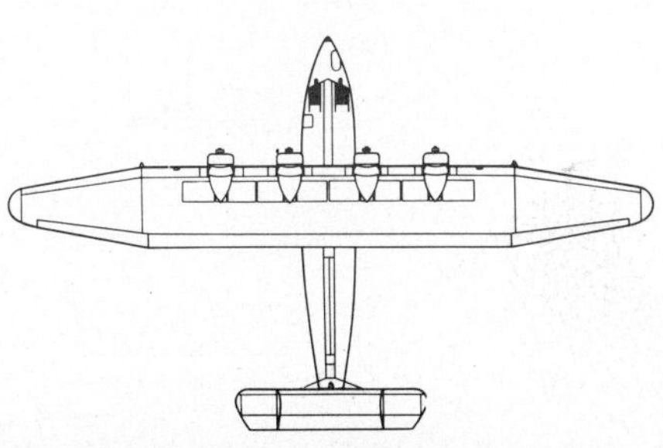

TUPOLEV ANT-25

Outstanding among the long-range single-engined monoplanes of very high aspect ratio built between the wars by France, Great Britain, Italy and Russia for attempts on the world's long-distance record was the Russian ANT-25. This was a design of Andrei Nikolaevich Tupolev, whose more recent productions are prominent today in the service of the Soviet and other air forces as well as in the State airline Aeroflot and other civil fleets.

Although the ANT-25 did not achieve its ultimate distinction until 1937 it was designed as early as 1932. It was completed at the beginning of 1935 and was prepared for a flight from Moscow to San Francisco, across the North Pole. An oil leak prevented the machine from proceeding far. Special equipment included cockpit heating; flotation bags; metal propeller; special water system for the engine, to enable it to function in extremely low temperatures; short-wave radio, with a range of 9,000 m (5,590 miles); and a new type of compass for trans-polar flying. In 1936 the machine was used in an attempt to beat the international distance record over a closed circuit, and it remained airborne for 56 hr 20 min. The distance covered, however, was short of the figure of 6,587 miles (10,601 km) set by France in 1932. In 1937 an ANT-25 flew from Moscow across the Arctic to California, an achievement which gained recognition as a world record for distance in a straight line. The actual recording read "Airline Distance. International Record. 10,148 kilometres (6,295·662 miles). Col. Mikhail Gromov, Comdt. Andrei Youmachev and Ing. Sergei Daniline, U.S.S.R., ANT-25 monoplane, AM-34 860 hp engine, from Moscow, U.S.S.R. to San Jacinto, California, July 13–15, 1937." Less than a month previously another ANT-25 had flown over the North Pole to Vancouver, Washington, covering 5,228 miles in 63 hr 17 min. These two great Polar flights carried forward the pioneering achievements of Amundsen and Ellsworth, Byrd and Floyd Bennett, Sir Hubert Wilkins and others.

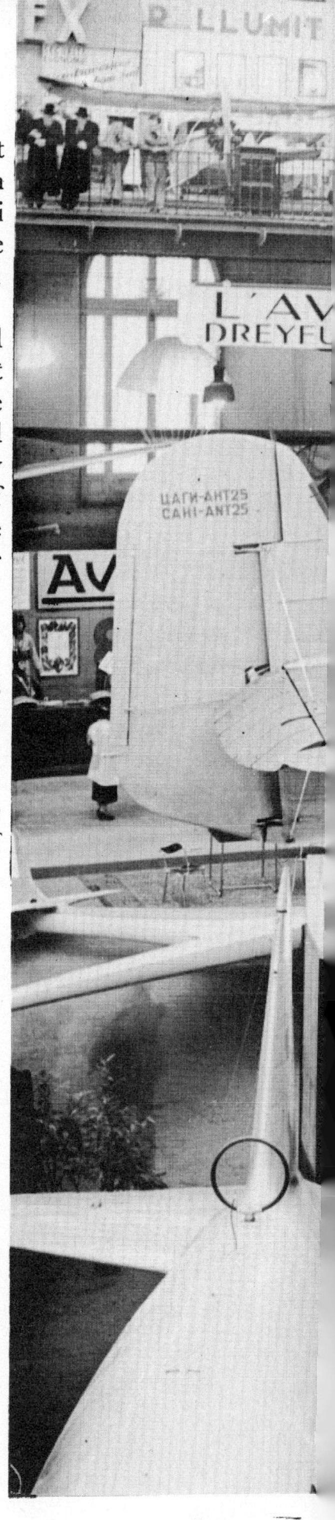

The starkness of this scene contrasts with the larger picture

Centrepiece of this USSR stand in the Grand Salon, Paris, where many historic aircraft had been displayed before it, was the broad-winged ANT-25

TYPE:
Single-engined long-range monoplane.

WINGS:
Low-wing cantilever monoplane. Wing in three sections. Three-spar structure, front and second spars in the inner portions boxed in to form fuel tanks. Structure completed by leading-edge girder and trailing-edge ribs. Entire wing covered with corrugated "Koltchougalumin" and a final covering of doped fabric to give a smooth exterior. Aerodynamically and statically balanced ailerons, each in four sections.

FUSELAGE:
Oval-section structure of built-up bulkheads, open-section stringers and metal skin, all of "Koltchougalumin".

TAIL UNIT:
Braced monoplane type. All-metal structure, with corrugated sheet covering and final covering of doped fabric. Balanced elevators and rudder. Trailing-edge tabs for trimming and aerodynamic balance.

LANDING GEAR:

Retractable type, each unit consisting of a pair of wheels carried by single oleo-pneumatic shock-absorber, strut-braced laterally and aft. Wheels retracted backwards into lower surface of wing, a portion remaining below and being faired aft. Fixed tail-wheel, faired into fuselage.

POWER PLANT:

One 950 hp M.34-R 12-cylinder Vee water-cooled engine driving three-blade metal propeller. Fuel tanks formed by wing spars. Header tank in fuselage. Tanks fitted with quick-release panels.

ACCOMMODATION:

Pilot's compartment over wing leading-edge, with provision for sleeping quarters behind. Navigator's compartment next, and further aft a compartment with emergency auxiliary controls, used also during a change of pilots. Radio installation in navigator's compartment. Streamline roof cupola for astronomical observations. Electric equipment supplying landing gear mechanism, lights, radio, etc. Emergency flotation gear, comprising inflatable rubberised bags, in wings and fore part of fuselage. Collapsible raft, lifejackets, electrically-heated flotation suits, emergency rations, etc.

DIMENSIONS:

Wing span 111 *ft* 6 *in* (33·98 *m*)
Length overall 43 *ft* 11 *in* (13·38 *m*)
Height overall 18 *ft* (5·49 *m*)

WEIGHTS:

Weight empty 9,240 *lb* (4,191 *kg*)
Weight loaded 24,750 *lb* (11,226 *kg*)

PERFORMANCE:

Max speed 149 *mph* (240 *kmh*)
Duration 65 *hr*

VICKERS WELLESLEY

The Wellesley was a significant aircraft for two reasons: it was the first aeroplane in the world built entirely on the geodetic principle; and its efficiency was such that, although a standard RAF bomber, it established a world's long-distance record with a minimum of modification. The system of construction utilised was the creation of Mr. B. N. (later Sir Barnes) Wallis. It was the claim of Vickers-Armstrongs, Ltd. that this put the material used in the most advantageous position for developing the maximum stiffness of structure, and also in the most efficient form for resisting large loads and developing high stress. It was pointed out that aircraft built on this principle combined in a marked degree great stiffness and strength with a structure weight so low as to give range and load-carrying figures that had hitherto been considered unattainable. A further inherent advantage claimed was the absence of bulkheads, frames and ribs, leaving the interior of wings and fuselage entirely unobstructed.

The first Wellesley was a private venture and was initially flown on 19 June 1935. In September the Air Ministry ordered the first batch of a total of 176 constructed. On 5 November 1938 three special Wellesleys of the RAF Long-Range Development Unit left Ismailia, Egypt, to fly to Darwin, Australia. One landed prematurely at Kupang before crossing the Timor Sea, but the other two reached Darwin on 7 November having covered 7,162 miles (11,430 km) in just over 48 hours. These three machines, which had all surpassed the record of the ANT-25, differed from the standard Wellesley bomber in having Pegasus XXII engines in a special installation, with long-chord cowling; revised cockpit arrangements; provision for a third crew-member; and Rotol constant-speed propellers. Take-off weight was increased to 18,400 lb (8,346 kg).

Wellesley bombers served mainly in the Middle East and were employed against the Italian forces in East Africa. The system of construction introduced on this aircraft was applied to the twin-engined Wellington, one of the most notable bombers of the Second World War.

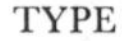

TYPE:
Single-engined bomber.

WINGS:
Low-wing cantilever monoplane. Aspect ratio 8·85:1. Duralumin construction on Vickers-Wallis geodetic principle. One main girder spar and two auxiliary spars fore and aft, with attached panels built up of geodetic members. Panels covered with fabric before assembly. Hinged metal leading-edge. Fabric-covered Frise ailerons over half span. Split flaps from ailerons to fuselage.

FUSELAGE:
Oval-section metal structure, built up of intersecting geodetic members assembled in jigs on four tubular longerons. Fuselage built in series of short sections joined by screwed unions. Fabric covering over longitudinal stringers.

TAIL UNIT:
Cantilever monoplane type. Conventional structure built up of duralumin spars and diagonal ribs, the whole covered with fabric. Trim-tabs in elevators and rudder.

LANDING GEAR:
Retractable type. Two cantilever legs incorporating Vickers oleo-pneumatic shock-absorbers, retracting inwardly into wing. Apertures closed by fairing plates on legs and wheels. Hydraulic retraction. Intermediate-pressure wheels. Vickers pneumatic wheel-brakes. Non-retracting tail-wheel.

POWER PLANT:
One Bristol Pegasus XX nine-cylinder air-cooled radial engine rated at 800/835 hp at 8,500 ft (2,600 m). Bristol combined exhaust and ring cowling. Three-blade de Havilland constant-speed metal propeller. Riveted Alclad fuel tanks (425 Imp gallons =

1,930 litres) in wings. Engine-driven pump feed to gravity tank in fuselage.

ACCOMMODATION:

Enclosed, widely separated, cockpits for pilot and observer, with intercommunicating space. Wheel control for pilot. Automatic pilot.

ARMAMENT:

One fixed Vickers or (later) Browning 0·303 in machine-gun, fired by pilot, in starboard wing outside propeller arc. One Lewis or Vickers Class K gas-operated gun on special Vickers pillar-type mounting in rear cockpit. Gun housed within fairing when stowed. Bombs carried in "bomb nacelles" strut-mounted one beneath each wing and sighted from prone position. Max load 2,000 lb. Provision could be made for carrying one 18-inch torpedo externally beneath the fuselage.

DIMENSIONS:

Wing span 74 *ft* 7 *in* (22·73 *m*)
Overall length 39 *ft* 3 *in* (11·96 *m*)
Height overall 12 *ft* 4 *in* (3·76 *m*)
Wing area 630 *sq ft* (58·53 m^2)

WEIGHTS AND LOADING:

Weight empty 6,369 *lb* (2,889 *kg*)
Weight loaded 11,000 *lb* (5,035 *kg*)
Wing loading 17·6 *lb/sq ft* (86·10 kg/m^2)
Power loading 12·33 *lb/hp* (5·60 *kg/hp*)

PERFORMANCE:

Max speed at 6,560 *ft* (2,000 *m*) 198 *mph* (319 *kmh*)
Max speed at 19,680 *ft* (6,000 *m*) 228 *mph* (367 *kmh*)
Landing speed 57 *mph* (92 *kmh*)
Initial rate of climb 1,200 *ft/min* (366 *m/min*)
Climb to 13,120 *ft* (4,000 *m*) 11·4 *min*
Absolute ceiling 35,250 *ft* (10,750 *m*)
Range with 1,000 *lb* (454 *kg*) *of bombs* 1,110 *miles* (1,790 *km*)
Max range with 1,000 *lb of bombs in overload condition* 2,590 *miles* (4,170 *km*)

Operational Wellesleys, with their characteristic "bomb nacelles", are seen above. Below are Wellingtons in production, showing the geodetic construction brought to fruition in the Wellesley by Sir Barnes Wallis (centre). Crews of the RAF Long-Range Development Unit are also seen

MIGNET POU du CIEL

Post-war Mignet HM.390

Croses Criquet, 1965-vintage Pou

There are remarkable analogies between the aircraft now under review and the Demoiselle of Santos-Dumont. In both instances the inventor was working in France; the type concerned was an ultra-light; and it was offered freely for private construction. Moreover, both machines utilised an unorthodox control system, and in both the pilot was seated pendulum-fashion beneath the wing. In the present instance the 1935 edition of *Jane's All the World's Aircraft* is relevant; thus: "M. Henri Mignet has for some years been concerned in the design and construction of light aeroplanes. He started with gliders and has progressed through a series of light aeroplanes to his ninth production, a single-seat monoplane of novel design known as the 'Pou du Ciel' ("Sky Louse"). In this machine M. Mignet has incorporated the simplest possible type of control. To obtain longitudinal stability he uses two surfaces, a main wing mounted on a steel-tube pylon forward, and a fixed wing, or large tailplane, mounted very close to and slightly below the main wing. The front or main wing is hinged to the pylon at the front spar and its angle of incidence is controlled by wires from the trailing-edge to the control column, to give fore-and-aft control. Ailerons have been abolished. Directional control is by rudder, which is operated by sideways movement of the control column. Laterally the machine looks after itself. The span of the main wing is small and it has a marked dihedral. A reflexed wing section with small C.P. movement is used and the C.G. is some way below the wings, and so has the steadying effect of a pendulum.

"M. Mignet has published a book describing how to build the 'Pou du Ciel', and he grants permission for anybody to build according to his instructions, so long as such machines are not built for financial gain. The only firm which has been granted the licence to build and sell the 'Pou du Ciel' is the Etablissements F. Louis . . . the 'Pou du Ciel' has attracted world-wide attention, and large numbers are being built by amateurs all over Europe and in many places abroad."

The golden prospect implicit in these lines was never to be fully realised, for a series of fatal accidents led to an investigation of the design which disclosed that at angles of incidence of $-15°$, and with the control column hard back, there was insufficient pitching moment to raise the nose. By that time 83 "Permits to Fly" (first introduced for the "Pou") had been issued in Britain alone. Nevertheless, another excerpt from *Jane's*, and this time the 1968/69 edition, will show that the dream of Santos-Dumont and Henri Mignet has not yet been extinguished; thus: "M. Lederlin, an architect, has designed and built a two-seat light aeroplane based on the familiar 'Pou du Ciel' formula. . . . M. Lederlin intends to make plans available to other constructors".

The first aircraft of the type was built in 1933, and the following description of the "standard" machine is based on the 1935 *Jane's*.

TYPE:

Single-seat light monoplane.

WINGS:

High-wing braced monoplane. Main wing hinged to steel-tube pylon over nose of fuselage and cable-braced laterally to fuselage. Wing tilted fore-and-aft by cables from trailing-edge to control column, to give fore-and-aft control. Box-spars of spruce and plywood, plywood ribs and fabric covering. No ailerons.

FUSELAGE:

Rectangular spruce framework covered with plywood.

TAIL UNIT:

Large fixed tailplane with leading-edge below trailing-edge of main wing. Same structure as main wing. Cable-bracing to bottom of fuselage. Rudder the only movable surface, hinged to vertical tail-post of fuselage. Wooden framework with fabric covering.

LANDING GEAR:

Two main wheels on axle-tube passing through slots in sides of fuselage and sprung by rubber shock-absorber cord to bottom longerons. Two small wheels on rudder-post, steered by rudder controls.

POWER UNIT:

One 17 hp Aubier & Dunne 540 cc two-cylinder in-line inverted two-stroke geared air-cooled engine on a triangulated steel-tube mounting over sloping nose of fuselage. Fuel tank (4·6 Imp gallons = 21 litres) in wing, with gravity feed to engine. Other engines of similar output fitted.

ACCOMMODATION:

Single open cockpit below wing. Control column, fore-and-aft movement tilting wing and lateral movement operating rudder.

DIMENSIONS:

Wing span 19 *ft* 7 *in* (6·00 *m*)
Tailplane span 13 *ft* 1½ *in* (4·00 *m*)

WEIGHTS:

Weight empty 220 *lb* (100 *kg*)

PERFORMANCE:

Max speed 62 *mph* (100 *kmh*)
Cruising speed 50 *mph* (80 *kmh*)
Climb to 3,280 *ft* (1,000 *m*) 19 *min*
Take-off run 328 *ft* (100 *m*)

American interest is here evinced in a pre-war British-built version of the singular French creation "Pou du Ciel"

Ju 87s usually operated in formations

JUNKERS Ju87

The Junkers J1 of the First World War has already been instanced both as an example of early all-metal construction and as a specialised type of military aircraft – a heavily armoured two-seater for supporting friendly ground forces by attacking those of the enemy. In the Second World War another highly specialised Junkers two-seater served with far greater distinction and notoriety. This was the Ju87 single-engined dive-bomber, which bore the generic appellation *Stuka* (*Sturzkampfflugzeug*), signifying a class of aircraft fostered by the German Air Ministry following the successful development in the USA of bombers capable of delivering their load in a very steep diving attack. This technique had been practiced by British fighter pilots in the 1914–18 war.

The first Ju87 was powered with a British Rolls-Royce Kestrel engine (as were a number of other German prototypes of the period) and was initially tested in the spring of 1935. This machine had twin fins and rudders, but the tail collapsed on diving trials and the second machine (Junkers Jumo 210 engine) had a single fin and rudder. Development proceeded, largely at the instigation of Ernst Udet, and the German *Stukagruppen*, equipped with aircraft of the B series, were engaged in many of the historic actions of the early months of war. With its relatively low performance and light defensive armament the Ju87 proved highly vulnerable to fighter attack, as did its British near-counterpart the Fairey Battle, but with numerous modifications the type continued in service throughout the war.

The Ju 87 had an unmistakable silhouette

Principle variants were:

Ju87A. Junkers Jumo 210 engine. Heavy bomb carried under fuselage on displacing gear. One fixed gun, one free gun.

Ju87B. Jumo 211 engine. Most components, except wings and tail surfaces, redesigned. Cantilever landing gear. Provision for wing bombs. Two fixed guns. Special variants with armour for close-support, tropical equipment, ski landing gear, etc.

Ju87C. Naval carrier-borne version, intended for service in the *Graf Zeppelin*. Jettisonable undercarriage for emergency alightings, folding wings. One example fitted experimentally with 88 mm recoilless gun.

Ju87R. Non-sequential suffix letter signified *Reichweite* (range), this variant having increased fuel tankage for anti-shipping operations. Otherwise generally as Ju87B.

Ju87D. Jumo 211J engine. Oil-cooler moved from top cowling to below engine, coolant radiator transferred to wing centre-section. Redesigned cockpit enclosure, with provision for twin rear guns. Revised landing gear and increased armour. Increased bomb load and provision for under-wing weapon containers (machine-guns, cannon or anti-personnel bombs). D-7 variant specially equipped for night attack.

Ju87G. Converted from Ju87D to carry two 37 mm (1·45 in) anti-aircraft guns under wing for anti-tank operations.

The following description relates to the Ju87B, the variant which first made history.

TYPE:

Two-seat dive-bomber.

WINGS:

Low-wing cantilever monoplane. Centre-section built integral with fuselage and set at coarse anhedral angle. Outer wing panels, tapering in chord and thickness, set at coarse dihedral angle. Two-spar all-metal structure with closely-spaced ribs and stressed-skin covering. Entire trailing-edge of wings and centre-section hinged on Junkers "double-wing" principle, outer portions acting as ailerons and inner portions as landing flaps. Dive-brakes beneath front spars outboard of landing gear. Brakes hinged clear of under-surface of wings, in normal flight edge-on to airstream, but for diving attacks turned through 90° to present flat-plate area.

FUSELAGE:

Oval-section structure of light-metal construction, made in two halves, joined on horizontal centre-line. Smooth metal skin riveted to Z-section frames and open-section stringers. Stringers continuous through frames. Small angle brackets riveted to frames and stringers where stringers passed through. Two halves joined by two internal angles, riveted together.

TAIL UNIT:

Braced monoplane type. Junkers "double-wing" tailplane and elevator. Tailplane braced to fuselage by two struts on each side. All-metal structure with smooth sheet covering. Trim-tabs in movable surfaces.

LANDING GEAR:

Fixed divided type, each unit incorporating oleo-pneumatic suspension, with legs attached to extremities of centre-section. Legs and wheels faired. Steerable tail-wheel.

POWER PLANT:

One Junkers Jumo 211Da 12-cylinder liquid-cooled inverted-Vee engine giving 1,200 hp for take-off. Three-blade VDM controllable-pitch propeller. Radiator in duct beneath engine, with controllable cooling flaps.

ARMAMENT:

Two fixed MG 17 machine-guns in wings, firing outside propeller arc. One free MG 15 machine-gun on manually operated mounting in rear cockpit. Two standard bomb loads: either one 500 kg (1,100 lb) bomb under fuselage or one 250 kg bomb under fuselage and four 50 kg (110 lb) bombs under wings. Fuselage bomb on displacement arms. Bombs aimed and released by pilot.

DIMENSIONS:

Wing span 45 *ft* 3 *in* (13·79 *m*)
Length overall 36 *ft* 5 *in* (11·10 *m*)
Height overall 13 *ft* 2 *in* (4·01 *m*)

WEIGHTS:

Weight empty (equipped) 6,085 *lb* (2,760 *kg*)
Weight loaded 9,560 *lb* (4,336 *lb*)

PERFORMANCE:

Max speed at S/L 211 *mph* (339 *kmh*)
Max speed at 16,000 *ft* (4,880 *m*) 210 *mph* (338 *kmh*)
Cruising speed 175 *mph* (282 *kmh*)
Max range with 500 *kg* (1,100 *lb*) *bomb* 370 *miles*

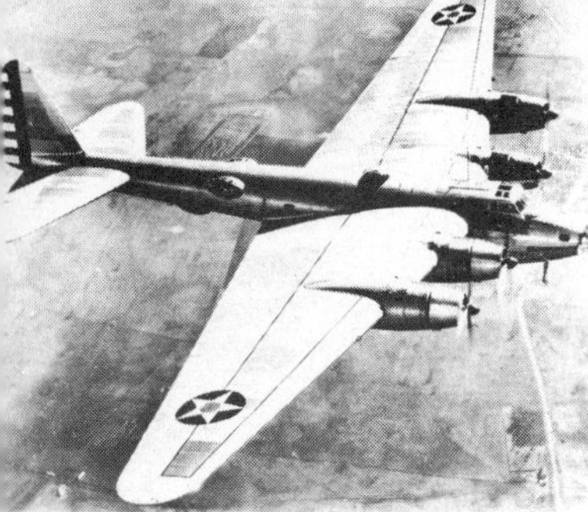

The XB-15, flown after the B-17

BOEING B-17

Excellence of performance at height and adaptability to operational demands of increasing stringency were salient factors in the success of the B-17 four-engined bomber in the Second World War. The massive employment of the type in operations over Europe, Africa, the Pacific and Japan has sometimes obscured the fact that the first prototype was flown as early as 28 July 1935. This aircraft (Model 299) embodied features of the Model 247 transport and the much larger Boeing XB-15 experimental bomber, and although it was by no means the first four-engined machine of its class it marked a striking new departure from the traditional twin-engined bombers of the inter-war years. This came about because of a broad interpretation of the term "multi-engined" used in the specification to which it was built. The "Flying Fortress", as it was called (although armament was later to prove deficient), attracted great public attention on the occasion of its delivery flight to Wright Field, when it flew 2,000 miles non-stop at a speed of 252 mph. This historic aeroplane was later destroyed in a crash. The first of thirteen development aircraft (Y1B-17) was delivered in March 1937, but a month of greater significance was January 1939, when an experimental Y1B-17A with turbo-supercharged engines was handed over. This form of supercharging was largely developed and exploited in the USA and to this development the operational success of the B-17 in terms of altitude performance and range can be largely attributed. The same form of supercharging was used on the B-17's hardly less famous companion type, the Consolidated B-24 Liberator.

The first B-17 (above) was a private venture. Below, B-17G

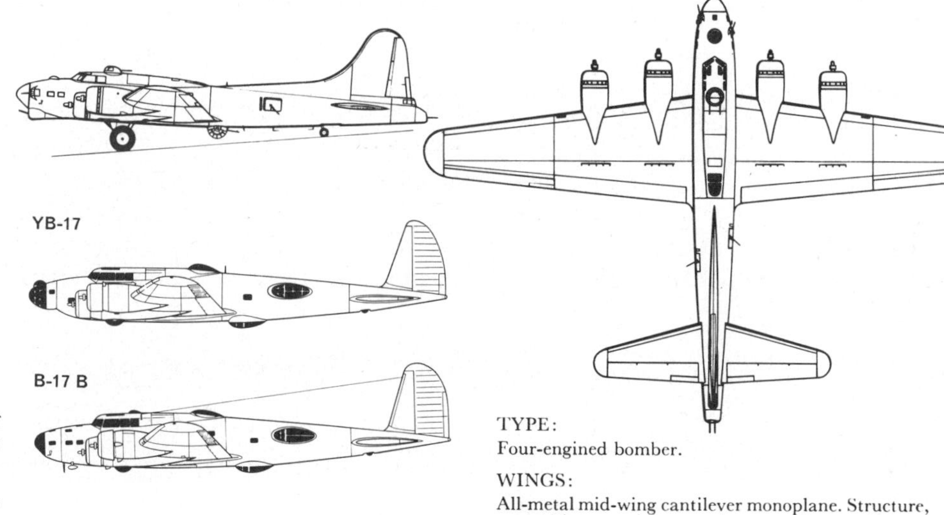

Production of B-17s totalled 12,726 machines of numerous sub-types, and of these 6,981 were built by Boeing. Other builders were Douglas and Vega. Principle variants were:

B-17B. First production model, with larger rudder, larger flaps, new nose and extensive internal changes.

B-17C. Revised gun installations, and number of guns increased from five to seven. Self-sealing fuel tanks and armour. First in combat with RAF (Service name Fortress) 24 July 1941.

B-17D. Numerous internal changes, and cowling flaps fitted.

B-17E. Thirty per cent redesign from original. Enlarged tail surfaces. Two-gun turret added aft and two-gun turret in bottom of fuselage. Two guns in manual installation behind tail. Bottom turret at first utilised periscopic sighting from sighting blister aft of turret, but Sperry ball turret substituted.

B-17F. Moulded Plexiglass nose assembly and many other changes. Two guns in forward cheeks, sometimes additional to gun firing through nose window. One gun in radio compartment.

B-17G. Forward "chin" turret. Staggered waist guns, to minimise interference between gunners, and staggered forward guns. Tail-gun position revised during production.

Experimental versions and adaptations of the B-17 were very numerous. The following description is representative of the type as in service at the end of the war.

Firepower was impressively augmented. Seen on this B-17G are "chin" and "cheek" installations in the nose and dorsal, ventral and tail turrets

TYPE:
Four-engined bomber.

WINGS:
All-metal mid-wing cantilever monoplane. Structure, comprising two inner sections carrying engine nacelles, two outer sections and two detachable tips, chiefly of aluminium-alloy, with two spars, ribs and stressed-skin covering. Electrically-operated split trailing-edge flaps on inner wing sections, ailerons on outer sections. Flaps and ailerons fabric-covered. Trim-tabs in ailerons. De-icers on leading-edges.

FUSELAGE:
All-metal semi-monocoque structure, consisting of bulkheads and circumferential stiffeners, the whole covered with a smooth metal stressed skin. De-icers on leading-edges of tailplane and fin.

TAIL UNIT:

Cantilever monoplane type. Aluminium-alloy framework, with fixed surfaces covered with smooth metal sheet and movable surfaces with fabric. Control and trim-tabs in elevator and rudder.

LANDING GEAR:

Retractable type. Air-oil shock-absorber units. Hydraulic wheel-brakes. Electrical retraction. Retractable tail-wheel.

POWER PLANT:

Four 1,200 hp Wright R-1820-97 nine-cylinder radial air-cooled engines with General Electric Type B-22 exhaust-driven turbo-superchargers installed in undersides of engine nacelles. Hamilton-Standard three-blade constant-speed full-feathering propellers 11 ft 7 in (3·54 m) diameter. Self-sealing fuel tanks in wings. Normal fuel capacity carried in six tanks in inner wing sections 1,700 US gallons (6,437 litres). Nine self-sealing auxiliary feeder tanks in outer wings. Two self-sealing droppable ferry tanks could be carried in bomb-bay. Maximum capacity of all wing tanks 2,780 US gallons (10,524 litres). Self-sealing hopper oil tank in each nacelle. Oil capacity 148 US gallons (560 litres).

ACCOMMODATION:

Normal crew six to ten. Bomb-aimer's compartment in nose. Flight compartment with dual controls forward of wing leading-edge. Upper electrically-operated two-gun turret aft of flight compartment. Radio-operator amidships. One two-gun electrically-operated turret beneath fuselage and two guns in extreme tail. Equipment included automatic pilot, two-way radio, radio homing equipment, oxygen equipment with supply-points for each crew-member and two collapsible dinghies.

ARMAMENT:

Eight or more 0·5 in (12·7 mm) Browning belt-fed machine-guns, two, remotely controlled, in "chin" turret beneath plastic bomb-aiming position in nose; two in "cheek" mountings, one on each side of nose; one through nose window; two in electrically operated turret on top of fuselage aft of cockpit; one through skylight in top of fuselage above radio-operator's compartment; two in Sperry electrically-operated "ball" turret below fuselage; two firing through side ports, one on each side, midway between wings and tail; and two in extreme tail. Internal bomb-stowage in fuselage between main spar frames. Normal capacity 6,000 lb (2,722 kg). Largest bomb carried internally 2,000 lb (907 kg).

DIMENSIONS:

Wing span 103 *ft* 9 *in* (31·62 *m*)
Length overall 74 *ft* 9 *in* (22·78 *m*)
Height overall 19 *ft* 1 *in* (5·82 *m*)
Wing area 1,420 *sq ft* (132·5 m^2)

WEIGHTS (B-17E):

Weight empty 33,279 *lb* (15,095 *kg*)
Normal loaded weight 40,260 *lb* (18,262 *lb*)
Max overload weight 53,000 *lb* (24,040 *kg*)

PERFORMANCE (B-17E):

Max speed 317 *mph* (510 *kmh*) *at* 25,000 *ft* (7,620 *m*)
Cruising speed 210 *mph* (338 *kmh*)
Service ceiling 36,600 *ft* (11,125 *m*)
Time of climb to 10,000 *ft* (3,050 *m*) 7·1 *min*
Range with 4,000 *lb* (1,8150 *kg*) *of bombs* 2,000 *miles*

B-17s of the United States Army Air Force were first in action over the Andaman Islands and others soon became operational over Europe, Africa and Japan

SUPERMARINE SPITFIRE

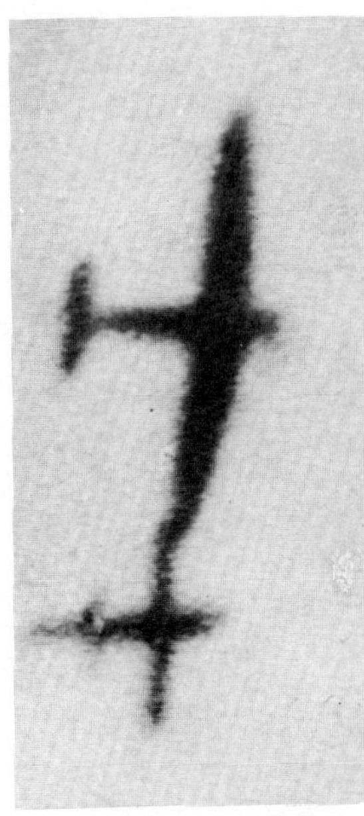

Spitfire upsetting flying bomb by direct action

The origins of the Spitfire, dating back to 1925, have been noted under the heading Supermarine S.4. The evolutionary process from this racing seaplane can now be traced through later types of metal construction. First of these was the S.5 which, in September 1927 won the Schneider Trophy for Britain at a speed of 281·65 mph (452·6 kmh). Next came the S.6 which was victorious in the 1929 event at 328·63 mph (528 kmh), and last—for it won the Trophy outright at 340·08 mph (553·6 kmh)—was the S.6B. This final contest took place in 1931 and in the same year an S.6B became the first aircraft in the world to exceed 400 mph. Yet in a single-seat Supermarine fighter built to an official specification issued in 1930 little of the grace and aerodynamic refinement of the Schneider racers was apparent, although R. J. Mitchell had been responsible for the whole series of designs. Tentatively named Spitfire, this new four-gun fighter was unimpressive, and the heritage from the seaplane racers was not again manifest until the greatly differing prototype of the historic Spitfire eight-gun fighter first took the air on 5 March 1936. This aeroplane is generally acknowledged to have been one of the most beautiful ever constructed; yet this beauty was reconciled with an ample wing area (in the interests of manoeuvrability and altitude performance), structural integrity and, as remarked, an eight-gun armament as never previously mounted in a single-seater. Three months after the maiden flight the Air Ministry ordered 310 Mk I Spitfires and by October 1939 4,000 were on order. Production continued until October 1947 when the last of 20,351 was completed. In addition to these 2,408 "navalised" machines (Seafire) had left the production lines.

Together with the Hawker Hurricane, which preceded it by several months (first flight 6 November 1935) the Spitfire endures in memory primarily for its part in the Battle of Britain, but the following summary of variants is adequate testimony to the diverse employment and adaptability of the type, which may be regarded as the most famous fighting aeroplane of all time.

Spitfire I

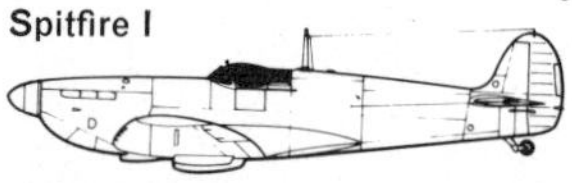

Spitfire IX

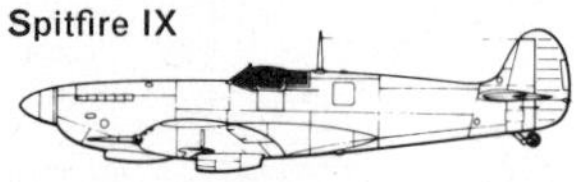

Spitfire LF XIVe

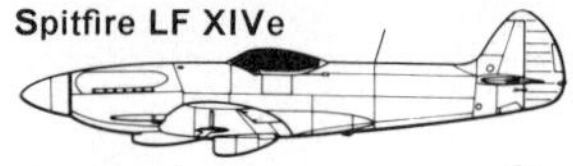

Spitfire 22

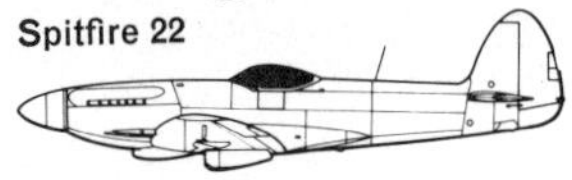

Spitfire Mk I. Rolls-Royce Merlin II or III engine driving two-blade fixed-pitch wooden propeller, or, later, de Havilland three-blade metal two-position controllable-pitch propeller. Armament (Mk IA) eight 0·303 in Browning machine-guns, or (Mk IB) four of these guns and two 20 mm British Hispano cannon.

Spitfire Mk II. Rolls-Royce Merlin XII engine, driving Rotol three-blade constant-speed propeller. Mks IIA and IIB otherwise similar to Mks IA and IB respectively.

Spitfire PR. Mk IV. Merlin 46 engine. Mk IA airframe with extra fuel in leading-edges, extra oxygen and no armament. Two vertical cameras, one oblique.

Spitfire Mk V. Merlin 45, 46, 50, 50A, 55 or 56 engine. Rotol or D.H. three-blade constant-speed propeller. In other respects Mks VA and VB similar to Mks IA and IB respectively. Mk VC fitted with "universal" wings, with normal armament of two 20 mm and four 0·303 in guns. Tropical equipment and drop-tanks installed as required. "Clipped" wings and special engines for low-altitude fighting. Provision for 250 lb (110 kg) or 500 lb (220 kg) bomb on drop-tank fittings.

Spitfire Mk VI. Merlin 47 or 49 engine, driving Rotol four-blade constant-speed propeller. Similar to Mk VB but with pressure cabin, strengthened spar and extended wing-tips. Span 40 ft 2 in (12·24 m).

Spitfire Mk VII. Merlin 61, 64 or 71 engine, with two-speed two-stage supercharger. Rotol four-blade constant-speed propeller. Nose lengthened, pressure cabin, larger rudder, retractable tail-wheel. Long-span wings. Twin radiator ducts under wings, port duct housing coolant radiator and oil-cooler and starboard duct coolant radiator and super-charger intercooler.

Spitfire PR. Mk VII. Rolls-Royce Merlin 61 engine. Long-span wings. Additional fuel in rear fuselage. Three cameras.

Spitfire Mk VIII. Designed from outset for engine with two-stage supercharger. Merlin 61, 63 63A, 66 or 70 engine. Three standard versions fighter Merlin 61, 63 or 63A and standard wings low-altitude fighter with Merlin 66 and extended wings; high-altitude fighter with Merlin 70 and extended wings. New pointed rudder and retractable tail-wheel.

Spitfire Mk IX. Adaptation of Mk VC, but with power plant installation as Mk VII. Standard low-altitude and high-altitude fighter versions Ultimately adapted to take "E" wings, with two 20 mm and two 0·5 in guns.

Fixed-pitch wooden propellers identify these Spitfires as early Mk Is. Ports for four of the eight wing-mounted Browning machine-guns are visible on the second machine in line. Note also ejector exhausts for Rolls-Royce Merlin engine

The Spitfire F Mk 22 was one of the last variants. Engine, Rolls-Royce Griffon

Spitfire PR. Mk X. Merlin 64, 71 or 77 engine driving Rotol four-blade propeller. Pressure cabin. Fuel in leading-edge. No armament. "Universal" camera installation.

Spitfire PR. Mk XI. Merlin 61, 63, 63A or 70 engine. Power plant installation as Mk VII, wings as Mk X.

Spitfire Mk XII. First Service variant with Rolls-Royce Griffon engine (Griffon III or IV). Similar to Mk VC, but with clipped wings , strengthened fuselage, pointed rudder.

Spitfire PR. Mk XIII. Similar to Mk VB, but Merlin 32 engine for low-level operation. Four machine-guns, three cameras.

Spitfire Mk XIV. Griffon 65 engine, with two-speed two-stage supercharger. Rotol five-blade constant-speed propeller. New fin and rudder of larger area. Usual three fighter versions, standard fighter with two 20 mm and two 0·5 in guns. Later aircraft had rear-view hood. Oblique camera in fighter-reconnaissance version. Bomb under fuselage, occasionally under wings also (2 × 250 lb = 2 × 110 kg).

Spitfire Mk XVI. Packard-built Merlin 266 engine. Low-altitude fighter-bomber with "clipped" wings. Some aircraft with pointed rudder, rear-view hood and/or additional fuel in rear fuselage. Wings normal or "clipped".

Spitfire PR. Mk XIX. Griffon 65 or 66 engine driving Rotol five-blade propeller. Photographic-reconnaissance version of Mk XIV. Extra fuel in wings. Max speed 460 mph (740 kmh). Ceiling over 43,000 ft (13,100 m). Range 1,500 miles (2,415 km).

Spitfire F. Mk 21. Major redesign. Griffon 61, 64 or 85 engine. Wings of new shape. Revised landing gear. Four 20 mm guns.

Spitfire F. Mk 22. As F. Mk 21, but with rear-view hood.

Spitfire F. Mk 24. Final production version. Zero-length launchers for rocket projectiles. Tail similar to Spiteful (later Supermarine type with laminar-flow wings).

The following description is representative of the Spitfire generally, and comparative data are quoted for the first and late-production versions.

TYPE:

Single-seat fighter.

WINGS:

Low-wing cantilever monoplane. Standard wings elliptical in plan but wings of shorter span with squared tips or of longer span with pointed tips could be fitted for low-altitude or high-altitude work respectively. Structure chiefly of light alloy. Single spar with tubular flanges and plate web. Forward of spar wing covered with heavy-gauge light-alloy sheet, forming with the spar, a very stiff and strong torsion box. Aft of spar covering of thinner gauge, supported by light-alloy girder webs. Standard wings had detachable tips. Split flaps between ailerons and fuselage.

FUSELAGE:

All-metal semi-monocoque structure, consisting of transverse frames, four main longerons, intercostal longitudinals and flush-riveted Alclad skin. Foremost frame formed a fireproof bulkhead, with centre portion of main wing spar built in. Aft portion of fuselage, with tail unit, detachable.

TAIL UNIT:

Cantilever monoplane type. Fin integral with rear fuselage. All-metal tailplane with smooth skin covering. Elevators and rudder with light-alloy frames and fabric covering. Trim-tabs in rudder and elevator.

LANDING GEAR:

Retractable type, consisting of two Vickers cantilever oleo-pneumatic shock-absorber legs raised outwardly into underside of wings. Hydraulic retraction with emergency lowering device. Fully castoring tail-wheel, retractable in some marks.

POWER PLANT:

One Rolls-Royce Merlin or Griffon twelve-cylinder Vee liquid-cooled engine on steel-tube mounting. Three-, four-, or five-blade propeller. Two fuel tanks (85 Imp gallons = 386 litres) in fuselage, with direct feed to engine pumps. Auxiliary "slipper" tank frequently carried beneath fuselage. (See introduction for additional information on power plant, propeller and fuel supply.)

ACCOMMODATION:

Enclosed cockpit over trailing-edge. Sliding canopy and hinged panel in port side for entry or exit. Adjustable seat and rudder pedals. Tropical versions had improved ventilation and stowage for desert equipment, water and emergency rations behind cockpit. Pressure cabin in some marks.

ARMAMENT:

See introductory notes for gun and bomb combinations. All guns free-firing from wings. Some early machines had ring-and-bead sights, but reflector sight standard. Gyro sight fitted in later machines.

DIMENSIONS (Spitfire Mk I):

Wing span 36 *ft* 10 *in* (11·23 *m*)
Length overall 29 *ft* 11 *in* (9·12 *m*)

DIMENSIONS (Spitfire F. Mk 22):

Wing span 36 *ft* 11 *in* (11·25 *m*)
Length overall 32 *ft* 11 *in* (10·03 *m*)

WEIGHTS (Spitfire Mk I):

Weight loaded 5,332 *lb*–5,784 *lb* (2,418 *kg*–2,622 *kg*)

WEIGHTS (Spitfire F. Mk 22):

Weight loaded 9,900 *lb* (4,490 *kg*)

PERFORMANCE (Spitfire Mk I):

Max speed 355 *mph* (571 *kmh*) *at* 19,000 *ft* (5,790 *m*)
Time of climb to 15,000 *ft* (4,570 *m*) 6·2 *min*
Ceiling 34,000 *ft* (10,360 *m*)

PERFORMANCE (Spitfire F. Mk 22):

Max speed 454 *mph* (731 *kmh*) *at* 26,000 *ft* (7,925 *m*)
Time of climb to 20,000 *ft* (6,100 *m*) 8 *min*
Ceiling 43,500 *ft* (13,230 *m*)

Hawker Hurricane, Spitfire's partner

"Caledonia" was a special long-range version for Atlantic trials

"Canopus" was the first of a magnificent family of flying-boats

SHORT EMPIRE FLYING-BOAT

In marine-aircraft development for commercial purposes the Short Empire flying-boat (otherwise known as the C-Class Boat, Empire Boat or Imperial Flying-Boat) was the next notable advance on the Sikorsky S-42. The first machine of the class, named *Canopus*, made its initial flight from the River Medway on 3 July 1936. Performance was comparable with that of contemporary landplanes and passenger comfort of an exceptional order. Although misfortunes were encountered (eight aircraft of the class were lost during the first two years of operations) the technical merit of the "Empire Boat" was beyond all doubt, and was further reflected in its military counterpart the Sunderland, perhaps the most successful craft of its kind ever built.

The original type of Empire flying boat, bearing the Short type number S.23, was ordered "off the drawing board" by Imperial Airways, a company which had received eminently satisfactory service from the Calcutta and Kent class biplane flying-boats of the same manufacture. Twenty-eight machines were involved, the cost of the entire fleet being £1,750,000. The first scheduled fiight, from Alexandria to Brindsi, was made on 30 October 1936. Another significant date was 5 March 1937 when the new Imperial Airways flying-boat base at Hythe, near Southampton, was formally opened. From that date onwards the Empire landplane services from the historic airport at Croydon ceased and the "Empire Boats" were in their full ascendancy. By 1938 seven services a week were being operated to Egypt, four to India, three to East Africa and two each to South Africa, Malaya and Australia.

For experimental Atlantic flights two of the boats were modified for operation at higher all-up weight (45,000 lb = 20,412 kg) and were fitted with extra tanks in the hull. The first of a number of flights was made by *Caledonia* on the night of 5/6 July 1937. Additional boats of improved type were built for Imperial Airways and Qantas. Development potential was realised in the S.30 variant with Bristol Perseus XIIC sleeve-valve engines, which, operating at a weight of 53,000 lb (24,040 kg) offered the same accommodation and more than double the range.

The forward lounge seated seven and was smaller than cabins aft

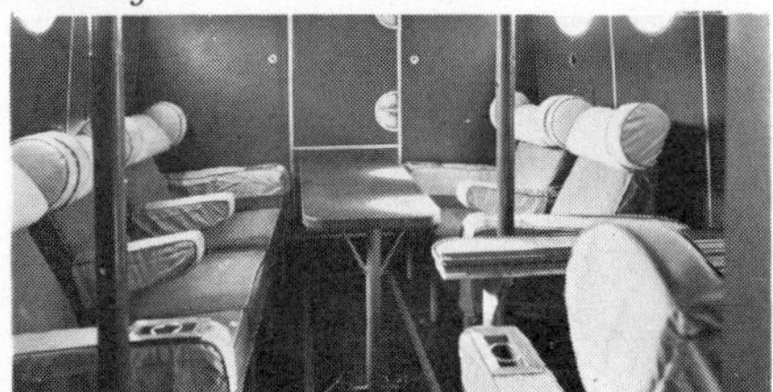

During 1938–39 special Empire boats operated a mail service across the Atlantic, using the British-developed Flight Refuelling technique. Converted Harrow bombers were employed as tankers. Boats of the same class rendered valuable service in the war of 1939 as did a scaled-up development known as the G class.

After the Empire flying-boat had been introduced into service the mail load was increased, an extra 1,000 lb being stowed in the forward passenger cabin. Seventeen passengers only were then carried. As originally laid out, and as now described, the type carried by day a crew of four or five, twenty-two passengers, baggage and 1½ tons of mail.

TYPE:
Four-engined commercial flying-boat.

WINGS:
High-wing cantilever monoplane. Structure composed of central girder comprising two spars of Hiduminium extruded sections braced by tubular struts and interconnected by light former ribs. Separate nose and rear sections of light alloy. Whole of wings, with exception of ailerons, covered with smooth metal sheet with joggled joints and flush

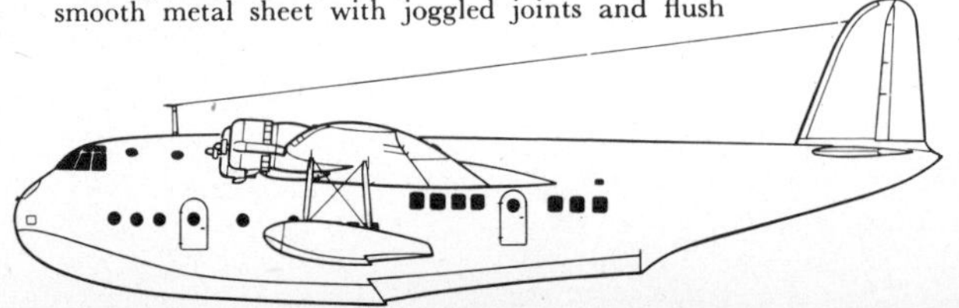

riveting. Flaps of Gouge type, giving increased wing area as well as flap effect when extended.

HULL:

Two-step type, with closely spaced rings and continuous longitudinal stringers, the whole covered with smooth metal panels. Countersunk riveting and joggled lap joints used throughout. Lateral stabilising floats mounted well inboard under wing on two struts, with additional wire-bracing to shock-absorbing link.

TAIL UNIT:

Cantilever monoplane type. Light alloy framework, sheet-metal leading-edges, fabric covering. Balanced rudder and elevator, incorporating trimming tabs.

POWER PLANTS:

Four Bristol Pegasus XC nine-cylinder radial air-cooled engines giving maximum of 790 hp at 5,500 ft (1,680 m). NACA cowlings with controllable trailing-edge flaps. De Havilland two-pitch three-blade metal propellers. Standard fuel capacity 652 Imp gallons (2,964 litres) in two near-cylindrical tanks within wing-spar truss between nacelles. Sections of wing leading-edge arranged to hinge down for use as maintenance platforms.

ACCOMMODATION:

Upper deck forward of wing spar with flight compartment for captain and first officer, with side-by-side dual controls, and radio operator. Also at this station was an auxiliary power unit driving a generator for electrical services when the main engines were stopped. Flight engineer carried only on special long-range flights. Also on this deck was stowage for mail-bags (access through hatch on starboard side), a desk for a purser and a cupboard for "ship's papers". This section of the hull reached by ladder from steward's pantry below. Access through wing spar to a hold for stowage of bedding. Below flight compartment, in extreme bow, was a mooring compartment with hatch, retractable bollard, and retractable landing light. This station accessible by ladder from flight compartment. Aft of bow station, below flight compartment, was a smoking lounge, seating five passengers facing inwards and two facing forward. All seats with tables for meals. Aft of this cabin, to port, was the forward passenger-access door, with lobby, and with two toilets adjoining. To starboard was the steward's pantry, or galley, with corridor leading to midships cabin. This midships cabin was between the main-spar bulkheads, and had seats for three passengers by day, the seats being convertible to bunks by night. Additional bunk arranged to fold into ceiling. Promenade cabin accessible through aft bulkhead, this cabin having eight seats, with tables, and a spacious promenade to port, with elbow rail. One step up from this cabin was the rear passenger-access door, and another step up, following the sweep of the hull, the after cabin, seating six. Freight hold behind, with hatch on starboard side. All passenger seats of special type developed by Imperial Airways and embodying a pneumatic cushion. Main cabins lit by large rectangular windows. Fitted carpets and leathercloth trim.

DIMENSIONS:

Wing span 114 *ft* (34·77 *m*)
Length overall 88 *ft* (26·84 *m*)
Wing area 1,500 *sq ft* (139·35 *m*²)

WEIGHTS:

Weight empty 23,500 *lb* (10,670 *kg*)
Weight loaded 40,500 *lb* (18,380 *kg*)

PERFORMANCE:

Max speed 200 *mph* (322 *kmh*) *at* 5,500 *ft* (1,680 *m*)
Max cruising speed 160 *mph* (256 *kmh*)
Minimum speed 69 *mph* (110 *kmh*)
Initial rate of climb 1,275 *ft/min* (389 *m/min*)
Absolute ceiling 20,000 *ft* (6,100 *m*)
Take-off time (full load) 20 sec
Range 760 *miles* (1,245 *km*)

Like many fine transport aircraft before it, the Stratoliner was closely related to a bomber, in this instance the B-17

BOEING STRATOLINER

The Boeing Model 307 Stratoliner, which made its initial flight on 31 December 1938, was the first airliner with a pressurised cabin to enter service. The purpose of such a cabin was to afford the passengers comfortable breathing conditions at the operating heights becoming possible at the period by virtue of engine supercharging and other techniques. The first full-scale cabin of the type was built into the Lockheed XC-35, a development of the twin-engined Lockheed Electra powered with supercharged Pratt & Whitney Wasp engines and equipped to maintain at all altitudes an internal pressure equivalent to that pertaining at 12,000 ft (3,660 m).

The Stratocruiser was derived from the Boeing B-17C bomber, but had an entirely new fuselage, and, after development, a new tail also. Eight Stratoliners were delivered to commercial operators, three Model 307s to Pan American Airways and five Model 307-Bs to Transcontinental and Western Air, Inc. Differences between these two variants were minor. One special machine, with Wright R-2600 engines, was built for Howard Hughes. In January, 1942 the five 307-Bs were converted for military use and given to the US Army designation C-75. In February of the same year they initiated the first transocean services on behalf of Air Transport Command, firstly to Cairo across the South Atlantic and Africa and later across the North Atlantic to Great Britain. These services were operated by TWA under contract to ATC. In the summer of 1944 the five C-75s were returned to Boeing for reconversion and return to TWA. In 2½ years as military transports they had flown nearly 45,000 hours and covered 7½ million miles without trouble or casualties. In the process of reconversion the 307-Bs were fitted with B-17G wings, power units, landing gear and tailplane. The cabin was completely redesigned, only the forward of the four former separate compartments, which could be used for freight or cargo when necessary, being retained. Seating capacity was increased from 33 to 38 and the cabin supercharging system was removed. These aircraft were then designated SA-307-B1. At least four were flying as recently as 1964.

TYPE:

Four-engined airliner.

WINGS:

Low-wing cantilever monoplane. Wing in six sections: two inner sections, two outer sections and two tips. Structure mainly of aluminium alloy, built up of two spars, ribs and stressed-skin covering. Split trailing-edge flaps. Trim-tabs in ailerons. Flaps and ailerons fabric-covered.

FUSELAGE:

Semi-monocoque structure of circular cross-section, consisting of aluminium-alloy rings and partition bulkheads and longitudinal stiffeners, the whole covered with smooth Alclad skin. In original design fuselage was sealed for high-altitude operation with moderate supercharging. Automatically controlled supercharging and pressure-regulating equipment for operation at altitudes of 14,000–20,000 ft (4,270–6,100 m), with a pressure differential of 2½ lb/sq in (0·17 kg/cm²) between outside atmospheric pressure and inside pressure. At an actual height of 14,700 ft (4,480 m) cabin conditions designed to be equivalent to a height of 8,000 ft (2,440 m). Pressurising equipment later removed.

TAIL UNIT:

Cantilever monoplane type. Aluminium-alloy framework. Fixed surfaces covered with smooth metal skin and movable surfaces with fabric. Trim-tabs in elevators and rudder.

LANDING GEAR:

Two main wheels electrically retractable into inner engine nacelles. Auxiliary manual control. Hydraulic brakes. Retractable tail-wheel.

POWER PLANT:

Four 1,100 hp Wright Cyclone GR-1820-G102 (Model 307) or 1,200 hp GR-1820-G666 (Model SA-307-B1) nine-cylinder radial air-cooled engines in semi-monocoque nacelles in wing leading-edges. Hamilton-Standard three-blade constant-speed full-feathering propellers. Fuel tanks in inner wings.

ACCOMMODATION:

Crew of five, and 33 (Model 307) or 38 (Model SA-307-B1) passengers. Main passenger cabin of Model 307 divided into four compartments, each accommodating 6 day passengers or 4 night passengers in transverse bunks, on right side of central aisle, with 9 individual reclining chairs on left side of aisle. Separate dressing-rooms for men and women. Fully-equipped galley. Cargo compartments with capacity for 6,590 lb (2,990 kg) beneath cabin floor and accessible from inside or out. Rebuilt SA-307-B1 accommodated 38 passengers in main cabin, which was not compartmented as in Model 307.

DIMENSIONS:

Wing span 107 *ft* (32·61 *m*)
Length overall 74 *ft* 4 *in* (22·65 *m*)
Height overall 20 *ft* 9½ *in* (6·32 *m*)

WEIGHTS:

Weight empty 30,000 *lb* (13,608 *kg*)
Weight loaded 45,000 *lb* (20,412 *kg*)

PERFORMANCE:

Max speed at 6,000 *ft* (1,830 *m*) 241 *mph* (388 *kmh*)
Cruising speed at 10,000 *ft* (3,050 *m*) *on* 2,500 *hp* 215 *mph* (346 *kmh*)
Service ceiling 23,300 *ft* (7,100 *m*)
Absolute ceiling with any two engines 10,500 *ft* (3,200 *m*)
Max range at 10,000 *ft* (3,050 *m*) *at* 50 *per cent power* 1,750 *miles* (2,816 *km*) *at* 184 *mph* (296 *kmh*)

Though of pre-war design Stratoliners rendered excellent service after the conflict

MITSUBISHI KARIGANE

In April 1937, a Japanese Mitsubishi monoplane bearing the type name Karigane (Wild Goose) and the individual name *Kamikaze* (*Divine Wind*) flew from Tokyo to London, a total distance of 9,900 miles, in 94½ hours. On a more leisurely return flight the following month the aircraft carried pictures of the coronation of King George VI, and these served to heighten the interest of the flight in the eyes of the Japanese people. The true significance of the flight to London and back was that it marked the emergence of Japanese aviation as a momentous force that was to be sorely felt by the USA at Pearl Harbor and by the Western Allies in the warfare that followed. Although the Karigane bore the stamp of Western influence it was a fine aeroplane in its own right and may be considered a precursor of the brilliantly designed Mitsubishi Type O (Zero) fighter (page 97). The design of the Zero dated, in fact, from 1937–38 although Japanese secrecy was such that not until 1942 did the Allied Powers become fully aware of its qualities.

The Karigane *Kamikaze* used for the Tokyo–London flight was built, together with another of the same type named *Asakaze* (*Morning Wind*), for the Tokyo *Asahi* Press, the completion date being toward the end of March 1937. In 1938 a Mk II version appeared, powered by an 800 hp Mitsubish A.14 fourteen-cylinder radial engine in place of the Nakajima Kotobuki III of 550 hp as fitted in the *Kamikaze*.

Friendly hands awaited at London's Croydon airport

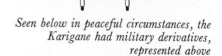

TYPE:
Two-seat high-performance monoplane.

WINGS:
Low-wing cantilever monoplane. Metal structure of multi-spar cellular type, with flush-riveted smooth sheet-metal covering. Metal-framed fabric-covered ailerons. Split trailing-edge flaps under fuselage and wings.

FUSELAGE:
Semi-monocoque metal structure of oval section. Smooth flush-riveted skin.

TAIL UNIT:
Cantilever monoplane type. Metal structure, fin and tailplane covered with flush-riveted smooth metal sheet. Rudder and elevator fabric-covered. Fin integral with fuselage. Fixed tailplane. Trim-tabs in elevators. Balanced rudder.

LANDING GEAR:
Fixed cantilever type. Oleo legs and wheels in streamline casings. Fixed tailwheel.

POWER:
One Nakajimi Kotobuki III nine-cylinder air-cooled radial engine, delivering 550 hp at 13,120 ft (4,000 m). Short-chord ring cowling. Two-blade metal propeller.

ACCOMMODATION:
Enclosed tandem cockpits, with pilot above wing and navigator aft of trailing-edge. Covers above occupants hinged on starboard side. Rear of enclosure merged into fin. Normal flying controls. Navigational equipment included radio with fixed aerial, compass, flight instruments, Demec navigation lights, a drift window and a new type of combined slide-rule and calculator carried in a pocket. Pilot's instruments included artificial horizon, turn indicator and rate-of-climb indicator, as well as two compasses, one of direct-reading bowl type and one of verge-ring type, mounted on floor.

DIMENSIONS:
Wing span 39 *ft* 4¾ *in* (12·00 *m*)
Overall length 27 *ft* 11 *in* (8·50 *m*)
Wing area 258 *sq ft* (24·00 m^2)

WEIGHT:
Weight loaded 5,060 *lb* (2,300 *kg*)

PERFORMANCE:
Max speed 310 *mph* (500 *kmh*)
Cruising speed 200 *mph* (320 *kmh*)
Range 1,490 *miles* (2,400 *km*)

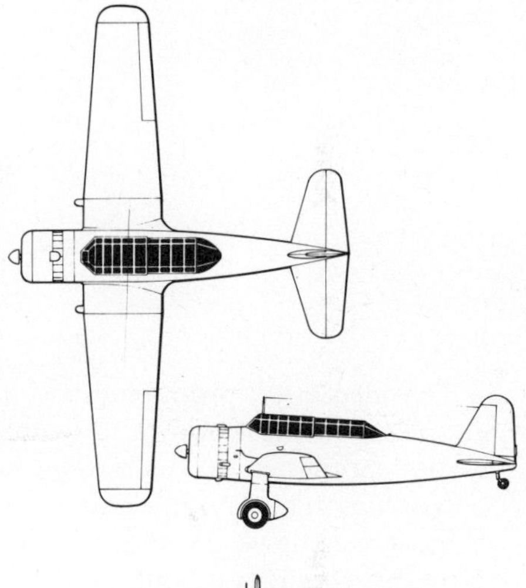

Seen below in peaceful circumstances, the Karigane had military derivatives, represented above

HEINKEL He 178

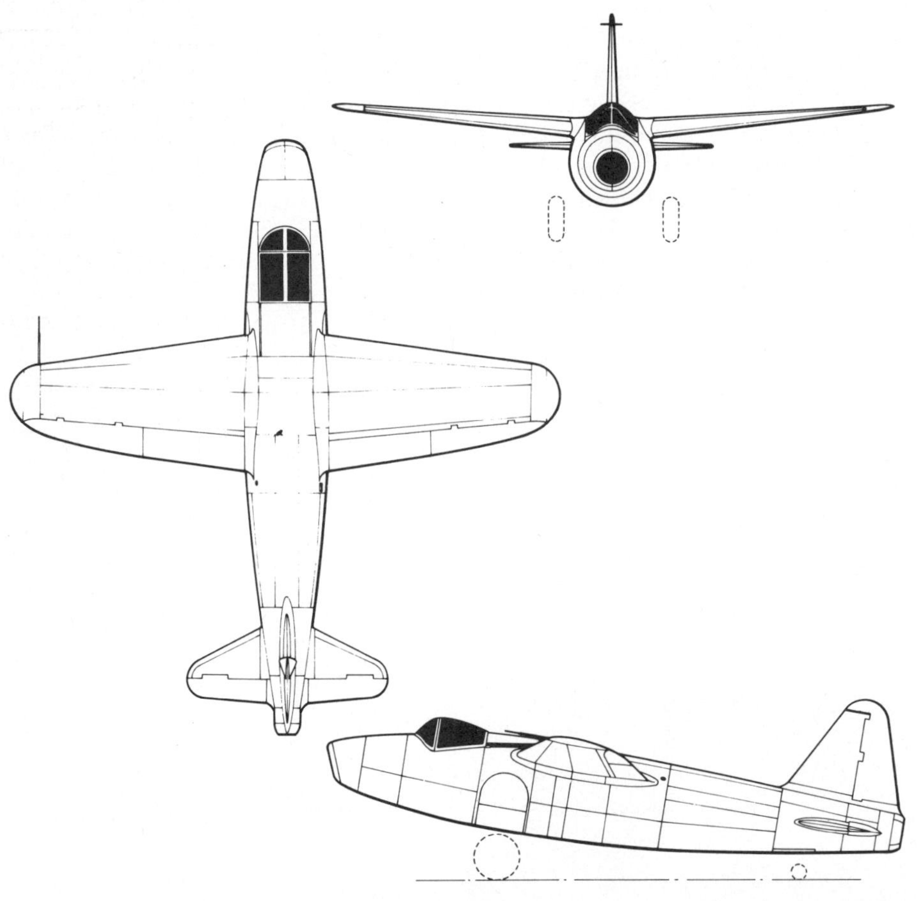

A film record of the He 178 survives

He 178: world's first turbojet aircraft

The idea of jet propulsion was already old when the Heinkel He 178 became the first aeroplane in the world to fly with a turbojet engine. The date was 24 August 1939. The earliest proposals for jet propulsion came in the eighteenth century, or earlier, and a patent was taken out in England by Frank (later Sir Frank) Whittle in 1930. Unknown to Whittle was the work undertaken in Germany by Dr. Pabst von Ohain and his technical assistant, Hahn. It was an engine of von Ohain's devising which powered the He 178 on the historic first flight already mentioned. The first flight with a Whittle engine was on 15 May 1941 (Gloster E.28/39). The use of a gas turbine for jet propulsion was proposed by Frank Whittle in 1928 and the patent already mentioned was published in 1932.

The first Whittle engine ran on the test-bench in 1937. In 1936 von Ohain joined the Heinkel company and in that year also original work on turbojets was initiated by the Junkers concern. In the context of this early work on gas turbines for aircraft it must be recorded that Dr. A. A. Griffith had produced a new aerodynamic theory of turbine design at the Royal Aircraft Establishment, Farnborough, as early as 1926, and the ideas of Dr. Griffith led to the building of an axial compressor in 1936.

Although very great success was achieved by British centrifugal-flow turbojet engines of classic Whittle type, and engines of this kind were very extensively built in the USA and the USSR, the axial-flow variety eventually prevailed. The Vickers Viscount—the world's first airliner with turboprop engines—is later described, but this had been preceded by the wholly experimental Gloster Meteor with two Rolls-Royce Trent turboprops, the first aircraft in the world to fly with engines of this kind.

It has been mentioned that von Ohain joined Heinkel in 1936. A secret department for the development of gas turbines was thereupon established and the first such engine was run under the direction of van Ohain in 1937. This was designated He S1. One year later the greatly improved He S3 was run and in another six months He S3A units were performing satisfactorily. After extensive tests the first He S3B was mounted under a Heinkel He 118, but although this installation was tested in flight the turbojet was not used for take-off or landing. This He S3B was eventually burnt out. Thereupon a second unit of the type, characterised by an axial inducer, centrifugal compressor, reverse-flow combustion chambers and a single-stage radial-inflow turbine, was installed in the specially designed He 178. The first flight with this unit was made by Captain Warsitz early on the morning of 24 August 1939, as already recorded, and a longer flight took place on 27 August. This latter date has generally been quoted as the date of the first flight.

The early work on the Heinkel had been undertaken without the knowledge of the German Air Ministry, and no great interest was displayed officially after news of the first flight was broken to selected individuals. In October 1939 the aircraft was inspected by high-ranking German officers and numerous flights were subsequently made in connection with the development of the He 280 twin-jet single-seat fighter. This aircraft generally resembled in layout the Messerschmitt Me 262 A (which see) and the British Gloster Meteor, having its turbojet engines installed one on each wing. It was not to achieve quantity production although the distinction can be claimed for it that it was the world's first jet fighter, the initial flight having been made on 2 April 1941. The He 280, moreover, was the first aeroplane in the world to have an ejection seat. This was operated by compressed air. On 13 January 1942, after being towed off the ground by two Me 110s to serve in the role of test-bed for the pulse-jet type of unit as later employed in the FZG-76 ("V-1") flying bomb, the aircraft encountered icing trouble and the pilot made the first emergency use of an ejection seat in history.

In general layout the He 280 bore a striking resemblance to the early Dayton-Wright racer, already described, in that it was a high-wing monoplane having its landing gear attached to, and retracting into, the fuselage. The turbojet installation was of "straight-through" type, that is, with nose intake and jet outlet at the rear of the fuselage.

Although the He 178 was the first turbojet aircraft to fly it was not the first jet-propelled Heinkel. This was, in fact, the He 176 which had an historic significance of its own—that of being the first aircraft to fly on the thrust of a liquid-fuel rocket. The flight took place in June 1939. Earlier flights by rocket-powered aircraft recorded in the context of the Messerschmitt Me 163B had been accomplished with solid-fuel rockets.

MITSUBISHI TYPE O FIGHTER

Just as the Focke-Wulf Fw 190 single-seat fighter came as an unexpected, and highly disagreeable, surprise to the Royal Air Force in Europe so did the Mitsubishi Type O carrier-borne fighter (Allied code-name "Zeke") present itself as an acute embarrassment to the American forces in the Pacific. The full significance of the type is implicit in the term "carrier-borne", for the Type O ("Zero" or "Zero-Sen") showed for the first time that a machine which carried the handicap of naval impedimenta could show superiority over land-based counterparts. The excellence of design which made this possible has already been instanced in the Mitsubishi Karigane, which had given the world notice of mounting Japanese technical potential by its Tokyo–London flight of April 1937.

Endurance was increased by an auxiliary tank

The prototype of the Type O carrier-borne fighter was first flown on 1 April 1939, this having a Mitsubishi MK2 Zuisei engine with which it attained slightly over 300 mph. The third prototype was fitted with the more powerful Nakajima NK1C Sakae, this bearing the official designation A6M2, whereas the earlier machines were A6M1s. In the summer of 1940 the A6M2 was adopted by the Japanese Navy as the Type O Carrier Fighter, Model 11, and was first in action in China during August 1940. All opposing fighters were shot down over Chungking, but although the USAAF received warning of the new Japanese fighter's capability the first encounters with the type in the Pacific came, as already intimated, as a complete surprise. The next variant was the A6M2 Model 21, which had folding wing-tips, and in June 1941 came the A6M3, powered with a Sakae 21 engine having a two-speed supercharger. On this version the span was reduced by removing the folding tips, and the A6M3 was taken into service as the Type O Fighter Model 32. This version had an improved rate of roll but suffered marginally in other respects. With fuel tanks added in the wings and the folding tips restored this version became the Model 22, and a two-seat trainer derivative of the A6M2 Model 21 was the A6M2-K. The Nakajima company produced a floatplane version as the A6M2-N. The A6M5 was derived from the A6M3 Model 32 and was produced as the Type O Fighter, Model 52, and more of this model and its derivatives were produced than of any other version.

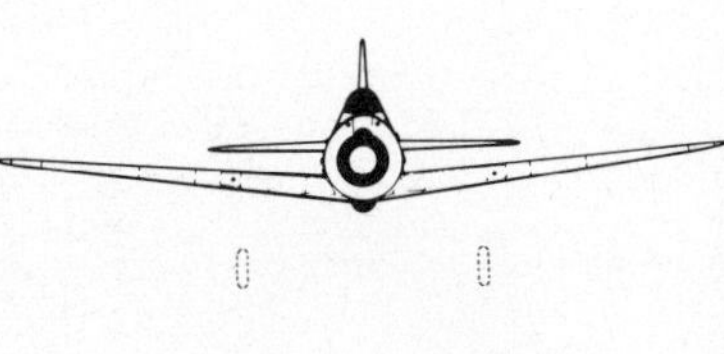

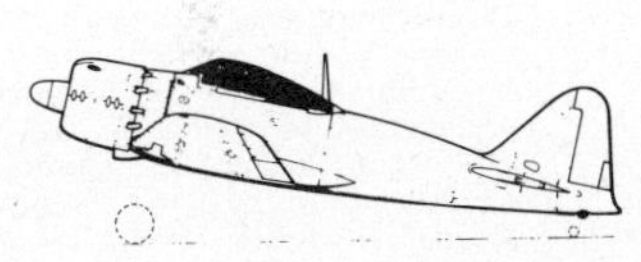

The following description applies to the A6M2 Model 21.

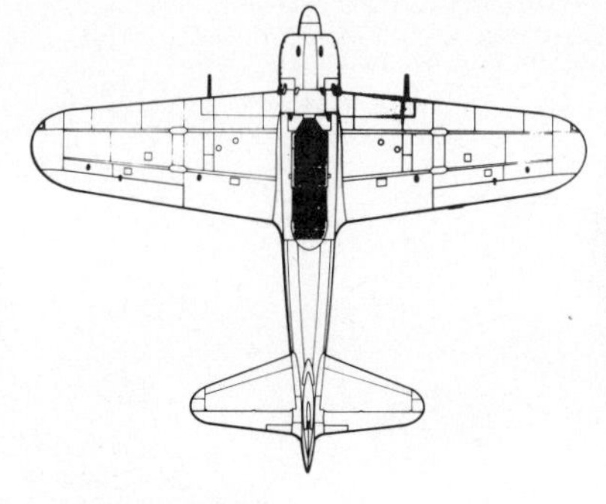

Type O Fighter, Model 52: a captive specimen

TYPE:
Single-seat carrier-borne fighter.

WINGS:
Low-wing cantilever monoplane. Main portion of wing built integrally with forward section of fuselage. All-metal two-spar construction. Spars with extruded booms and sheet webs. Stressed-skin covering. Hydraulically operated split trailing-edge flaps between long-span ailerons and fuselage.

FUSELAGE:
Semi-monocoque structure of light-alloy. Oval section. In two sections, divided at vertical bulkhead aft of cockpit. Forward section built integrally with wing, upper surface of which formed floor of cockpit. Front and rear sections butt-jointed and secured by bolts.

TAIL UNIT:
Cantilever monoplane type. All- metal framework with metal-covered fixed surfaces and fabric-covered movable surfaces. Controllable trim-tabs in elevator. Rudder trim-tab adjustable on ground.

LANDING GEAR:
Retractable type. Hydraulic retraction, main wheels being raised inwardly. Fairing plates on oleo legs and hinged doors under wing closing apertures when wheels raised. Deck-arrester hook flush with fuselage forward of tail-wheel.

POWER PLANT:
One Nakajima Sakae 12 fourteen-cylinder air-cooled radial engine of 925 hp driving three-blade Mitsubishi-Hamilton variable-pitch propeller. Long-chord cowling with controllable cooling flaps. Unprotected fuel tanks in fuselage and wing. Provision for jettisonable tank under fuselage.

ACCOMMODATION:
Pilot's enclosed cockpit, with all-round visibility, above wing. No armour plate or bullet-proof windscreen.

ARMAMENT AND EQUIPMENT:
Two synchronised 7·7 mm Type 97 (Vickers pattern) guns in fuselage, firing through ports in cowling each gun having 500 rounds. Two 20 mm Type 99 (Oerlikon pattern) guns, each with 60 rounds, in wing outboard of propeller. Under-wing provision for two 30 kg (66 lb) or 60 kg (132 lb) bombs. Two watertight compartments in each wing and canvas bag in rear fuselage for emergency flotation.

DIMENSIONS:
Wing span 39 *ft* 4½ *in* (11·99 *m*)
Length overall 29 *ft* 8¾ *in* (9·06 *m*)
Height overall 11 *ft* 5¾ *in* (3·50 *m*)

WEIGHTS:
Weight empty 3,704 *lb* (1,680 *kg*)
Weight loaded 5,313 *lb* (2,410 *kg*)

PERFORMANCE:
Max speed 332 *mph* (534 *kmh*) *at* 16,570 *ft* (5,050 *m*)
Cruising speed 207 *mph* (333 *kmh*) *at* 13,120 *ft* (4,000 *m*)
Time of climb to 19,685 *ft* (6,000 m) 7 *min* 27 *sec*
Service ceiling 33,790 *ft* (10,300 *m*)

VOUGHT-SIKORSKY VS-300

The work of Igor Sikorsky has already been instanced in respect of very large landplanes and flying-boats, but his fullest contribution to aeronautical progress is perhaps to be seen in his establishment of the helicopter as a practical tool and weapon.

Mr. Sikorsky built his first helicopter in Russia in 1909. This had two contra-rotating rotors, representing his first attempt to cancel out torque, which he was eventually able to do on the VS-300, constructed in 1940, by adopting what has been described as the "penny-farthing" formula (single main rotor with small anti-torque rotor at the tail) as tried by Von Baumhauer in 1924. Sikorsky's helicopter of 1909 never left the ground, and one he built in the following year lifted only itself. His active work on helicopters then lapsed in favour of more conventional aircraft. Having settled in the USA in 1919, following the 1917 revolution, he resumed his aeronautical work, and in 1923 established the Sikorsky Aero Engineering Corporation.

Early tethered test

Control of the company passed in 1929 to the United Aircraft Corporation, famous for its Pratt & Whitney engines, Hamilton Standard propellers and Chance Vought aircraft, and it was at this time that he produced the S-40 "Clipper", referred to in the description of the S-42. In 1931 his continuing interest in helicopters began to take tangible form again when he applied for a patent which, in his own words, "included nearly all major features of the VS-300." He has further related: "Late in 1938, in line with my recommendation, the management of United Aircraft decided to embark upon the development of a direct lift aircraft. It was most interesting, I would say thrilling, to resume a certain engineering development where it was discontinued thirty years earlier, not only in another country, but even in a different world.

"The type of aircraft which I was developing on paper since 1929 was a simple helicopter with one main lifting screw and one small auxiliary rotor situated at the end of the fuselage and used mainly to counteract the torque of the main lifting screw. The machine included a system of controls for changing the pitch of each of the propellers and also for varying the incidence of the blades of the main rotor along certain sections of the disc of rotation. These latter movements, that are sometimes called the cyclic control, enable the pilot, by moving the stick, to feather the blades so that their pitch is increased at any given point in their cycle of rotation, while at the opposite point in the cycle, the pitch is simultaneously decreased. This arrangement was expected to form the means for longitudinal and lateral control, while the change of the pitch of the auxiliary rear propeller would provide directional control."

The first brief "hops" were made in November 1939, but control was deficient and in 1940 the cyclic-pitch control was temporarily discarded. The system substituted involved the fitting of two horizontal rotors on outriggers to give fore-and-aft control (including forward motion) and lateral control. In this form the VS-300 flew successfully on 13 May 1940. On 6 May 1941, flown by Igor Sikorsky, the helicopter set up a new world helicopter record (previously held by the remarkable German Focke-Achgelis Fw 61) by remaining airborne for 1 hr 32 min 36. Other alterations followed. In June 1941 cyclic-pitch lateral control was provided, and a single horizontal rotor was fitted at the tail for fore-and-aft control. In December 1941 came the final major improvement: the horizontal rotor was removed and the main rotor was given full cyclic-pitch control.

Mounted on rubber floats, the VS-300 had the additional distinction of becoming the world's first amphibious helicopter. It was placed in the Edison Museum, Dearborn, Mich, in 1943.

TYPE:

Single-seat experimental helicopter.

ROTOR SYSTEM:

In the condition in which it made its first successful flights lifting and control members of the machine consisted of a single three-bladed lifting rotor and three small auxiliary rotors, all engine-driven. One of three auxiliary rotors carried on horizontal axle on structure at rear of fuselage, acting as anti-torque rotor. Variation of pitch provided directional control. Two other auxiliary rotors carried on vertical shafts at extremities of outriggers. Variation of pitch of these rotors in the same direction produced longitudinal control, whereas variation in opposite directions gave lateral control. With power off, main rotor and two horizontal auxiliary rotors autorotated.

FUSELAGE:

Open structure of steel tubes. In late stages of development nose fairing enclosed cockpit and partial fabric covering extended aft.

POWER UNIT:

One 75 hp Lycoming (later 100 hp Franklin) four-cylinder air-cooled engine mounted in fuselage beneath main rotor pylon.

LANDING GEAR:

Tricycle type, or two large rubber bags.

DIMENSIONS (Final version):

Rotor diameter 30 *ft* 0 *in* (9·14 *m*)
Length overall 27 *ft* 10 *in* (8·48 *m*)
Height overall 10 *ft* 0 *in* (3·05 *m*)

WEIGHT (Final version):

Weight loaded 1,290 *lb* (585 *kg*)

PERFORMANCE (Final version):

Cruising speed 40–50 *mph* (64–80 *kmh*)
Range 50–75 *miles* (80–120 *km*)

The second Sikorsky helicopter (1910)

In later years trees again formed a setting (Mr Sikorsky in VS-300)

ILYUSHIN Il-2 STORMOVIK

The most remarkable aircraft employed by Russia against the attacking German forces after 1941 was a heavily armoured ground-attack machine which may be compared with the Junkers J 1 of 1917, already described. Not the least of its notable characteristics was its armament of air-to-ground rocket projectiles, in the development and employment of which the USSR was foremost.

Displayed on this example are Polish markings and rocket rails

The application of armour to military aircraft dated back to before the First World War and harassment of enemy troops by non-specialised aircraft occurred in the early phases of that conflict. The earliest use of bombs by aircraft has been mentioned in the context of the Caproni Bomber. The history of rocket propulsion for aircraft will be traced in connection with the Me 163 B and a note on the use of the rocket as a weapon is now in order.

That the rocket was a Chinese invention dating from the twelfth century is generally conceded and war rockets are known to have been used in the battle for the island of Chiozza (1379). The name of the Englishman Sir William Congreve is most closely associated with the development of the modern war rocket and the first rockets used for offensive purposes from aircraft were of the Le Prieur type, so named after their French inventor. These were employed during the war of 1914–18 against kite balloons used for artillery spotting and were fixed to the interplane struts of the carrier aircraft. Rockets for air-to-ground attack was first employed by the Il-2, now under review. This type of armament was thereafter adopted by the other contending Powers.

In recognition of his success as an aircraft designer Sergei Ilyushin, who was responsible for the Il-2, was made 'Hero of Soviet Labour' in 1941. The design of the Il-2 was quite conventional but, as already indicated, it had special provision for the attack of enemy forces, including armoured vehicles, from low level. About 35,000 Il-2s were built.

TYPE:

Single-seat or two-seat ground-attack aircraft.

WINGS:

Low-wing cantilever monoplane. Very thick section on inboard portions, moderate taper in plan, sharp taper in thickness. Moderate dihedral. All-metal construction, including covering. Split flaps between ailerons and wing-root fillets. Inset ailerons in two sections, with trim-tabs on inner sections.

FUSELAGE:

Oval-section composite structure. Forward part of metal, with metal covering. Rear part of wood.

TAIL UNIT:

Cantilever monoplane type. Tailplane/elevator assembly very sharply tapered in plan. Two trim-tabs in elevator, one in rudder. Mass balance on top of rudder. Fixed surfaces metal-covered, movable surfaces fabric-covered.

LANDING GEAR:

Retractable tail-wheel type. Main wheels retracted rearwards into under-wing fairings, leaving part of each wheel exposed. Twin oleo-pneumatic shock-absorber legs for each main wheel. Non-retractable castoring tail-wheel with partially faired leg.

POWER PLANT:

One 1,300 hp AM-38 twelve-cylinder Vee liquid-cooled engine driving three-blade constant-speed metal propeller. Dog for Hucks starter at tip of spinner. Coolant radiator below fuselage, oil cooler in top cowling.

ACCOMMODATION:

Pilot, or pilot and gunner, under short canopy over wing. Canopy extensively protected by armour-plate or armoured glass. Armour-plate shell enclosing engine, radiator and oil cooler, fuel tanks and crew. Total weight of armour exceeded 1,540 lb, representing about 15 per cent of loaded weight.

ARMAMENT:

Two 20 mm cannon and two 7·6 mm machine-guns in wing, with barrels of cannon projecting forward of leading-edge. One 12·7 mm gun for gunner on free mounting. Attachment points under wings for guide rails for eight 56 lb (25·40 kg) rocket projectiles. Four bomb cells in wing inboard of landing gear fairings. Provision for 880 lb (400 kg) of bombs. Bombs and rocket projectiles could be carried simultaneously.

DIMENSIONS:

Wing span 47 *ft* 10 *in* (14·58 *m*)
Length overall 38 *ft* 1 *in* (11·60 *m*)

PERFORMANCE:

Max speed 270 *mph* (434 *kmh*)

On the two-seater there was a 12·7 mm gun

The short canopy for the pilot and gunner was extensively protected by armour-plate or armoured glass and there was additional armouring

NORTH AMERICAN MUSTANG

The Mustang single-seat fighter achieved an unassailable eminence in World War II by reason of its technical excellence, adaptability and extent of employment. It was designed, at the suggestion of the North American company, to meet a requirement stated by the British Air Purchasing Commission in April 1940. Delays notwithstanding, the first test flight took place on 26 October 1940. By this time a contract for 320 aircraft, bearing the maker's designation NA-73, had been placed, and the fifth and tenth off the production lines were taken over by the US Army as XP-51s. In RAF service the appellation became Mustang I. The American Allison engine at that time installed was rated to deliver its power at relatively low levels, and though the fighting potential of the Mustang was fully appreciated the Mustang I entered service with Army Co-operation Command. Subsequent development is best outlined by specific reference to the principal variants. It must first be noted that the Mustang's extraordinary aerodynamic efficiency was manifest not only in its high speed but in range capability also, and the type will always be remembered as a pre-eminent escort fighter of the 1939–45 war. In this role it was extensively operated with Lockheed Lightnings and Republic Thunderbolts. With the adoption of the Rolls-Royce Merlin engine its ultimate wartime potential was realised, and the later forms of the aircraft (the P-51 D and K are described) represented one of the highest achievments in Anglo-American co-operation.

P-51 (Mustang 1 A)

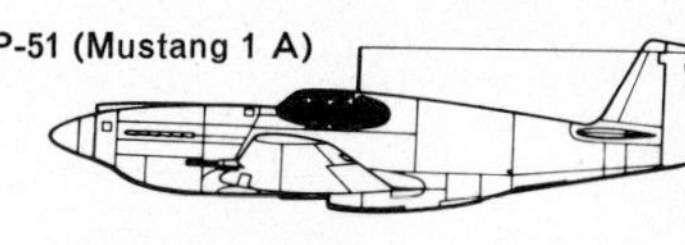

P-51 B (Mustang III) + Malcolm Hood.

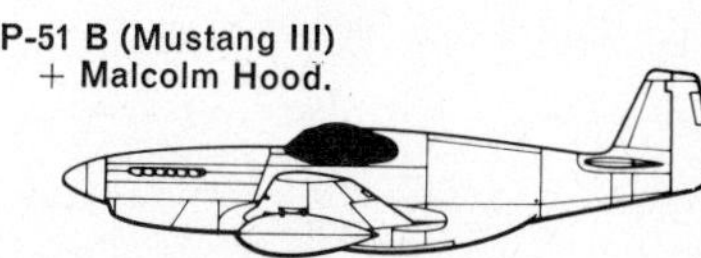

P-51 D (Mustang IV)

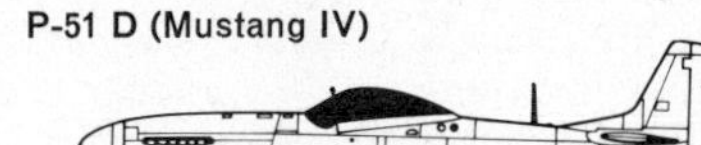

P-51 H

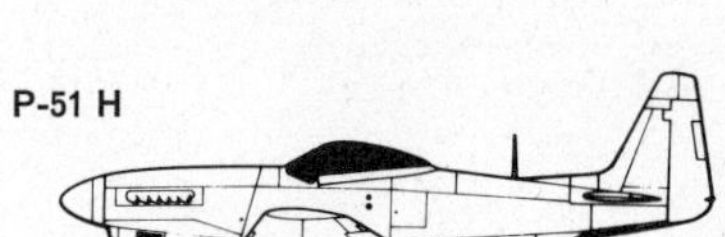

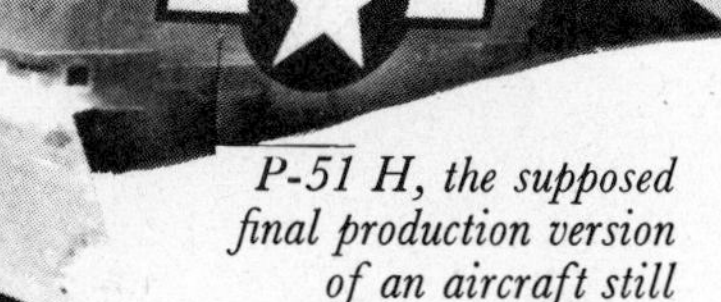

P-51 H, the supposed final production version of an aircraft still being manufactured today. Engine, Packard Merlin V-1650-9

Production during and immediately after the war totalled 14,819 aircraft, but such was the excellence of the basic design that, in addition to marketing a tandem two-seat business and sporting conversion of the F-51 D bearing the name Cavalier, the Cavalier Aircraft Corporation today holds a major contract to supply new F-51 Ds to the USAF for counter-insurgency duties. The corporation has also developed a new attack version known as the Mustang II and another having a Rolls-Royce Dart turboprop. The main production variants of the Mustang were:

Mustang I. Allison V-1710-F3R engine. Four 0·50 in and four 0·30 in guns. Operated by RAF with F.24 camera mounted obliquely aft of cockpit.

Mustang IA (P-51). Allison V-1710-81 engine. Four 20 mm wing-mounted guns. Some fitted with two K-24 cameras and designated F-6A.

Mustang II (P-51 A). Four 0·50 wing-mounted guns and provision for under-wing bombs or drop-tanks. Max bomb load two 500 lb (225 kg).

A-36 A. Developed specifically as a dive-bomber, deliveries beginning September 1942. Wing-mounted dive-brakes (rendered inoperative in service), two 500 lb bombs, six 0·50 in guns.

P-51 B and C (Mustang III). Identical sub-types, suffix denoting factory. First Merlin-powered operational versions. Merlin originally fitted experimentally in Great Britain to improve Mustang's altitude capability. Production aircraft had Packard V-1650-3 or -7 version of Merlin, with two-speed two-stage supercharger. Strengthened airframe, revised radiator, extra internal fuel tankage, four 0·50 in guns. Some modified for tactical reconnaissance, with two cameras. Malcolm backward-sliding cockpit hood later fitted to improve pilot's view.

P-51 D and K. Packard V-1650-7 engine. Two variants differed solely in propeller, K having Aeroproducts type instead of Hamilton Standard. Most noticeable difference from earlier variants was sliding bubble canopy and cut-down rear fuselage. Dorsal fin. Six 0·50 in guns, two 500 lb or 1,000 lb (450 kg) bombs, or six 5 in (12·7 cm) rockets.

XP-51 F. Experimental. Complete redesign as "lightweight" fighter. Structure weight reduced by 1,600 lb (726 kg). Reduced fuel capacity and four 0·50 in guns only.

XP-51 G. Experimental. Merlin V-1650-9 engine in longer fuselage. Six 0·50 in guns.

P-51 H. "Final" production version (see above). Similar to XP-51 F. Short bubble canopy. Integral engine mounting for V.1650-9 engine delivering war-emergency power with water injection of 2,218 hp at 10,200 ft and conferring a speed of 487 mph at 25,000 ft (7,620 m).

TYPE:

Single-seat fighter.

WINGS:

Low-wing cantilever monoplane. NAA-NACA laminar-flow section. Wing in two sections, bolted together on centre-line of fuselage, upper surface of wing forming floor of cockpit. Two-spar all-metal structure with smooth Alclad skin. Spars with single plate flanges and extruded booms. Remaining structure consisting of pressed ribs with flanged lightening holes and extruded spanwise stringers. Non-metallic fuel cells between spars, with structural door in undersurface of each wing to facilitate installation and removal. Metal-covered ailerons, port aileron with trim-tab. Hydraulically operated slotted flaps.

FUSELAGE:

All-metal structure of oval section in three parts: engine section, main section, tail section. Construction entirely of aluminium-alloy extrusions except for cockpit armour. Engine section consisting of two Vee-type cantilever bearers built up of plate webs and top and bottom extruded members, each attached at two points to front fireproof bulkhead of main section. Main section consisting of two beams, each side beam comprising two longerons, forming the caps, and the skin, reinforced by vertical frames, forming the webs. Aft of cockpit longerons extended into semi-monocoque structure reinforced by vertical frames. Structure of rear portion of main section continued in detachable tail-section.

TAIL UNIT:

Cantilever monoplane type. One-piece tailplane with detachable tips. Tailplane and fin structure comprising two spars, pressed ribs and extruded stringers, with Alclad skin. Rudder and elevator with aluminium-alloy frames and fabric covering. Trim-tabs in control surfaces.

LANDING GEAR:

Retractable type. Cantilever air-oil shock-absorber legs hinged to large forged fittings bolted to reinforced ribs and retracted inwardly forward of main spar. Hydraulic retraction. Raised gear covered by plates on legs and doors. Hydraulic wheel-brakes. Swivelling, steerable, retractable tail-wheel.

POWER PLANT:

One 1,590 hp Packard V-1650-7 (Rolls-Royce Merlin 69) twelve-cylinder Vee liquid-cooled engine on built-up cantilever mounting. Four-blade Hamilton Standard or Aeroproducts constant-speed propeller. Coolant and oil radiators in scoop under fuselage aft of cockpit. Thermostatically controlled exit flaps. Self-sealing fuel cells in wings and one in fuselage behind cockpit. Jettisonable ferry or combat tanks could be installed on bomb carriers.

ARMAMENT:

Six 0·50 in Browning machine-guns, three in each wing. Detachable faired carrier under each wing for bomb up to 1,000 lb (450 kg). Electrical fusing.

EQUIPMENT:

Moulded blister-type sliding hood with optically flat 5-ply laminated glass bullet-proof front panel. Stainless-steel sheet and armour-plate fireproof bulkhead forward of cockpit and two armour plates behind pilot. Electrical system (24 V), radio, oxygen,

DIMENSIONS:

Wing span 37 *ft* 0¼ *in* (11·28 *m*)
Length overall 32 *ft* 3¼ *in* (9·83 *m*)
Height overall 13 *ft* 8 *in* (4·16 *m*)

WEIGHTS:

Weight empty 7,125 *lb* (3,232 *kg*)
Weight loaded (*normal*) 10,100 *lb* (4,580 *kg*)
Weight loaded (*max*) 12,100 *lb* (5,490 *kg*)

PERFORMANCE:

Max speed 437 *mph* (703 *kmh*) at 25,000 *ft* (7,620 *m*)
Time of climb to 20,000 *ft* (6,095 *m*) 7·3 *min*
Range (*with drop tanks*) 1,650 *miles* (2,655 *km*)

DE HAVILLAND MOSQUITO

The Mosquito was the realisation of an ideal: an unarmed bomber that would depend for its defence on sheer performance. It proved to be even more than this, and the following notes on variants (excluding Canadian and Australian but including Sea Mosquito) attest to its exceptional versatility. As an example of wooden construction it was pre-eminent.

The layout was planned in 1938 and the prototype bomber flew on 25 November 1940, eleven months from the start of detail design. In July 1941 the first three Mosquitoes were delivered to the RAF, and in that month also a production scheme was planned to include the Canadian de Havilland plant. Nine months later plans to manufacture the type in Australia were completed. Total production was 7,781 aircraft.

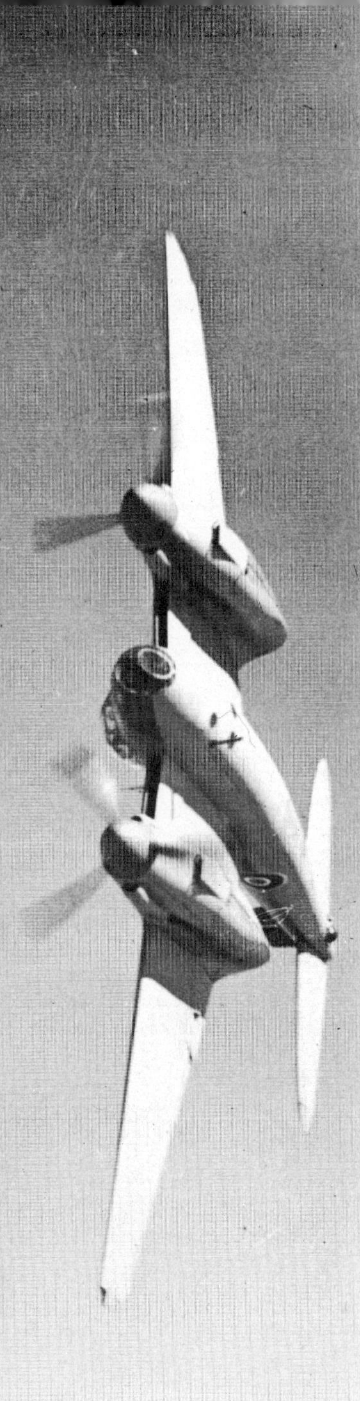

Breakaway: Mosquito B Mk IV

Mosquito PR. Mk I. Two Rolls-Royce Merlin 21 engines with two-speed single-stage superchargers and D.H. Hydromatic constant-speed propellers. Short engine nacelles. Four cameras.

Mosquito F. Mk II. Merlin 21 or 23 engines. Fighter with four 20 mm British Hispano cannon and four 0·303 in machine-guns.

Mosquito T. Mk III. Two-seat dual-control trainer. Modified from Mk. II.

Mosquito B. Mk IV. Merlin 21 or 23 engines. Unarmed bomber. First ten were converted Mk I airframes fitted to carry four 250 lb (113 kg) bombs. Later production series had lengthened nacelles and carried four 500 lb (227 kg) bombs with shortened vanes. Many converted to carry one 4,000 lb (1,814 kg) bomb and some had strengthened wings for two 50 Imp gallon (227 litres) drop tanks. Pathfinder version had special radar.

Mosquito PR. Mk IV. Unarmed reconnaissance version with four cameras instead of bombs.

Mosquito B. Mk V. Merlin 21 engines. Prototype development of B. Mk IV with new "Standard Wing" to take two 50 gallon drop tanks or two 500 lb bombs. Not produced in United Kingdom, but formed basis of Canadian B. Mk VII.

Mosquito FB. Mk VI. Merlin 21, 23 or 25 engines. Developed from F. Mk II as fighter-bomber with standard fighter armament and space for two 500 lb bombs in rear half of bomb-bay. Provision for two 50 gallon drop tanks or two 500 lb bombs or eight 60 lb (27 kg) rocket projectiles under wings.

Mosquito PR. Mk VIII. First high-altitude Mosquito. Converted from Mk IV by fitting Merlin 61 engines with two-speed two-stage superchargers and providing for two 50 gallon drop tanks.

Mosquito B. Mk IX. Merlin 72 engines with two-speed two-stage superchargers. High-altitude unarmed bomber. Four 500 lb bombs in fuselage and two 500 lb bombs under wings. Extra fuselage tanks and two 50 gallon drop tanks as alternatives to bombs. Later converted to take one 4,000 lb bomb and two 50 gallon (later 100 gallon) drop tanks. Pathfinder version had special radar.

Mosquito PR. Mk IX. Photographic-reconnaissance version of B. Mk. IX.

Mosquito NF. Mk XII. Merlin 21 or 23 engines. Four-cannon night fighter similar to F. Mk II but with radar in place of machine-guns.

Mosquito NF. Mk XIII. Merlin 21 or 23 engines. Four-cannon night fighter.

Mosquito NF. Mk XV. Merlin 73 or 77 engines. Special high-altitude fighter developed from prototype PR. Mk VIII. Pressure cabin, extended wing-tips, reduced fuel, four 0·303 in machine-guns in blister.

Mosquito B. Mk XVI. Merlin 72 or 76 (starboard) or 73 or 77 (port) engines, port engine driving cabin supercharger. Development of B. Mk IX. Original bomb load 3,000 lb (1,360 kg). Converted to take one 4,000 lb bomb with two 50 gallon drop tanks or four 500 lb bombs with two 100 gallon drop tanks.

Mosquito PR. Mk XVI. Photographic reconnaissance verion of B. Mk XVI. Fitted with astrodome.

Mosquito NF. Mk XVII. Merlin 21 or 23 engines. Version of NF. XII with American radar.

Mosquito FB. Mk XVIII. Merlin 25 engines. Development of FB. Mk VI with fuselage modified to take adaptation of 6-pounder (57 mm) anti-tank gun instead of four 20 mm cannon. Two 500 lb bombs or eight rocket projectiles or two 50 gallon or 100 gallon drop tanks under wings.

The Mosquito B Mk IV was the first bomber version to enter service. A 4,000 lb bomb was later carried

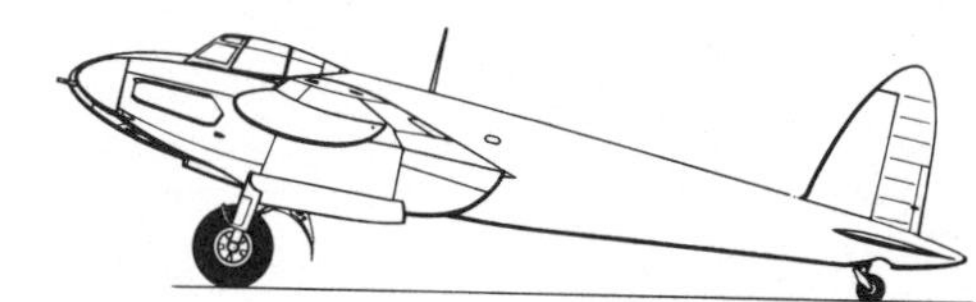

Pilot's station in Mosquito B Mk IV. The bomb-aimer's station is visible at right, though this is incomplete

The first test flight of the Mosquito prototype depicted was made by Geoffrey de Havilland, son of Sir Geoffrey, on 25 November 1940

Mosquito NF. Mk XIX. Merlin 25 engines. Night fighter developed from NF. Mk XIII but with engine change and ability to take either British or American radar.

Mosquito NF. Mk 30. Merlin 72 or 76 engines. British or American radar.

Mosquito PR. Mk 32. Lightened version of PR. Mk XVIII with extended wing-tips. No crew armour or fuel tank protection. Reduced photographic equipment.

Sea Mosquito TF. Mk 33. First production Sea Mosquito. Two Merlin 25 engines driving four-bladed constant-speed full-feathering propellers. Upward-folding wings. Torpedo, bomb or mine under fuselage or bombs in bomb-bay and under wings. Rocket projectiles under wings. American radar.

Mosquito PR. Mk 34. Very-long-range development of Mk. XVI. Merlin 113/114 engines. One 4,000 lb bomb with two 50 gallon drop tanks or four 500 lb bombs with two 100 gallon drop tanks.

Mosquito B. Mk 35. High-altitude development of B. Mk XVI. Merlin 113/114 engines. One 4,000 lb bomb with two 50 gallon drop tanks or four 500 lb bombs with two 100 gallon drop tanks.

Mosquito NF. Mk 36. Development of N.F. Mk. 30 with Merlin 113 engines.

Sea Mosquito TF. Mk 37. Replacement for T.F. Mk. 33. British radar.

Mosquito TT. Mk 39. Target tug with lengthened nose and dorsal cupola.

TYPE:

High-performance multi-purpose military monoplane.

WINGS:

Mid-wing cantilever monoplane. Wing in one piece, with sharply swept-forward trailing-edge. All-wood structure comprising two box spars with laminated spruce flanges and plywood webs, spruce and plywood compression ribs, spanwise spruce stringers and plywood skin. Double skin on upper surface, with upper stringers sandwiched between the two skins. False leading-edge, built up of nose rib formers and a D-skin, attached to front spar. Entire wing screwed, glued and pinned and finally covered with fabric over the plywood. Hydraulically operated slotted flaps between ailerons and engine nacelles and between nacelles and fuselage. Slotted ailerons, with trim-tab in port aileron.

FUSELAGE:

Oval-section all-wood structure, jig-built in two vertical halves, each completely equipped before joining. Seven bulkheads built up of two plywood skins, kept apart by two spruce blocks, carrying outer skin comprising a sandwich of balsa wood between two layers of plywood. At points where bulkheads attached balsa core replaced by spruce ring. Where attachments made to skin, bakelite plug inserted into balsa, a plywood flange glued to the inner surface distributing the load. Two halves of fuselage scarfed together with Vee notches reinforced by ply inserts above and below and an additional overlapping ply strip on the inside of the joint. After assembly, whole fuselage covered with fabric and doped. Underside cut out to accept wing, attached to four pick-up points. Lower part of cut-out section replaced after assembly.

TAIL UNIT:

Cantilever monoplane type. All-wood structure with plywood-covered fixed surfaces and fabric-covered rudder and elevators. Aerodynamically and statically balanced control surfaces. Automatic rudder bias by spring-loaded telescopic strut linked to trim-tab. Trim-tabs in elevator.

LANDING GEAR:

Retractable type. Two units comprising two legs with rubber-in-compression springing and one large wheel. Units retracted hydraulically into tails of engine nacelles. Apertures closed by hinged doors. Hydraulic wheel-brakes. Dunlop-Marstrand non-shimmying retractable tail-wheel.

POWER PLANT:

Two Rolls-Royce Merlin twelve-cylinder Vee liquid-cooled engines on welded steel-tube mountings cantilevered from wing spars. D.H. three-blade constant-speed full-feathering propellers 12 ft (3·66 m) diameter. Radiators in thickness of wing inboard of nacelles, with intakes along leading-edge and outlets controlled by flaps under wing surface ahead of front spar. Each radiator in three parts, outboard section forming oil cooler, middle section coolant radiator and inboard section cabin heater. Fuel in ten protected tanks, two (68 Imp gallons = 309 litres each) in fuselage between wing spars, two (79 and 65 Imp gallons = 359 and 295 litres each) on either side of fuselage inboard of nacelles, and two (32 and 24 Imp gallons = 145 and 109 litres each) outboard of each nacelle. Three additional tanks in long-range versions, one in fuselage and two under wing.

ACCOMMODATION:

Fighter and fighter-bomber: Side-by-side seating for crew of two in nose, pilot to port. Armoured bulkhead in solid nose and flat bullet-proof windscreen. Entrance through door on starboard side. Unarmed bomber and photographic reconnaissance: Accommodation as for fighter. Transparent nose with optically flat panel for bomb-aimer. Vee windscreen with two layers of glass with constant flow of dried air passing between to prevent misting and icing, and spectacle-type control instead of stick-type column in Fighter. Entrance through hatch in floor. Supercharged and heated cabin in some marks.

DIMENSIONS:

Wing span 54 *ft* 2 *in* (16·51 *m*)
Length overall 44 *ft* 6 *in* (13·56 *m*)
Height (*over rudder in flying position*) 17 *ft* 5 *in* (5·31 *m*)

WEIGHTS AND LOADINGS (Mk 34):

Weight empty 14,622 *lb* (6,632 *kg*)
Normal loaded weight 22,587 *lb* (10,245 *kg*)

PERFORMANCE (Mk 34):

Max speed 425 *mph* (684 *kmh*)
Cruising speed 315 *mph* (507 *kmh*) at 30,000 *ft* (9,145 *m*)
Max still-air range 3,500 *miles* (5,633 *km*)

B IV

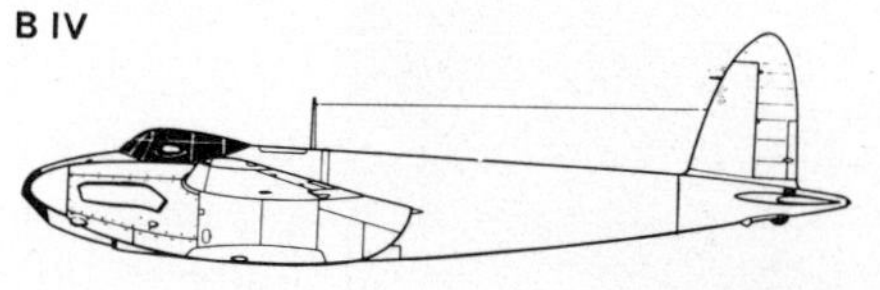

PR 34

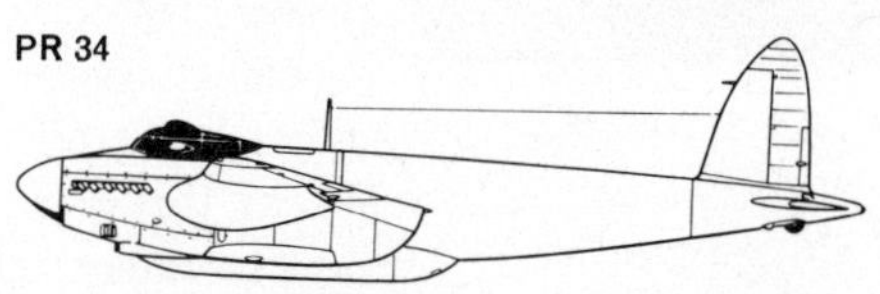

FB VI

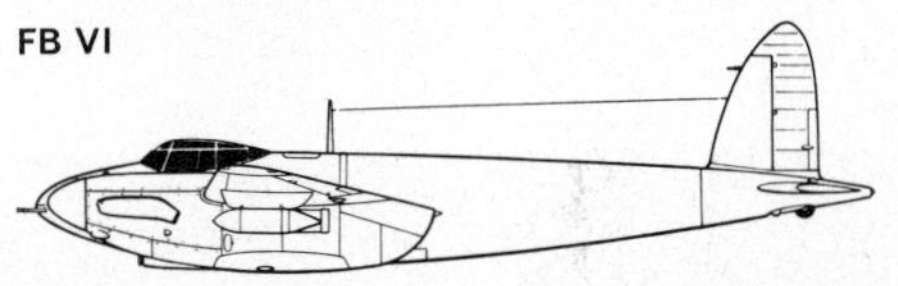

NF 36

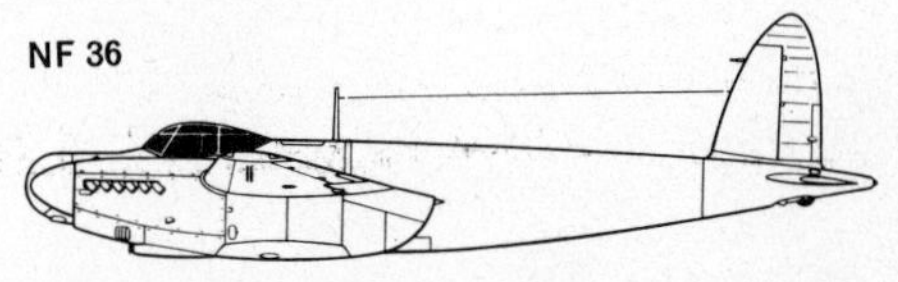

Mosquito rundown (photographs): B Mk IV; TT Mk 39; B Mk IV; Sea Mosquito TF Mk 37

MESSERSCHMITT Me 262 A

Professor Willy Messerschmitt, seen congratulating the pilot of a record-breaking Me 109, was designer of the Me 262,

The place of the Me 262 in history is secured more by reason of the technical excellence of its design than by its service record, for relatively few of the 1,433 examples constructed ever saw battle. Moreover, many of those which ultimately reached operational units were, it is now recognised, misemployed in the secondary role of ground attack. Had singleness of purpose matched technical merit this aircraft might well have restored German ascendency in the air. In having two wing-mounted turbojet engines the type resembled the British Gloster Meteor, a fighter which, notwithstanding assertions to the contrary, was in operational squadron service before the Me 262. Apart from its propulsive system the Me 262 was notable in exploiting the German development of wing sweepback, in the interests of speed.

The Messerschmitt company was instructed to proceed with the design in 1938 and three prototypes were ordered in March 1940. These airframes were completed before turbojet engines became available for them, and the first was initially flown, on 4 April 1941, with a Junkers Jumo 210 piston engine. On 25 November of the same year the second prototype was tested with two BMW 003 turbojet engines, but with the piston engine retained as a safety measure. The turbojets failed, and flight was not achieved. True jet flight, solely on turbojet power, was first accomplished by the third prototype on 18 July 1942, the engines on this occasion being of the Junkers Jumo 004 type, which was to become standard. For early trials the prototypes were handicapped by having a tail-down landing gear, but a nose-wheel was fitted to the fifth example. Other prototypes were built but production of the first production version (Me 262 A) was delayed, in part by bombing.

This Me 262 A-1 was the first German jet-propelled fighter to be captured intact

The two basic variants of the A sub-type later described were the A-1 fighter, with four guns, and the A-2 bomber with two guns. There were several non-standard variations, involving the following installations, among others: two cameras instead of guns; one 50 mm MK 214A cannon in nose; two 30 mm MK 103, two 30 mm MK 108 and two 20 mm MG 151/20 guns; extra radio equipment for bad-weather fighting; under-wing racks for twenty-four 50 mm R4M rocket projectiles; extra fuel tanks, including one under the forward fuselage. One machine was converted to accommodate a prone bomb-aimer in the nose, and there were several versions of the Me 262 B two-seater. The following description relates to the Me 262 A-1 and A-2.

TYPE:
Single-seat fighter (A-1) or bomber (A-2).

WINGS:
Low-wing cantilever monoplane. One-piece wing fitting in recess in underside of fuselage. Inner sections, between fuselage and jet nacelles, with swept-back leading-edge and swept-forward trailing-edge. Outer panels tapered and swept back. Detachable square-cut tips. All-metal structure, with single built-up I-section main spar in two halves and smooth flush-riveted stressed skin. Frise-type ailerons in two sections on each wing. Slotted flaps inboard of ailerons, moving rearwards as well as down. Full-span automatic leading-edge slots.

FUSELAGE:
All-metal semi-monocoque structure of near-triangular section with rounded corners and with wing passing through broad base. Four sections: steel nose cone housing guns and ammunition, centre-section, including cockpit, rear fuselage and tail section.

TAIL UNIT:
Cantilever monoplane type. Tailplane mounted half-way up fin and electrically adjustable. Rudder and elevator mass-balanced. Geared tab in rudder also used for trimming. Trim-tabs in elevators.

LANDING GEAR:
Retractable tricycle type. Main wheels raised inwardly into underside of wings and nose-wheel backwards into fuselage. Hydraulic retraction by pump on port engine. Hydraulic brakes on all wheels.

POWER PLANT:
Two Junkers Jumo 004 B-1 eight-stage axial-flow turbojet engines in nacelles underslung from wings. Starting by small Riedel two-stroke engine built in to each engine. One 3,000 Watt generator on each engine. Fuel used J-2 diesel oil. Four fuel tanks in fuselage, two of 198 Imp gallons (900 litres), one of 38 Imp gallons (170 litres) and one of 132 Imp gallons (600 litres) capacity. Quantity of fuel varied according to armament load. Provision under fuselage for two R1 502 assisted take-off rockets.

ARMAMENT:
Four (A-1) or two (A-2) MK 108 30 mm short-barrelled guns. Electro-pneumatic cocking, electric firing. Ammunition carried varied according to load condition. Max capacity 360 rounds, 100 each for upper guns, 80 each for lower guns. Reflector gun-sight. A-2 had two Messerschmitt combined carrier-slips, each for a 250 kg (550 lb) bomb.

EQUIPMENT:
FuG 16 ZY VHF radio for air-to-air and air-to-ground traffic. FuG 25 A IFF equipment. Two Very pistols. Special seat-type parachute, combining emergency oxygen set, stomach belt and shoulder strap with quick-release fitting. Pilot protected by 15 mm armour plate front and rear and by 90 mm bullet-resisting windscreen.

DIMENSIONS:
Wing span 41 *ft* 0 *in* (12·50 *m*)
Length overall 34 *ft* 9½ *in* (10·60 *m*)
Height overall 12 *ft* 7 *in* (3·85 *m*)

WEIGHTS:
Max loaded weight (A-1) 15,565 *lb* (7,060 *kg*)
Max loaded weight (A-2) 15,432 *lb* (7,000 *kg*)

PERFORMANCE (A-1):
Max speed 540 *mph* (870 *kmh*) *at* 19,680 *ft* (6,000 *m*)
Time of climb to 26,240 *ft* (8,000 *m*) 11 *min*
Service ceiling 39,360 *ft* (12,000 *m*)

The controls of an Me 262

AVRO LANCASTER

Wartime Lancaster sorties totalled some 156,000

Compactness was a marked Lancaster characteristic

The military significance of the Avro 683 Lancaster four-engined bomber is, perhaps, best conveyed in a declaration by the chief of the RAF's wartime Bomber Command that it was the greatest single factor in winning the Second World War. With its companion type, the Handley Page Halifax, of essentially similar layout, the Lancaster certainly brought into being a new concept of strategic bombing. Whereas the Halifax had been designed from the outset as a four-engined aircraft, the Lancaster was a derivative of the twin-engined Manchester, and the first Lancaster was, in fact, a Manchester airframe with four Rolls-Royce Merlin X engines in underslung nacelles in place of the two Rolls-Royce Vultures of the standard Manchester. Originally known as the Manchester III, this aircraft was first flown on 9 January 1941. The first production-type Lancaster was initially flown on 1 October 1941, and showed such excellence of performance and load-carrying ability that massive production was initiated with the greatest urgency. The first operational sortie by Lancasters was the laying of mines in the Heligoland Bight on 3 March 1942. New bombing techniques combined with the audacity of aircrews to make military history on a massive scale. Lancasters breached the Mohne and Eder dams and sank the German battleship *Tirpitz* and a single aircraft destroyed the Bielefeld Viaduct with one 22,000 lb (9,980 kg) bomb. The total of wartime sorties was of the order of 156,000 and on 21 March 1945 the number of Lancaster squadrons in Bomber Command was 56. Lancasters found more merciful employment in the repatriation of 75,000 prisoners of war and in air-sea rescue duties and rendered service also as flying test beds. Many were supplied to foreign powers. The civil Lancastrian and the York freighter were derivative types and salient features of the Lancaster were reproduced in its successor the Lincoln.

The following were the principal variants of the Lancaster.

Lancaster Mk I. Rolls-Royce Merlin 20 or 22 engines.

Lancaster Mk I (Special). Adapted to carry 8,000, 12,000, or 22,000 lb (3,630, 5,440, or 9,980 kg) bomb. No H2S radar.

Lancaster Mk I (FE.). Intended for operation against Japan in the Far East. Increased tankage.

Lancaster Mk II. Bristol Hercules VI engines.

Lancaster Mk III. Packard-built Merlin 28, 38 or 244 engines.

Lancaster Mk VI. Merlin 87 engines driving four-blade propellers. Nose and dorsal turrets deleted. Special radar-jamming devices.

TYPE:

Four-engined bomber.

WINGS:

Mid-wing cantilever monoplane. Wing in five main sections: centre-section of parallel chord and thickness integral with fuselage centre-section, two tapering outer sections, and two almost semi-circular wing-tips. Subsidiary units: detachable leading- and trailing-edge sections of outer wings and centre-section, flaps and ailerons. All units built up individually, with all fittings and equipment, before assembly. Two-spar structure, each spar having a top and bottom extruded boom bolted on to a single thick-gauge web-plate. Ribs were aluminium-alloy pressings flanged and swaged for stiffness. Covering of smooth aluminium-alloy. Ailerons with metal noses, but fabric-covered aft of hinges. Split flaps between ailerons and fuselage.

FUSELAGE:

All-metal structure of oval section, in five separately-assembled main sections. Backbone formed by pairs of extruded longerons located half-way down the cross-section of the three middle sections. Cross-beams between these longerons supported the floor and formed the roof of the bomb compartment. U-frames and formers bolted to longerons carried smooth skin covering. Remaining sections built up of oval frames and formers and longitudinal stringers, with flush-riveted metal covering. All equipment and fittings installed before final assembly of separate units.

TAIL UNIT:

Cantilever monoplane type with twin oval fin-and-rudder assemblies at extremities of tailplane. Tailplane in two sections, built up as wings. Tailplane spars joined together on fuselage centre-line. All surfaces metal-covered except elevator (fabric). Trim-tabs in elevators and rudders.

LANDING GEAR:

Retractable main wheels, fixed tail-wheel. Main wheels hydraulically retracted into inboard engine nacelles. Apertures closed when wheels raised by hinged doors connected to retracting gear.

POWER PLANT:

Four Rolls-Royce Merlin twelve-cylinder Vee liquid-cooled engines or four Bristol Hercules fourteen-cylinder radial air-cooled engines (see introductory notes). Welded steel-tube mountings cantilevered from front wing-spar. Three-blade de Havilland or Rotol constant-speed full-feathering propellers. Six protected fuel tanks in wings. Oil tank in each nacelle.

ACCOMMODATION:

Crew of seven. Bomb-aimer in nose below front gun-turret. Pilot above and behind to port, beneath raised canopy, with wide all-round view. Fighting controller's position immediately aft. Navigator's station aft of this, with table, chart stowage and astrodome in roof. Radio operator's station just forward of front spar, at rear of navigator's table. Rest room with bed within centre-section. Mid-upper and mid-lower turrets aft of rear spar, together with stowages for flares, emergency rations, etc. Walkway along entire length of fuselage. Entrance door on starboard side, just forward of tailplane. Radar navigation and bombing aids introduced as war progressed.

ARMAMENT:

Up to ten Browning 0·303 in machine-guns in four hydraulically operated Nash & Thompson turrets, one in nose, two amidships (ventral turret later deleted), one in extreme tail. Tail turret with four guns, others with two. Tail turret supplied along ammunition tracks from boxes in rear fuselage. Bomb compartment 33 ft long. Typical load 14,000 lb. Design provision made for 4,000 lb bombs. Later adaptations for 12,000 lb, 12,000 lb deep-penetration Tallboy and 22,000 lb Grand Slam. Armoured bulkhead across centre-section of fuselage arranged to open for passage through on either side of centre-line. Armour plating behind pilot's head, and seat armoured. Several other vulnerable parts also armoured. Bullet-proof glass in fighting controller's station. Full night-flying equipment, radio, flares, oxygen, de-icing equipment, etc. Dinghy carried in centre-section trailing edge, automatically released and inflated in emergency alighting in sea, but could also be operated by hand.

DIMENSIONS:

Wing span 102 *ft* 0 *in* (31·08 *m*)
Length overall 69 *ft* 6 *in* (21·18 *m*)
Height overall 20 *ft* 0 *in* (6·09 *m*)

WEIGHTS:

Weight empty 36,900 *lb* (16,737 *kg*)
Weight loaded 68,000 *lb* (30,844 *kg*)

PERFORMANCE:

Max speed 287 *mph* (462 *kmh*) at 11,500 *ft* (3,505 *m*)
Cruising speed 210 *mph* (338 *kmh*)
Time of climb to 20,000 (6,095 *m*) 41·6 *min*
Range with 14,000 *lb of bombs* 1,660 *miles* (2,670 *km*)
Service ceiling 24,500 *ft* (7,467 *m*)

Luminous in an otherwise drab setting are the fighting controller's position and two of the three gun turrets

DOBLHOFF WNF 342

Spinning test of early rotor

It is sometimes asserted that the Doblhoff helicopter of 1943 was the first to have a jet-propelled rotor, and though it will be shown that this is not strictly correct it was the first successful machine of the type. The initial full-scale experiments with a jet-driven rotor were made in 1915 by Papin and Rouilly. Their water-borne helicopter had a single hollow blade, counterweighted by a fan driven by an 80 hp Le Rhône engine and delivering air through the blade. The air was ejected from an L-shaped tube and there was a small auxiliary pipe for directional control. Tests were made on Lake Cercey, Côte d'Or, on 31 March 1915, but the pilot had to abandon the machine when it became unstable and it afterwards sank. Very much earlier—in 1842—W. H. Phillips caused a model helicopter to rise from the ground by the power of steam-jets emanating from the rotor blades.

The first WNF 342 had a Walter Mikron engine

Bombing caused the scene of experiments to be moved out of Vienna

The work of Friedrich L. Doblhoff with the Wiener Neustadter Flugzeugwerke dated from 1942. A piston engine was adapted to drive the supercharger rotor of an Argus engine, the air compressed being mixed with fuel before being delivered through hollow rotor blades to steel combustion chambers at the tips. The effectiveness of the system was demonstrated when the rotor became airborne with the attachment intended to anchor it to the light-alloy test rig, which was itself attached to an anvil. The first prototype Doblhoff helicopter, the WNF 342 V1, made its initial flight in the spring of 1943. A 60 hp Walter Mikron II engine was fitted and it was hoped that the helicopter might be developed to meet a German Navy requirement for a submarine-borne observation aircraft of this class. The first prototype was a single-seater with a loaded weight of 360 kg (795 lb). It was of welded steel-tube construction, and had a tricycle landing gear. Twin fins and rudders were fitted and the rotor had

Hovering test of the second prototype

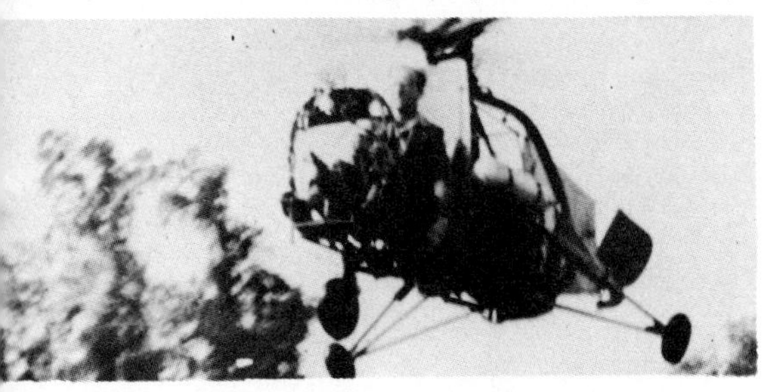

flapping and drag hinges. This historic first prototype, which was the first manned helicopter to take-off by means of a jet-driven rotor, proved to have insufficient side area but, apart from its very high fuel consumption, proved generally satisfactory. It was damaged during an air raid on Vienna and the scene of the experiments was moved to quieter surroundings. A second prototype was built in 1944 and was likewise a single-seater, though having a 90 hp engine and flying at a weight of 460 kg (1,015 lb). There was a large single fin and a very long rudder, pivoted horizontally. During 1945 a third prototype was constructed, having the same jet-propulsion system but also a propeller for use in horizontal flight. Thus the engine (a Siemens-Halske Sh.14 A of 150 hp) could either drive the air compressor for jet propulsion or drive the propeller, the rotor then free-wheeling in autorotation. This system was introduced in the recognition that fuel

consumption in the earlier machines was prohibitively high and that the tip drive was best employed for take-off, hovering and landing only. This third version—a cabin single-seater with twin tail-booms and twin fins and rudders—was destroyed by its own violent oscillations. Its flying weight was 548 kg (1,210 lb). Also during 1945 came a fourth prototype which had steel-strip leaf-springs connecting the rotor blades to the hub and a propeller as on the third machine. This version was a two-seater with twin booms and a single fin and rudder.

It had completed some 25 hours' flying when it was USA. Flying weight was 640 kg (1,410 lb).

Although these Doblhoff helicopters had no direct successors the abilities of Friedrich Doblhoff and his collaborators A. Stepan and Theodor Laufer found useful employment. Doblhoff himself joined the McDonnell organisation in the USA,

The second prototype flying in 1944

The third prototype flying in 1945

contributing to the development of the XV-1 convertiplane which had jets at the rotor-blade tips and was the first aircraft of its class to make a transition from vertical to horizontal flight (April 1955). Stepan joined the Fairey company in England and participated in work which led to the Fairey Rotodyne (page 138). Laufer went to SNCASO in France and made his own further contribution to helicopter progress.

The fourth of the prototypes was captured by American forces and shipped to the USA

MESSERSCHMITT Me 163 B

The Me 163 B was the world's first rocket-propelled fighter, but not the first rocket-propelled aeroplane. The right to the latter distinction was gained on 11 June 1928 by a tail-first glider propelled by rockets from the Wasserkuppe in western Germany. There was, however, a very real connection between the two aircraft, for directing the 1928 experiments with the glider was Professor Alexander Lippisch, and it was this same eminent aerodynamicist who was mainly responsible for the Me 163 B. Before the development of that aircraft is described it must be recorded that Fritz von Opel, who had been associated with the flight of 1928, constructed a special rocket-powered glider with which, on 30 September 1929, he made a flight of some ten minutes duration, attaining a speed of about 100 mph (160 kmh). This glider was launched from a rocket-propelled cradle.

The Me 163 had a predecessor in the DFS 194, built in 1938 as a flying test bed for rocket engines. This aircraft was designed by Prof. Lippisch and completed by the Messerschmitt works. It was flown in 1940 with a Walter HWK R.1 rocket unit and formed the basis for the Me 163 prototypes. The first of these made its initial flight under rocket power in August 1941 and results thereafter were sufficiently encouraging for the German Air Ministry to sponsor an operational interceptor version. The earliest Me 163s used a Walter rocket fuelled by hydrogen peroxide and water, with calcium permanganate as a catalyst, but better results were promised with a new type of rocket using hydrazine-hydrate and methanol. This was the power plant chosen for the Me 163 B, the designation Me 163 A having been reserved for a small number of trainer variants. Me 163 Bs were first in action in the summer of 1944. Although they achieved a measure of success as "target-defence" interceptors the nature of their fuels rendered them dangerous to their crews. Flight endurance under rocket power was eight minutes only, and pilots were obliged to protract their airborne time by periods of gliding. To mitigate this deficiency the HWK 509 C rocket unit was developed, this having an auxiliary "cruising chamber" which increased powered endurance to 12 minutes.

The following description relates to the production-type Me 163 B-1.

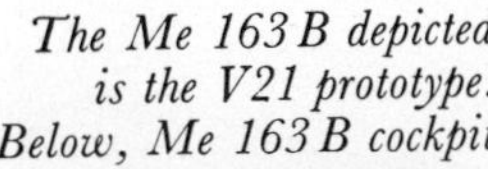

The Me 163 B depicted is the V21 prototype. Below, Me 163 B cockpit

TYPE:
Rocket-propelled interceptor fighter.

WINGS:
Mid-wing cantilever monoplane. Swept-back wings with marked wash-out of incidence towards tips. Wooden construction, with 8 mm plywood skin covered with doped fabric. Built-up main spar of laminated wood. Fixed "pillar-box" slot in leading-edge extending from about semi-span to tip sections. Lateral and longitudinal control by differentially operated "elevons" of composite construction in positions of normal ailerons. Large fabric-covered trimming surfaces inboard of elevons, operated by a screw-jack. Split flaps in undersurfaces of wings forward of trimming surfaces.

FUSELAGE:
Short all-metal semi-monocoque structure, mainly of approximately oval cross-section, built in two halves, the rear half, containing the rocket engine, being detachable.

TAIL UNIT:
No horizontal tail surfaces. Single fin-and-rudder assembly above fuselage with balanced rudder having an adjustable trim-tab.

LANDING GEAR:
Aircraft normally took-off under its own power on a jettisonable two-wheel chassis. Retractable landing skid extended during take-off and retracted when wheels dropped automatically. Castoring tail-wheel faired into lower portion of fin.

POWER PLANT:
One Walter HWK 109 A-2 bi-fuel liquid rocket engine of 3,750 lb (1,700 kg) static thrust in fuselage behind pilot. Unit just over 7 ft (2·13 m) long and supplied ready for mounting. Two main assemblies: forward assembly consisting of housing for turbine, two worm-type pumps for delivering fuel, central unit, pressure-reducing valve and electric starter-motor. Small cylindrical unit attached to forward housing for producing steam to drive the turbine by the action of a solid catalyst on the hydrogen-peroxide ("T-stoff"). Second assembly comprising the combustion-chamber unit. Fuels used were concentrated hydrogen-peroxide ("T-stoff") and a solution of hydrazine-hydrate in methanol ("C-stoff"). Tankage in fuselage for about 226 Imp gallons (980 litres) of "T-stoff" and in wings for about 110 Imp gallons (500 litres) of "C-stoff".

ACCOMMODATION:
Pilot's cockpit in line with leading-edges. Mechanically jettisonable hinged Plexiglass moulding forming cockpit cover. Main instrument panel hinged to give access to equipment in armoured nose-cone.

ARMAMENT:
Two 30 mm MK 108 guns, one in each wing root. Ammunition, 60 rounds per gun, in two boxes under detachable fairing in fuselage.

DIMENSIONS:
Wing span 30 *ft* 6 *in* (9·30 *m*)
Length overall 19 *ft* 5 *in* (5·90 *m*)

WEIGHTS:
Weight empty 4,200 *lb* (1,905 *kg*)
Weight loaded 9,500 *lb* (4,310 *kg*)

PERFORMANCE:
Max speed 596 *mph* (960 *kmh*) *at* 10,000 ft–30,000 *ft* (3,050 *m*–9,145 *m*)
Time of climb to 30,000 *ft* (9,145 *m*) 2·6 *min*
Service ceiling 39,500 *ft* (12,040 *m*)
Endurance under power 8 *min*

MESSERSCHMITT Me 323

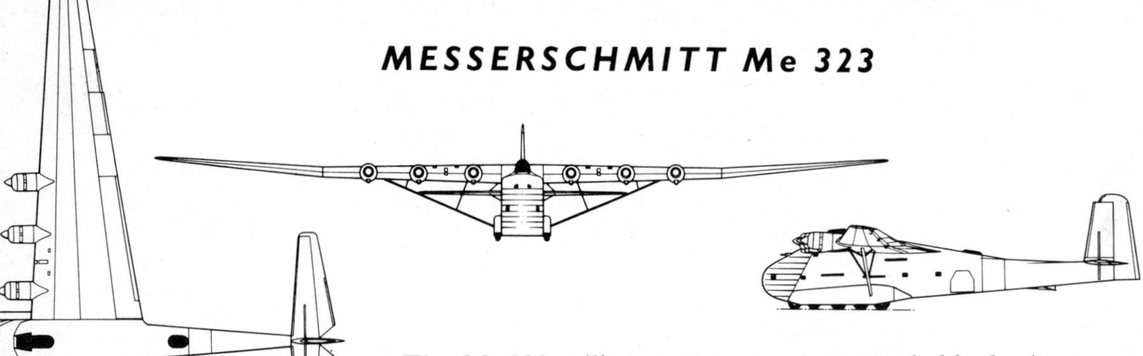

The Me 323 military transport was remarkable for its great size and capacity; for its introduction of features reproduced in later transport aeroplanes (nose-opening doors and multi-wheel fuselage-mounted landing gear); and not least for the fact that it was developed from a towed glider. The glider was designated Me 321 and was popularly known as the Gigant, a name which was perpetuated for the Me 323 powered development. The fact that the first series of Me 323s bore the series letter D is explained by the fact that the suffix letters A, B and C were allocated to variants of the Me 321.

Rapid handling of heavy and bulky loads governed Me 323 design features

The Me 321 could be towed by a single large aircraft or by a team of three Me 110 twin-engined heavy fighters, but the benefits to be derived from tractive power of its own were obvious and the Gnome-Rhône 14 N fourteen-cylinder two-row radial engine, which was in production in occupied France, was chosen as the power unit in order not to interfere with production of aero-engines in Germany. The complete power "eggs", of which there were six per aircraft, were the same as those designed for the Bloch 175 twin-engined military monoplane before the complete occupation of France in November 1942. After the abolition of the line of demarcation production of these complete power units was continued by S.N.C.A.S.O.

The following description applies in general to the Me 323 D.

TYPE:

Six-engined military transport.

WINGS:

High-wing semi-cantilever monoplane. Wide-span centre-section, supporting engines, braced by single strut on each side. Tapered in chord and thickness, upper surface flat. Taper continued on outer cantilever panels, but these set at dihedral angle. Structure comprising a single rectangular girder spar built up of four steel-tube members connected by N-braces, wooden ribs and plywood and fabric covering. Centre-section entirely plywood-covered, outer panels with plywood over leading-edge and back to spar, remainder fabric-covered. Entire trailing-edge hinged, outer portions acting as ailerons and inner portions as flaps. Flaps and ailerons carried on steel-tube outriggers projecting from spar. Ailerons each in two sections and having combined servo- and trim-tabs. Aileron movement assisted by electric servo-motor in each wing.

FUSELAGE:

Welded steel-tube structure of rectangular section with fabric covering over secondary wooden fairing structure. Floor in forward portion supported by cross girders.

TAIL UNIT:

Braced monoplane type. Wooden construction. Entire unit hinged to rear fuselage and moved hydraulically to change tail incidence over range $+2\frac{1}{2}$ to $-5°$.

LANDING GEAR:

Multi-wheel type comprising ten wheels and designed to overcome obstacles like a caterpillar track. Wheels in tandem alongside lower edges of fuselage and enclosed in elongated "paddle-box" fairings. Wheels attached to girders sprung by coil springs and so disposed that aircraft remained horizontal irrespective of load. When centre of gravity was correctly placed aircraft could be made to rock about rear pair of wheels. Six main wheels had pneumatic brakes.

POWER PLANT:

Six Gnome-Rhône 14 N 48/49 fourteen-cylinder radial air-cooled engines, each rated at 990 hp at 12,200 ft (3,720 m). Long-chord cowlings. Variable-pitch metal or fixed-pitch wooden propellers. Six self-sealing fuel tanks in wing. Occasionally additional tankage in back of freight compartment. Two engineers' positions, one in each wing-root leading-edge, each engineer controlling three engines. Provision under wings for four assisted take-off rockets, electrically fired by pilot.

ACCOMMODATION:

Crew comprising two pilots, two engineers and one radio operator. Side-by-side dual control in armoured pilots' compartment, forward of leading-edge and above main fuselage structure. Radio operator's cabin inside main spar on port side. Engineers' cabins as mentioned above. Main hold 36 ft (10·97 m) long, 10 ft 3 in (3·12 m) wide and 11 ft (3·35 m) high occupying full cross-section of fuselage. Access to hold through vertically-split nose forming two outwardly-hinging doors 11 ft (3·35 m) high. Loading ramps carried in aircraft. Additional door in each side of hold. Possible loads: one 88 mm anti-aircraft gun with full equipment, 8,700 loaves of bread, fifty-two 200 litre (44 Imp gallon) drums of fuel, 130 men, 60 stretcher cases.

ARMAMENT:

Normal scheme provided for five 13 mm MG 131 machine-guns but firepower could be augmented by troops carried.

DIMENSIONS:

Wing span 181*ft* 0 *in* (55·17 *m*)
Length overall 93 *ft* 4 *in* (28·45 *m*)
Wing area 3,229 *sq ft* (300 *m²*)

WEIGHTS:

Weight empty 61,750 *lb* (28,010 *kg*)
Weight loaded 99,210 *lb*) 45,000 *kg*)

PERFORMANCE:

Cruising speed at 5,000 *ft* (1,525 *m*) 129 *mph* (208 *kmh*)
Rate of climb at S/L 236 *ft/min* (73 *m/min*)

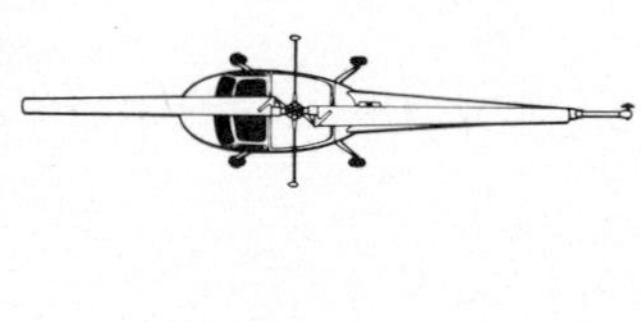

BELL MODEL 47

The 1947 edition of *Jane's All the World's Aircraft* contained the following historic entry: "The Bell Aircraft Corporation had an experimental helicopter (Model 30) flying in the middle of 1943 following two years of development work. The Model 30 was tested by the U.S. Army under the designation XR-12. This model was superseded late in 1945 by the first of the Model 47 series. On March 8, 1946, this helicopter received the first commercial licence (NC-1H) to be granted by the C.A.A., and on March 8, 1946, received Helicopter Type Certificate No. 1 from the C.A.A.

In 1946 the company began production of the Model 47 helicopter for commercial, industrial and government uses. Eighteen are on order for the US Army and ten for the Navy.

"A feature of this helicopter is the stabilizing system. The position of the rotor, which is mounted on the mast by a cardan universal joint, is governed by a stabilizing bar mounted just below the rotor hub and set at right angles to the two rotor blades. This stabilizing bar, which in the Model 47 is about 5 ft (1·52 m) long and weighted at the ends, is linked to the rotor in such a way that it tends to determine the plane of the rotor and maintain it generally horizontal irrespective of the angle of the mast. The rotor blades are not articulated but are rigidly connected to the hub, which is rocked about its longitudinal axis to control the rotor."

While initial success was in some degree assured by the historic certification already noted only technical merit of a very high order could ensure for the Model 47 the continuing production it enjoys today. Current versions are the 47G-3B-2 three-seater, with outstanding high-altitude performance over a wide range of temperatures; 47G-4A basic three-seat utility helicopter: 47G-5 low-cost model in which non-essential structures and components have been eliminated to reduce initial price and increase max useful load to 1,200 lb (544 kg); Ag-5 agricultural version of the last-named; OH-13S observation version for US Army; and TH-13T two-seat instrument training version.

The following description applies to the original production version of the Model 47:

TYPE:

Two-seat cabin helicopter.

ROTORS:

Two-blade main rotor and auxiliary two-blade controllable-pitch anti-torque propeller. Main rotor hub mounted on transmission mast by universal joint and provided with a stabilizing bar below and at right angles to the blades. Swash-plate revolving with the mast but free to move up and down providing cyclic pitch-control. Lower half of swash-plate which did not revolve altered pitch of the blades differentially for directional control. Main rotor drive through a centrifugal clutch and a two-stage planetary transmission with a 9:1 reduction ratio. Free-wheeling mechanism incorporated in transmission. Anti-torque propeller driven by a tubular shaft and controlled by cables and pulleys. Main rotor blades, of symmetrical aerofoil section, of laminated wood with a steel insert in leading edge for strength and mass-balance. Anti-torque propeller blades likewise of laminated wood.

FUSELAGE:

In two sections. Forward section was a welded tubular steel framework which provided for mounting the engine and supporting the metal and Plexiglass cabin. Rear section also a tubular structure, triangular in cross-section and serving as a support for the anti-torque rotor drive-shaft.

LANDING GEAR:

Four-wheel type. The two forward self-castoring wheels capable of swivelling through 360°, the two rear whels fixed.

POWER PLANT:

One vertically-mounted 175 hp Franklin 6ALV-335 six-cylinder horizontally-opposed air-cooled engine with clutch, drive shaft and rotor assembly in an integral unit in a steel tube framework with the engine supported in rubber mounts at the top and bottom and attached to the welded framework of the forward fuselage. Engine-mounting structure with three attachment points for the rear fuselage.

ACCOMMODATION:

Enclosed cabin seating two side-by-side. Dual flight controls, including cyclic and collective pitch controls and anti-torque pedals. Cyclic control tilted main rotor and regulated translational flight. Collective pitch control lever, at left of each seat, controlled absolute angle of main rotor blades and incorporated a grip-type throttle. Anti-torque pedals controlled pitch of anti-torque rotor and determined heading.

DIMENSIONS:

Diameter of main rotor 33 *ft* 7½ *in* (10·24 *m*)
Diameter of tail rotor 5 *ft* 5 *in* (1·65 *m*)

WEIGHTS:

Useful load 612 *lb* (278 *kg*)
Weight loaded (*max*) 2,100 *lb* (953 *kg*)

PERFORMANCE:

Cruising speed (75% *power*) 80 *mph* (129 *kmh*)
Service ceiling 9,700 *ft* (2,957 *m*)
Range (*with* 32 *US gallons* = 121 *litres*) *of fuel* 200 *miles* (322 *km*)

Military exterior, civil interior

FAIRCHILD PACKET

A requirement for specially designed, as distinct from adapted, military transport aircraft quickly became apparent during the Second World War and in 1941 work was begun on a Fairchild twin-engined high-wing monoplane then known as the XC-82. The prototype flew on 10 September 1944 and was in full quantity production at the war's end. Since that time the basic layout has been reproduced with success in the Armstrong Whitworth Argosy and Nord Noratlas. Late in 1947 a new and improved version of the C-82 was flown. Designated C-119 this had increased power and capacity and a relocated flight deck giving improved vision for formation flying and troop and supply dropping. The wings were strengthened to permit an increase in flying weight to 74,000 lb (33,570 kg) and the capacity of the freight hold was increased to 3,095 cu ft (87·60 m³).

Steward-Davis jet-augmented C-119

C-119 of the Royal Canadian Air Force delivering a snowmobile at Goose Bay, Labrador

The original versions of the Packet were:

C-82A. Two 2,100 hp Pratt & Whitney R-2800-85 engines. Production model of the XC-82. By the end of 1947 over 150 had been delivered to the USAF, practically all of which were assigned to Troop-Carrier Squadrons of the 9th Air Force.

C-119A. Prototype modified from standard C-82A to test the new nose configuration and new power-plant. Did not incorporate widened fuselage. First flew in November 1947.

C-119B. Two Pratt & Whitney R-4360-20 twenty-four cylinder radial engines with two-stage blowers, rated at 2,650 hp to 6,000 ft (1,830 m), 2,300 hp at 18,000 ft (5,480 m) and with 3,250 hp available for take-off. Production version of C-119A. 99 ordered, the first delivered in 1948.

The following description applies to the C-82A as originally taken into service:

TYPE:

Twin-engined military transport.

WINGS:

Cantilever high-wing monoplane. Two-spar structure in three main sections consisting of anhedral centre-section let into fuselage and carrying engine nacelles and tail-booms, and two outer wings. Detachable tips. Centre-section and outer wings each in three main sections comprising leading-edge, inter-spar section and trailing-edge. Two-spar all-metal structure. Metal ailerons on outer wings in two sections each side arranged to droop with flaps. Controllable trim-tab in inner section of port aileron. Electrically-operated NACA slotted trailing-edge flaps between ailerons and fuselage divided by tail-booms.

FUSELAGE:

All-metal semi-monocoque structure, in six main sections comprising main body, sides, upper front, upper rear, nose compartment, and rear cargo door compartments. Structure consists of Alclad vertical frames, longitudinal stringers and longitudinal and transverse beams, with smooth Alclad skin. Seven longitudinal beams taking floor and tie-down loads beneath a ply-covered floor. Rear compartment split on vertical centre-line, the halves hinging outwards to allow direct loading of freight.

Special doors were provided for paratroops

TAIL BOOMS:

All-metal structures of circular cross-section forward tapering to oval-section aft. Each in two main sections. Forward section of semi-monocoque construction with pressed light alloy channel-section frames, top-hat section longitudinal stringers and light-alloy skin. Forward section bolted to engine nacelle structure aft of trailing-edge. Aft section similarly constructed with heavy frames and bulkheads and stressed light alloy skin, and bolted to forward section at leading-edge of tailplane.

TAIL UNIT:

Cantilever monoplane type with twin fins and rudders extending above and slightly below tail-booms. All-metal structures. Tailplane and fins each with two light-alloy spars pressed chordwise ribs and stressed metal skin. One-piece metal-framed elevator and rudders each have single spar, metal nose and fabric covering over all. Controllable elevator trim-tab each side of centre-line and in each rudder.

LANDING GEAR:

Retractable tricycle type. Each main wheel carried between pair of oleo shock-absorber legs retracting into engine nacelles and enclosed by twin doors. Nose-wheel carried in, half-fork on oleo shock-absorber leg retracting into nose and enclosed by twin doors. Hydraulic operation, and emergency lowering gear. Hydraulic brakes on main wheels.

POWER PLANT:

Two Pratt & Whitney R-2800-85 eighteen-cylinder two-row radial air-cooled engines each rated at 1,700 hp. Tapered long-chord NACA cowlings with controllable trailing-edge gills. Steel-tube bearers in monocoque nacelles terminating in tail-booms. Hamilton Standard Hydromatic three-blade full-feathering propellers. Four fuel tanks in outer wings between spars.

ACCOMMODATION:

Flight deck with two seats side-by-side for pilot (on port) and co-pilot; navigator on centrally-placed seat facing to starboard with table behind co-pilot's seat, and radio-operator's position on port side aft of navigator. Auxiliary flight deck aft of main flight deck accommodating radio equipment. Access ladder on port side of main compartment with hatch leading to flight deck. Emergency escape hatch in roof. Forty-one folding canvas side-seats in troop transport version. Seats removable and entire space usable for freight transport. Floor reinforced to take heavy loads and provided with tie-down rings. For ambulance duties provision made for 34 litters and 4 attendants. Automatic monorail-system for rapid delivery of parachute supplies. Paracans suspended from electrically-operated trolleys running the length of the hold and dropped through doors in floor of fuselage. Rear cargo doors opened vertically on centre-line. Adjustable ramps permitting vehicles to be driven in, and freight to be loaded from bed of truck. Forward access door on port side.

DIMENSIONS:

Wing span 106 *ft* 5 *in* (32·44 *m*)
Length overall 77 *ft* 1 *in* (23·49 *m*)
Height overall 26 *ft* 4 *in* (8·03 *m*)

WEIGHTS:

Weight empty 32,500 *lb* (14,742 *kg*)
Weight loaded (normal) 50,000 *lb* (22,680 *kg*)
Max overloaded weight 54,000 *lb* (24,500 *kg*)

PERFORMANCE:

Max speed 248 *mph* (399 *kmh*) *at* 17,500 *ft* (5,310 *m*)
Cruising speed (75% *power*) 218 *mph* (351 *kmh*) *at* 10,000 *ft* (3,050 *m*)
Service ceiling 21,200 *ft* (6,450 *m*)

Dropping a 105 mm howitzer and jeep from a C-82 at Fort Bragg, North Carolina

DHC-2 BEAVER

A class of aircraft always identified with Canadian "bush" flying, which has, indeed, made significant contributions to the opening-up of important areas of the North American continent, is the robust, single-engined high-wing monoplane as represented in the 1930s by the Fairchild 71, with its Pratt & Whitney Wasp engine. The qualities of hardiness, tractability and adaptability of this class of aircraft have been perpetuated with particular success in the past twenty years by The de Havilland Aircraft of Canada in their DHC-2 Beaver.

The Beaver can operate with wheels, floats, skis, amphibious gear or combined wheel-ski gear

The excellence of the Beaver's field performance, especially in its latest Mark III Turbo-Beaver form, ranks it among the most successful STOL (short take-off and landing) utility aircraft ever built, although no elaborate high-lift devices are used to make this possible. It may be noted, as a point of historical interest, that although many early aeroplanes of ordinary work-a-day type could, by their very nature, be grouped within the STOL class, and although the Handley Page leading-edge slot came as a boon in the 1920s, in the context of slow flying and short take-off and landing it was the German Fieseler Fi 156 of 1936 which first demonstrated what could be achieved in these respects in an aircraft suitable for every-day use.

Although the Beaver was designed to meet the requirements of Canadian operators (the final layout being based on the results of a survey of some eighty "bush" operators from coast to coast), it was destined to achieve wide international acceptance. The prototype flew for the first time on 16 August 1947, only ten months after the design was begun. The total of Mark I production aircraft delivered was 1,657, of which 968 were supplied to the US Armed Forces. A single Beaver Mark II was built with a 570 hp Alvis Leonides piston engine and the Mark III Turbo-Beaver has a Pratt & Whitney (VAC) PT6A turboprop engine.

The following description relates to the Beaver as first produced.

TYPE:

Single-engined utility transport.

WINGS:

High-wing braced monoplane. High-lift wing section. All-metal structure of constant chord and thickness. Single bracing struts on each side. Entire trailing-edge hinged. Slotted ailerons and flaps interconnected so that when flaps are lowered to maximum angle of 40° the ailerons droop progressively to about 15° while retaining full lateral control. Hydraulic flap operation.

FUSELAGE:

Rectangular all-metal structure, the forward section to back of cabin a tubular structure with removable metal panels and the rear fuselage a stressed-skin monocoque.

TAIL UNIT:

Cantilever monoplane type. All-metal structure, including covering.

LANDING GEAR:

Interchangeable floats, wheels and skis. Oleo-sprung cantilever single-leg wheel gear with steerable tail-wheel. Twin Edo Model 4580 all-metal floats. Float base (C/L of floats) 9 ft 6¾ in (2·92 m).

POWER PLANT:

One 450 hp Pratt & Whitney R-985 Wasp Junior nine-cylinder radial air-cooled engine driving a two-blade Hamilton Standard controllable-pitch propeller 8 ft 6 in (2·59 m) diameter. Fuel tanks (3) in fuselage suspended from floor structure and easily removable for servicing. Tank fillers in fuselage sides to permit refuelling from ground or floats. Maximum fuel capacity 80 Imp gallons (363 litres). Oil tank and cooler in engine compartment. Worth oil-dilution system. Hand and electric-starters. Remote-control fire-extinguishing system in engine compartment.

ACCOMMODATION:

Pilot's compartment with pilot on port side and removable seat on starboard. Dual rudder pedals and Y-type control column with throw-over wheel. Entrance door with automobile-type sliding windows on each side. Cabin may seat six passengers. Cabin heating by combustion-heater. Floor stressed for freight-carrying and lightweight collapsible bush-seats are interchangeable with cargo attachments. Two side doors, one on each side, wide enough to roll a 45-gallon petrol drum into cabin on its side. Hatches in rear wall of cabin to enable long pieces of freight, such as 10 ft drilling-rods, to be loaded and stowed. Adequate baggage space at back of cabin, with separate locker aft for emergency rations, etc. Total cabin capacity 144 cu ft (4·03 m³). Capacity available for freight payload 120 cu ft (3·35 m³).

EQUIPMENT:

24V electrical system charged by engine-driven 1,500-watt generator. Batteries in rear fuselage on removable tray accessible through fuselage side. Provision for navigation lights, instrument lighting, anchor riding light and cabin lights. Fittings on floats chassis for 16 ft canoe. Extra equipment to operators specifications include radio and built-in engine pre-heater.

DIMENSIONS:

Wing span 48 *ft* 0 *in* (14·63 *m*)
Length overall (*landplane*) 30 *ft* 3 *in* (9·22 *m*)
Length overall (*seaplane*) 32 *ft* 9 *in* (9·98 *m*)

WEIGHTS (landplane):

Weight empty 2,784 *lb* (1,262 *kg*)
Weight loaded 4,500 *lb* (2,041 *kg*)

WEIGHTS (seaplane):

Weight empty 3,029 *lb* (1,374 *kg*)
Weight loaded 4,750 *lb* (2,155 *kg*)

PERFORMANCE (landplane):

Max speed 179 *mph* (288 *kmh*)
Cruising speed at 5,000 *ft* (1,524 *m*) 146 *mph* (235 *kmh*)
Initial rate of climb 1,310 *ft/min* (396 *m/min*)

PERFORMANCE (seaplane):

Max speed 155 *mph* (249 *kmh*)
Cruising speed at 5,000 *ft* (1,524 *m*) 137·5 *mph* (221 *kmh*)
Initial rate of climb 1,200 *ft/min* (336 *m/min*)

BELL X-1

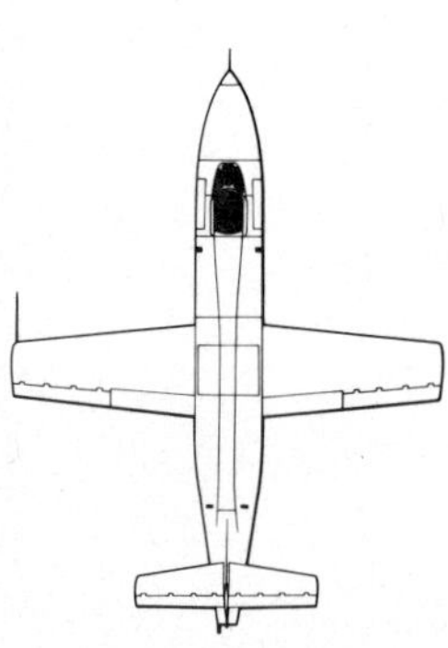

The X-1A had a raised cockpit. A Mach number of 2.42 was attained

Larry Bell greets Major Yeager after his 1,650 mph flight

The first manned aircraft to exceed the speed of sound (Mach 1) in level flight was America's Bell X-1 rocket-propelled research aircraft. The date was 14 October 1947, the Mach number 1·06 and the pilot Captain Charles E. Yeager, United States Air Force. This aircraft, the first of three of the type, was built in 1945 and is now in the National Air and Space Museum of the Smithsonian Institution. Construction was sponsored by the National Advisory Committee for Aeronautics (later National Aeronautics and Space Administration) and by the US Army Air Corps, its purpose being research into high-speed aerodynamics. It was the first rocket-propelled aircraft in the world designed for this purpose, the German DFS 194 of 1938, already mentioned, having been a flying test-bed for rocket engines. One claim sometimes advanced on the X-1's behalf—that it was America's first rocket-propelled aircraft—cannot, however, be admitted, for that distinction belongs to the Northrop MX-324 which, on 5 July 1944 was towed into the air by a Lockheed Lightning and having been cast off at 10,000 ft (3,050 m) made a four-minute rocket-powered flight. The Northrop aircraft had an additional distinction in that the pilot lay prone, as on the Wright *Flyer*.

The cockpit enclosure of the X-1 was flush with the upper surface of the fuselage

The X-1 was initially launched from a Boeing B-29 Superfortress but later took-off under its own power

During 1946 the X-1 was carried to altitude by a Boeing B-29 Superfortress and allowed to glide to earth. After one such drop, on 9 December 1946, the aircraft first flew under its own power. The first take-off under power was on 5 January 1949. The take-off run was 2,300 ft (700 m) and the time to climb to 23,000 ft (7,015 m) was 1 min 40 sec.

The third X-1 had the turbine-pump fuel system for which the type had originally been intended, and construction was authorised of four additional aircraft of the same general type (X-1 A, B, C and D). The third of these was never built, but the second machine of the original batch of three was redesigned by the NACA as the X-1E. This variant had af thinner wing, revised cockpit and the fuel system of the third example.

On 12 December 1953, the X-1A attained a speed of 1,650 mph (2,655 kmh) at 70,000 ft (21,335 m) and in the following year reached a height of 94,000 ft (28,650 m). The third X-1 was destroyed by an explosion in 1951 before its first powered flight. Both the X-1A and the X-1D were destroyed by fire.

TYPE:

Single-seat rocket-propelled monoplane for supersonic research.

WINGS:

Cantilever mid-wing monoplane. Thickness/chord ratio 10%. Aspect ratio 6. Aluminium-alloy structure with straight taper and square tips. Trailing-edge flaps between ailerons and fuselage.

FUSELAGE:

All-metal structure of oval cross-section.

TAIL UNIT:

Cantilever monoplane type with tailplane mounted on fin. Dorsal fin extending forward to cockpit. Tailplane incidence adjustable in flight. Balanced rudder and elevators. Trim-tab in rudder.

LANDING GEAR:

Retractable tricycle type. Main wheels carried on shock-absorber legs, retractable into fuselage and enclosed by hinged doors. Nose-wheel retractable into fuselage. Compressed-air springing and retraction.

POWER PLANT:

Reaction Motors E6000-C4 rocket unit, consisting of four cylinders burning alcohol and liquid oxygen, with a total static thrust of 6,000 lb (2,722 kg). Power output controlled by selection of the number of cylinders to be fired at any one time, giving a thrust of 1,500, 3,000, 4,500 or 6,000 lb (720, 1,361, 2,081 or 2,722 kg) at will. Rocket outlet in extreme tail of fuselage, under rudder. Aircraft originally designed to be powered with a rocket unit wherein fuel would be forced into the burners by a turbine pump, but as this had not been fully developed a pressurised system was employed. In this system nitrogen under pressure forced the fuels into the burner but as compared with the turbine-pump system it reduced fuel endurance from 4 to 2½ min at full power. Third aircraft had low-pressure propellant system using a hydrogen peroxide steam-turbine-driven pump.

ACCOMMODATION:

Enclosed pressurised cabin in nose for pilot. Access door on starboard side ahead of wing.

DIMENSIONS:

Wing span 28 *ft* 0 *in* (8·54 *m*)
Length overall 31 *ft* 0 *in* (9·45 *m*)
Length overall (*X-1C*) 36 *ft* 0 *in* (10·97 *m*)

WEIGHTS AND LOADING:

Fuel weight (*first two aircraft*) 8,177 *lb* (3,709 *kg*)
Weight loaded (*first two aircraft*) 13,400 *lb* (6,078 *kg*)
Weight loaded (*third aircraft*) 15,000 *lb* (6,804 *kg*)
Weight loaded (*X-1C*) 17,000 *lb* (7,710 *kg*)
Landing weight (*first two aircraft*) 5,200 *lb* (2,359 *kg*)

PERFORMANCE:

See introductory notes.

The larger 0.21 had an unusual landing gear

LEDUC 0.10

The greatest contributions toward the development of the ramjet type of powerplant for aircraft and missile propulsion were made in France and Germany. This powerplant may be described as a tube in which fuel is continuously burnt with air rammed in at the front by forward speed. A variant is the pulsejet, as used in the German FZG-76 (V-1) flying bomb, a piloted version of which was flown.

First air-launched powered flight of the 0.10 was from a Languedoc on 21 April 1949

The name first associated with the ramjet is that of René Lorin who in 1906 proposed an impracticable scheme for reaction propulsion and later propounded his ideas for a catapult-launched radio-directed flying bomb powered by a ramjet—a remarkable prevision of the German weapon already mentioned. In 1935 Lorin's fellow-countryman René Leduc was successful in producing a small ramjet unit which developed a thrust of 4 kg (8·82 lb) at 300 m (985 ft/sec). His first complete ramjet-driven aircraft was the 0.10 monoplane, powered by a Leduc unit developing a thrust of about 2,250 kg (4,960 lb) at 900 kmh (560 mph) at sea level. The 0.10 was first released as a glider from the top of a four-engined Languedoc monoplane in October 1947. On 21 April 1949 the aircraft was released from a Languedoc at 3,050 m (10,000 ft) over Toulouse, proceeding to fly for twelve minutes and reaching a speed of 680 kmh (423 mph) on only half power. In a later flight, likewise on half power, a speed of over 800 kmh (500 mph) was attained at a height of 11,000 m (36,090 ft), at which height the climbing speed was 2,440 m/min (8,000 ft/min).

Three prototypes were built. The first two were identical, but the third, the 0.11, which was air-launched for the first time on 8 February 1951, was originally intended to be fitted with two Turboméca Piméné turbojet engines, one at each wing-tip. These were, in fact, at one time fitted, but were later removed. Their purpose was to serve as stand-by units for use in the air or for landing. During early tests much difficulty was encountered owing to misting of the pilot's windows. A larger version, the 0.21, was completed in the spring of 1953. It was first air-launched on 16 May 1953. Development of the 0.22 supersonic interceptor was abandoned when official support was withdrawn at a period of financial stringency in 1957. The first machine of this type, which had swept wings, was initially tested on 26 December 1956 and by March 1957 had made more than thirty flights on the power of a SNECMA Atar turbojet engine.

The following description relates to the Leduc 0.10.

The penalties imposed on airframe design by the large diameter of the thermo-propulsive duct may be judged from the exit diameter apparent

TYPE:
Two-seat experimental ramjet monoplane.

WINGS:
Cantilever mid-wing monoplane. All-metal structure. Central sealed two-spar box girder serving as integral fuel tank, passing through fuselage. Detachable leading-edge forward and slotted flaps and ailerons aft of box.

FUSELAGE:
Tubular open-ended fuselage duct was a double-skinned light-alloy structure. Suspended in the forward end by cross wires was the pilot's compartment.

TAIL UNIT:
Cantilever monoplane type. Light-alloy structure. Fin and halves of tailplane attached to fuselage duct by external fittings.

LANDING GEAR:
Retractable tail-wheel type. Wheels stowed in under-wing fillets and when lowered turned through 45°. Manual operation.

POWER PLANT:
Leduc thermo-propulsive fuselage duct (ramjet). Air entered annular opening surrounding pilot's cockpit, passed to centre of fuselage where it entered a series of five internal cylindrical ducts of increasing size, the leading-edge of each duct being ringed with fuel injectors. Total of 500 burners. The resultant mixture was ejected from the rear end of the fuselage as a high-velocity jet. Fuel feed by electrically-driven pump. Fuel (1,135 litres = 250 Imp gallons) carried in wing.

ACCOMMODATION:
Sealed compartment in front end of fuselage duct seating two in tandem. Perspex nose cone forward vision and corresponding circular windows in compartment and outer duct, two on each side, providing lateral vision. Two doors giving access to seats. Air-conditioning and heating. Pilot's cockpit and forward portion of fuselage duct could be detached in emergency and lowered by parachute stowed above wing in after portion of compartment, which also enclosed small Leduc auxiliary gas-turbine for driving generator.

DIMENSIONS:
Wing span 34 *ft* 6 *in* (10·52 *m*)
Length overall 33 *ft* 7 *in*

WEIGHT:
Weight loaded 6,173 *lb* (2,800 *kg*)

The one heavy and two medium-calibre guns were so located that their barrels were largely external under the nose

MiG-15

The first combat between manned jet-propelled aircraft occurred over Korea in 1951, the aircraft engaged being a Soviet-designed MiG-15 and an American Lockheed F-80 Shooting Star. It quickly became apparent thereafter that the F-80 was utterly outclassed and the MiG presented itself as an embarrassment which paralleled that experienced when the Mitsubishi Type O was first encountered in the earlier eastern war. The high performance of the Soviet fighter was attributable to excellence of design, utilising German aerodynamics (swept-back wings) and a basically British (Rolls-Royce) centrifugal-flow turbojet engine. The merit of the design is further exemplified by the estimate that production totalled over 15,000, thus ranking this aircraft as the most widely produced jet fighter in the world.

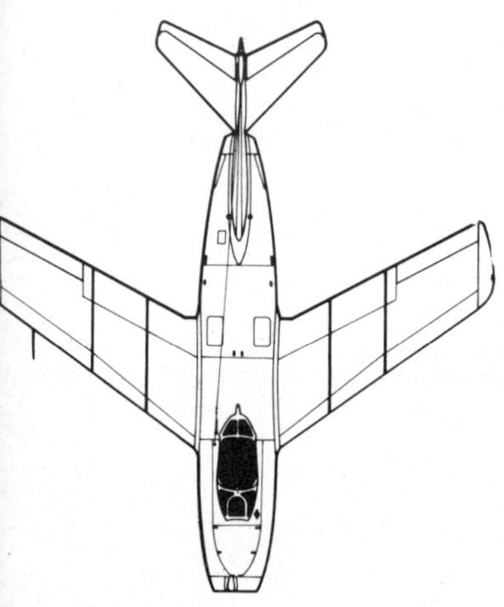

The first MiG-15 was initially tested in 1947 and production began in 1948. The type's American counterpart was the North American F-86 Sabre over which it demonstrated points of superiority, notwithstanding the all-round excellence of the American fighter. Rate of climb and acceleration were both in favour of the MiG whereas the F-86 was stronger, faster in the dive, more tractable in manoeuvre and benefited from its radar gun-laying equipment. Variants of the original MiG-15 design were the MiG-15 *bis*, with Klimov VK-1 turbojet engine of higher thrust and other refinements, and the MiG-15 UTI two-seat trainer. The basic design features were retained in the MiG-17, production of which began in 1953.

TYPE:
Single-seat fighter.

WINGS:
Mid-wing cantilever monoplane. Sweepback at leading-edge 42°. Dihedral −3°. Thickness/chord ratio 11% constant. All-metal light-alloy stressed-skin structure with two main I-section spars. Hydraulically-operated Fowler split flaps. Ailerons with both mass and sealed aerodynamic balances. Two fences on each wing.

FUSELAGE:
Semi-monocoque light alloy stressed-skin structure. In two main units, a forward assembly of nose and mid sections, and a rear section, joined by quick-release bolts at the rear wing spar attachment points, the rear fuselage being easily detachable for engine servicing. Air-brakes on rear fuselage.

TAIL UNIT:
Cantilever monoplane type with high-mounted tailplane. Sweepback on fin and tailplane leading-edges 42°. Tailplane incidence adjustable on ground only. Elevators and rudders of stressed light-alloy construction. Electrically-operated trim-tab in port elevator. Both upper and lower rudders mass-balanced.

LANDING GEAR:
Retractable tricycle type. Air-oil shock absorbers. Main wheels, with levered suspension, raised inward, nose wheel forward. Hydraulic retraction, with emergency pneumatic system. Hydraulic brakes.

POWER PLANT:
One RD-45 centrifugal-flow turbojet engine (2,740 kg = 6,040 lb st). Bifurcated nose air-inlet. Fuel tanks in mid fuselage section between divided air intake ducts. Total internal fuel capacity 1,250 litres (330 US gallons). Drop-tanks 600 litres (160 US gallons) each optional, one under each wing.

ACCOMMODATION:
Pressurised cockpit forward of wing leading-edge with sliding canopy. Oxygen system for emergency use. Ejection seat not fitted in earliest machines but later standardised.

ARMAMENT:
Two NS (Nudelmann-Suranov) 23 mm guns below side of nose and one 37 mm N (Nudelmann) gun below starboard. Guns mounted in cradle or "pack" which could be lowered for easy maintenance on the removal of a panel. Gyro gun-sight. Attachments for rocket projectiles or bombs beneath wings. Some aircraft of the type had a vertical camera aft of gun pack.

DIMENSIONS:
Wing span 33 *ft* 1½ *in* (10·10 *m*)
Length overall 36 *ft* 5 *in* (11·10 *m*)
Height overall 11 *ft* 2 *in* (3·40 *m*)

WEIGHTS:
Weight empty 8,333 *lb* (3,780 *kg*)
Weight loaded (combat) 11,288 *lb* (5,120 *kg*)
Max loaded weight (with external fuel or bombs) 14,350 *lb* (6,465 *kg*)

PERFORMANCE:
Max speed approx 666 *mph* (1,072 *kmh*)
Stalling speed 109 *mph* (175 *kmh*)
Initial rate of climb 10,400 *ft/min* (3,170 *m/min*)
Service ceiling 51,000 *ft* (15,550 *m*)

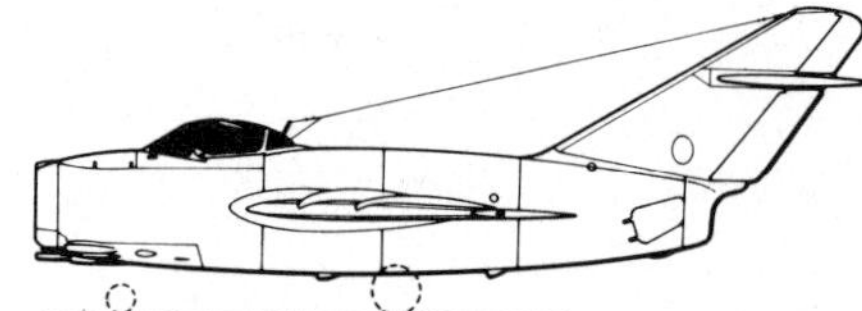

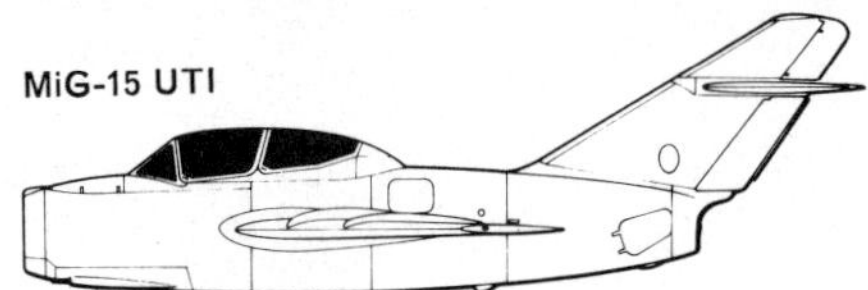

MiG-15 UTI

The MiG-17, as seen in Indonesia retained basic MiG-15 features

Basic design features of the MiG-15 were retained in the MiG-17, production of which began in 1953

Early Viscount V.700

Viscount V.816, proclaiming manufacturer and operator

Typifying turboprop travel for world airlines: Viscounts for VASP (Brazil)

VICKERS VISCOUNT

The original Viscount prototype was the world's first turboprop airliner. Bearing the company designation V.630 it was initially flown on 16 July 1948. As first conceived in 1945 the design provided for only 24 passengers, but when the intended Rolls-Royce Dart turboprop engine reached practical form it was found capable of yielding 1,000 shp instead of 800 shp and it was decided to build the V.630 as a 32-passenger aircraft. The second prototype (V.663) was powered by two turbojet engines, having been diverted as a development aircraft for the Rolls-Royce Tay, but the third prototype (V.700), which flew on 19 April 1950, had four Rolls-Royce Dart R.Da.3 turboprop engines. The airframe had by this time been "stretched" to accomodate 40–48 passengers. The fuselage was lengthened by 6 ft 8 in (2·03 m) and the wing span was increased by 5 ft (1·52 m). The first production Viscount, a 53-seat V.701 for BEA, was flown on 20 August 1952. The world's first passenger services operated by turboprop aircraft were inaugurated by the first of twenty-six Viscounts of this type on 18 April 1953. In the V.700D variant the airframe remained unaltered but the engines were of the Dart R.Da.6 (510) type, of 1,670 ehp. The V.770D was the North American version with US equipment and alterations to meet CAA requirements. Of the Viscount 700 Series a total of 287 aircraft was produced, marking a signal success for this new form of air travel.

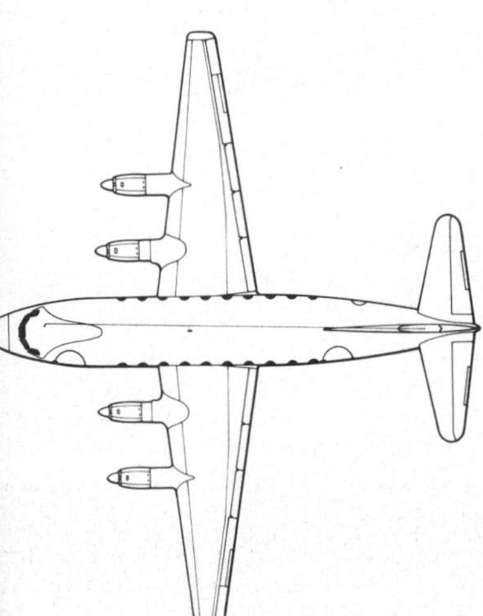

On 27 July 1956 a new version of the Viscount was first flown. This was the first of the 800 Series (actually a V.802 for BEA). In the new Series the fuselage length was increased by 3 ft 10 in (1·17 m). Provision was made for mounting the forward bulkhead and pantry on rails, enabling the cabin capacity to be adjusted between passengers and freight. In the still later 810 Series Dart 525 engines were installed and structural modifications were made to permit operation at increased weights and speeds. First-class accommodation was for 52 passengers. Alternative arrangements were for up to 65 tourist-class or 70 coach-class passengers. The higher power of the new Dart engines (1,990 ehp each) allowed an economical cruising speed of 352 mph (566 kmh) at 18,000 ft (5,485 m). Of the 800 Series 67 aircraft were built and of the 810 Series, 84.

The following description applies in general to the 700 Series, this being the form in which the Viscount introduced turboprop travel to the world.

TYPE:

Four-engined airliner.

WINGS:

Low-wing cantilever monoplane. Aerofoil section NACA 63 modified. Aspect ratio 9·17. All-metal structure with stressed Alclad skin. Double-slotted flaps between Irving-type ailerons and fuselage. Thermal de-icing. Gross wing area 963 sq ft (89·30 m).

FUSELAGE

All-metal stressed-skin structure. Entire fuselage except nose-wheel retraction bay and extreme rear pressurised.

TAIL UNIT:

Cantilever monoplane structure. All-metal construction. Single fin and rudder and 15° dihedral on tailplane. Spring tabs in all control surfaces. Thermal de-icing.

LANDING GEAR:

Retractable tricycle type, hydraulically operated. All units with single Vickers shock-absorbers supporting twin wheels. Dunlop or Goodyear wheels and brakes.

The first Viscount of all: the V.630 flying temporarily in British Service markings

POWER PLANT:

Four Rolls-Royce Dart 504 turboprop engines, each driving a four-blade Rotol fully-feathering propeller of 10 ft (3·05 m) diameter. Max output per engine 1,400 shp plus 365 lb (165 kg) of jet thrust. Total fuel capacity 1,720 Imp gallons (7,820 litres) in bag-type tanks forward and aft of main wing spar. Water-methanol system for boosted take-off. Total water capacity 75 Imp gallons (341 litres).

ACCOMMODATION:

Normal seating for 40 passengers, but up to 62 in high-density version. Deep oval windows. Normal crew of three or four, comprising two pilots and one or two stewards. Separate crew station for radio-operator/navigator optional. When not carried, radio and radar operated from second pilot's seat by remote control. Pantry forward of main cabin, toilet compartment at rear. Three large freight and luggage compartments, one forward of main cabin, one aft with separate door on starboard side, one below floor level forward, with two access doors. Combined pressurisation, air-conditioning and temperature control, giving ground-level conditions up to 15,000 ft (4,575 m) and 8,000 ft (2,440 m) conditions at 30,000 ft (9,150 m). Air-conditioning system operative on ground without running engines.

DIMENSIONS:

Wing span 94 *ft* 0 *in* (28·65 *m*)
Length overall 81 *ft* 2 *in* (24·74 *m*)
Height overall 26 *ft* 9 *in* (8·15 *m*)

WEIGHTS (3-crew, 40-passenger layout):

Weight empty (equipped) 33,115 *lb* (15,020 *kg*)
Max payload 13,589 *lb* (6,164 *kg*)
Max loaded weight 58,500 *lb* (26,535 *kg*)
Max landing weight 52,000 *lb* (23,587 *kg*)

PERFORMANCE:

Normal operational cruising speed at 20,000 *ft* (6,095 *m*) *at* 50,000 *lb* (22,680 *kg*) 321 *mph* (514 *kmh*)
Rate of climb at 58,500 *lb* (26,535 *kg*), *ICAN conditions flaps up, on four engines*, 930 *ft/min* (284 *m/min*) *at S/L and* 370 *ft/min* (113 *m/min*) *at* 15,000 *ft* (4,575 *m*)
Service ceiling at 52,000 *lb* (23,587 *kg*) 26,700 *ft* (8,145 *m*)
Take-off distance to 50 *ft* (15·2 *m*) *at* 58,500 *lb* (26,535 *kg*), *ICAN sea level conditions, four engines*, 4,560 *ft* (1,387 *m*)
Landing distance from 50 *ft* (15·24 *m*) *at* 52,000 *lb* (23,587 *kg*), *ICAN conditions*, 2,658 *ft* (805 *m*)

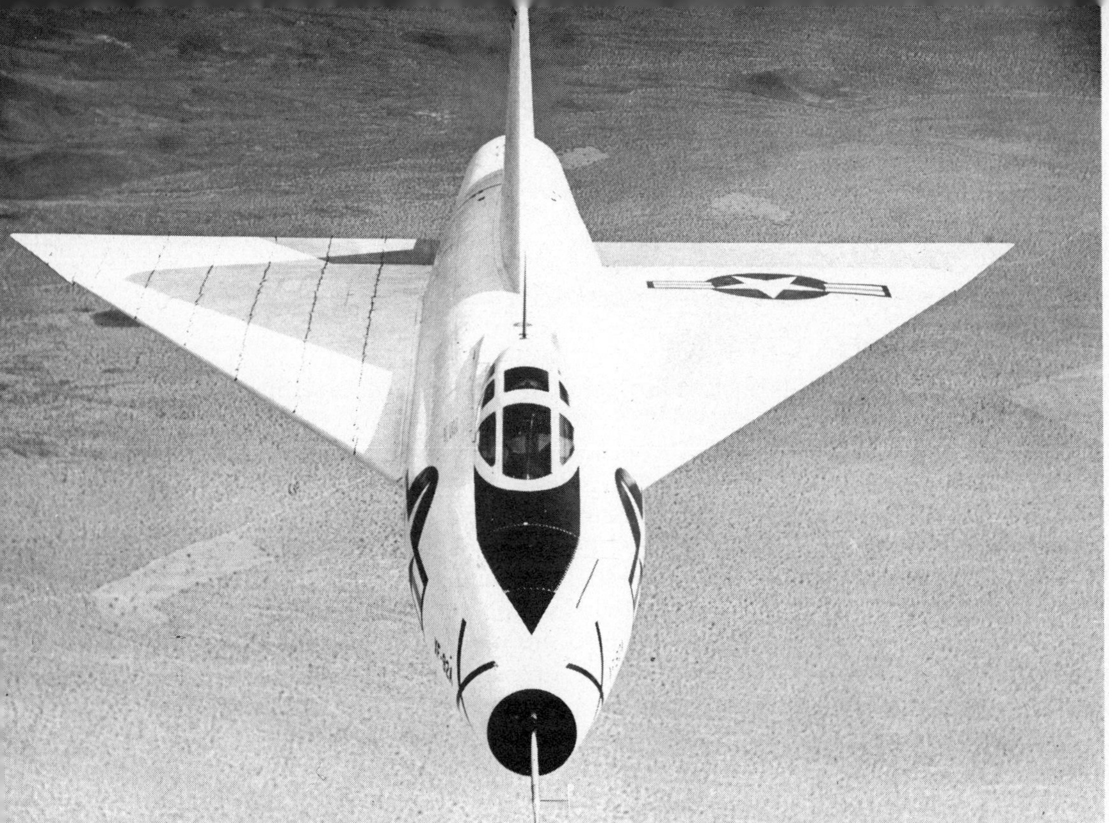

Wool tufts on the starboard wing of the XF-92A were photographed by a camera in the tail fin

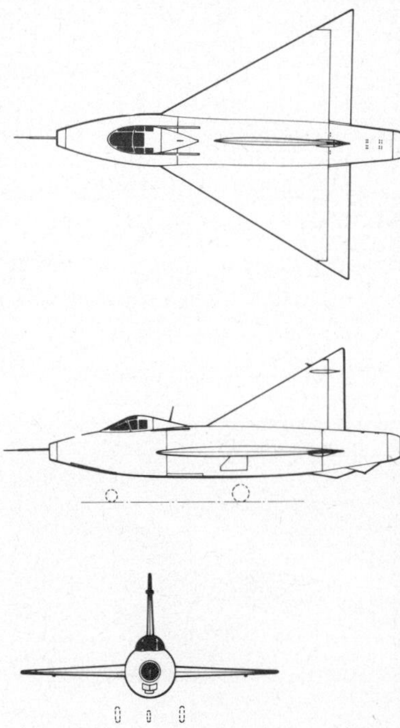

CONVAIR XF-92 A

There are significant links between the aircraft now under review and two earlier, contrasting, and yet related types already described. These types are the Dunne D.5 and Messerschmitt Me 163 B. The essential feature of the D.5 was that it had wings of Vee plan-form and achieved stability without the aid of a tail unit. This same formula was revived in the 1920s by the *Pterodactyls* of the British Professer G. T. R. Hill, and research along similar lines in Germany was associated with Lippisch and Koehl. The name of Alexander Lippisch has already been linked with the tailless rocket-propelled Me 163 B, but in modern aerodynamics this same man is more particularly associated with the "delta" wing, one, that is, having a triangular plan-form. This wing form has sometimes, and quite correctly, been likened to the schoolboy's paper dart, and the name "dart" has, in fact, been perpetuated in the modern aeronautical world by the Convair F-102 Delta Dart interceptor fighter.

North American XB-70

Avro Vulcan

This machine is closely related to the General Dynamics Hustler bomber later described and was a derivative of an earlier delta-wing interceptor, the F-102 Delta Dagger. This in turn was based on the design of the Convair XF-92 A research aircraft. Before the XF-92 A is described the origins of the Lippisch delta-wing formula must be traced.

The first Lippisch aircraft having a wing of this form was initially flown in 1931. It had a 32 hp Bristol Cherub engine and wing-tip fins and rudders. Other experimental deltas were built, but it was not until the advent of jet propulsion that the triangular wing form, with its great strength and low thickness-chord ratio, came into its own. The first jet-propelled delta-wing aircraft was the American Convair XF-92 A, described below.

The XF-92 A was originally known as the Convair Model 7002 and was built as a flying mock-up of the projected "mixed-power" XF-92 fighter. The contract for the XF-92 was cancelled, and the Model 7002 was thereupon designated XF-92 A. Its first flight was on 18 September 1948. This historic aeroplane was designed in collaboration with Dr. Lippisch and was a precursor not only of the American deltas already mentioned, and of the very large North American XB-70 of 1964, but of the Avro Vulcan which, first flown in 1952, remains in service with the RAF. Much basic research work on the delta wing-form was undertaken by the Avro company (now Hawker Siddeley).

The aerodynamic significance of the XF-92 A and its Convair successors extends beyond the delta wing-form. Mention has already been made of the F-102 Delta Dagger. This was intended to attain supersonic speed, but test flights showed that this predicted performance could not be achieved. It was at this stage that Mr. James Whitcomb came forward with his "area rule" for "waisting" the fuselage (the so-called "Coke-bottle" formula) to permit an airflow reconcilable with supersonic speed. Redesign took 117 working days and Mach 1 was first exceeded by the YF-102 A on 21 December 1954.

The following particulars relate to the XF-92 A. Data are approximate.

TYPE:

Single-seat delta-wing research aircraft.

WINGS:

Mid-wing cantilever monoplane. All-metal structure of triangular plan-form. Sweepback on leading-edge 60°. Straight trailing-edge, pointed tips. Sharp taper in thickness. "Elevons", serving both as elevators and ailerons, on trailing-edge and tip sections.

FUSELAGE:

All-metal semi-monocoque structure of almost symmetrical form. Nose air-intake for turbojet engine. Door-type air brakes on sides beneath wings.

TAIL UNIT:

No horizontal surfaces. Very large vertical surfaces resembling wings in shape but with rounded tip to balanced rudder carried at trailing-edge. Small under-fin.

LANDING GEAR:

Retractable tricycle type with nose-wheel retracting forwards into fuselage and main wheels outwards into wings. Tail bumper, necessitated by very steep take-off and landing attitude.

POWER PLANT:

One Allison J-33-A-29 centrifugal-flow turbojet with water injection. "Straight-through" duct installation.

DIMENSIONS:

Wing span 31 *ft* 0 *in* (9·45 *m*)
Length overall 41 *ft* 0 *in* (12·49 *m*)
Height overall 18 *ft* 0 *in* (5·49 *m*)

WEIGHT:

Designed loaded weight 15,000 *lb* (6,800 *kg*)

PERFORMANCE:

The XF-92 A was not capable of supersonic speed.

The original Comet had four de Havilland Ghost turbojet engines and two main wheels. When a four-wheel bogie landing gear was adopted, outward retraction was retained

BOAC were the first Comet operators

DE HAVILLAND COMET

The Comet was the world's first jet airliner. The general layout was finished in 1947 and the first flight took place on 27 July 1949. Remarkable performances were quickly achieved. On 25 October 1949 the aircraft flew from England to Castel Benito, Libya, at an average speed of 440 mph (708 kmh) for the 1,491 miles (2,400 km). The return flight was made the same day at a speed of 457 mph (735 kmh). A flight from London to Rome and back on 16 March 1950 occupied a total of 4 hr 7 min flying time—the outward flight, at 448 mph (721 kmh) over 911 miles (1,466 km) was made with 17 passengers and a crew of five, and considerably exceeded the current FAI point-to-point record between the two capitals. During a flight to Africa for tropical trials the Comet, on 24 April 1950, flew non-stop from Hatfield, north of London, to Cairo Airport, a distance of 2,168 miles (3,490 km) in just under 5 hr 9 min. This flight likewise constituted an FAI inter-city record. On this occasion a payload of 8,000 lb (3,630 kg) was carried, this being the equivalent of 34 passengers and baggage. The next day it flew to Nairobi, covering 2,182 miles (3,512 km) non-stop in 5 hr 15 min.

Important operating advantages, actual or potential, soon became apparent. High speed had not been secured by the sacrifice of slow-flying ability; wing loading was moderate (less than that of some contemporary propeller-driven airliners) and stalling speed was correspondingly modest. Thus, although the Comet cruised at high speed "above the weather", it could descend steeply through cloud at slow forward speed and circuit, approach and land in the manner of other airliners of the period. Operation was possible from normal airports along the main trunk routes. The simplicity of the four de Havilland Ghost turbojet engines was reflected throughout the airframe and allowed a marked simplification of the controls in the cockpit, the pressurising and de-icing systems, and a reduction in the size and weight of the undercarriage. The absence of vibration from the engines was found to have a most beneficial effect on the life of components such as radio and instruments.

Production of the first sixteen Comets was laid down directly from the design stage, a policy which resulted in a considerable saving in time. Comets were ordered by the British Ministry of Supply, BOAC, Canadian Pacific Airlines and the French company UAT. The first for BOAC was initially flown on 9 January 1951 and the world's first jet passenger service was inaugurated on 2 May 1952. It was established that the Comet could reach Tokyo in 36 hours compared with 86 hours by piston-engined airliners.

For nearly two years Comets were operated with encouraging results, rendered the more so by the introduction of the Rolls-Royce Avon axial-flow turbojet in the Series 2, but in January 1954 a Comet IA of BOAC took off from Rome and disappeared near Elba. All aircraft of the type were withdrawn from service, but operations were resumed in March. In April another Comet IA of BOAC took off from Rome and disappeared near Naples. All were withdrawn from service. These disasters led to historic salvage operations by the Royal Navy and investigations at the Royal Aircraft Establishment at Farnborough which disclosed structural weakness in the form of metal fatigue. Based on the findings of a Court of Enquiry, set up to study the circumstances of the two accidents which had occurred to Comet IAs of BOAC, and following statements by the British Government in February 1955, a new production programme for the Comet was drawn up, concentrated mainly on the Comet 4. Aircraft of this greatly developed series have rendered excellent service, but these aircraft differ in many salient respects from the Comet 1 and 1A now described.

TYPE:

Four engined medium-range jet airliner.

WINGS:

Low-wing cantilever monoplane with moderate sweepback. Two turbojet engines in each stub wing, passing through front and rear spar webs. Integral fuel tanks and thermal de-icing. Air brakes on wings. Plain flaps outboard of engines and split flaps inboard, with hydraulic operation. Extensive use of Redux metal-to-metal bonding. Chord 29 ft 6 in (8·99 m) at root, 6 ft 9 in (2·06 m) at tip. Gross wing area 2,015 sq ft (187·20 m^2).

FUSELAGE:

Semi-monocoque structure of circular cross-section, 10 ft (3·05 m) in diameter throughout length of cabin. Aft end of cabin sealed by pressure dome. Redux bonding used extensively.

TAIL UNIT:

Cantilever monoplane type with single fin and rudder and small dorsal fin. Main fin insulated from stub, to contain HF aerial. VHF and ILS aerials housed in di-electric tips of fin and tailplane.

LANDING GEAR:

Retractable tricycle type of de Havilland design, each main unit with four-wheel bogie retracting outwards into wings. Doors retracted when gear down. Steerable twin-wheel nose unit retracting backwards into fuselage. Hydraulic retraction.

POWER PLANT:

Four de Havilland Ghost 50 (5,050 lb = 2,290 kg st each) (Series 1) or Ghost 50 Mk. 2 with water/methanol injection (5,050 lb = 2,290 kg st each) (Series 1A). Hinged panels below wings exposing installations for easy servicing from ground. Quickly-detachable air intake and tail pipe connections and special disconnect-joints in engine-control connecting rods. Installation split into three temperature zones, each zone being separated by fireproof bulkhead and having its own ventilators and fire-extinguishing system. Fuel in integral wing tanks and flexible bag tanks in centre-section, with pressure refuelling. Fuel capacities: Series 1 6,000 Imp gallons (27,276 litres), Series 1A 7,000 Imp gallons (31,820 litrs).

ACCOMMODATION:

Flight deck forward, with facilities for two pilots with full dual control, flight engineer and radio-operator/navigator. Seating capacities: Series 1 36 passengers, Series 1A 44 passengers. Flight deck, cabin and freight compartments pressurised to $8\frac{1}{4}$ lb/sq in (0·58 kg/cm^2) by air tapped from engine compressors, giving cabin altitude of 8,000 ft (2,435 m) with aircraft at 40,000 ft (12,120 m). Toilet, wardrobe, and dressing amenities. Main passenger door in port side at end of cabin, crew door forward in port side.

DIMENSIONS:

Wing span 115 *ft* 0 *in* (35·00 *m*)
Length overall 93 *ft* 0 *in* (28·35 *m*)
Height (*on ground, over fin*) 28 *ft* $4\frac{1}{2}$ *in* (8·65 *m*)

WEIGHTS (Series 1):

Capacity payload 12,500 *lb* (5,670 *kg*)
Loaded weight 105,000 *lb* (47,630 *kg*)

WEGTHS (Series 1A):

Capacity payload 12,670 *lb* (5,747 *kg*)
Loaded weight 115,000 *lb* (52,163 *kg*)

PERFORMANCE (Series 1 and 1A):

Cruising speed 490 *mph* (789 *kmh*)

The first of the Comets was universally admired, for its purity of line and high finish

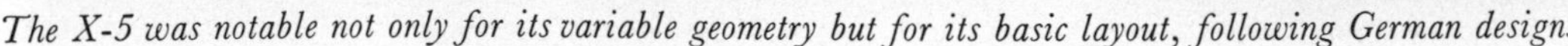

The X-5 was notable not only for its variable geometry but for its basic layout, following German designs

The time required to sweep the wings to their maximum angle was 30 seconds

BELL X-5

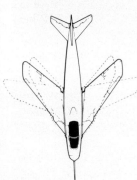

The Bell X-5 of 1951 was the first manned aircraft to have wings the sweepback of which could be varied in flight. It was used by the NACA to investigate the effects of such variation, the object being to reconcile high speed achieved by sweepback with the advantages of fixed-wing aircraft for take-off, landing and other flight regimes.

The idea of wings with variable geometry is by no means new. Aircraft have been flown with wings the span or angle of incidence of which could be altered in flight, and models were tested in the United Kingdom in 1946 the sweepback angle of which was variable, according to the ideas of Mr (now Sir) Barnes Wallis. In 1952 the Grumman F-10-F experimental naval fighter utilised a similar scheme, but the first operational type was the General Dynamics F-111. The company named was selected as prime contractor for the development of this aircraft (originally known as the TFX) with Grumman Aircraft as an associate. Data leading to the construction of this very advanced aircraft were collected during trials with the X-5 now described.

TYPE:
Single-seat variable-sweepback research aircraft.

WINGS:
Cantilever mid-wing monoplane. Wings tapered in plan and thickness. Operating mechanism for varying sweepback simultaneously compensated for the resultant shift of the centre of gravity. Specially designed fairing at each wing root to ensure that the root leading-edge presented a smooth aerofoil surface regardless of the angle of sweepback. Full-span leading-edge slats. Ailerons with inset tabs.

FUSELAGE:
Deep forward section housing pilot, air intake and power plant. Slender rear portion carrying tail. Hydraulically-operated dive brakes in sides of fuselage forward of cockpit, in the form of metal "doors" which could be opened to positions at nearly right angles to the fuselage.

TAIL UNIT:
Cantilever unit. All surfaces with moderate sweepback. Tailplane attached to fuselage. Small under-fin.

LANDING GEAR:
Retractable tricycle type. All three wheels retractable into fuselage.

POWER PLANT:
One Allison J-35-A-17 turbojet engine (4,900 lb = 2,680 kg st) mounted far forward beneath cockpit. Direct nose air intake with lipped upper edge in front of fuselage. Tail pipe efflux beneath rear fuselage.

ACCOMMODATION:
Pressurised and air-conditioned cockpit ahead of wings. Sliding Plexiglas canopy and pilot's seat both jettisonable in emergency. Ejection seat of cordite cartridge type. Long boom extending from nose housing yaw-measuring devices and pitot head.

DIMENSIONS:
Wing span (*wing at normal setting*) 32 *ft* 9 *in* (10·00 *m*)
Length overall 32 *ft* 4 *in* (10·16 *m*)
Height (*over fin*) 12 *ft* 0 *in* (3·66 *m*)

WEIGHT:
Weight loaded (*approx*) 10,000 *lb* (4,540 *kg*)

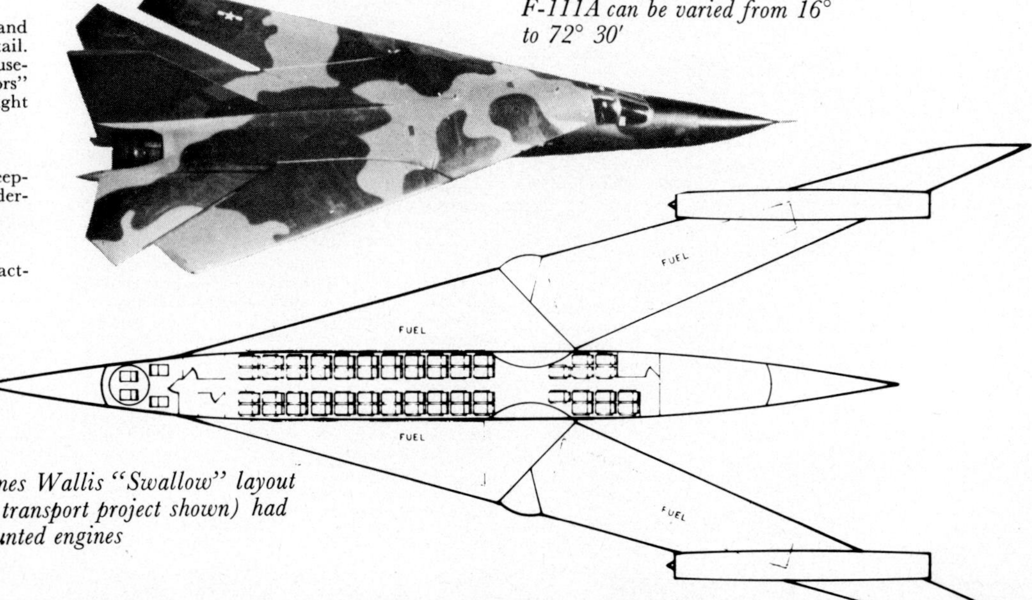

The outer wings of the General Dynamics F-111A can be varied from 16° to 72° 30′

The Barnes Wallis "Swallow" layout (56-seat transport project shown) had wing-mounted engines

Historically the Jet Provost is significant in having been the chosen type for the introduction of "all-through" jet training

The aerobatic qualities of the Jet Provost have become internationally renowned, in large measure due to performances by the RAF's "Red Pelicans", seen here in action during 1964. The type has been developed not only for training but for ground attack

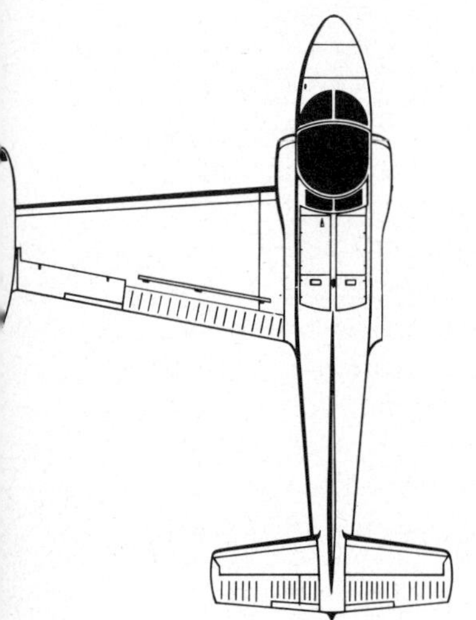

HUNTING (BAC) JET PROVOST

The Jet Provost is significant in aeronautical history not only because it was the means of making the Royal Air Force the first Service in the world to adopt the principle of "all-through" jet training but because of its commercial success as a light multi-purpose military aircraft. These facts are the more remarkable in view of the fact that the type was a direct development of the piston-engined Provost.

The prototype Jet Provost T. Mk 1 flew for the first time on 26 June 1954. The turbojet engine installed was the Bristol Siddeley Viper ASV.5 (1,640 lb = 745 kg st). Of this version a small pre-production batch was ordered by the RAF for evaluation by Flying Training Command. Development resulted in production of the T. Mk 2 version which had a redesigned rear fuselage, shorter landing gear, hydraulic instead of pneumatic services and the higher-powered Viper ASV.8 engine. The following versions remain in service:

Jet Provost T.Mk 3. Development of Mk 2, with one-piece moulded windscreen, Martin-Baker light-weight ejection seats, wing-tip fuel tanks and detail refinements.

Jet Provost T.Mk 4. Similar to Mk 3, but with Viper Mk 202 turbojet and detail changes. The T.Mk 4 was developed to meet the RAF requirement to extend the basic syllabus and thus economise in the use of the more expensive advanced trainer.

Jet Provost T.Mk 51. Armed export version of Mk 3, with two 0·303 in machine-guns in engine intake walls, gun camera in nose and underwing attachments for rockets or small bombs.

Jet Provost T.Mk 52. Armed export version of Mk 4, with same operational equipment as Mk 51.

Other variants of the Jet Provost are the greatly developed BAC 145 and BAC 167. The former is known by the RAF designation Jet Provost T.Mk 5.

The description and specification which follow refer to the Jet Provost T.Mk 4.

TYPE:

Two-seat jet primary and basic trainer.

WINGS:

Cantilever low-wing monoplane. All-metal structure, with main and subsidiary spars. Metal-covered ailerons, with trim-tabs. Slotted flaps. Air-brakes on wings at rear spar position ahead of flaps. Air-brakes and flaps hydraulically-operated.

FUSELAGE:

All-metal semi-monocoque stressed-skin structure.

TAIL UNIT:

Cantilever all-metal structure. One-piece tailplane, interchangeable elevators, fin and rudder. Fixed surfaces covered with smooth and movable surfaces with fluted alloy skin. Trim and balance tabs in elevators; combined trim and balance tab in rudder.

LANDING GEAR:

Hydraulically-retractable tricycle type. Main wheels retract inward into wings, nose-wheel forward. Dowty oleo-pneumatic shock-absorbers. Dunlop wheels and tyres. Dunlop hydraulic disc brakes.

POWER PLANT:

One Rolls-Royce (Bristol) Viper Mk 202 turbojet engine (2,500 lb = 1,134 kg st) in fuselage aft of cockpit. Lateral intakes on each side of forward fuselage. Normal internal fuel capacity (three tanks in each wing) 182 Imp gallons (827 litres). Two 48 Imp gallon (218 litres) wing-tip tanks may be fitted to order. Oil capacity 14 pts (8 litres).

ACCOMMODATION:

Enclosed cockpit seating two side-by-side with dual controls. Martin-Baker Type 4P lightweight ejection seats. Single centrally-placed blind-flying panel. Rearward sliding jettisonable canopy is manually-operated.

SYSTEMS AND EQUIPMENT:

Cockpit is air-conditioned. Oxygen is turned on automatically at 8,000 ft (2,440 m). RAF aircraft fitted with UHF radio and Rebecca Mk 8. Alternatives include VHF radio and radio-compass.

ARMAMENT:

Provision for a 0·303 in machine-gun in the base of each engine air intake, with 600 rounds per gun, a cine camera-gun in nose and two standard reflector sights. Additional alternative weapon loads include an under-fuselage pack of two 0·50 in guns with 100 rounds per gun, or, on underwing attachments, 24 Sura Mk 3 rockets, six 60 lb rockets, twelve 25 lb rockets, twelve 8 cm Oerlikon rockets, eight 25 lb bombs or two 100 lb bombs.

DIMENSIONS, external:

Wing span over tanks 36 *ft* 11 *in* (11·25 *m*)
Length overall 32 *ft* 5 *in* (9·88 *m*)
Height overall 10 *ft* 2 *in* (3·11 *m*)

WEIGHTS:

Basic weight 4,650 *lb* (2,110 *kg*)
Normal T-O weight 7,400 *lb* (3,356 *kg*)
Max landing weight 7,250 *lb* (3,288 *kg*)

PERFORMANCE (at max T-O weight, except where indicated)

Max level speed at 20,000 *ft* (6,100 *m*) (½ *fuel*) 410 *mph* (660 *kmh*)
Stalling speed 75 *mph* (120 *kmh*)
Rate of climb at S/L 3,400 *ft* (1,035 *m*) *min*
Time to 10,000 *ft* (3,050 *m*) 3·5 *min*
Time to 20,000 *ft* (6,100 *m*) 7·7 *min*
T-O to 50 *ft* (15 *m*) 2,200 *ft* (670 *m*)
Landing from 50 *ft* (15 *m*) 2,050 *ft* (625 *m*)
Range with max fuel at 30,000 *ft* (9,150 *m*) 700 *miles* (1,130 *km*)

ROLLS-ROYCE TMR (FLYING BEDSTEAD)

Mention has already been made, in the context of the Heinkel He 178, of Dr. A. A. Griffith and his aerodynamic theory of turbine design (1926). During 1939 Dr. Griffith joined the Rolls-Royce company and in a memorandum of June 1945 advanced a number of ideas which formed the basis of the very successful Avon axial-flow turbojet engine. In that same paper mention was also made of the possibility of installing a turbojet power plant at the rear of the aircraft fuselage.

The prospect of a light, powerful engine of small diameter and located in this manner led Dr. Griffith to conceive the idea of a supersonic interceptor fighter which could take-off vertically, and designs were prepared in December 1945. As early as April 1941 he had written of the possibility of "jump take-off" and what he termed "thistledown landing" by jet deflection, but it was his study of a small, lightweight expendable turbojet suitable for missile application that led to his most important investigations into VTOL (vertical take-off and landing) possibilities. It was now his firm intention to replace wing-lift by jet-thrust, the wing area being reduced to suit only the cruise condition. His first study, for a ship-borne aircraft, was compromised by having small engines mounted on the wing flaps and his next was for the supersonic interceptor fighter already mentioned. This was to have its lift engines arranged in two groups, six forward and four aft. Numerous designs followed. To achieve the necessary control in roll and pitch Dr. Griffith proposed compressed-air jets suitably located and directed and controlled by gyroscopic or other devices, the air being obtained by bleeding the compressors of the lift engines. To investigate such a system he required a source of compressed air capable of sustaining itself in the atmosphere and the notion occurred to him to build a framework carrying two turbojet engines modified to provide the required control air, fuel for 18 minutes' duration of hover, a pilot and instruments. On 27 March 1952 a preliminary design was commenced, using two Rolls-Royce Nene centrifugal-flow engines arranged back to back, with their jet pipes meeting at the centre of gravity of the rig. Here the pipes were fitted with cascades of deflecting vanes and the exhaust gases were directed downwards to provide vertical lift. Compressed air bled from the compressors was fed to downward-pointing control nozzles arranged fore and aft and laterally on outrigger supports. From the preliminary drawing the total weight, including fuel and pilot, was estimated in order to verify that a test-rig design having a lift-thrust suitably in excess of weight was feasible. The Aeronautical Research Council endorsed the suggestion that the rig should be built and a contract was placed. On 3 July 1953 the completed rig was run out on a gantry for tethered tests and the engines were run. The first free flight was made on 3 August 1954, the rig being airborne at a height of 8 to 10 feet (2·5–3 m) and successfully controlled by the compressed-air nozzles for a period of 8½ minutes. Many subsequent flights were made and modifications introduced as required.

Tremendous publicity attended the early flights and the name *Flying Bedstead* became famous throughout the world, although the device was known to Rolls-Royce as the TMR (thrust-measuring rig). Nine months before the first free flight Dr. Griffith was so confident of its eventual success that he designed in great detail a supersonic jet-lift transport aircraft to cruise at Mach 2·6 at 60,000 feet (18,290 m).

Soon after the first free flight of the TMR Rolls-Royce commenced the design of the first small turbojet engine specifically intended for jet-lift. This was designated RB.108 and enabled Short Brothers and Harland to build the S.C.1 research aircraft for the further investigation of Dr. Griffith's ideas on lift and control. The first of two S.C.1s constructed was initially flown, as a conventional aircraft, on 2 April 1957. A series of hovering tests in a special gantry preceded the first free vertical take-off, from an open platform, on 25 October 1958. The S.C.1 was a delta-winged monoplane with four RB.108 lift engines and one special RB.108 for propulsion. The lift engines had an extremely rapid response to throttle movements, a very necessary quality for the landing operation and transition.

In the context of the early British work described it is fitting to mention the American Bell VTOL aircraft which achieved its first free vertical flight on 16 November 1954. This had two Fairchild J44 turbojet engines mounted one on each side of the fuselage pointing directly downwards for take-off and arranged to be tilted into the horizontal position for forward flight. Experiments with an unmanned device using a jet engine for direct lift were made by Ryan Aeronautical Co. in May 1951.

The first free VTOL flights were made on the TMR by Rolls-Royce test pilot R. T. Shepherd

The historic Rolls-Royce "Flying Bedstead" is now in the Science Museum, London

LOCKHEED F-104 STARFIGHTER

Notwithstanding the extremely advanced nature of its design, featuring an unswept wing of extremely short span and thinness, the first Starfighter—one of two XF-104s—made its initial flight only eleven months after the contract was awarded. The date was 7 February 1954. Since that time massive production has been undertaken not only by Lockheed but by other manufacturers, as detailed in the following notes. The prototypes differed from the subsequent variants in having a Wright J65-W-6 turbojet engine. The nose-wheel retracted rearwards and a downward-ejection seat was installed.

Subsequent versions so far announced are:

F-104A. Single-seat fighter. Similar to XF-104, but with air-intake shock-cones, forward-retracting nose-wheel and other refinements. General Electric J79-GE-3B turbojet engine with afterburning. Ventral fin. Flap-blowing system and Lockheed in-flight refuelling equipment with removable probe. Deliveries to the USAF Air Defense Command began on 26 January 1958. After a period, these aircraft were withdrawn and issued to American Air National Guard. Some now back in service with Air Defense Command, and 27 of these are being re-engined with J79-GE-19 turbojets.

NF104A. Three F-104A fitted with a Rocketdyne AR-2 auxiliary rocket-engine in tail, above jet-pipe, is helping to train USAF pilots for flight at heights up to 130,000 ft (39,500 m). Other modifications included the fitting of F-104G type fin and rudder, forward extension of the engine air intake cones and introduction of HTP reaction jet controls at nose, tail and wing-tips. Each wing-tip has been extended by 2 ft (0·61 m).

F-104B. Tandem two-seat development of F-104A, for use as both combat aircraft and operational trainer. Greater fin area and full-powered rudder.

F-104C. General Electric J79-GE-7A turbojet. Fighter-bomber for USAF Tactical Air Command.

F-104D. Two-seat version of F-104C for USAF Tactical Air Command. Similar to F-104B but with power plant, in-flight refuelling equipment and other modifications introduced in F-104C.

F-104DJ. Similar to F-104D. Lockheed built 20 for Japan Air Self-Defence Force.

F-104F. As F-104D, but some equipment changes. Thirty built by Lockheed for Federal German Air Force.

F-104G (Lockheed Model 683-10-19). Single-seat multi-mission fighter, based on F-104C. General Electric J79-GE-11A turbojet engine. Strengthened structure and different operational equipment. Lockheed Model C-2 upward-ejection seat. Vertical tail surfaces enlarged by 25%. Fully-powered rudder. Manoeuvring flaps added to reduce turning radius by one-third at height of 5,000 ft (1,525 m). Extra fuel tank interchangeable with fixed armament of 20-mm Vulcan gun. Larger tyre size than earlier versions to reduce UCI pressure.

A total of 977 were ordered from three groups of European manufacturers. One group, known as Arge Süd and comprising the German companies of Messerschmitt, Heinkel, Siebelwerke and Dornier, has produced 210 for the Federal German Air Forces. A second group, Arge Nord, made up of the Dutch companies of Fokker and Aviolanda and the German companies of Hamburger Flugzeugbau and Vereinigte Flugtechnische Werke, has built 255 for the German Air Force and 95 for the RNAF, with Fokker handling all final assembly. The Belgian companies of SABCA and Avions Fairey have completed a total of 188, of which 89 were for the German Air Forces and 99 for the Belgian Air Force. In Italy, Fiat and Aermacchi have collaborated in the production of 229 for the air forces of Italy (154), the Netherlands (25) and Germany (50). In addition to European production, Lockheed has built 96 F-104G's for Germany, one each for Italy and Belgium, and 81 similar F-104G(MAP) aircraft for other nations participating in the Mutual Assistance Programme. Recipients of these aircraft, and others built by Canadair (see CF-104 entry below), include Norway, Nationalist China, Spain, Denmark, Greece and Turkey. In November 1968, West Germany announced an order for an additional 50 F-104Gs.

RF-104G. F-104G fitted with internal camera pack for reconnaissance.

TF-104G. (Lockheed Model 583-10-20). Total of 137 two-seat conversion trainers bearing this designation were ordered from Lockheed for the Federal German Air Force, 14 for the Netherlands and 29

Initial deliveries of F-104s were made to the USAF Air Defense Command, but the type has found an incomparably wider acceptance in the air forces of other nations

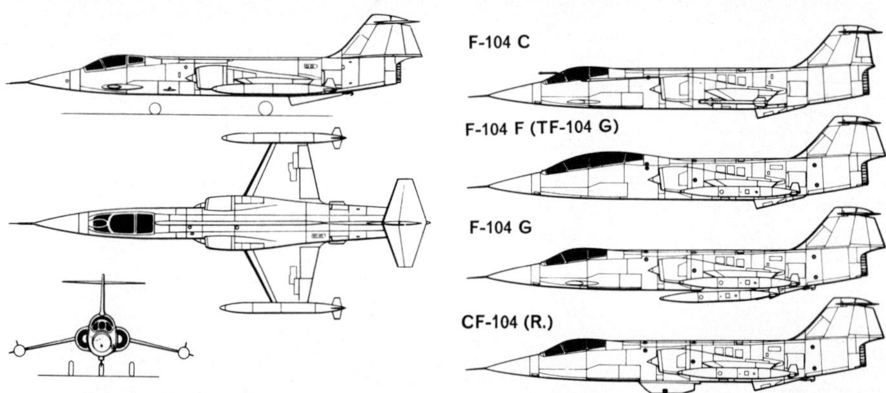

Streaming its drag parachute, this RF-104G of the Royal Netherlands Air Force also exhibits an electronic reconnaissance pod under the fuselage

for other MAP nations, including Belgium, Italy and Denmark. They are equipped with NASARR and full operational equipment, including the same fittings for under-wing and wing-tip stores as the F-104G, with optional fuselage bomb carrier.

RTF-104G1. Reconnaissance version of the TF-104G trainer, to meet Federal German *Luftwaffe* requirement. An advanced reconnaissance aircraft equipped with cameras, infra-red and sideways-looking radar for all-weather day and night missions.

F-104J. As F-104C except for equipment. Planned production of three by Lockheed and 207 by Mitsubishi for Japan Air Self-Defence Force, of which the first 20 were shipped by Lockheed as parts for assembly in Japan.

F-104N. Astronaut proficiency trainer for NASA. Three delivered.

F-104S. Developed from F-104G Starfighter, primarily as interceptor. General Electric J79/J1Q turbojet with redesigned afterburner. Nine external attachments for stores, including rockets, bombs and Sidewinder missiles. Normal primary armament will consist of Raytheon Sparrow air-to-air missiles. Total of 165 being built under licence in Italy for Italian Air Force. Max speed Mach 2·4.

CF-104. Single-seat strike-reconnaissance aircraft, basically similar to F-104G. Total of 200 built by Canadair for RCAF. Provision for two Sidewinders. Advanced navigation/fire-control system. Lockheed have developed for this version an under-fuselage reconnaissance pod containing four Vinten cameras and Computing Devices of Canada electronic control systems. Canadair also produced 110 similar aircraft as F-104G (MAP) under contract to USAF for nations participating in Military Aid Programme.

CF-104D. Total of 38 two-seat aircraft ordered from Lockheed by RCAF.

QF-104. Remotely-controlled recoverable target drone conversion of F-104A for missile evaluation and firing practice.

On all standard versions of the Starfighter an automatic pitch control system is fitted to sense and prevent pitch-up, together with a three-axis auto-stabiliser. A boundary layer control system is used to decrease landing speed.

In June 1963, an experimental zero-length launching of a piloted F-104, using a specially-developed Rocketdyne solid-propellent booster rocket, was made successfully.

Details given below refer specifically to the single-seat F-104G version.

TYPE:

Single-seat supersonic fighter.

WINGS:

Cantilever mid-wing monoplane. Bi-convex supersonic wing section with a thickness/chord ratio of 3·36%. Aspect ratio 2·45. Anhedral 10°. No incidence. Leading-edge nose radius of 0·016 in (0·041 cm) and razor-sharp trailing-edge. All-metal structure with two main spars, 12 span-wise intermediate channels between spars and top and bottom one-piece skin panels, tapering from thickness of 0·25 in (6·3 mm) at root to 0·125 in (3·2 mm) at tip. Each half-wing a separate structure cantilevered from five forged frames in fuselage. Full-span electrically-actuated drooping leading-edge. Entire trailing-edge hinged, with inboard sections serving as landing flaps and outboard sections as ailerons. Ailerons are of aluminium, each powered by a servo control system manufactured by Bertea. The control is irreversible and hydraulically-powered, each aileron being actuated by ten small hydraulic cylinders. Trim control is applied to position the aileron relative to the servo control position. An electric actuator positions the aileron trim. Flaps are of aluminium, actuated electrically. Above each flap is the air delivery tube of a boundary layer control system, which ejects air bled from the engine compressor over the entire flap span when the flaps are lowered to the landing position.

A new concept of fighter design and performance was established when the Starfighter made its appearance early in 1954. The most notable aerodynamic and structural feature was the extremely thin unswept wing, with a thickness/chord ratio of 3·36 per cent, aspect ratio of 2·45 and anhedral angle of 10 degrees

FUSELAGE:

All-metal monocoque structure. Hydraulically-operated aluminium air-brake on each side of rear fuselage.

TAIL UNIT:

T-type cantilever unit with "all-flying" one-piece horizontal tail surface hinged at mid-chord point at top of the sweptback vertical fin and powered by a hydraulic servo. Tailplane has similar profile to wing and is all-metal. Rudder is fully-powered by a hydraulic servo manufactured, like the tailplane unit, by Bertea. Trim control is applied to position the tailplane relative to the servo control position, by means of an electric actuator. Rudder trim is operated by an electric actuator located in the fin. The rudder itself is trimmed in the same way as the tailplane. Narrow-chord ventral fin to improve stability.

LANDING GEAR:

Retractable tricycle type. H. M. Loud (Dowty patent) liquid-spring shock-absorbers. Hydraulic actuation. Main wheels raised in and forward. Steerable nose-wheel retracts forward into fuselage. Main wheel legs are hinged on oblique axes so that the wheels lie flush within the fuselage skin when retracted. Bendix hydraulic disc brakes with Goodyear anti-skid units. Drag parachute in lower part of fuselage near end of tailpipe.

POWER PLANT:

One General Electric J79 turbojet engine with afterburner. Electrical de-icing elements fitted to air intakes. Most of the aircraft's hydraulic equipment mounted inside large engine access door under fuselage to facilitate servicing. Internal fuel in five bag-type fuselage tanks. Provision for external fuel in two pylon tanks and wing-tip tanks. In-flight refuelling can be provided through Lockheed-designed probe-drogue system.

ACCOMMODATION:

Pressurised and air-conditioned cockpit well forward of wings. Canopy hinged to port for access. Lockheed Model C-2 ejection seat.

SYSTEMS:

Air-conditioning package by AiResearch (single-seat) or Hamilton Standard (two-seat), using engine-bleed air. Two separate hydraulic systems, using engine-driven pumps. No. 1 system operates one side of tailplane, rudder and ailerons, also the automatic pitch control actuator and autopilot actuators. No. 2 system operates other half of tailplane, rudder and ailerons, also the landing gear, wheel brakes, speed brakes, nose-wheel steering and constant-frequency electrical generator. Emergency ram air turbine supplies emergency hydraulic pump and electric generator. Electrical system supplied by two engine-driven variable-frequency generators. Constant-speed hydraulic motor drives generator to supply fixed-frequency AC. DC power supplied by two batteries and an inverter.

ARMAMENT (F-104G):

Bomb carrier under fuselage for store weighing up to 2,000 lb (907 kg). Under-wing pylons can each carry a 1,000 lb (453 kg) store, fire bomb, rocket pod, Sidewinder, air-to-air missile, AGM-12B Bullpup air-to-surface missile or 195 US gallon (740 litres) fuel tank. Provision for two Sidewinders under fuselage and either a Sidewinder or fuel tank on each wing-tip. Vulcan gun (20 mm) interchangeable with extra fuel tank.

ELECTRONICS AND EQUIPMENT:

Integrated electronics system in which various communications and navigation components may be installed as a series of interconnecting but self-sustaining units which may be varied to provide for different specific missions. Equipment includes autopilot with "stick steering", which includes modes for preselecting and holding altitude, speed, heading and constant rate of turn; multi-purpose NASARR radar system; fixed-reticule gunsight; bomb computer; air data computer; dead reckoning navigation device; TACAN radio air navigation system; provision for data link-time division set and UHF radio; lightweight fully-automatic inertial navigation system; and provision for fitting a camera pod under the fuselage for reconnaissance duties.

DIMENSIONS:

Wing span without tip-tanks 21 *ft* 11 *in* (6·68 *m*)
Length overall 54 *ft* 9 *in* (16·69 *m*)
Height overall 13 *ft* 6 *in* (4·11 *m*)

WEIGHTS AND LOADING:

Weight empty 14,082 *lb* (6,387 *kg*)
Max T-O weight 28,779 *lb* (13,054 *kg*)
Max wing loading 148 *lb/sq ft* (723 *kg/m*²)

PERFORMANCE:

Max level speed at 36,000 *ft* (11,000 *m*) *Mach* 2·2 = 1,450 *mph* (2,330 *kmh*)
Max cruising speed Mach 0·95
Econ cruising speed Mach 0·85
Rate of climb at S/L 50,000 *ft* (15,250 *m*) *min*
Service ceiling 58,000 *ft* (17,680 *m*)
Zoom altitude over 90,000 *ft* (27,400 *m*)
Time to accelerate to Mach 2·0 3 *min*
Radius with max fuel 745 *miles* (1,200 *km*)
Ferry range (excluding flight refuelling) 2,180 *miles* (3,510 *km*)

15 July 1954: maiden flight of the first Model 707, familiar today, after massive production, as the "Dash 80"

The half-million-dollar cabin mock-up

Early engine-icing rig on "Dash 80"

BOEING MODEL 707

The prototype of the Boeing Model 707 was the first jet transport to be flown in the USA (15 July 1954). Designated Model 367-80, it was built as a private venture and was used to demonstrate the potential of commercial and military developments. One such development was ordered in large numbers for the USAF as the KC-135 tanker-transport. In July 1955 Boeing was given clearance by the USAF to build commercial derivatives. These have the basic designations 707 and 720 and are operated today in numerous versions. The 720 was developed for medium- and short-haul operations and has wing modifications to permit higher cruising speeds at low altitudes and better field performance. External appearance notwithstanding, the differences from the 707 are so extensive that description is not warranted under the present heading. The number of 707s and 720s delivered or ordered by the end of April 1969 was 834.

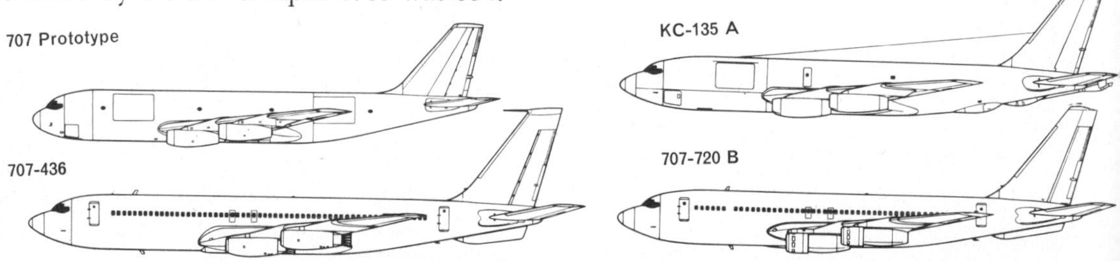

Prior to rollout and delivery to Pan American World Airways is seen the 1,000th jet aircraft (including tankers) built by the Boeing Company's Transport Division, a 707-320C

The basic civil versions of the 707 are as follows:

367-80. The prototype tanker-transport, used very extensively for development flying and already historic as the "Dash 80". Powered originally with Pratt & Whitney JT3P turbojets (each 9,500 lb = 4,300 kg st). Emphasis of development flying since 1960 on advanced control systems.

707-120. First production version. Primarily for continental use, but capable of full-load over-ocean operation on many routes. Four Pratt & Whitney JT3C-6 turbojets (each 13,500 lb = 6,124 kg st). Longer and wider fuselage than prototype. Accommodation for up to 180 passengers. First production aircraft, a 707-121 for Pan American World Airways, flew for first time on 20 December 1957. The 707-138 for Qantas is the only version with the optional shorter fuselage.

707-120B. Development of 707-120, with four 17,000 lb (7,718 kg) Pratt & Whitney JT3D-1 or 18,000 lb (8,165 kg) st JT3D-3 turbofan engines and design improvements incorporated originally in 720. These include new inboard wing leading-edge and four additional segments of leading-edge flaps, which lessen runway requirements and raise the max cruising speed to Mach 0·91. The 707-138B for Qantas was the only model with optional shorter fuselage. Production completed.

707-220. Generally identical with 707-120 but with four Pratt & Whitney JT4A-3 engines (each 15,800 lb = 7,167 kg st).

707-320 Intercontinental. Long-range over-ocean version with increased wing span and longer fuselage. Four Pratt & Whitney JT4A-3 or -5 (each 15,800 lb = 7,167 kg st), or JT4A-9 (each 16,800 lb = 7,620 kg st), or JT4A-11 (each 17,500 lb = 7,945 kg st) turbojet engines. Accommodation for up to 189 passengers.

707-320B Intercontinental. Development of 707-320 with four Pratt & Whitney JT3D-3 or -3B turbofan engines (each 18,000 lb = 8,165 kg st), fitted with double thrust reversers. New leading- and trailing-edge flaps, low-drag wing-tips and other refinements.

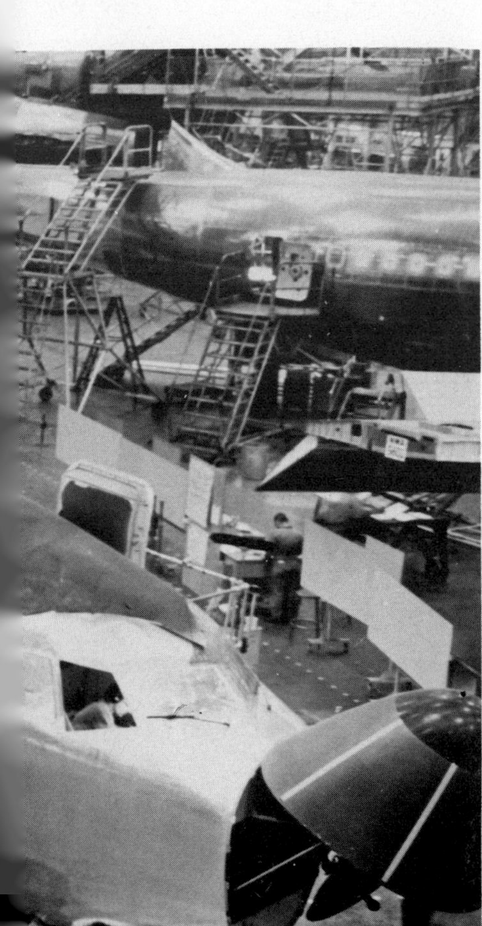

707-320C Intercontinental. Cargo or mixed cargo-passenger version of 707-320B with forward cargo door and Boeing-developed cargo loading system, using pallets or containers. Cargo space comprises 8,074 cu ft (228 m³) on full upper deck and 1,700 cu ft (48 m³) in two lower-deck holds.

707-420 Intercontinental. As 707-320 but with four Rolls-Royce Conway Mk 508 turbofan engines (each 17,500 lb = 7,945 kg st).

The following description applies in general to all models of the Boeing 707.

TYPE:

Four-engined jet airliner.

WINGS:

Cantilever low-wing monoplane. Sweep-back at quarter-chord 35°. All-metal two-spar fail-safe structure. Centre-section continuous through fuselage. Normal outboard aileron and small inboard aileron on each wing, built of aluminium honeycomb panels. Two Fowler flaps and one split fillet flap of aluminium alloy spoilers on each wing forward of ailerons. Primary flying controls aerodynamically balanced and manually operated through spring-tabs. Lateral control at low speeds by all four ailerons, supplemented by spoilers interconnected with the ailerons. Lateral control at high speeds by inboard ailerons and spoilers only. Operation of flaps adjusts linkage between inboard and outboard ailerons to permit outboard operation only with extended flaps. Spoilers may also be used symmetrically as speed brakes. Thermal anti-icing on leading-edges.

One of hundreds of Model 707s delivered to the airline operators of the world

FUSLAGE:

All-metal semi-monocoque fail-safe structure with cross-section made up of two circular arcs of different radii, the larger above, faired into smooth-contoured ellipse.

TAIL UNIT:

Cantilever all-metal structure. Anti-balance tab and trim tab in rudder. Trim and control tabs in each elevator. Electrically and manually operated variable-incidence tailplane. Powered rudder. Small ventral fin (except on 707-320B and C).

LANDING GEAR:

Hydraulically-retractable tricycle type. Main units are four-wheel bogies which retract inwards into underside of thickened wing-root and fuselage. Dual nose-wheel unit retracts forward into fuselage. Landing gear doors close when legs fully extended. Gear can be extended in flight to give maximum rate of descent of 15,000 ft/min (4,570 m/min) when used in conjunction with spoilers. Boeing oleo-pneumatic shock-absorbers. Multidisc brakes by Bendix on 707-120, -120B, -220, by Goodrich on 707-320, -320B, -420 and by Goodyear on 707-320C. Hydro-air flywheel detector type anti-skid units.

POWER PLANT:

Four turbojet or turbofan engines mounted in pods under the wings (details under "series" descriptions). Fuel in four main, two reserve and one centre main integral wing tanks. Fuel capacity varies with model. (707-320, -320B, -320C, -420: 23,855 US gallons = 90,299 litres).

ACCOMMODATION (707-120, -120B, -220):

Flight compartment seats pilot and co-pilot side-by-side, with stations for flight engineer and navigator behind. Main cabin can seat up to 181 passengers in six-abreast economy configuration. Typical arrangement has 36 first-class and 95 coach-class seats, with four galleys and four toilets. Two passenger doors, forward and aft on port side. Baggage compartments fore and aft of wing in lower segment of fuselage. Entire accommodation, including baggage compartments, air-conditioned and pressurised.

Flight compartment of a military 707 variant

ACCOMMODATION (707-320, -320B, -320C, -420):

Basically as for 707-120. Max accommodation for 189 economy-class passengers in all except 707-320C which can seat up to 202 passengers. Typical arrangement has 24 first-class seats and 123 coach-class seats, with four galleys and five toilets.

SYSTEMS:

Air-cycle or vapour-cycle air-conditioning and pressurisation system, using three AiResearch engine-driven turbo-compressors. Electrical system includes four 30kVA or 40kVA 115/200V 3-phase 400 c/s AC alternators and four 75A transformer-rectifiers giving 28V DC. No APU.

DIMENSIONS:

Wing span:
120, 120B, 220 130 *ft* 10 *in* (39·87 *m*)
320, 420 142 *ft* 5 *in* (43·41 *m*)
320B, 320C 145 *ft* 9 *in* (44·42 *m*)

Length overall:
120, 220 144 *ft* 6 *in* (44·04 *m*)
120B 145 *ft* 1 *in* (44·22 *m*)
320, 320B, 320C, 420 152 *ft* 11 *in* (46·61 *m*)

WEIGHTS:

Basic operating weight, empty:
120 118,000 *lb* (53,520 *kg*)
120B 123,151 *lb* (55,861 *kg*)
220 122,000 *lb* (55,340 *kg*)
320 135,000 *lb* (61,235 *kg*)
320B 138,385 *lb* (62,771 *kg*)
320C (*all cargo*) 133,874 *lb* (60,725 *kg*)
420 133,000 *lb* (60,330 *kg*)

Max T-O weight:
120, 120B 257,000 *lb* (116,575 *kg*)
220 247,000 *lb* (112,037 *kg*)
320, 420 312,000 *lb* (141,520 *kg*)
320B 327,000 *lb* (148,325 kg)
320C (*all cargo*) 331,000 *lb* (150,138 *kg*)

PERFORMANCE (at average cruising weight):

Max level speed:
120, 220, 320, 420 623 *mph* (1,002 *kmh*)
120B, 320B, 320C 627 *mph* (1,010 *kmh*)

Max permissible diving speed Mach 0·95

Econ cruising speed:
120 549 *mph* (884 *kmh*)
120B 557 *mph* (897 *kmh*)
220 538 *mph* (865 *kmh*)
320 545 *mph* (876 *kmh*)
320B, 320C 550 *mph* (886 *kmh*)
420 531 *mph* (854 *kmh*)

Rate of climb at S/L:
120 2,400 *ft* (731 *m*) *min*
120B 5,050 *ft* (1,539 *m*) *min*
220 4,300 *ft* (1,310 *m*) *min*
320 3,500 *ft* (1,067 *m*) *min*
320B 3,550 *ft* (1,082 *m*) *min*
320C 2,940 *ft* (896 *m*) *min*
420 2,900 *ft* (884 *m*) *min*

Range with max payload, allowances for climb and descent, no reserves:
120 3,217 *miles* (5,177 *km*)
120B 4,235 *miles* (6,820 *km*)
220 3,260 *miles* (5,245 *km*)
320 4,784 *miles* (7,700 *km*)
320B 6,160 *miles* (9,915 *km*)
320C 3,925 *miles* (6,317 *km*)
420 4,865 *miles* (7,830 *km*)

SUD-AVIATION SE 210 CARAVELLE

The Caravelle first introduced into common use the practice of mounting jet engines (in this instance two) at the rear of the fuselage, attached to the sides in nacelles. It has proved a notable technical and commercial success and has the further operational distinction that, since the Spring of 1968, aircraft of the type, equipped with the Sud/Lear Phase IIIA all-weather landing system, have been authorised to land, in commercial operation, under zero ceiling conditions and 200 m (656 ft) forward visibility.

The Caravelle was ordered in prototype form by the French Secretariat d'Etat a l'Air in January 1953, and the first of two prototypes was initially flown on 27 May 1955.

An early design study had been made of a "tri-jet" layout, as later adopted internationally.

Caravelle I and IA. Initial production series with Rolls-Royce Avon RA.29 Mk 522 (Series I) or Mk 522A (Series IA) engines. Series I entered service in mid-1959. All aircraft of these series later converted to Caravelle III standard.

Caravelle III. Second production version with 11,400 lb (5,170 kg) st Avon RA.29 Mk 527 engines. Standard accommodation for 64–80 passengers.

Caravelle VI-N. Two Avon RA 29 Mk 531 engines (each 12,200 lb = 5,535 kg st). Accommodation for 16–20 first class and 55–60 economy class passengers.

Caravelle VI-R. Similar to VI-N, but with modified windscreen for improved visibility. Avon 523R or 533R engines (each 12,600 lb = 5,725 kg st) fitted with thrust reversers and spoilers in three sections on the trailing-edge of each wing to reduce effect of high-lift devices and increase wheel pressure on the ground during landing.

Caravelle 10 R. Similar to VI-R but powered by two Pratt and Whitney JT8D-7 turbofan engines (each 14,000 lb = 6,350 kg st) fitted with thrust reversers. Change in fuselage structure, consisting of replacement of slanting floor bracing struts by vertical struts, giving considerable increase of capacity in lower holds. Landing distances reduced by new-type wheels and use of Sud-Aviation cascade thrust reversers of type developed for Super Caravelle.

Caravelle 11 R. Mixed passenger/freight transport, derived from Caravelle 10 R and powered by two Pratt & Whitney JT8D-7 turbofan engines. Load distribution facilitated by increase of 36·6 in (0·93 m) in length of front fuselage. Floor strength increased and number of cargo attachment rails increased from four to seven. Cargo door.

Super Caravelle. A much-refined development of the Caravelle with two Pratt & Whitney JT8D-7 turbofan engines. Fuselage 3 ft 3½ in (1·0 m) longer, providing accommodation for up to 104 tourist class passengers. Aerodynamic refinements include an extension of the wing leading-edge near the root; an increase in the operating travel of the flaps, which are of double-slotted type; the addition of a bullet fairing at the intersection of the rudder and elevators; and an increase in tailplane span. Optional installation of additional centre fuel tank.

Caravelle 12. Super Caravelle airframe with fuselage lengthened to seat up to 128 passengers.

Main access is through door under rear fuselage

TYPE:

Twin-jet medium-range airliner.

WINGS:

Cantilever low-wing monoplane. Sweepback at quarter-chord 20°. Wing in two sections joined on fuselage centre-line. All-metal three-spar structure, with spanwise stringers riveted to skin. Two-piece all-metal ailerons on each wing, operated hydraulically by duplicated Automotive Products actuators, with electric standby power. Hydraulically-actuated Fowler flaps. Air-brakes on upper and lower surfaces ahead of flaps. Three-section spoilers on trailing-edge of each wing of Series VI-R. Thermal de-icing.

FUSELAGE:

Circular-section all-metal semi-monocoque structure. Max diameter 10 ft 6 in (3·20 m). Length of pressurised section 84 ft 1 in (25·634 m).

TAIL UNIT:

Cantilever all-metal structure. Sweep-back on tailplane 30° at quarter-chord. Hydraulically-powered rudder and elevators, using duplicated Automotive Products actuators, with electric standby power. Thermal de-icing.

LANDING GEAR:

Retractable nose-wheel type. Hispano shock-absorbers. Twin nose-wheel unit retracts forward. Each main unit has a four-wheel bogie and retracts inward. Hydraulic retraction. Maxaret anti-skid brakes on main wheels.

POWER PLANT:

Two turbojet or turbofan engines mounted in nacelles on each side of the rear fuselage just ahead of tail unit (details under "Series" descriptions above). Fuel in four integral tanks in wings, with total capacity of 4,180 Imp gallons (19,000 litres).

ACCOMMODATION:

Crew compartment for two or three persons. Standard accommodation for up to 64 first class (four-abreast) or 80 tourist (five-abreast) passengers. Entire accommodation pressurised. Main access to cabin aft through door under rear fuselage with hydraulically-operated integral steps. Steps serve as tail support when lowered. Further door on port side at front of cabin. Two toilets, coat rooms and light baggage racks aft of cabin. Two galleys, one forward and one aft of cabin.

SYSTEMS:

Air-conditioning system utilises two turbo-compressors, driven by engine-bleed air, and includes a cold air unit. Pressure differential 8·25 lb/sq in (0·58 kg/cm²). Hydraulic system, pressure 2,500 lb/sq in (175 kg/cm²), for landing gear actuation, nose-wheel steering, brakes, flying controls and air-brakes. Electrical system includes two 30V DC engine-driven generators and inverters for 115V 400 c/s AC.

DIMENSIONS

Wing span 112 *ft* 6 *in* (34·30 *m*)
Length overall 105 *ft* 0 *in* (32·01 *m*)
Height overall 28 *ft* 7 *in* (8·72 *m*)
Tailplane span 34 *ft* 9 *in* (10·60 *m*)
Wheel track (c/l of shock-struts) 17 *ft* 0 *in* (5·21 *m*)
Wheelbase 38 *ft* 7 *in* (11·79 *m*)

WEIGHTS (Series 10 R):

Max payload 20,720 *lb* (9,400 *kg*)
Max T-O weight 114,640 *lb* (52,000 *kg*)
Max landing weight 109,130 *lb* (49,500 *kg*)

PERFORMANCE (Series 10 R):

Max cruising speed at 25,000 *ft* (7,620 *m*) *at* 94,800 *lb* (43,000 *kg*) 497 *mph* (800 *kmh*)
T-O distance at max T-O weight 6,400 *ft* (1,950 *m*)
Landing distance at max landing weight 5,120 *ft* (1,560 *m*)
Range with max payload, 300 miles (480 *km*)
diversion and SR427 reserves 1,800 *miles* (2,900 *km*)

The windows of the Caravelle are of characteristic "Gothic" form. Four-abreast seating allows for up to 64 passengers

HAWKER SIDDELEY TRIDENT

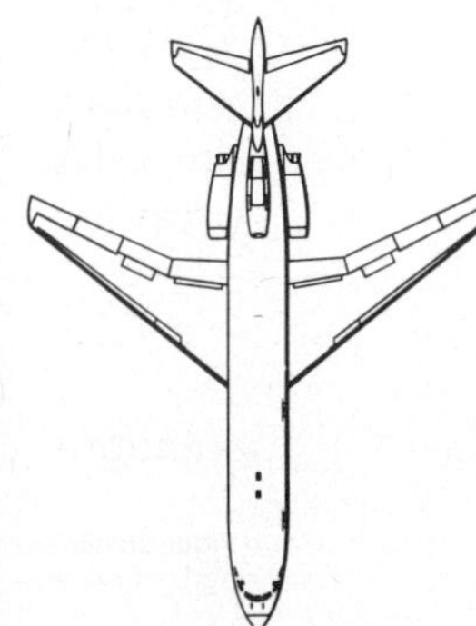

The three-engined transport aeroplanes which were employed by the leading world airline operators in the late 1920s and early 1930s have already been represented by the Fokker FVII-3m and Ford Tri-motor. Another notable aircraft of this class, although it did not achieve international success, was the de Havilland Hercules, a wooden biplane which rendered excellent service on the African routes of Imperial Airways. The Hercules bore the de Havilland type number 66 and the D.H. 121 airliner, the first example of which was initially flown on 9 January 1964, marked a modern reversion to the three-engined formula. The type, later named Trident, was ordered into production initially to meet BEA's requirements for a short-haul 600-mph airliner for service from 1963–64 onwards. The Boeing 727 was the first US design to follow the same layout, with three rear-mounted engines.

On 10 June 1965, a BEA Trident 1 made the first automatic touch-down on a commercial airline service, at London Airport, using its Smiths Auto-flare equipment.

TYPE:
Three-engined jet airliner.

WINGS:
Cantilever low-wing monoplane. Main wing is continuous from wingtip to wingtip, and comprises a six-cell centre-section box extending across the fuselage, a two-cell box from the wing root out to 40% of the semi-span, and from there a single-cell box to the wingtip. The entire wing box is subdivided to form integral fuel tanks. Extensive use is made of Reduxing between skins and stringers. Ailerons actuated by triplexed power control system without manual reversion. Three independent hydraulic systems work continuously in parallel and power three separate jacks of Fairey manufacture at each primary flying control surface. Two all-metal double-slotted trailing-edge flaps on each wing. Krueger leading-edge flap at each wing-root. All flaps operated by screw jacks and hydraulic motors of Hobson manufacture. One all-metal spoiler, forward of outer flap on each wing, acts also as airbrake/lift dumper. Lift dumpers forward of inner flaps. No trim-tabs. Srs 1 has leading-edge droop; Srs 1E and 2E have full-span leading-edge slats.

FUSELAGE:
Consists of a pressure shell extending back to the engines and a rear fuselage carrying the engines and tail unit. Semi-monocoque fail-safe structure of aluminium-copper alloys, using Redux bonding to attach stringers to skin throughout the pressure cell.

TAIL UNIT:
Cantilever all-metal structure, with tailplane mounted at tip of fin. All-moving tailplane with geared slotted flap on trailing-edge to assist in providing high negative lift coefficient for take-off and landing. No trim-tabs. Power control system as for ailerons. Thermal de-icing of leading-edges.

LANDING GEAR:
Retractable tricycle type. Hydraulic retraction. Hawker Siddeley (main units) and Lockheed (nose) oleo-pneumatic shock-absorbers. Each main unit consists of two twin-tyred wheels mounted on a common axle: during retraction the leg twists through nearly 90°and lengthens by 6 in (15 cm), enabling wheels to stow within the circular cross-section of the fuselage. Nose unit has twin wheels and is offset 2 ft 0 in (61 cm) to port, retracting transversely.

POWER PLANT:
Three Rolls-Royce Spey turbofan engines (details under "Series" descriptions). Two in pods, one on each side of rear fuselage; one inside rear fuselage. Trident 1 has four integral fuel tanks in wings: on Trident 1E there is also an integral tank in centre-section.

ACCOMMODATION:
(Trident 1) Crew of three on flight deck. (Mixed-class version has bar (stbd), galley (stbd) and toilet (port) at front, then a 16-seat first-class compartment, with seats in pairs on each side of central aisle, two galleys (stbd) and coat stowage (port), 61-seat tourist-class cabin with three-seat units on each side of aisle, and two toilets at rear. All-tourist version has 103 seats, six-abreast, with 39 seats in forward cabin, 64 seats in rear cabin, galley, and toilet at front and two toilets at rear.

The Trident introduced a vogue for the now familiar "tri-jet" layout

ACCOMMODATION:
(Trident 1E, 2E): Basically as for Trident 1, with four-abreast first-class seats and six-abreast tourist seating. Mixed-class version has toilet (port) and galley (stbd) at front, 12-seat first-class cabin, two galleys (port), 79-seat tourist cabin and two toilets at rear. Tourist version has 115 seats, with galley and toilet at front and two toilets at rear.

ACCOMMODATION:
(Trident 1E-140): Basically as for Trident 1E, but seats of new design allowing ample leg-room for up to 139 passengers at closer pitch. Seven-abreast (four/three) seating in forward cabin.

DIMENSIONS:

Wing span:
Srs 1 89 *ft* 10 *in* (27·38 *m*)
Srs 1E 95 *ft* 0 *in* (28·96 *m*)
Srs 2E 98 *ft* 0 *in* (29· 87 *m*)
Length overall 114 *ft* 9 *in* (34·98 *m*)
Height over tail 27 *ft* 0 *in* (8·23 *m*)

WEIGHTS:
Operating weight, empty:
Srs 1 67,500 *lb* (38,618 *kg*)
Srs 1E 71,500 *lb* (22,432 *kg*)
Srs 2E 73,200 *lb* (33,203 *kg*)
Max T-O weight:
Srs 1 115,000 *lb* (52,163 *kg*)
Srs 1E 135,500 *lb* (61,462 *kg*)
Srs 2E 143,500 *lb* (65,090 *kg*)

PERFORMANCE (at max T-O weight):
Typical high-speed cruise:
Srs 1 *Mach* 0·85 *at* 25,000 *ft* (7,620 *m*= 589 *mph* (948 *mph*)
Srs 1E, 2E *Mach* 0·88 *at* 27,000 *ft* (8,230 *m*) = 605 *mph* (972 *kmh*)
Range with max fuel (with reserves):
Srs 1 *with* 7,480 *lb* (3,393 *kg*) *payload* 2,555 *miles* (4,108 *km*)
Srs 1E *with* 16,020 *lb* (7,266 *kg*) *payload* 2,445 *miles* (3,934 *km*)
Srs 2E *with* 16,020 *lb* (7,266 *kg*) *payload* 2,500 *miles* (4,025 *km*)

On 10 June 1965 a Trident of BEA, as depicted, made the first automatic touchdown on a commercial service

G91 Y twin-engined development of the earlier G91 described

FIAT G91

The G91 light attack fighter was chosen, as the result of competitive trials in 1957, as a standard NATO tactical aircraft. The operational requirements were issued by NATO in the spring of 1954. While the aircraft was still in the project stage Fiat was awarded a contract for the construction of three prototypes and 27 pre-production aircraft, all powered by the Bristol Siddeley Orpheus turbojet. This first prototype flew on 9 August 1956.

"T" two-seater and "R" single-seater, respectively, for training or tactical use for photographic reconnaissance

In the technical evaluation trials carried out at Brétigny, France, in the autumn of 1957, the G91 proved itself able to meet the requirements of the official specification when operated from semi-prepared airstrips, with and without external stores. As the result, it was ordered into production as stated.

Versions of the G91 are as follows:

G91. Basic single-seat ground-attack fighter, with Orpheus 801 turbojet. Internal armament four 0·50 in machine-guns. Evaluation by 103 Squadron of the Italian Air Force began in February 1959.

G91R/1. Similar to G91, but equipped for photographic-reconnaissance. Three Vinten cameras for front and lateral oblique photography by day at high speed and low altitude. Vertical photography from high altitude also possible. Orpheus 80302 turbojet.

G91R/3. Similar to G91R/1, but with two 30 mm guns and equipment changes, including installation of Bendix Doppler and Computing Devices of Canada Position and Homing Indicator.

G91R/4. Similar to G91/R1, but with equipment changes.

G91N. Modified to evaluate various navigation aids, to determine the most suitable aids for lightweight ground-attack fighters.

G91T/1. Tandem two-seat version of G91 for advanced training at transonic speeds. Suitable also for use as tactical fighter. Similar to G91 except for two seats, rear one slightly raised, under electrically-operated two-section canopy. Two under-wing pylons only.

G91T/3. Similar to T/1 but with equipment changes.

G91PAN. Special aerobatic version for Italy's National Aerobatic Team. No armament. Smoke tanks under wings.

The latest development of the type is the twin-engined G91Y, now being built for the Italian Air Force. This has two General Electric J85 turbojet engines with afterburning and compared with the original G91 has approximately 60% greater take-off thrust at the cost of only a relatively small increase in power plane weight.

The following description relates specifically to the original G91, but is generally applicable to other versions.

TYPE:

Single-seat ground-attack fighter.

WINGS:

Cantilever low-wing monoplane. Laminar-flow aerofoil section. Sweepback at 25% chord approx 37°. All-metal two-spar structure in three portions, of which the centre-section is integral with fuselage. Outer wings easily detachable for transport or replacement. Ailerons fitted with irreversible hydraulic servo-control, with artifical feel and trimmer. Electrically-actuated slotted flaps.

FUSELAGE:

All-metal semi-monocoque structure. Rear portion detachable for engine replacement. Two hydraulically-actuated door-type air-brakes side-by-side under centre fuselage.

TAIL UNIT:

Cantilever monoplane type. All-metal structure. Rudder and elevator statically and dynamically balanced. Electrically-actuated variable-incidence tailplane. Elevator fitted with irreversible hydraulic servo-control and artificial feel. Rudder fitted with electrically-actuated balance-tab.

LANDING GEAR:

Retractable tricycle type. Hydraulically-actuated. Low-pressure tyres. Nose-wheel equipped with hydraulic anti-shimmy device, releasable manually for ground manoeuvring. Hydraulic brakes. Braking parachute stowed at base of rudder.

POWER PLANT:

One Fiat-built Bristol Siddeley Orpheus 80302 turbojet engine (2,270 kg = 5,000 lb st) in all versions but early G91s, which had Orpheus 801. Fuel in armoured fuselage tankage. Provision for auxiliary tanks.

ACCOMMODATION:

Pilot on Martin-Baker Mk 4 fully-automatic ejection seat in armoured, pressurised and air-conditioned cabin. Electronic and manual temperature control. Electrically-operated jettisonable rearward-hinging canopy. Automatically-controlled oxygen system.

ARMAMENT:

Normal fixed armament of four 0·50 in Colt-Browning machine-guns in fuselage, two on each side of cockpit, or two 30 mm guns, one on each side. Four underwing pylons for the following loads: Inner pylons 500 lb bombs, nuclear weapons, Nord 5103 air-to-air guided missiles, clusters of 6 × 3 in air-to-ground rockets, honeycomb packs of 31 air-to-ground folding-fin rockets, pods containing one 0·50 in machine-gun and 250 rounds of ammunition. Outer pylons Nord 5103 air-to-air guided missiles, 250 lb bombs, honeycomb packs of 19 air-to-ground folding-fin rockets, pods containing one 0·50 in machine-gun and 250 rounds of ammunition.

DIMENSIONS:

Wing span 28 *ft* 1 *in* (8·56 *m*)
Length overall 33 *ft* 9 *in* (10·29 *m*)
Height overall 13 *ft* 1 *in* (4·00 *m*)

WEIGHTS:

Weight empty 6,702 *lb* (3,040 *kg*)
Weight loaded (*with external stores*) 11,465 *lb* (5,202 *kg*)

PERFORMANCE:

Max speed at low altitude 650 *mph* (1,045 *kmh*)
Max diving speed above Mach 1 *at* 30,000 *ft* (9,150 *m*)
T-O distance to 50 *ft* (15 *m*) 3,870 *ft* (1,180 *m*)
Landing distance from 50 *ft* (15 *m*) 2,020 *ft* (615 *m*)

The international character of the G91 was accentuated from the time of its initiation by the fitting of a Fiat-built Bristol Orpheus turbojet engine, the intake for which is among G91R features apparent here

Fiat G91 Rs. Production by Fiat has been completed, but the company is prime contractor for 165 Lockheed F-104S Starfighters and has G91 developments in hand

OPTICAL GLASS
CAMERAS COMPARTMENT

GENERAL DYNAMICS B-58 HUSTLER

In design, construction and performance the Hustler was the most distinctive bomber of its era

Among remarkable design features is the two-component disposable armament and fuel pod

The delta-wing Hustler was the world's first supersonic bomber, and an aircraft of great technical, as well as military, distinction. Its origins were in a USAF design-study competition won in 1949 and in a contract awarded in 1952 to produce the aircraft as a "weapon system" management concept which made the company responsible not only for the airframe but for managing the development of all systems except engines. An important part of the "minimum size" concept, which also governed the design, is the two-component disposable armament and fuel pod carried beneath the fuselage. The lower component carries only fuel, and in combat would be dropped as soon as the fuel became exhausted. The upper component contains both fuel and one weapon, either nuclear or conventional. Additional weapons are carried under the wings. With weapons released the aircraft is not only "clean" aerodynamically but is carrying no useless empty structure within itself. The Hustler was also the first aircraft to have individual escape capsules for the crew, for emergency use at supersonic speeds. The first manned ejection test was on 28 February 1962, and since that date capsules have been fitted retrospectively.

The sharp temperature rise from aerodynamic friction associated with the Mach 2 performance of the Hustler made necessary an entirely new approach to the design and manufacture of the skin and primary structures. The heat- and fatigue-resistant skin is made of a glass-fibre, aluminium and stainless steel honeycomb, sandwiched between two layers of metal. About 90 per cent of the wing surface is made of honeycomb sandwich panels.

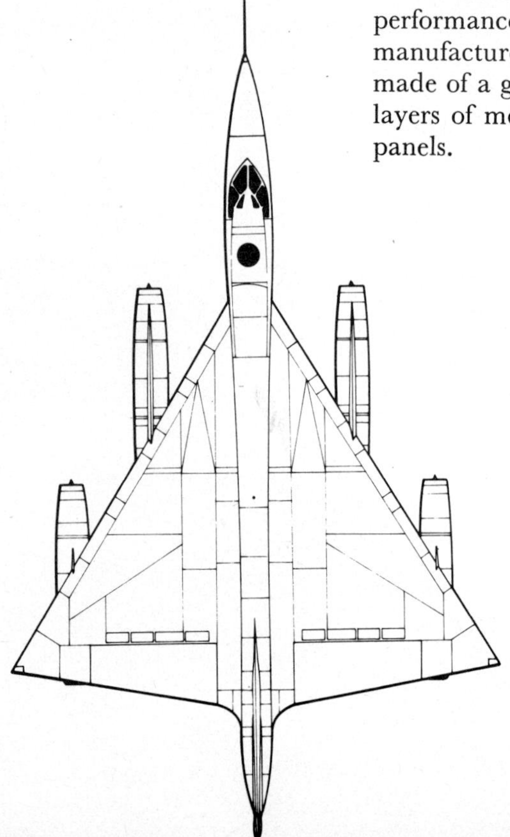

The following versions have been produced since the first prototype made its initial flight on 11 November 1956:

B-58A. Standard production version. Of 30 service-test models the first eight had General Electric J79-GE-1 turbojets. The remainder had J79-GE-5 turbojets, like the fully operational B-58A, of which 86 were built before production ended in the Autumn of 1962. In addition to these 86, ten service-test models were brought up to operational standard. Eight more were converted into TB-58A trainers.

NB-58A. One service test B-58A adapted as a flying test bed for the General Electric J93-GE-3 turbojet, in an under-fuselage pod.

TB-58A. Eight service-test models converted as dual-control trainers. Extended cockpit windows. Military equipment deleted but flight refuelling equipment retained.

During flight trials, Hustlers attained speeds up to Mach 2·09 (equivalent to 1,380 mph = 2,220 kmh) at 50,000 ft (15,250 m). Low-level capabilities were demonstrated with a 1,400-mile (2,250 km) flight at nearly 700 mph (1,126 kmh) while never exceeding 500 ft (150 m) above the ground. In January 1961 six international closed-circuit speed records were set up by Hustlers. On 12 January, Major Henry J. Deutschendorf and crew averaged 1,061·81 mph (1,708·82 kmh) round a 2,000-km circuit, carrying a 2,000 kg (4,409 lb) payload. This raised the records also for 1,000 kg payload and no payload over this distance. Two days later, Major Harold E. Confer and crew set up records for 2,000 kg payload, 1,000 kg payload and no payload over a 1,000-km circuit with an average speed of 1,284·73 mph (2,067·58 kmp).

On 10 May 1961, another B-58A, piloted by Major Elmer E. Murphy, flew at a sustained speed of 1,302 mph (2,095 kmh) for 30 minutes, thereby winning the Aero Club de France Blériot Trophy for the first aircraft to average 2,000 kmh for 30 minutes. The same aircraft, piloted by Major W. R. Payne, flew non-stop 3,669 miles (5,905 km) from New York to Paris in 3 hours, 19 min, 41 sec, on 26 May 1961, at an average speed of 1,105 mph (1,778 kmh). This was one leg of a non-stop flight of 5,183 miles (8,341 km) during which the Hustler was three times refuelled in flight.

Three more official records were set on 5 March 1962, during a Los Angeles to New York return flight, covering speed in both directions and the return trip. The Los Angeles–New York leg was

LANDING GEAR:

Retractable tricycle type. Each main unit has an eight-wheel bogie which retracts vertically upward into wings. Nose-unit has twin wheels and retracts rearward.

POWER PLANT:

Four General Electric J79-GE-5B turbojet engines (each 15,600 lb = 7,075 kg st with afterburning) in underwing pods with variable air-inlet ducts. Fuel in wings and under-fusalge pod. Normal fuel capacity more than 15,000 US gallons (56,780 litres). Flight refuelling socket for "flying boom" system on port side of fuselage nose.

ACCOMMODATION:

Crew of three (pilot, navigator-bombardier and defence systems operator) in separate tandem cockpits with individual hinged canopies and individual self-contained emergency escape capsules capable of being used at Mach 2.

SYSTEMS AND EQUIPMENT:

Bendix electronic powered-control and autopilot system which continually senses and computes maximum control surface movement permitted by structural limitations over the entire speed range. Sperry bombing-navigation system, providing automatic internal guidance. Hamilton Standard automatic air conditioning and pressurisation system provides cooling for the cockpits, wheel wells and electronic installations, controls heating, de-humidifies the cabin air and provides demisting and rain removal air for windscreen.

Pilot, navigator-bombardier and defence systems operator have individual self-contained emergency escape capsules capable of operation at Mach 2

timed at 2 hr, 58·7 sec. On 14 September 1962, a Hustler climbed to 85,360·84 ft (26,018 m), establishing records for height with 5,000 kg and 2,000 kg payloads. The total of speed and altitude/payload records was brought up to 19 on 16 October 1963. Most significant of the new records was the longest supersonic flight made up to that date, from Tokyo to London, in 8 hr 53 min. The officially recognised distance for this flight is 8,028 miles (12,920 km) measured as a great circle route between the two cities. In fact, the Hustler covered a considerably greater distance, in order to keep over friendly territory.

TYPE:

Three-seat medium bomber.

WINGS:

Cantilever mid-wing monoplane of delta-configuration. All-metal structure making extensive use of honeycomb sandwich skin panels. Conical camber leading-edge. Wide-chord elevons from wing-root fairings to outboard engine pods.

FUSELAGE:

All-metal semi-monocoque structure, conforming with the Area Rule and making extensive use of honeycomb skin panels. Large ribbon braking parachute housed under tail.

TAIL UNIT:

Vertical fin and rudder only. All-metal construction.

ARMAMENT:

One General Electric T-171E3 Vulcan 20-mm multi-barrel cannon in flexible mounting in fuselage tail-cone.

DIMENSIONS, external:

Wing span 56 *ft* 10 *in* (17·32 *m*)
Length overall 96 *ft* 9 *in* (29·49 *m*)
Height overall 29 *ft* 11 *in* (9·12 *m*)

WEIGHT:

Max T-O weight over 160,000 *lb* (72,570 *kg*)

PERFORMANCE (at max T-O weight):

Normal max speed at 44,000 *ft* (13,400 *m*)
Mach 2 (1,324 *mph* = 2,118 *kmh*)
Service ceiling over 60,000 *ft* (18,300 *m*)

Each main unit of the landing gear has an eight-wheel bogie retracting vertically upward into the wings

DASSAULT MIRAGE III

"Mixed-power" interceptor fighters, having rocket engines in addition to turbojet engines, were being designed and developed in Germany during 1945 and rocket-boosted versions of the Me 262 were actually flown. One of these was fitted with "mixed-power units" made by BMW and comprising a standard turbojet and a bi-fuel rocket. Another had a jettisonable rocket unit under the fuselage. In post-war years the mixed-power formula has been favoured in France.

During 1954 the S.O. 9000 Trident was tested with a rocket unit in the fuselage and a turbojet on each wing-tip, but this type was never built in quantity. The first machine of the class to achieve this status was the Dassault Mirage III, an all-weather delta-wing single-seater designed initially as a high-altitude interceptor but developed to perform ground-support missions from small airstrips. The first prototype was initially flown on 17 November 1956, powered by a SNECMA Atar 101G turbojet with afterburner. In this form, on 30 January 1957, it exceeded Mach 1·5 in level flight at an altitude of 36,380 ft (11,000 m). Later it was fitted with an SEPR 66 auxiliary rocket engine and reached a speed of Mach 1·9 with this in use, supplementing the turbojet. On 24 October 1958 one of the pre-series Mirage III-As exceeded Mach 2 in level flight at 41,000 ft (12,500 m). The Mirage III-B was a two-seater development and the III-C

A braking parachute is a feature

was the production version of the III-A, an all-weather interceptor and day ground attack fighter with SNECMA Atar 9B turbojet engine and optional SEPR 841 rocket engine. Aircraft of this series, and also of the later, slightly longer III-E series, have achieved remarkable success in the export market. The Mirage III-E has a normal magnetic detector mounted in the fin, and a central gyro and "black boxes" to provide accurate and stabilised heading information. The pilot's equipment determines at any instant the geographical co-ordinates of the aircraft and compares them with the co-ordinates of the target, the difference between the two being presented to the pilot as a "course to steer" and "distance to run". Associated with this facility is a rotative magazine in the cockpit in which it is possible to insert up to 12 plastic punch-cards. Each card represents the co-ordinates of a geographical position. Therefore it is possible before take-off at Point A to select point B on the rotating magazine. During take-off, i.e. after reaching 173 mph (278 kmh), the computer will switch on and the heading and distance to point B will be presented to the pilot. When overhead point B (assuming a pure navigational sortie) he can select either point A or the next turning point, or if required this sequence can continue until a maximum of twelve pre-set turning points have been used. Another facility available in the computer is known as the "additional base". Assuming that between points A and B the pilot receives instructions by radio to go to point C (and that there is no punch card in the magazine for point C) the pilot can, by means of setting knobs, "wind on" the bearing and distance of point C from point B; then, when he selects the switch "additional base", the heading to steer and distance to run to point C will be indicated.

Marconi Doppler equipment provides the ground speed and drift information for the above, while TACAN is presented as a "bearing and distance" on an indicator.

The Mirage III was the precursor of an entire family of military aircraft, including the Mirage IV supersonic bomber for the French Air Force and experimental VTOL and "swing-wing" developments. The latest development is the Mirage 5 (M.5) ground attack aircraft, with simplified electronics, greater fuel capacity and extended stores carrying capability.

The following data refer to the Mirage III-E, but are generally applicable to all versions.

TYPE:

Single-seat fighter.

WINGS:

Cantilever low-wing monoplane of delta planform, with conical camber. Thickness/chord ratio 4·5% to 3·5%. Aspect ratio 1·94. Anhedral 1°. No incidence. Sweepback on leading-edge 60° 34′. All-metal torsion-box structure with stressed skin of machined panels with integral stiffeners. Elevons are hydraulically powered by Dassault twin-cylinder actuators with artificial feel. Air-brakes, comprising small panels hinged to upper and lower wing surfaces, near leading-edge.

FUSELAGE:

All-metal structure, "waisted" in accordance with the Area Rule.

TAIL UNIT:

Cantilever fin and hydraulically-actuated powered rudder only. Dassault twin-cylinder actuators with artificial feel.

LANDING GEAR:

Retractable tricycle type, with single wheel on all units. Hydraulic retraction, nose-wheel rearward, main units inward. Messier shock-absorbers and hydraulic disc brakes. Main wheel tyre pressure 85·5–142 lb/sq in (6–10 kg/cm²). Braking parachute.

POWER PLANT:

One SNECMA Atar O9C turbojet engine (13,670 lb = 6,200 kg st with afterburner), plus optional and jettisonable SEPR 844 single-chamber rocket motor (3,300 lb = 1,500 kg st) or interchangeable fuel tank. Movable half-cone centre-body in each air

The two-seater has a one-piece canopy

The Royal Australian Air Force is among the Services equipped with one of France's most notable products

intake. Total internal fuel capacity 733 Imp gallons (3,330 litres) when rocket motor is not fitted. Provision for this to be augmented by two 132, 285 or 374 Imp gallon (600, 1,300 or 1,700 litre) underwing drop-tanks.

ACCOMMODATION:

Single seat under rearward-hinged canopy. Hispano-built Martin-Baker Type RM.4 zero-altitude ejection seat.

SYSTEMS:

Two separate air-conditioning systems for cockpit and electronics. Two independent hydraulic systems, pressure 3,000 lb/sq in (210 kg/cm^2), for flying controls, landing gear and brakes. Power for DÇ electrical system from 24V 40Ah batteries and a 26·5V 9kW generator. AC electrical system power provided by one 200V 400 c/s transformer and one 200V 400 c/s 9kVA alternator.

ELECTRONICS AND EQUIPMENT:

Duplicated UHF, TACAN, Doppler, CSF Cyrano II fire-control radar in nose, navigation computer, bombing computer, automatic gunsight.

ARMAMENT:

Normal interceptor armament comprises one MATRA R.530 air-to-air missile under fuselage. Provision for two 30-mm DEFA cannon in fuselage, each with 125 rounds of ammunition, and two Sidewinder air-to-air missiles in addition to R.530. Ground attack armament consists normally of the 30-mm guns and two 1,000 lb bombs, or an AS.30 air-to-surface missile under the fuselage and 1,000 lb bombs under the wings. Alternative underwing stores include JL-100 pods, each with 18 rockets, and 55 Imp gallon (250 litre) fuel tanks.

DIMENSIONS:

Wing span 27 *ft* 0 *in* (8·22 *m*)
Length overall 49 *ft* 3½ *in* (15·03 *m*)
Height overall 13 *ft* 11½ *in* (4·25 *m*)

WEIGHTS AND LOADING:

Weight empty 15,540 *lb* (7,050 *kg*)
Max T-O weight 29,760 *lb* (13,500 *kg*)
Max wing loading 75·85 *lb sq/ft* (370 kg/m^2)

PERFORMANCE (Mirage III-E, in "clean" condition with guns installed):

Max level speed at low altitude 870 *mph* (1,400 *kmh*)
Approach speed 211 *mph* (340 *kmh*)
Landing speed 168 *mph* (270 *kmh*)
Time to 36,100 *ft* (11,000 *m*), *Mach* 0·9 3 *min*
Time to 49,200 *ft* (15,000 *m*), *Mach* 1·8 6 *min* 50 *sec*
T-O run, according to mission 2,295–5,250 *ft* (700–1,600 *m*)
Landing run, using brake parachute 2,295 *ft* (700 *m*)
Max combat radius:
low level throughout 305 *miles* (490 *km*)
high-low-high 398 *miles* (640 *km*)
high level throughout 472 *miles* (760 *km*)

Since the first prototype of the Mirage III made its initial flight on 17 November 1956 the type has been developed as a two-seater trainer, fighter-bomber and reconnaissance aircraft. Primary mission was interception

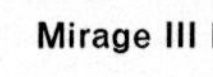

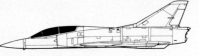

Mirage III B

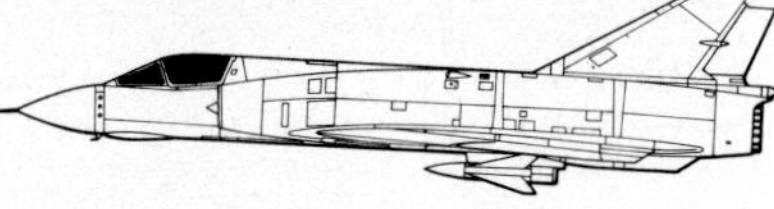

Mirage III E

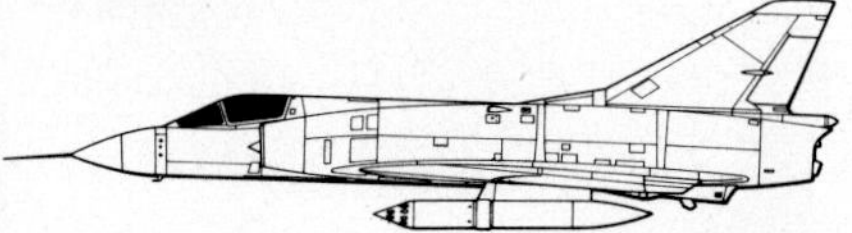

Mirage III C

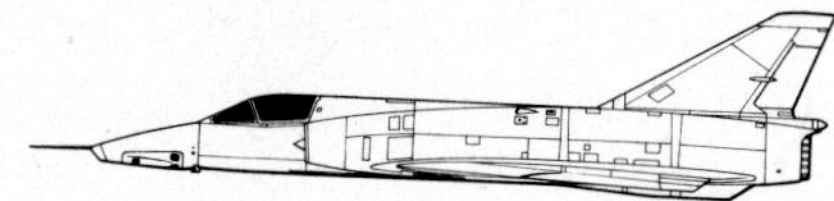

Mirage III R

CESSNA MODEL 150

The name of Clyde V. Cessna, who flew his first aeroplane in 1911, lives on today in the Cessna Aircraft Company. Already a familiar figure in American aeronautics, Clyde Cessna became president of the Travel Air Company in 1925, then being associated with Walter Beech and Lloyd Stearman. Like Clyde Cessna, Walter Beech had been a "barnstormer" pilot, and his name likewise lives on today in the Beech Aircraft Corporation, which shares with the Cessna and Piper companies the distinction of supplying the greatest numbers of private and corporate aircraft to world markets. An aircraft of particular note in this context is the Cessna Model 150, the prototype of which flew for the first time in September 1957. By January 1969, a total of 12,319 Model 150s had been delivered.

The Model 150J now described is available in standard, trainer and commuter versions, on wheels or floats. The trainer has as standard equipment dual controls, a Cessna 300 series 90-channel nav-com installation, rate of climb indicator, a turn co-ordinator that provides visual presentation of turn information, and landing lights.

The 10,000th Cessna 150, delivered in December 1967, displaying the long wheel fairings and raked tail surfaces which characterise late models in the 150 series

The commuter has the same equipment as the trainer, plus a vacuum system with directional and horizon gyros, wheel fairings, individual seats, heated pilot and "omni-flash" beacon.

Although nominally a two-seater, the 150J can be fitted with a "family seat", aft of the main seats, for one or two children with a combined weight not exceeding 120 lb (54 kg).

Compared with earlier versions, the 150J has an extensively revised instrument panel with an integral central pedestal and all electrical switches and circuit breakers relocated to a panel unit in front of the pilot, a key starter and more knee room for pilot and passenger. Optional extras include a wing levelling stability augmentation system, winterisation kit, control-wheel mounted map light, advanced design dry vacuum pump, ground service plug for external battery connection, and handle and step for floatplane refuelling.

Data relate to the standard landplane.

TYPE:

Two-seat cabin monoplane.

WINGS:

Braced high-wing monoplane. Wing section NACA 2412 (tips symmetrical). Aspect ratio 7. Chord 5 ft 4 in (1·63 m) at root, 3 ft 8½ in (1·12 m) at tip. Dihedral 1°. Incidence 1° at root, 0° at tip. All-metal structure, with formed Royalite tips. Modified Frise all-metal ailerons. Electrically-actuated NACA single-slotted all-metal flaps.

FUSELAGE:

All-metal semi-monocoque structure.

TAIL UNIT:

Cantilever all-metal structure, with sweptback vertical surfaces. Trim-tab in starboard elevator.

LANDING GEAR:

Non-retractable tricycle type. "Land-o-Matic" spring-steel cantilever main legs. Steerable nose-wheel on oleo-pneumatic shock-absorber strut. Size 6·00 × 6 wheels, with nylon tube-type tyres, on main wheels; size 5·00 × 5 nose-wheel, with nylon tube-type tyre. Tyre pressure 30 lb/sq in (2·11 kg/cm²). Toe-operated single-disc hydraulic brakes. Optional wheel fairings for all three units (standard on commuter). Floats optional.

POWER PLANT:

One 100 hp Continental O-200-A four-cylinder horizontally-opposed air-cooled engine. McCauley two-blade metal fixed-pitch propeller, diameter 5 ft 9 in (1·75 m) on landplane, 6 ft 3 in (1·90 m) on floatplane version. Two all-metal fuel tanks in wings. Total standard fuel capacity 26 US gallons (98 litres); optional long-range tanks increase total capacity to 38 US gallons (143·8 litres). Oil capacity 1·5 US gallons (5·7 litres).

ACCOMMODATION:

Enclosed cabin seating two side-by-side. Dual controls standard in trainer and commuter, optional in standard model. Baggage compartment behind seats, backs of which hinge forward for access. Baggage capacity 120 lb (54 kg). Alternatively, "family seat" can be fitted in baggage space, for two children not exceeding 120 lb (54 kg) total weight. Door on each side. Heating and ventilation standard. Winterisation kit optional.

ELECTRONICS AND EQUIPMENT:

Optional equipment includes Cessna 90-channel nav/com 300 installation (standard on trainer and commuter); nav/omni 300 with full VOR/LOC/ glideslope receiver and optional marker beacon; nav/com 300R; ADF 300; blind-flying instrumentation (standard on commuter model); dual controls (standard in trainer and commuter); and "omni-flash" beacon (standard on commuter). Wing levelling stability augmentation system optional.

DIMENSIONS:

Wing span 32 *ft* 8½ *in* (9·97 *m*)
Length overall 23 *ft* 0 *in* (7·01 *m*)
Height overall 8 *ft* 7½ *in* (2·63 *m*)

WEIGHTS:

Weight empty 975 *lb* (442 *kg*)
Max T-O weight 1,600 *lb* (726 *kg*)

Floats demand extra fin area

PERFORMANCE:

Max speed at S/L 122 *mph* (196 *kmh*)
Max cruising speed (75% *power*) *at* 7,000 *ft* (2,133 *m*) 117 *mph* (188 *kmh*)
Stalling speed, flaps down 48 *mph* (78 *kmh*)
Service ceiling 12,650 *ft* (3,850 *m*)
Range at econ cruising speed, normal tankage 565 *miles* (909 *km*)

Pre-rollout shot of 3,000th model 150

FAIREY (WESTLAND) ROTODYNE

The rear end of the fuselage comprised clamshell-type loading doors

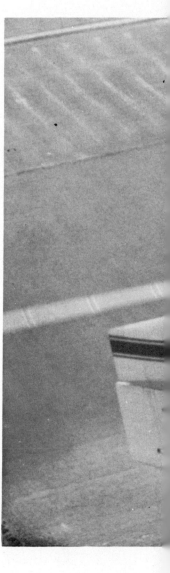

A design for a "convertiplane", that is an aircraft having horizontal screws or rotors for vertical lift and propellers for propulsion, was published by the Englishman Sir George Cayley in 1843, and this design had the further distinction that the rotors were intended to close, in order to form wings. The idea of such an aircraft, which would reconcile the virtues of the fixed-wing aeroplane with those of the helicopter, persisted, and in April 1955 the McDonnell XV-1 gained for America the credit of achieving the first "translation" from vertical to horizontal flight. In 1957 the British Fairey company, founded by Richard (later Sir Richard) Fairey in 1915 and already mentioned in the context of the Curtiss R2C-1 Navy Racer and Hawker Hart, themselves produced an aircraft of this "compound helicopter" class which, though never brought to fruition, was a highly significant achievement in aeronautical engineering. This prototype (later called Rotodyne Y) was based on experience gained with the Fairey Jet Gyrodyne. It flew for the first time on 6 November 1957 and on 5 January 1959 established a world's speed record for rotorcraft with a speed of 307·22 kmh (191 mph) over a closed circuit of 100 km.

This aircraft was considerably smaller than the intended production version (Rotodyne Z) which was to be powered with two Rolls-Royce Tyne turboprop engines and carry 54–70 passengers. Interest was aroused by the Rotodyne among operators throughout the world, for it was rightly perceived as the world's first vertical take-off airliner, and a £4 million development contract was awarded to Westland Aircraft (still eminent among the world's constructors of rotary-wing aircraft) following its take-over of the Rotodyne development programme in 1960. As in the first prototype, the Tyne-engined production version was to have its engines coupled to auxiliary air compressors through a clutch. The compressors would deliver air to pressure-jet units at the tips of the rotor blades where fuel would be burned to produce thrust for rotation. It was recognised that noise would be a factor which could militate against the utilisation of the Rotodyne for civil purposes and considerable research into noise reduction led to the development of suppressors which offered a 90 per cent reduction at a distance of 200 ft (60 m) for a loss of only 5 per cent thrust. It was estimated that the noise level of production aircraft at this distance would be 95 decibels, which was no greater than for large twin-engined helicopters with piston engines.

The Rotodyne could be flown as a pure helicopter, with tip-jets alight and propellers giving zero thrust, or as an autogyro, with engine power being delivered to the propellers only, the rotor being in autorotation. For take-off and landing tip-jet power was normally used, whereas for cruising flight the rotor would be autorotating. The first transition from

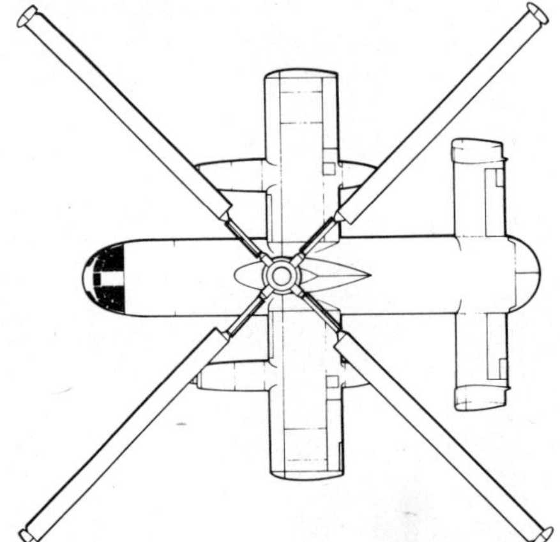

vertical flight to horizontal flight was accomplished on 10 April 1958 and development went ahead as already described, but financial and other considerations compelled the Westland company to abandon the programme in 1962.

The following particulars relate to the Rotodyne Y, as actually flown.

TYPE:
Large transport compound helicopter.

The Rotodyne was designed, built and initially developed by the Fairey company, but later development was the responsibility of Westland Aircraft Ltd, which today is actively studying designs for very advanced V.TOL aircraft of other types

Practical investigations of the Rotodyne's possibilities were made

ROTOR SYSTEM:

Single four-blade main rotor of all-metal (mainly stainless steel) construction carried above fuselage on massive pylon structure, fully faired early in 1960. No anti-torque rotor.

ROTOR DRIVE:

Pressure-jet units of Fairey design at rotor-blade tips.

WINGS:

Cantilever high-wing monoplane. All-metal two-spar construction. Ailerons fitted, and angle of incidence increased, during 1959.

FUSELAGE:

All-metal semi-monocoque structure of rectangular cross-section.

TAIL UNIT:

Braced monoplane type, mounted on top of fuselage. Three fins and two rudders (central fin added early 1960). All-metal construction.

LANDING GEAR:

Retractable tricycle type with main wheels retracting into engine nacelles. Oleo-pneumatic shock-absorbers.

POWER PLANT:

Two Napier Eland N. E1.3 turboprop engines of 3,000 ehp maximum rating mounted in nacelles underslung from wing and driving de Havilland four-blade propellers. Fairey pressure-jet on tip of each rotor blade. Fuel in wings.

ACCOMMODATION:

Flight compartment with dual controls in nose of fuselage. Unrestricted main cabin with clamshell-type loading doors at rear. Accommodation possible for 40 passengers.

DIMENSIONS:

Rotor diameter 90 *ft* 0 *in* (27·43 *m*)
Wing span 47 *ft* 0 *in* (14·32 *m*)

WEIGHTS:

The Rotodyne Y flew at weights up to 33,000 *lb* (14,968 *kg*)

PERFORMANCE:

The Rotodyne Y established a world's speed record of 307·22 *kmh* (191 *mph*)
Range 285 *miles* (459 *km*)

The RF-4C reconnaissance version has a special nose

McDONNELL PHANTOM II

The first McDonnell Phantom was a US Navy fighter produced in 1946, and the Phantom II is an entirely new design, though likewise originally built for the US Navy. It is an aircraft of exception versatility and has found very wide international acceptance. The prototype (XF4H-1) flew for the first time on 27 May 1958 and achieved the very remarkable speed of Mach 2·6 during its flight trials. Subsequent development is best related in the following notes on variants built to date.

F-4A. (formerly F4H-1F). The 11th production F-4B was equipped for trials in the ground attack role under this designation. During one test, it carried a total of twenty-two 500 lb bombs under its fuselage and inner wings. Further F-4Bs were subsequently equipped to F-4A standard. After evaluation of this version, the USAF decided to order land-based versions of the F-4A under the designations F-4C and RF-4C.

F-4B. (formerly F4H-1). Standard all-weather fighter for US Navy and Marine Corps. Development series of 23 followed by first production models in 1961. First 40 F-4Bs were each powered by two General Electric J79-GE-2A turbojets. Subsequent aircraft have J79-GE-8's. About 550 built by mid-1965.

RF-4B. (formerly F4H-1P). Multi-sensor reconnaissance version of F-4B for US Marine Corps. No dual controls or armament. J79-GE-8 engines. High-frequency single side-band radio. Twelve ordered under 1963 fiscal year budget. Overall length increased to 63 ft (19·2 m).

F-4C. (formerly F-110A). Two-seat fighter for USAF, developed from F-4A, with J79-GE-15 turbojets, cartridge starting, wider-tread low-pressure tyres, larger brakes, Litton inertial navigation system, APQ-100 radar, APQ-100 PPI scope, LADD timer, Lear Siegler AJB-7 bombing system, GAM-83 controls, dual controls and boom flight refuelling instead of drogue (receptacle in top of fuselage, aft of cockpit). Folding wings and arrester gear retained. For close support and attack duties with Tactical Air Command, PACAF and USAFE.

RF-4C. (formerly RF-110A). Multiple-sensor reconnaissance version of F-4C for USAF, with radar and photographic systems in modified nose which increases overall length by 2 ft 9 in (0·84 m). Three basic reconnaissance systems are: side-looking radar to record high-definition radar picture of terrain on each side of flight path on film; infra-red detector to locate enemy forces under cover or at night by detecting exhaust gases and other heat sources; forward and side-looking cameras, including panoramic models with moving-lens fitments for horizon-to-horizon pictures. Films can be processed in flight and ejected over ground command post. Systems are operated from rear seat. HF single side-band radio.

F-4D. Development of F-4C for USAF, with J79-GE-15 turbojets, APQ-109 fire-control radar, ASG-22 servoed sight, ASQ-91 weapon release computer, ASG-22 lead computing amplifier, ASG-22 lead computing gyro, 30kVA generators, and ASN-63 inertial navigation system.

F-4E. Multi-role fighter for USAF, capable of performing air superiority, close-support and interdiction missions. Has internally-mounted M-61A1 20-mm multi-barrel gun, improved (AN/APQ-120) fire-control system and J79-GE-17 turbojets. Additional fuselage fuel cell.

F-4G. Development of F-4B for US Navy, with AN/ASW-21 data link communications equipment. Interim model pending availability of F-4J.

F-4J. Development of F-4B for US Navy and Marine Corps, primarily as interceptor but with full ground attack capability. J79-GE-10 turbojets. Increased flap area, 16½° drooping ailerons and slotted tail give reduced approach speed in spite of increased landing weight. Westinghouse AWG-10 Doppler fire-control system. Lear Siegler AJB-7 bombing system, 30kVA generaors.

F-4K. Development of F-4B for Royal Navy, with improvements evolved for F-4J plus other changes. The Westinghouse AN/AWG-10 pulse Doppler fire-control radar system has been modified to allow the antenna to swing around with the radome. Two Rolls-Royce Spey RB.168-25R Mk 201 turbofans with 70% reheat. The air intake ducts are 6 in (15·2 cm) wider than on US models to cater for these more powerful engines. Drooped ailerons. Tailplane has reduced anhedral and incorporates a leading-edge fixed slot. Strengthened main landing gear. Nose landing gear strut extends to 40 in (1·02 m), compared to 20 in (0·51 m) on the F-4J, to permit optimum-incidence catapulting. Martin-Baker ejection seats. Weapons include Sparrow air-to-air missiles and Martel air-to-surface missiles.

F-4M. Version for Royal Air Force. Generally similar to F-4K, but with larger brakes and low-pressure tyres of F-4C. Folding wings and arrester gear retained.

The Phantom II has set up many official records since December 1959, including World Speed and Height Records of 1,606·48 mph (2,585·425 kmh) and 98,556 ft (30,040 m) respectively.

The following details apply specifically to the F-4B:

TYPE:

Twin-engined two-seat all-weather fighter.

WINGS:

Cantilever low-wing monoplane. Average thickness/chord ratio 5·1%. Sweep-back 45°. Outer panels have extended chord, giving "dog-tooth" leading-edge, and dihedral of 12°. Centre-section and centre wings form one-piece structure from wing fold to wing fold. Portion that passes through fuselage comprises a torsion-box between the front and main spars (at 15% and 40% chord) and is sealed to form two integral fuel tanks. Spars are machined from large forgings. Centre wings also have forged rear spar. Centre-line rib, wing-fold ribs, two intermediate ribs forward of main spar and two aft of main spar are also made from forgings. Wing skins machined from aluminium panels 2½ in (6·35 cm) thick,with integral stiffening. Trailing-edge is a one-piece aluminium honeycomb structure. Flaps and ailerons of all-metal construction, with aluminium honeycomb trailing-edges. Inset ailerons limited to down movement only, the "up" function being supplied by hydraulically-operated spoilers on upper surface of each wing. Ailerons and spoilers fully powered by two independent hydraulic systems. Hydraulically-operated trailing-edge flaps and leading-edge flap on outboard half of each inner wing panel are "blown" Hydraulically-operated air-brake under each wing aft of wheel well. Outer wing panels fold upward for stowage.

FUSELAGE:

All-metal semi-monocoque structure, built in forward, centre and rear sections. Forward fuselage fabricated in port and starboard halves, so that most internal wiring and finishing can be done before assembly. Keel and rear sections make extensive use of steel and titanium. Double-wall construction under fuel tanks and for lower section of rear fuselage, with ram air cooling.

TAIL UNIT:

Cantilever all-metal structure, with 23° of anhedral on one-piece all-moving horizontal surfaces (anhedral on RAF and RN versions is reduced to 15° and leading-edge incorporates a fixed slot). Ribs and stringers of horizontal surfaces are of steel, skin of titanium and trailing-edge of steel honeycomb. Rudder interconnected with ailerons at low speeds.

LANDING GEAR:

Hydraulically-retractable tricycle type, main wheels retracting inward into wings, nose unit rearward. Single wheel on each main unit, with tyres size 30 × 7·7; twin wheels on nose unit which is steerable and self-centering, and can be lengthened pneumatically to increase the aircraft's angle of attack for take-off. Brake-chute housed in fuselage tail-cone.

POWER PLANT:

Two General Electric J79-GE-8 turbojet engines (each 16,500 lb = 7,485 kg st with afterburning). Variable-area inlet ducts monitored by air data computer. Integral fuel tankage in wings, between front and main spars, and in six fuselage tanks, with total capacity of 2,000 US gallons (7,569 litres). Provision for one 600 US gallon (2,270 litres) external tank under fuselage and two 370 US gallon (1,400 litre) underwing tanks. Equipment for probe-and-drogue and "buddy tank" flight refuelling, with retractable probe in starboard side of fuselage.

ACCOMMODATION:

Crew of two in tandem on Martin-Baker Mk H5 ejection seats, under individual rearward-hinged canopies. Optional dual controls.

SYSTEMS:

Three independent hydraulic systems, pressure 3,000 lb/sq in (210 kg/cm²). Pneumatic system for canopy operation, nose-wheel strut extension and ram air turbine extension. Primary electrical source is AC generator. No battery.

ARMAMENT:

Six Sparrow III, or four Sparrow III and four Sidewinder, air-to-air missiles on four semi-submerged mountings under fuselage and two underwing mountings. Provision for carrying alternative loads of up to about 16,000 lb (7,250 kg) of nuclear or conventional bombs and missiles on five attachments under wings and fuselage. Typical loads include eighteen 750-lb bombs, fifteen 680-lb mines, eleven 1,000-lb bombs, seven smoke bombs, eleven 150 US gallon napalm bombs, four Bullpup air-to-surface missiles and fifteen packs of air-to-surface rockets.

ELECTRONICS:

Eclipse-Pioneer dead-reckoning navigation computer, Collins AN/ASQ-19 communications-navigation-identification package, AiResearch A/A 24G central air data computer, Raytheon radar altimeter, General Electric ASA-32 autopilot, RCA data link, Lear attitude indicator and AJB-3 bombing system. Westinghouse APQ-72 automatic radar fire-control system in nose. ACF Electronics AAA-1 infra-red detector under nose.

DIMENSIONS, external:

Wing span 38 *ft* 5 *in* (11·70 *m*)
Width, wings folded 27 *ft* 6½ *in* (8·39 *m*)
Length overall 58 *ft* 3 *in* (17·76 *m*)
Height overall 16 *ft* 3 *in* (4·96 *m*)
Wheel track 17 *ft* 10½ *in* (5·30 *m*)

AREA:

Wings, gross 530 *sq ft* (49·2 *m*²)

The brake-chute is housed above the horizontal tail surfaces

WEIGHTS:

T-O weight (clean) 46,000 *lb* (20,865 *kg*)
Max T-O weight 54,600 *lb* (24,765 *kg*)

PERFORMANCE:

Max level speed with external stores over Mach 2
Approach speed 150 *mph* (240 *kmh*)
Combat ceiling 71,000 *ft* (21,640 *m*)
T-O run (interceptor) 5,000 *ft* (1,525 *m*)
Landing run (interceptor) 3,000 *ft* (915 *m*)
Combat radius:
interceptor over 900 *miles* (1,450 *km*)
ground attack over 1,000 *miles* (1,600 *km*)
Ferry range 2,300 *miles* (3,700 *km*)

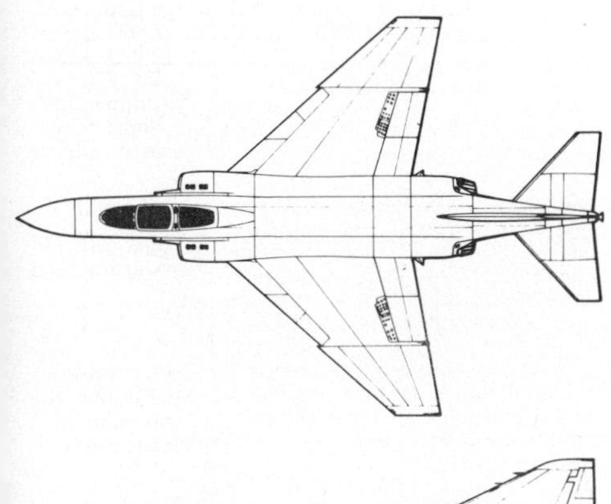

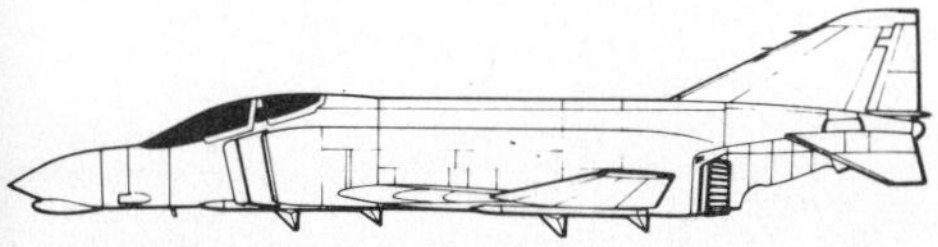

F-4 C

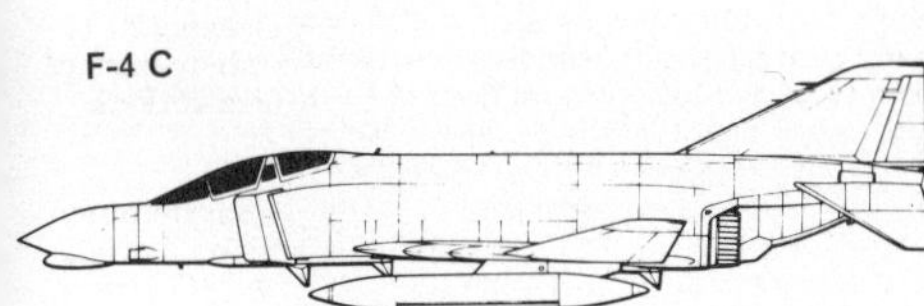

F-4 E

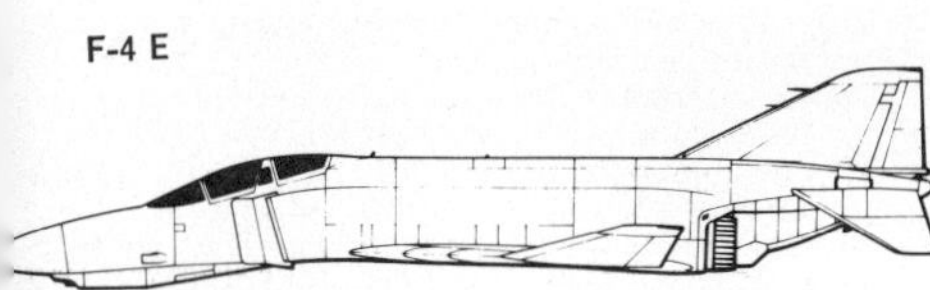

F-4 M

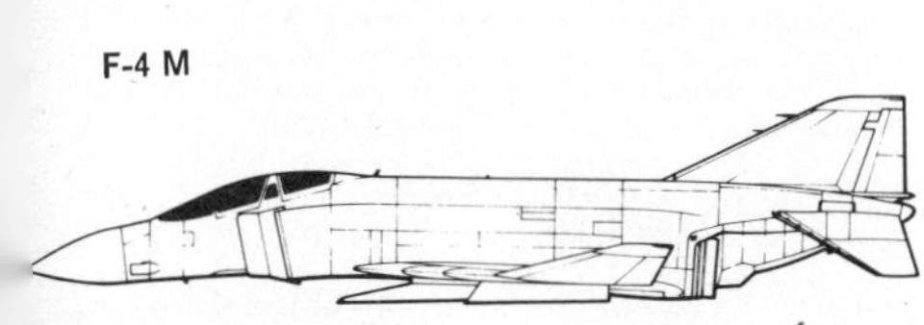

Formerly designated F4H-1, the F-4B is a standard all-weather fighter of the US Navy and Marine Corps. These examples belong to USS "Forrestal"

NORTH AMERICAN X-15A

The X-15A rocket-powered research aircraft was flown faster and higher than any other manned aeroplane. Technical characteristics were extremely advanced and are later described in detail. Piloting skill of an exceptional order was demanded, but twelve different pilots participated in the flying programme. Not the least remarkable aspect of the aircraft was that it flew above the effective atmosphere and depended for control on small rockets, a feature it shared with spacecraft.

A Boeing B-52 Stratofortress got the X-15A airborne

Although it was an outgrowth of the experimental programmes involving earlier US aircraft of the "X" series the X-15A may be considered to date from 1955 when, following preliminary studies by the NACA and an industry-wide design competition, North American was awarded a USAF/USN/NACA contract for three manned research aircraft with a design speed of at least Mach 7 and capable of reaching an altitude of at least 264,000 ft (80,500 m). Known as the X-15A this aircraft was to furnish data particularly with regard to heating, stability, control and the problems of re-entry into the atmosphere.

Initial flight tests with the first two X-15As were made with two Reaction Motors LR11-RM-5 rocket motors (each 8,000 lb = 3,630 kg st) installed in place of the single large Reaction Motors XLR99-RM-2 motor, which was not ready for service. Both aircraft were later re-engined with the XLR99, rated at 57,000 lb (25,855 kg) st at sea level and about 70,000 lb (31,750 kg) st at peak altitudes. The propellant consumption of this engine exceeded 10,000 lb/min at full throttle. The third X-15A was fitted with an XLR99 engine from the start.

The first X-15A flew for the first time under the starboard wing of its B-52 Stratofortress "mother-plane" on 10 March 1959. It was not released on that occasion and its first free flight, without power, was made on 8 June 1959. The first powered test flight was made with the second X-15A on 17 September 1959, when it reached a speed of Mach 2·1 (1,350 mph = 2,172 kmh) in a shallow climb to 52,341 ft (15,953 m). The pilot for these initial tests was North American test pilot Scott Crossfield.

During the third powered flight with No 2 X-15A, on 5 November 1959, there was an engine explosion and it broke its back in landing. It resumed flying on 4 February 1960, after repairs. Meanwhile, the first X-15A had also completed its first powered flight on 23 January 1960.

After March 1960 much of the flight development with the first two X-15A's was taken over by Major Robert White of the USAF, Joseph Walker, chief test pilot for NASA, and Lt Cdr Forrest Petersen, USN.

By 20 October 1960, more than 20 successful flights had been made, using the interim LR11 rocket-engines. On 4 August 1960 Mr Walker achieved an unofficial speed record of 2,196 mph (3,534 kmh), equivalent to Mach 3·31, in the first X-15A. On 12 August 1960 Major White flew the same aircraft to an unofficial altitude record of 136,500 ft (41,605 m).

The first XLR99 engine was delivered in late May 1960 and was installed in the third X-15A. On 8 June 1960, the engine blew up during a ground test run, causing very substantial damage to the aircraft.

The first flight with the XLR99 engine was made by Mr Crossfield in the second X-15A on 15 November 1960. Although the engine was held down to its lowest power and the airbrakes were extended fully, the X-15A achieved a speed of nearly 2,000 mph (3,200 kmh).

Since then numerous flights have set up new unofficial international performance records. On 30 March 1961 Mr Walker reached a height of 169,600 ft (51,695 m). On 21 April Major White attained a speed of 3,074 mph (4,947 kmh). Mr Walker reached 3,307 mph (5,322 kmh) on 25 May and the first "mile per second" flight was made by Major White, who recorded 3,603 mph (5,798 kmh) on 23 June. The first X-15A rejoined the programme, with its XLR99 engine installed, in August 1961. On 9 November 1961, Major White attained 4,093 mph (6,587 kmh), at which temperatures of up to 1,147°F were recorded on the wing leading-edges, and on 30 April 1962 Mr Walker took the X-15A's unofficial altitude record to 246,700 ft (75,200 m). On 27 June 1962, in the first X-15A, Mr. Walker reached a speed of 4,159 mph (6,693 kmh) after the engine burned for 89 seconds instead of the normal 84 seconds. On 17 July 1962, in No 3 aircraft, Major White climbed to a height of 314,750 ft (95,935 m), or 59·6 miles and thereby qualified for his US Astronauts "Wings" by travelling more than 50 miles above the earth. Other pilots later qualified and Mr Walker set a new record by attaining a height of 354,200 ft (107,960 m), or 67·08 miles, on 22 August 1963.

The No 2 aircraft was involved in an accident on 9 November 1962, and the decision was taken to rebuild it in a new form, for even more advanced research. The modifications to the design were finalised in January 1963. Construction began on 13 May 1963, and the aircraft flew for the first time in its new form, as the X-15A-2, on 28 June 1964. First flight with external fuel tanks fitted (see below) was made in early November 1965, the tanks being jettisoned at a speed of 1,400 mph (2,250 kmh) at 71,000 ft (21,650 m). On this occasion, the tanks were empty. On 18 November 1966, the aircraft attained a speed of Mach 6·33, equivalent to 4,250 mph (6,840 kmh), piloted by Major Pete Knight, USAF, and on 3 October 1967 he flew the X-15A-2 at a new unofficial record speed of Mach 6·72, equivalent to 4,534 mph (7,297 kmh).

The basic airframe remained much as before. About 65% of the structure was welded and the aircraft was made largely of titanium and stainless steel, although some aluminium was used internally where high heat and high loads were not a problem. The airframe was covered with an "armour skin" of Inconel X nickel alloy steel, to withstand temperatures ranging from +1,200°F to −300°F.

Test flights of the X-15A-2 encountered temperatures far beyond these limits, so the entire airframe was coated with Emerson Electric T-500 ablative material, like an ICBM nose-cone. The windscreen was modified to cater for the higher kinetic heating and each side was made an elliptical three-pane structure, with a middle pane of alumino-silicate and a fused silica outer pane.

A new extension of the centre fuselage provided accommodation for two propellent tanks containing liquid hydrogen for advanced ramjet engines which could be attached under the rear fuselage, in place of the normal ventral fin. A spherical tank mounted aft of the upper tail fin contained helium to pressurise the liquid hydrogen tanks. New equipment bays contained photographic and optical apparatus for "up-looking" and "down-looking" experiments at great heights.

The X-15A-2 retained its rounded "hot-nose" which was designed by Northrop to sense the angles of attack and side-slip during exit and entry phases of hypersonic flight in the upper atmosphere. The sensor contained a hydraulically-actuated sphere with multiple sensing ports and was designed to point directly into the relative wind at all times. Information displayed on the pilot's instument panel indicated attitude angles which had to be corrected to avoid excessive frictional heating.

The wings were of thin (5%) section, with an aspect ratio of 2·5. Pitch and roll control in the atmosphere were provided by the "all-moving" tailplane, the two parts of which could be moved together or differentially. There were no ailerons, but flaps were fitted on the inboard wing trailing-edges. The starboard wingtip was removable on the X-15A-2 to permit testing of new configurations and materials at hypersonic speeds.

The dorsal and ventral fins had a wedge section with a blunt trailing-edge no less than 12 in (0·30 m) wide. Each contained small split air-brakes. The upper fin was pivoted for directional control; the lower fin was jettisoned before landing. The control surfaces, flaps and air-brakes were all hydraulically-operated.

The landing gear comprised two retractable steel skids on the aft section, below the tailplane, and a conventional twin-wheel nose unit. The skids were lowered by a mechanical system. Retraction was manual. All three units were strengthened and lengthened on the X-15A-2 to provide 3 ft 3½ in (1·0 m) ground clearance and so make possible the mounting of the external ramjets to which reference has already been made.

The X-15A-2 was powered by a Thiokol (Reaction Motors) XLR99-RM-2 single-chamber throttlable liquid-propellent rocket-engine, with a thrust rating of 57,000 lb (25,855 kg) st at 45,000 ft (13,700 m).

Almost all of the fuselage between the cockpit and the rocket motor comprised integral tankage for the liquid oxygen and anhydrous ammonia propellents, which weighed a total of 18,000 lb (8,165 kg). This necessitated carrying the controls and pipelines externally in large wedge-shape fairings which also reduced airflow interference between the wings and fuselage.

External propellent tanks, carried on each side of the fuselage, are each 22 ft 0 in (6·70 m) long and 3 ft 1¾ in (0·96 m) in diameter. The propellents in these tanks were used first, taking the X-15A-2 to a speed of about 1,365 mph (2,195 kmh) at 70,000 ft (21,350 m). The empty tanks were then jettisoned and recovered by parachute, after which the internal propellents were used in the normal way.

Control during high-altitude flying, above the effective atmosphere, was achieved by means of 12 jet nozzles of the HTP rocket type, four in the wing-tips and eight in the nose. These were developed by Bell Aircraft and were controlled by a three-axis stick on the port side of the cockpit. Each produced from 40 to 110 lb (18·50 kg) of thrust.

Flight data were provided by an inertial system developed by Honeywell Military Products Group of the Minneapolis-Honeywell Regulator Co, originally for the abandoned X-20A Dyna-Soar space glider. Installed in the Autumn of 1964, it consisted of an inertial measuring unit, North American Autonetics Verdan computer and coupler electronics. Data were fed by the inertial unit into the computer which provided the pilot with information on altitude, speed, rate of climb and attitude, using a Lear Instrument display. The basic X-15A was also designed to carry more than 1,300 lb (590 kg) of research instrumentation, involving approximately 600 temperature pickups and 140 pressure pickups.

A total of 156 flights had been made by the three X-15As by the end of February 1966. Total time in free flight was then just over 24 hr, including 6 hr 29 min above Mach 3, 4 hr 13 min above Mach 4, 56 min above Mach 5 and 11 sec above Mach 6. The total number of flights had risen to 191 by 20 February 1968. On 15 November 1967, X-15A-3 was lost in a crash near Johannesburg, California.

The X-15 programme was finally terminated in November 1968.

DIMENSIONS, external (X-15A-2):
Wing span 22 *ft* 0 *in* (6·70 *m*)
Length overall 52 *ft* 5 *in* (15·98 *m*)

AREA:
Wings, gross 200 *sq ft* (18·6 m^2)

WEIGHTS (X-15A-2):
Max launching weight 50,914 *lb* (23,095 *kg*)
Max landing weight 17,120 *lb* (7,765 *kg*)

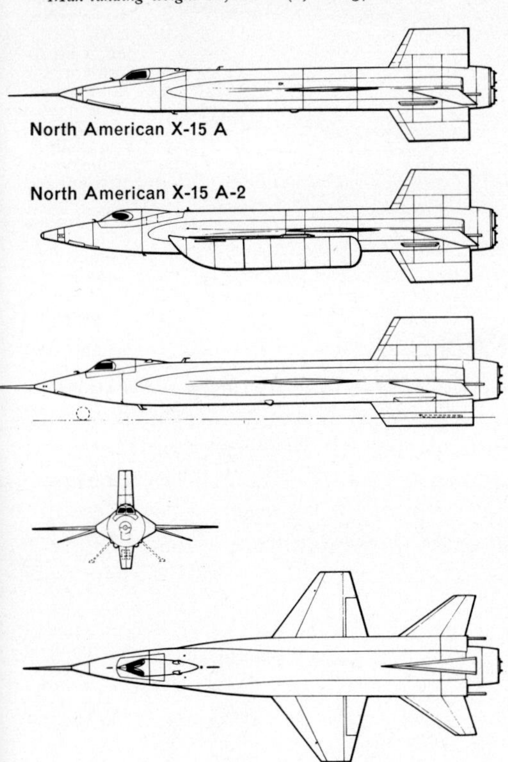

Technical responsibility for the X-15A was vested in NASA. The USAF administered design and construction

The "Grand", S-42, VS-300—and now the Skycrane. Igor Sikorsky installed at right

The original S-60 Skycrane had Pratt & Whitney piston engines and lifted a variety of loads, including the irrepressible Mr Sikorsky and senior engineers

SIKORSKY S-60 and S-64 SKYCRANE

Developed from the S-60 of 1959, the Skycrane is a heavy-lift helicopter of the class known as "universal-lift" or "flying crane". Though massive it is by no means the world's largest, that distinction being held by the Soviet V-12. Even the earlier Mi-10 has a rotor diameter of 114 ft 10 in (35·00 m). Designed for military transport duties, the first S-64 production model (S-64A) can be equipped with interchangeable "pods" for use as a 67-seat troop transport, a mine-sweeper, cargo or missile transport, or for anti-submarine or field-hospital operations.

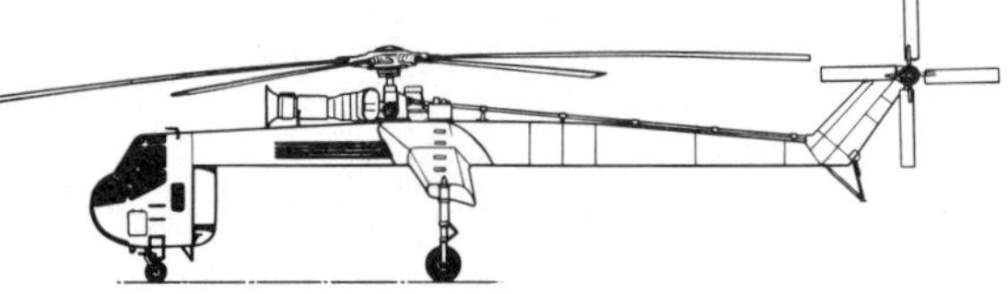

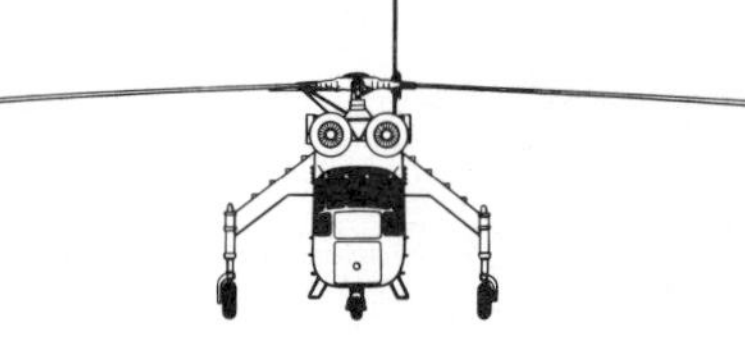

Equipment includes a removable 15,000 lb (6,800 kg) hoist, a sling attachment and a load stabiliser to prevent undue sway in cargo winch operations. Attachment points are provided on the fuselage and landing gear to facilitate securing of bulky loads. Pickup of loads is made easier by the pilot's ability to shorten or extend the landing gear hydraulically.

The first of three prototypes of the S-64A flew for the first time on 9 May 1962. The second and third prototypes were delivered to Federal Germany for evaluation by the German armed forces.

In June 1963, the US Army announced that it had ordered six S-64As, under the designation CH-54A, to investigate the heavy-lift concept, with emphasis on increasing mobility in the battlefield. Delivery of five CH-54As (originally YCH-54As) to the US Army took place in late 1964 and early 1965. A sixth CH-54A remained at Stratford, with a company-owned S-64 for a programme leading toward a restricted FAA certification, which was awarded on 30 July 1965. Further orders for some sixty CH-54s have since been placed.

The first CH-54As were assigned to the US Army in Vietnam. In April 1965 one of these aircraft established new international height records by reaching 21,374 ft (6,515 m) with a 5,000 kg payload, 28,743 ft (8,760 m) with 2,000 kg and 29,340 ft (8,943 m) with 1,000 kg. On 29 April an aircraft of the type lifted 90 persons, including 87 combat-equipped troops, in a detachable "van". This is believed to be the largest number ever carried by a helicopter. Apart from transporting heavy vehicles Skycranes have retrieved some hundreds of damaged aircraft.

Sikorsky Aircraft have developed, and are supplying, an all-purpose van known as the Universal Military Pod having a max loaded weight of 20,000 lb (9,072 kg), accommodating 45 combat-equipped troops or 24 stretchers and adaptable for several other duties. Length of the pod is 31 ft 5 in (9·58 m), width 9 ft 7 in (2·92 m) and height 7 ft 11 in (2·41 m). Entrance doors are provided on either side of the forward area of the pod, and a double-panelled ramp is located aft. Initial production deliveries were scheduled for July 1968.

A civilian "people pod", known as the XB-1 Skylounge, was built by he Budd Company for an evaluation programme which began in 1967. The Skyloung, which seated 23 passengers, was being developed for the Los Angels Department of Airports as a possible means of transporting people speedily between city centre and airport. It could be towed on the ground by a variety of vehicles, enabling passengers to be collected at various points in a city, heliport, flown to an airport by helicopter, and towed to a fixed-wing airliner, without changing from one vehicle to another.

On 15 February 1968, Sikorsky announced that it had received an order for two commercial Skycranes, designated **S-64E**, from Rowan Drilling Company Inc., of Houston, Texas. These will be operated by Rowan through a newly formed subsidiary, Rowan Air Cranes, Inc.

Important new developments are in prospect.

TYPE:

Twin-turbine heavy flying crane helicopter

ROTOR SYSTEM:

Six-blade fully-articulated main rotor with aluminium blades and aluminium and steel head. Four-blade tail rotor with titanium head and aluminium blades. Rotor brake standard.

ROTOR DRIVE:

Steel-tube drive-shafts. Main gearbox below main rotor, intermediate gearbox at base of tail pylon, tail gearbox at top of pylon.

FUSELAGE:

Pod-and-boom type of aluminium and steel semi-monocoque construction.

LANDING GEAR:

Non-retractable tricycle type, with single wheel on each unit.

POWER PLANT:

Two 4,500 shp Pratt & Whitney JFTD12A-4A shaft-turbine engines. Two fuel tanks in fuselage, forward and aft of transmission, each with capacity of 440 US gallons (1,664 litres). Total standard fuel capacity 880 US gallons (3,328 litres). Provision for auxiliary fuel tanks of 440 US gallons (1,664 litres) capacity, raising total fuel capacity to 1,320 US gallons (4,992 litres).

ACCOMMODATION:

Pilot and co-pilot side-by-side at front of cab. Aft-facing seat for third pilot at rear of cabin, with flying controls. The occupant of this third seat is able to take-over control of the aircraft during loading and unloading. Two additional jump seats available in cab. Payload in interchangeable pods (see above).

DIMENSIONS, external:

Diameter of main rotor 72 *ft* 0 *in* (21·95 *m*)
Diameter of tail rotor 16 *ft* 0 *in* (4·88 *m*)
Distance between rotor centres 44 *ft* 6 *in* (13·56 *m*)
Length overall 88 *ft* 6 *in* (26·97 *m*)
Length of fuselage 70 *ft* 3 *in* (21·41 *m*)
Width, rotors folded 21 *ft* 10 *in* (6·65 *m*)
Height to top of rotor hub 18 *ft* 7 *in* (5·67 *m*)
Overall height 25 *ft* 5 *in* (7·75 *m*)
Ground clearance under fuselage boom 9 *ft* 4 *in* (2·84 *m*)
Wheel track 19 *ft* 9 *in* (6·02 *m*)
Wheelbase 24 *ft* 5 *in* (7·44 *m*)

AREAS:

Main rotor disc 4,070 *sq ft* (378·1 m^2)
Tail rotor disc 201 *sq ft* (18·67 m^2)

WEIGHTS:

Weight empty 19,110 *lb* (8,668 *kg*)
Max T-O weight 42,000 *lb* (19,050 *kg*)

PERFORMANCE: (at normal T-O weight of 38,000 lb = 17,237 kg):

Max level speed at S/L 127 *mph* (204 *kmh*)
Max cruising speed 109 *mph* (175 *kmh*)
Max rate of climb at S/L 1,700 *ft* (518 *m*) *min*
Service ceiling 13,000 *ft* (3,960 *m*)
Hovering ceiling in ground effect 10,600 *ft* (3,230 *m*)
Hovering ceiling out of ground effect 6,900 *ft* (2,100 *m*)
Range with max fuel, 10% *reserve* 253 *miles* (407 *km*)

The main pilots' cab. There is an aft-facing seat for a third pilot at rear

The US Army has significantly increased its mobility by adopting the Skycrane

The Soviet Mi-10 is in the Skycrane category. Though bigger, it is not the biggest

The Universal Military Pod has a civilian counterpart in the XB-1 Skylounge

The expression of the Pregnant Guppy is as elegant as its name and shape

First flight of the Super Guppy, 31 August 1965. "World's Largest Airplane" was proclaimed on the nose

Mini Guppy not one of the aeroplanes which looks better in the air

AERO SPACELINES B-377 PREGNANT GUPPY

Post-war conversions of military aircraft for civil purposes have been numerous and there have been a few notable transformations of one form of civil aircraft into another. One of the best examples of these is the Aviation Traders Carvair, a specialised car ferry or mixed-traffic aircraft developed in Great Britain from the Douglas DC-4. More recently the American company Aero Spacelines Inc has undertaken developments of the Boeing Stratocruiser which, in terms of appearance, capacity and purpose, have caused a minor sensation in aeronautical circles.

Aero Spacelines Inc has developed two conversions of Boeing Stratocruiser/C-97 transport aircraft, under the names of Pregnant Guppy and Super Guppy respectively, to provide specialised transportation of large booster stages and other items used in America's national space programmes. The conversions were performed entirely with private capital and with no prior contracts or other commitments. The US government subsequently contracted for the exclusive use of both aircraft, and heavy utilisation by NASA and the Department of Defense has precluded their use for commercial transportation of outsize cargoes.

New advanced versions of the Super Guppy and Mini Guppy were announced late in 1968, and the first three of an eventual mixed fleet of ten or twelve of these two types are now in production and scheduled to be in service during 1969. The final fleet of aircraft is expected to be made up of equal numbers of Super Guppies and Mini Guppies.

The new aircraft will include a commercial version of the Super Guppy with a floor width of 13 ft 0 in (3·96 m), a diameter of 25 ft 6 in (7·77 m) and a cruising speed of 300 mph (483 kmh), carrying a 50,000 lb (22,680 kg) payload; and further Mini Guppies powered by turboprop engines to increase payload to 60,000 lb (27,215 kg).

Construction of the B-377 Pregnant Guppy was initiated in 1961 as a conversion of a Boeing B-377 Stratocruiser into a transport for large booster rockets of the kind being produced under US space programmes. The converted aircraft flew for the first time on 19 September 1962, and was given the designation B-377PG Pregnant Guppy.

The first stage that was flight tested involved lengthening the rear fuselage of the Stratocruiser, by inserting a 16 ft 8 in (5·08 m) section aft of the wing trailing-edge. The much more ambitious second stage entailed building a huge circular-section "bubble" structure over the top of the fuselage. This new structure has an inside height of 19 ft 9 in (6·02 m), compared with a normal headroom of just under 9 ft 0 in (2·74 m) for the upper deck of the aircraft, enabling it to accept cargo up to 19 ft 9 in (6·02 m) in diameter.

Initial flight tests of some 60 hours proved the B-377PG to be stable and controllable in all flight regimes. As a result, the conversion was completed in the Spring of 1963, when the original upper fuselage structure (inside the new structure) was removed and the tail of the aircraft was made removable, for straight-in loading of the booster rockets, carried on oversize pallets, through the medium of a bolt-joint aft of the wing. Volume of the cabin is now 29,187 cu ft (826·5 m²), which was larger than the cabin space available in any other aircraft in the world at the time of the conversions.

Test flying was resumed on 16 May and the B-377PG received FAA Supplemental Type Approval under Part 8 (special purpose) CAR on 10 July 1963. Immediately afterwards, it flew from Los Angeles to Cape Kennedy carrying an inert Saturn S-IV stage manufactured by Douglas Aircraft. This operation and subsequent regular flights have been made under NASA-Marshall Space Flight Center contracts awarded to Aero Spacelines.

The basic power plant consists of four Pratt & Whitney R-4360-B6 radial engines, each driving a Hamilton Standard Model 34E60-387 constant-speed propeller. Early in 1968, these engines were supplemented by attachments for four Aerojet-General 15KS-1000-A1 assisted take-off rockets, and flight tests have shown that these offer a considerable improvement in take-off performance from short runways.

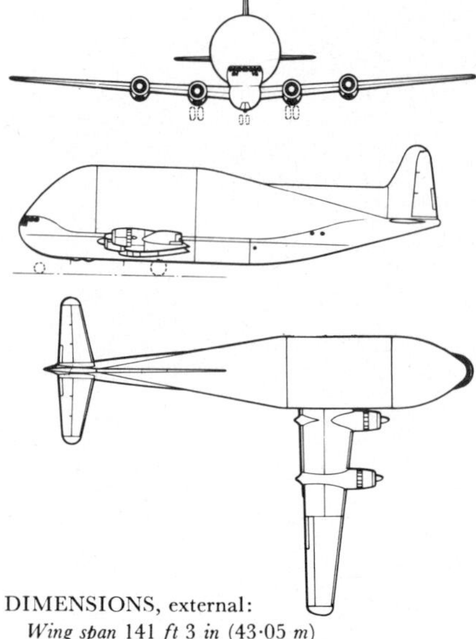

DIMENSIONS, external:

Wing span 141 *ft* 3 *in* (43·05 *m*)
Length overall 127 *ft* 0 *in* (38·71 *m*)
Height to top of fuselage 31 *ft* 3 *in* (9·53 *m*)
Height overall 38 *ft* 3 *in* (11·66 *m*)

DIMENSIONS, internal:

Cargo compartment:
Total length 80 *ft* 0 *in* (24·38 *m*)
Length of constant-section portion 30 *ft* 0 *in* (9·14 *m*)
Max width 19 *ft* 9 *in* (6·02 *m*)
Max height 19 *ft* 9 *in* (6·02 *m*)
Floor width 8 *ft* 7 *in* (2·62 *m*)

WEIGHTS:

Max payload 29,000 *lb* (13,155 *kg*)
Max T-O weight 133,000 *lb* (60,328 *kg*)*

**This will be increased to* 145,000 *lb* (65,770 *kg*) *after programmed modification.*

PERFORMANCE:

Normal cruising speed 225 *mph* (362 *kmh*)

First flight of the Pregnant Guppy, 19 September, 1962. This aircraft presented the most arresting spectacle in the sky—until the arrival of the Super Guppy

SAAB-37 VIGGEN

The aircraft produced by the Swedish SAAB organisation, established in 1937 by a group of industrial companies, are among the most efficient, and technically significant, in the world. The first product of original design was the Saab B.17 two-seat dive-bomber of 1940. The J 29 single-seat fighter of 1951 was a token of even more remarkable military types, and of these the Saab-32 A Lansen ranked as the first transonic all-weather ground-attack aircraft to enter service in western Europe. The Saab-35 Draken, with its characteristic "double-delta" wing form, was among the most advanced aircraft in the world, and the Saab-37 Viggen, hereafter described, is a "double-delta" of somewhat different form and of the highest technical merit.

The Viggen (Thunderbolt) is a multi-mission combat aircraft and is the most important component in System 37, the next manned weapon system for the Swedish Air Force.

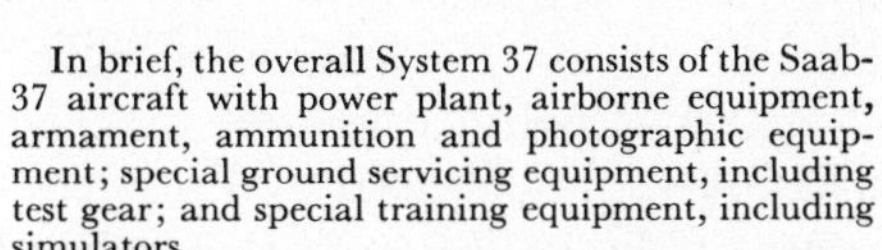

In brief, the overall System 37 consists of the Saab-37 aircraft with power plant, airborne equipment, armament, ammunition and photographic equipment; special ground servicing equipment, including test gear; and special training equipment, including simulators.

During development, particular attention is being paid to the optimum adaptation of System 37 to the SwAF base organisation and air defence control system (STRIL 60).

The Saab-37 has an extremely advanced aerodynamic configuration, using a foreplane, fitted with flaps, in combination with a main delta wing to convey STOL characteristics. The original intention of using flap-blowing on the foreplane has been abandoned.

By employing a Swedish supersonic development of the American Pratt & Whitney JT8D turbofan engine with a very powerful Swedish-designed afterburner, the Saab-37 is able to cruise economically at extremely low altitudes and, at the same time, possesses the acceleration performance required for interception work. The combination of advanced aerodynamic features with this powerful engine, thrust reverser and automatic speed control during landing, will enable the aircraft to be operated from narrow runways only 1,640 ft (500 m) long.

The structure is designed along conventional lines, similar to that of the Draken, using light-metal forgings and heat-resistant plastic bonding.

The planned production versions are as follows:

AJ 37. Single-seat attack aircraft, with interceptor capability. Will begin to replace the A 32A Lansen in 1971.

JA 37. Single-seat interceptor, with attack capability. Intended to replace the J 35 Draken, starting in the mid-seventies.

S 37. Single-seat reconnaissance aircraft. Intended to replace the S 32C Lansen.

Sk 37. Tandem two-seat trainer. Rear cockpit takes place of some electronics and forward fuselage fuel tank, and is fitted with bulged hood and periscope. This version will enter service simultaneously with AJ 37.

The first of seven prototypes of the Saab-37 flew for the first time on 8 February 1967, followed by the second machine on 21 September 1967 and the third (the first fully-equipped prototype) on 29 March 1968. On 20 March 1967, it was announced that the Swedish government had decided to order an initial production batch of 100 Viggen aircraft, comprising 83 AJ 37's and 17 Sk 37's, for delivery in 1971–74. Procurement of a further 75 Viggens was announced on 5 April 1968.

The following details refer specifically to the AJ 37 all-weather attack version of the Saab-37.

TYPE:

Single-seat all-weather attack aircraft.

WINGS:

Tandem arrangement of canard foreplane, with trailing-edge flaps, and rear-mounted delta main wing with powered elevons.

FUSELAGE:

Conventional all-metal semi-monocoque structure.

TAIL UNIT:

Vertical surfaces only, comprising main fin and powered rudder, the top section of which can be folded downwards, supplemented by a small ventral fin.

LANDING GEAR:

Retractable tricycle type. Twin-wheel steerable nose unit retracts forward. Each main unit has two wheels in tandem and retracts inward into wings. Main oleos shorten during retraction.

POWER PLANT:

One supersonic development of the Pratt & Whitney JT8D-22 turbofan engine (Swedish designation RM8), built by Svenska Flygmotor and fitted with a Swedish-developed afterburner and thrust reverser. Static thrust with afterburning approx 26,450 lb (12,00 kg). One fuel tank in each wing; saddle tank over engine; one tank in each side of fuselage and one aft of cockpit. Provision for external tank on centre pylon under fuselage.

ACCOMMODATION:

Pilot only, on ejection seat, in pressurised and air-conditioned cockpit. Rearward-hinged clam-shell canopy.

ELECTRONICS AND EQUIPMENT:

Computations in connection with various phases of an attack, including navigation, target approach and fire control calculations, will be handled by the Saab CK-37 miniaturised digital computer, thus freeing the pilot for concentration of tactics. By changing the computer programme, variations can be introduced to cater for new tactics, etc. Other equipment will include an automatic speed control system, SRA head-up display system for primary flight data. AGA aircraft attitude instruments and radio, Arenco air data unit and instruments, L.M. Ericsson radar, SRT radar altimeter and Philips navigation equipment.

ARMAMENT:

Primary armament will be the Swedish Rb 04 air-to-surface guided missile for use against naval targets or the Saab Rb 05 air-to-surface missile for use against both ground and naval targets, plus various types of air-to-surface rockets, bombs, 30-mm guns and mines. All armament will be carried externally on three attachments under fuselage and one under each wing. The attack version will also be able to perform interception missions armed with air-to-air missiles.

DIMENSIONS, external:

Wing span 34 *ft* 9¼ *in* (10·60 *m*)
Length overall (*incl probe*) 53 *ft* 5¾ *in* (16·30 *m*)
Height overall 18 *ft* 4½ *in* (5·60 *m*)
Height overall, vertical fin folded 13 *ft* 1½ *in* (4·00 *m*)

WEIGHT:

T-O weight with normal armament approx 35,275 *lb* (16,000 *kg*)

PERFORMANCE:

Max level speed above Mach 2
Time to 36,000 *ft* (11,000 *m*) *approx* 2 *minutes*

The second prototype Viggen with two Rb 04 air-to-surface missiles beneath the main delta wings

Although apparently a single-seater, this U-2D has a second seat, located under the prominent radome

LOCKHEED U-2

The de Havilland Mosquito has been instanced as an unarmed bomber and reconnaissance aircraft dependent upon sheer performance to elude opposing fighters. Even more specialised were the Junkers Ju 86 P and R of the *Luftwaffe*, with their diesel engines and pressure cabins, carrying only a light offensive or reconnaissance load but offering the severest challenge to opposing defences by reason of extreme altitude capability. The ultimate in such ultra high-altitude reconnaissance aircraft (it may be classed as such although used also for research) was the Lockheed U-2, maker of political as well as aeronautical, history. Even more remarkable was the Lockheed A-11, announced by President Johnson on 29 February 1964 and intended originally to supersede the V-2 in its clandestine reconnaissance work. Instead, it became SR-71A strategic reconnaissance aircraft.

U-2s have flown unseen over many lands. Glider-like design made this possible

Development of the U-2 began in 1954 and the prototype flew for the first time in the following year. A total of 25 of the basic single-seat version are reported to have been built in the Experimental Department of Lockheed's California Division. Some of these were delivered to the 4,028th and 4,080th Strategic Reconnaissance Squadrons of the USAF Strategic Air Command, based in Texas and Puerto Rico. Others were operated by Lockheed on behalf of the NASA (formerly NACA) and, apparently, the US Central Intelligence Agency. Several were lost, including the aircraft which is claimed to have been shot down near Sverdlovsk in the historic incident over the Soviet Union on 1 May 1960, and another shot down over China on 9 September 1962. The latter was stated to have been one of two purchased from the United States by Nationalist China in July 1960.

Early production U-2s were powered by a special Pratt & Whitney J57C turbojet engine with wide-chord compressor blades for flight at very high altitudes. Later models, of the type lost in Russia, had a Pratt & Whitney J75-P-13 turbojet, specially adapted to run on low-volatility fuel. Range could be extended by shutting off the engine and gliding. To make this possible, the U-2 had a sailplane configuration and great emphasis was placed on weight saving. This explains the unique landing gear, with underwing balancer units which were jettisoned after take-off.

Equipment varied considerably in different aircraft. Some were instrumented with equipment supplied by the NACA and the Wright Air Development Center to gather data on clear-air turbulence, convective clouds, wind shear, the jet stream, cosmic radiation and the concentration of certain elements in the atmosphere, including ozone and water vapour. Three U-2s with this kind of equipment, from the 4,080th Squadron, spent 18 months on meteorological research over the Argentine in 1958–59.

Soviet reports have stated that the Sverdlovsk U-2 carried an electromagnetic receiver for monitoring and recording radio and radar transmissions from the ground, made by Huggins Laboratories, Hewlett-Packard and Raytheon, a Lear A-10 autopilot and MA-1 compass, Bendix ARN-6 ADF, Magnavox ARC-34 UHF command radio and a Model 73B camera.

In mid-1961, a new two-seat conversion, designated U-2D, was displayed at Wright-Patterson AFB during Armed Forces Day.

TYPE:

High-altitude reconnaissance and research monoplane.

WINGS:

Cantilever mid-wing monoplane, with turned-down wingtips for use as skids during landing. Aspect ratio 14·3. All-metal structure. Trailing-edge flaps over approximately 60% of span. Wing area approximately 565 sq ft (52·5 m²).

FUSELAGE:

All-metal monocoque structure with thin-gauge skin. Forward-opening door-type air-brake on each side of fuselage aft of wings.

TAIL UNIT:

Cantilever monoplane type. All-metal structure. Control surfaces each with a trim-tab. Ventral fin under fuselage of some aircraft, immediately aft of wing.

LANDING GEAR:

Retractable tandem tail-wheel type. Main and tail units each fitted with dual wheels. Jettisonable balancer units under wings, each with dual wheels. Tail-wheels and underwing wheels very small, with solid tyres. Brakes on main wheels. Braking parachute in container under rudder.

POWER PLANT:

One Pratt & Whitney J57C (approximately 11,000 lb = 4,990 kg st) or J75-P-13 turbojet engine. Normal internal fuel capacity 785 US gallons (2,970 litres). Provision for two 105 US gallon (395 litre) external tanks on wing leading-edges.

ACCOMMODATION:

Pilot only, on ejector seat, under rearward-sliding transport canopy. Ventral periscopic sight for panoramic camera (usually Perkin-Elmer Type 501).

DIMENSIONS:

Wing span 80 *ft* 0 *in* (24·38 *m*)
Length overall 49 *ft* 7 *in* (15·11 *m*)

WEIGHTS (J57 engine):

T-O weight, internal fuel only 15,850 *lb* (7,190 *kg*)
Max T-O weight, with external tanks 17,270 *lb* (7,833 *kg*)

PERFORMANCE (J57 engine):

Max speed at cruising height 494 *mph* (795 *kmh*)
Cruising speed 460 *mph* (740 *kmh*)
Service ceiling approx 70,000 *ft* (21,350 *m*)
Range, internal fuel only, 100 *US gallons reserve* 2,200 *miles* (3,540 *km*)
Range, with external tanks, 100 *US gallons reserve* 2,600 *miles* (4,185 *km*)

Forward-opening air-brakes are fitted on each side of the fuselage aft of the wings

Side-by-side in the rear fuselage are two large afterburning turbojet engines and to each side of the jet nozzles are low-set all-moving horizontal surfaces

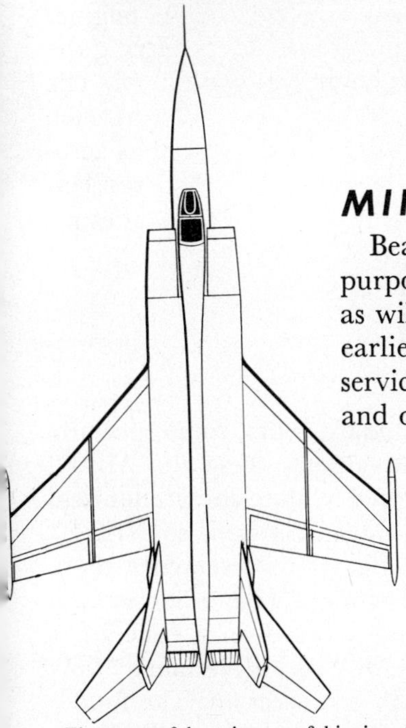

MIKOYAN MiG-23 (E-266)

Bearing the NATO code name "Foxbat", this twin-jet all-weather fighter or multi-purpose aircraft ranks as one of the most remarkable aeroplanes ever constructed, although, as will be noted, it embodies features reminiscent of a British and an American design of earlier years. It is one of several Soviet military aircraft now under development or in service which number among them V/STOL aircraft in the category of the Hawker Harrier and others using the principle of variable geometry.

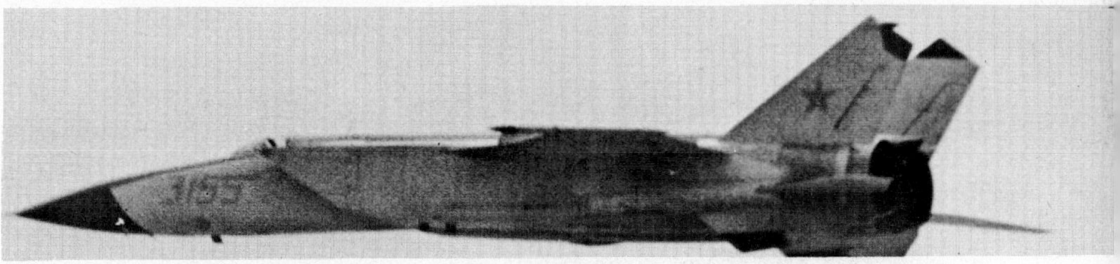

First news of the existence of this aircraft came in a Soviet claim, in April 1965, that a twin-engined aircraft designated E-266 had set up a new 1,000-km closed-circuit speed record of 1,441·5 mph (2,320 kmh), carrying a 2,000 kg payload. The attempt was made at a height of 69,000–72,200 ft (21,000–22,000 m) by Alexander Fedotov, who had earlier set up a 100-km record in the E-166.

The same pilot set up a new payload-to-height record of 98,349 ft (29,977 m) with a 2,000-kg payload in the E-266, on 5 October 1967, after an assisted take-off. This qualified also for the record with a 1,000-kg payload. Photographs of the E-266 issued officially in the Soviet Union identified it subsequently as the new twin-finned Mikoyan single-seat fighter of which four examples took part in the Domodedovo display in July 1967 and which is now known to be designated MiG-23 in the Soviet Air Force.

Its performance in level flight was demonstrated further on 5 October 1967, when M. Komarov set up a speed record of 1,852·61 mph (2,981·5 kmh) over a 500-km closed circuit. On 27 October, P. Ostapenko set up a 1,000-km closed circuit record of 1,814·81 mph (2,920·67 kmh) in an E-266, carrying a 2,000-kg payload and qualifying also for records with 1,000-kg payload and no payload.

On three of the aircraft shown at Domodedovo, the cut-off line of the dielectric nose-cone was vertical in side elevation; on the fourth aircraft the nose-cone was covered with paint, giving a sloping cut-off line. This, and detail differences in equipment such as antennae, may indicate that the aircraft were from a pre-production or early production series.

The comparatively low aspect ratio cropped delta wings, mounted high on the fuselage have compound landing-edge sweep and anhedral over the entire span. The twin tail fins were almost certainly adopted as being preferable to the single large and tall fin that would otherwise have been essential with such a wide-bodied supersonic design. The fins incline outward, as do the large ventral fins.

The basic fuselage is quite slim, but is blended into the two huge rectangular air intake trunks, which have wedge inlets of the kind used on the North American A-5 Vigilante. The inner walls of the intakes are curved at the top and do not run parallel with the outer walls; hinged panels form the lower lip of each intake, enabling the intake area to be varied.

It is likely that the landing gear is a retractable tricycle type, also similar to that of the Vigilante, with the main wheels retracting into the air intake trunks.

The power plant of the MiG-23 consists of a pair of large afterburning turbojet engines (each rated at 24,250 lb = 11,000 kg st), mounted side-by-side in the rear fuselage. To each side of the jet nozzles are low-set all-moving horizontal tail surfaces of characteristic MiG shape.

No pictures of the MiG-23 have yet been released showing it with external stores, and no weapons were visible on the aircraft at Domodedovo. The fact that the commentator referred to these as high-altitude all-weather interceptors confirms the probability that the MiG-23 was designed to intercept fast strike aircraft, possibly with "snap-down" missiles to deal with low-flying raiders. His claim that this design has a Mach 3 performance is supported by the latest speed records.

The MiG-23 would also appear to offer considerable potential in the strike role, except at very low altitudes. There is clearly sufficient room between the engines and intake ducts for an internal weapon bay or recessed nuclear weapon, as on the Mirage IV; but the only visible weapon attachments are four underwing hard-points.

DIMENSIONS (estimated):

Wing span 40 *ft* 0 *in* (12·20 *m*)
Length overall 69 *ft* 0 *in* (21·00 *m*)

The HL-10 in the upper views was one of two metal-built developments of the wooden M2-F1 glider immediately above

The HL-10 is generally similar to the M2-F2 but the straight side of its cross-sectional D shape forms the undersurface instead of being uppermost

NORTHROP M2-F2 and HL-10

Numerous types of manned aircraft, some adaptations of standard types, some specially constructed, have assisted in the US space programme, and among these the M2-F2 wingless lifting-body re-entry research vehicles has already earned a place in aeronautical history. It was one of two such aircraft built by Northrop under contract to NASA's Flight Research Center. A concept of the Ames Research Center, it represented a more refined metal development of the successful wooden M2-F1 glider. The other vehicle supplied to NASA is known as the Northrop/NASA HL-10 and is based on a concept of the Langley Aeronautical Laboratory. It was delivered to NASA on 19 January 1966. Both vehicles have a basic delta plan-form and are D-shaped in cross-section. The fundamental difference is that in the M2-F2 the straight side of the D is on top, whereas it forms the undersurface of the fuselage of the HL-10. When tested in 1967 the HL-10 encountered control problems, necessitating some redesign, and testing was resumed in March 1968.

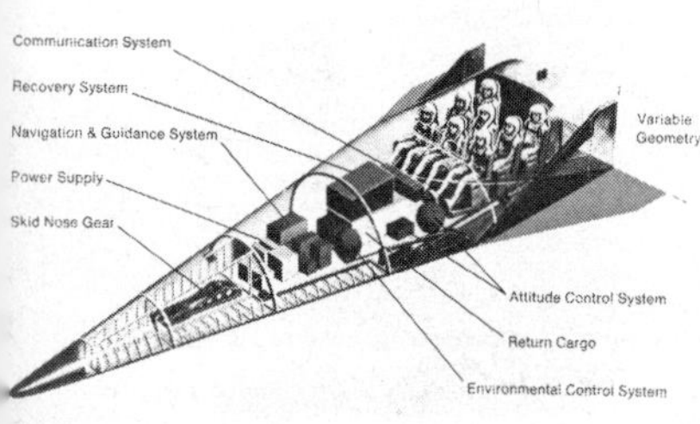

Layout of a possible wingless lifting-body vehicle

M2-F2. Northrop have long experience in the construction of unconventional tailless aircraft of "flying wing" type

Conventional semi-monocoque construction is used for the body of both aircraft and most of their systems are not only identical but utilise "off-the-shelf" components. For example, both aircraft are fitted with a retractable landing gear comprising a modified North American T-39 nose unit, Northrop F-5 main legs with T-38 wheels and brakes' and a Grumman F9F tail-bumper. The pilot sits on a modified version of the Weber lightweight rocket-powered ejection seat produced for the Cessna T-37, in a pressurised cockpit (differential 10 lb/sq in = 0·70 kg/cm²). UHF radio is fitted.

The M2-F2 is controlled by two thick-section rudders and two elevons hinged to the upper surface of the aircraft's boat-tail. For additional downward pitch force, there are pitch flaps under the boat-tail. All control surfaces are made of metal sandwich and are operated by fully-duplicated irreversible hydraulic actuators, with stability augumentation in all three axes.

Unlike the original wooden M2-F1, the M2-F2 was so designed that, after initial unpowered flight trials, it could be fitted with an 8,000 lb (3,630 kg) st Thiokol (Reaction Motors) XLR11 liquid-propellent rocket-engine of the kind fitted initially to the X-15A research aircraft. To enable it to be air-launched from beneath the starboard wing of a B-52 Stratofortress "mother-plane", it was designed to utilise an adaptor under the existing Z-15A carrier-pylon.

The M2-F2 was delivered to NASA on 15 June 1965. Following tests in the Agency's full-scale wind tunnel at Ames Research Center, it made its first unpowered flight on 12 July 1966, after release from the B-52 at 45,000 ft (13,700 m). Its pilot, Mr Milton O. Thompson, made a practice flare-out at about 25,000 ft (7,600 m) and, after completing two 90° turns, increased speed to 350 mph (560 kmh) in order to be able to flare out and slow the rate of descent from 250 ft/sec (76 m/sec) to under 10 ft/sec (3 m/sec) for the landing. Emergency thrusters, fitted for use during the flare, were not used and the M2-F2 was landed successfully four minutes after release at about 190 mph (305 kmh) on Rogers Dry Lake bed, near Edwards AFB, California.

During these unpowered flights, the rocket propellent tanks were available for water ballast. permitting tests over a range of all-up weights.

By the end of 1966, the M2-F2 had completed its initial programmed series of unpowered flight tests, having made a total of 14 flights. It was then fitted with the XLR11 rocket-engine. On 10 May 1967, it crashed on landing at Rogers Dry Lake, Edwards AFB, California, at the end of its 16th flight. Purpose of the unpowered flight had been to evaluate the effects of reduction in automatic damping for roll and yaw before the start of powered flight trials. The M2-F2 was severely damaged and was disassembled, preparatory to rebuilding for further flight trials.

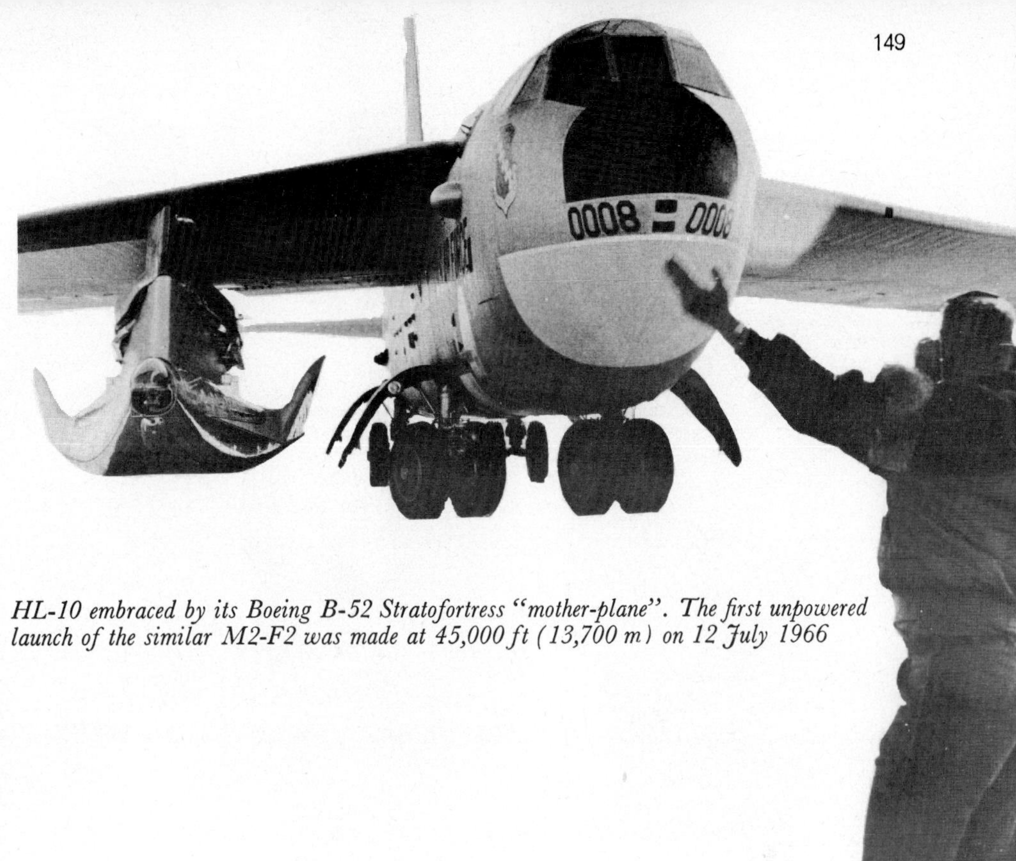

HL-10 embraced by its Boeing B-52 Stratofortress "mother-plane". The first unpowered launch of the similar M2-F2 was made at 45,000 ft (13,700 m) on 12 July 1966

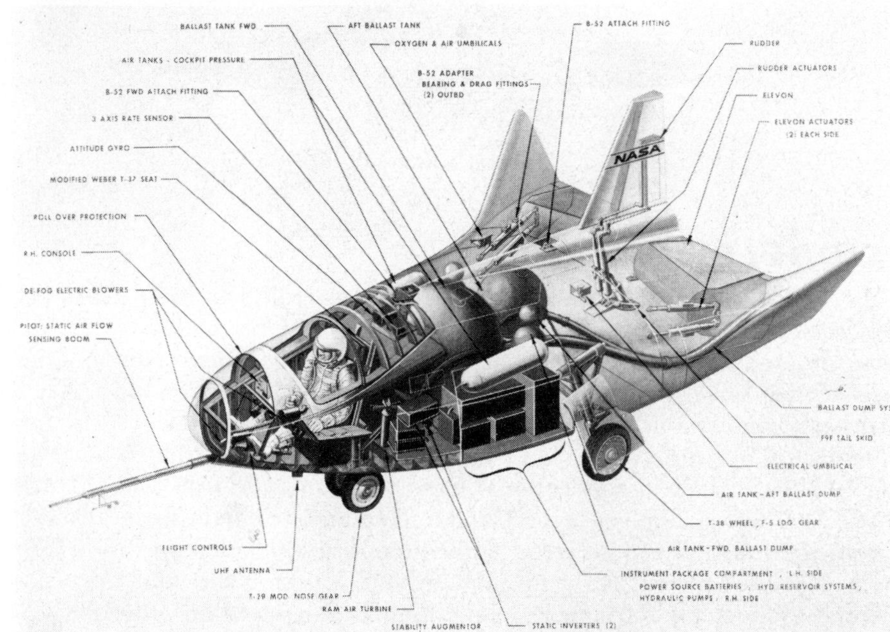

Official drawing showing salient HL-10 features, including provisions for attachment to the B-52 Stratofortress

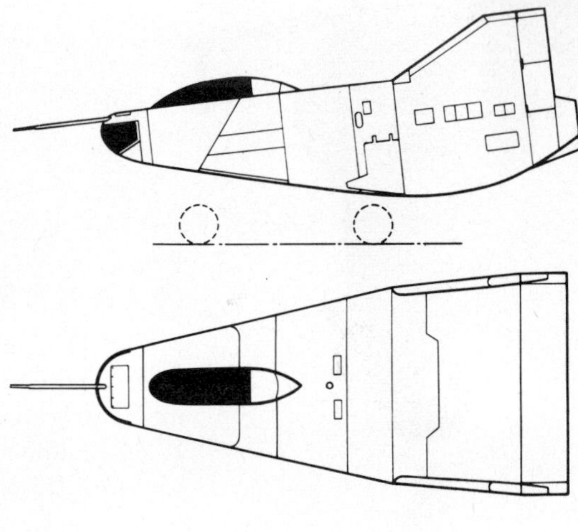

DIMENSIONS:

Max width 9 *ft* 7 *in* (2·92 *m*)
Length overall 22 *ft* 2 *in* (6·76 *m*)
Height overall 8 *ft* 10 *in* (2·69 *m*)

AREA:

Planform area 160 *sq ft* (14·86 *m*²)

WEIGHTS:

Max launching weight 9,000 *lb* (4,080 *kg*)
Min landing weight 4,700 *lb* (2,130 *kg*)
Max landing weight 8,000 *lb* (3,630 *kg*)

A forecast by Martin Marietta

The significance of the Hawker Siddeley V/STOL close-support and reconnaissance aircraft is great in both tactical and technical senses

P.1127 development aircraft

HAWKER SIDDELEY HARRIER

The Harrier V/STOL close-support and reconnaissance aircraft has been developed from a Hawker private-venture design begun in 1957. Two prototypes and four development aircraft were ordered in 1959–60, these being known by the Hawker designation P.1127. The basis of this novel, indeed revolutionary, type of military aircraft was a vectored-thrust turbojet engine, and the initial tests were of historic importance. The first prototype began tethered hovering tests on 21 October 1960. The first untethered hovering flight followed on 19 November, and conventional flight trials on 13 March 1961. Shortly afterwards the first P.1127 was joined by a second, and tests culminated in the first transitions from vertical to horizontal flight and vice versa. Subsequent trials included operation from the aircraft-carrier *Ark Royal* at sea, early in 1963. About a year before this operation Britain, the USA and the Federal German Republic jointly announced an order for nine field-evaluation aircraft. Design changes were made and the name Kestrel conferred. All nine Kestrels were delivered to a tripartite squadron in Britain between April and September 1965.

A new plan: a P.1127 showing the four rotatable exhaust nozzles for the Pegasus engine

Early in 1966 six Kestrels were shipped to the USA and spent four months flying with the US Army, US Navy and USAF. Four were later sent to Edwards AFB and the remaining pair to NASA's Langley facility. Meanwhile, the Kestrels in the UK had become associated with the flight development of the Harrier.

Although having a layout similar to that of the pioneer P.1127, and being known originally as the HS.1127 (RAF), the Harrier is virtually a new design. Only some 5 per cent of the structural drawings are common to both types. Six development aircraft were flying by the end of July 1967. On October 24 of that year a pre-production aircraft was flown on to, and took off vertically from, the helicopter platform on the stern of the Italian guided missile escort cruiser *Andrea Doria*. Production began in 1967 of a provisional quantity of 71 Harriers. Two operational versions have been announced, the Harrier GR.Mk 1 close-support and reconnaissance version and the T.Mk 2 operational trainer, which retains the full external load-carrying ability of the GR.Mk 1.

The basic design from which the Harrier has been derived is attributable to Sir Sydney Camm who was also responsible for such outstanding Hawker military types as the Hart (page 64), Fury, Hurricane (the first eight-gun fighter and among the most famous aircraft of the Second World War), Sea Hawk and Hunter.

The Harrier GR.Mk 1 is now described.

TYPE:

Single-seat V/STOL close-support and reconnaissance aircraft.

WINGS:

Cantilever shoulder-wing monoplane. Anhedral 10°. Sweepback 34° at quarter-chord. One-piece aluminium alloy three-spar structure. Entire wing unit removable to provide access to engine. Plain ailerons and flaps, of bonded aluminium-alloy honeycomb construction. Ailerons irreversibly operated by Fairey tandem hydraulic jacks. Jet reaction control valve built into front of each outrigger wheel fairing. Normal "combat" wingtips can be replaced by bolt-on extended tips to increase ferry range.

FUSELAGE:

Semi-monocoque structure, mainly of aluminium alloy, but with some titanium and steel adjacent to engine and in other special areas. Jet reaction control valves in nose and in extended tail-cone. Large forward-hinged dive brake aft of main-wheel well.

TAIL UNIT:

One-piece tailplane, with 10° of anhedral, irreversibly operated by Fairey tandem hydraulic jack. Rudder and trailing-edge of tailplane of bonded aluminium honeycomb construction. Rudder operated manually. Ventral fin under rear fuselage.

ELECTRONICS AND EQUIPMENT:

Avionics and electrical equipment in fuselage bay aft of wing trailing-edge. VHF/UHF and HF radio, TACAN and IFF standard. No conventional autopilot. Non-duplicated autostabilisation system for pitch and roll.

SYSTEMS:

Pressurisation system pressure differential 3·5 lb/sq in (0·25 kg/cm²). Dual hydraulic systems, pressure 3,000 lb/sq in (210 kg/cm²), actuate flying controls, landing gear, nose-wheel steering and air-brake, and include a retractable ram-air turbine inside top of rear fuselage, driving a small hydraulic pump for emergency power. AC electrical system with transformer-rectifiers to provide required DC supply. Two 4kVA alternators. Two 28V 25Ah batteries, one of which energises a 24V motor to start Rotax gas-turbine starter/APU.

ARMAMENT AND OPERATIONAL EQUIPMENT:

Optically-flat panel in nose, on port side, for F.95 oblique camera. No built-in armament. Combat load carried on four underwing and three under-fuselage hard-points. The inboard wing points and the centre fuselage point are stressed for loads of up to 1,200 lb (544 kg) each, and the outboard under-wing pair for loads of up to 650 lb (295 kg) each; the two outboard points under the fuselage can each carry a 30-mm gun pod and ammunition. At present, the Harrier is cleared for operations with a maximum external load of 5,000 lb (2,270 kg). A typical combat load is a pair of 30-mm Aden gun pods (interchangeable with under-fuselage strakes) and a 5-camera reconnaissance pod under the fuselage, and two Matra launchers, each with 57 × 68-mm SNEB rockets, and two pairs of Lepus flares or two 100 Imp gallon (455 litre) drop-tanks under the wings. A 1,000 lb (454 kg) bomb can be carried on the central fuselage pylon in combination with gun pods. Ferranti Fe 541 inertial nav/attack system, incorporating Specto head-up display, 6-in diameter moving-map display and position computer.

Their revolutionary design notwithstanding, the Kestrel/Harrier designs display features of the earlier Hawker Hunter

LANDING GEAR

Retractable bicycle type of Dowty Rotol manufacture, permitting operation from virtually any type of surface. Hydraulic actuation, with nitrogen bottle for emergency extension of landing gear and air-brake. Single steerable nose-wheel retracts forward, twin coupled main wheels rearward, into fuselage. Small outrigger units retract rearward into fairings slightly inboard of wing-tips. Nose-wheel leg of levered-suspension Liquid Spring type. Telescopic oleo-pneumatic main and outrigger gear. Dunlop wheels, low-pressure tyres, multi-disc brakes and anti-skid units.

POWER PLANT:

One Rolls-Royce Bristol Pegasus 101 vectored-thrust turbofan engine (approx 19,200 lb = 8,710 kg st), with four rotatable exhaust nozzles of the two-vane cascade type. The low-drag intake cowl, with inward-cambered lips, has automatic suction relief doors aft of the leading-edge to improve intake efficiency by providing extra air for the engine at low forward or zero speeds. Fuel in six integral tanks in centre-fuselage and wing centre-section, with total capacity of approx 650 Imp gallons (2,955 litres). This can be supplemented by two 100 Imp gallon (455 litre) underwing jettisonable combat tanks or two larger ferry tanks. Provision for in-flight re-fuelling probe above the port intake cowling.

ACCOMMODATION:

Pilot on Martin-Baker Type 9A Mk 1 zero-altitude zero-speed rocket ejection seat in a pressurised and air-conditioned cockpit. Liquid oxygen system of 1 Imp gallon (5 litres) capacity.

DIMENSIONS, external:

Wing span 25 *ft* 3 *in* (7·70 *m*)
Length overall 45 *ft* 8 *in* (13·92 *m*)
Height overall (11 *ft* 3 *in* (3·43 *m*)

AREA:

Wings, gross 210 *sq ft* (18·67 *m*²)

WEIGHTS (estimated):

Weight empty, equipped 12,000 *lb* (5,443 *kg*)
Max T-O weight (*hover*) 16,000 *lb* (7,257 *kg*)
Max T-O weight (*STOL*) 23,000 *lb* (10,433 *kg*)

PERFORMANCE (GR.Mk 1 development aircraft):

Max level speed over 720 *mph* (1,159 *kmh*)
Max diving speed over Mach 1·25
Ferry range approaching 2,300 *miles* (3,700 *km*)

Maker's drawing showing inboard profile of Kestrel FGA. Mk 1

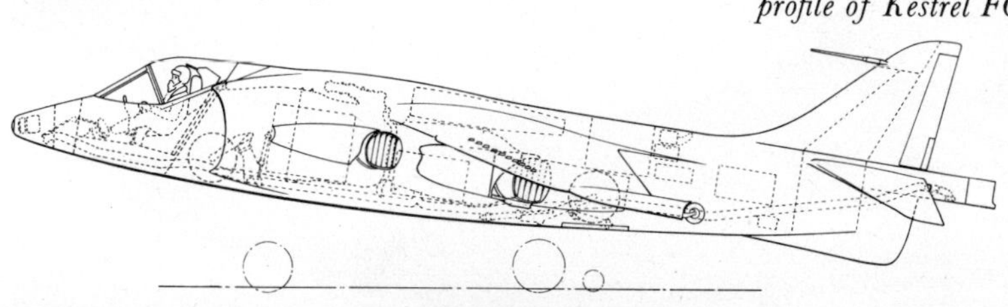

In 1969 the Harrier became the first V/STOL close-support and reconnaissance aircraft to enter regular squadron service

Of two test rigs built, the second (left) was called the "Big Rig"

DORNIER Do 31 E

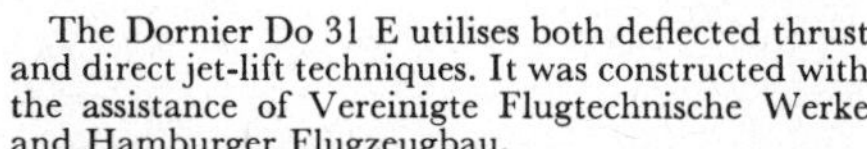

The past two decades have seen the production in several countries of experimental V/STOL transport aircraft of high significance, and though none has reached the stage of operational employment, as the Hawker Harrier has done in the military field, certain designs promise rewarding success in the years ahead. Among these the Dornier Do 31 E, later described, has a particular distinction. By way of historical background some mention may be made of other notable designs, among which the Fairey Rotodyne has already been instanced as an ambitious rotary-wing venture. Other transport, or quasi transport, types have been the McDonnell XV-1, Hiller X-18, Doak Model 16, Ryan XV-5A, Bell XV-3, LTV-Hiller-Ryan XC-142 A, Canadair CL-84 and Lockheed SV-4 B Hummingbird. The historic importance of the Rolls-Royce TMR and Short SC-1 in the development of V/STOL techniques has already been noted.

It must be reiterated that the Do 31 E is an experimental aircraft. The projected operational development (Do 131) differs considerably.

The Dornier Do 31 E utilises both deflected thrust and direct jet-lift techniques. It was constructed with the assistance of Vereinigte Flugtechnische Werke and Hamburger Flugzeugbau.

Initially, two Do 31 E aircraft have been constructed under a German Defence Ministry contract, and the first of these, the Do 31 E 1, made its first flight on 10 February 1967. Each of the Do 31 Es has as its primary power plant two Rolls-Royce Bristol Pegasus 5-2 vectored-thrust turbofan engines in nacelles under the wings. In addition there are wingtip pods for two groups of four Rolls-Royce RB 162-4D lift-jets, although these have not been fitted to the Do 31 E 1, which has been used for conventional flight trials only. The second aircraft, the Do 31 E 3, which made its first flight on 14 July 1967, and which has the full complement of engines, is being used to carry out an experimental programme of jet-borne flight, which started with successful vertical take-offs and landings and transition flights at the end of 1967. The first transition from vertical take-off to horizontal flight took place on 16 December 1967, and the first transition from horizontal flight to vertical landing on 21 December 1967. By the end of 1968, the E 1 had made approx. 60 flights, while the Do 31 E 3 had completed 70 flights, including many hovering flights and transitions. A third airframe, for static tests, is designated Do 31 E 2.

Continued testing in 1969 is aimed at optimising take-off and landing procedures, investigating noise levels, etc.

The location of the Pegasus engines is determined by the need to protect the fuselage from hot gases ejected from the side nozzles. The lift engines are at the wingtips to ensure effective compensation of the roll moment following a failure of an inboard engine in the vertical flight phase.

For pitch control, high-pressure bleed air from the Pegasus engines is ducted to nozzles at the stern of the aircraft, of which two point up and two down. Roll control is achieved by thrust modulation of the lift engines and yaw control by differential tilting of the lift engine nozzles. Rates of climb and descent are set with the throttle of the Pegasus engines. Attitude control in hovering flight is exercised through a unit developed by Bodenseewerk Perkin-Elmer.

TYPE:
Experimental V/STOL transport aircraft.

WINGS:
Cantilever high-wing monoplane. Wing section NACA 64 (A412)-412·5 at root, NACA 64 (A412)-410 at tip. Aspect ratio 5·05. Sweepback at quarter-chord 8° 30′. No dihedral or incidence. Three-spar riveted light alloy structure. Two-section ailerons, between propulsion engine pod and lift-jet pod on each wing, take form of camber-changing flaps with movement of ±25°. Conventional flap on each wing between fuselage and propulsion engine pod. Ailerons operated by duplicated hydraulic jacks, flaps by a hydraulic motor. No tabs.

FUSELAGE:
Conventional all-metal semi-monocoque structure of circular section (diameter 10 ft 6 in = 3·20 m), slightly flattened at bottom. Upswept rear fuselage incorporating rear-loading doors.

TAIL UNIT:
Cantilever all-metal structure with vertical surfaces swept back at 40° at quarter-chord. Fixed-incidence tailplane, with sweep of 15°, is mid-set on fin. Elevators in four sections; each with separate hydraulic actuator. Rudders in two sections, each with separate hydraulic actuator. No aerodynamic or mass balancing of control surfaces. No tabs.

LANDING GEAR:
Hydraulically-retractable tricycle type with twin wheels on each unit. All units retract rearward, main units into rear of propulsion engine nacelles. Oleo-pneumatic shock-absorbers. Multiple-disc brakes on main wheels. Steerable and fully-castoring nose unit. Brake parachute housed in rear loading ramp and ejected downward, for use during flight testing.

POWER PLANT:
Two Rolls-Royce Bristol Pegasus 5-2 vectored-thrust propulsion engines, each rated at 15,500 lb (7,000 kg) st, in pods under wings. Removable lift-jet pod on each wing-tip, each housing four Rolls- to engines is normally from centre-section tank, to which fuel is transferred equally from other tanks to maintain trim.

ACCOMMODATION:
Crew of two on flight deck, with dual controls. Folding seats for 36 fully-equipped troops are fitted as standard equipment along cabin side walls. Alternative payloads include 24 stretchers in tiers of four, with centre aisle; two or three jeeps; one Unimog type S or two Unimog type 410 1D vehicles; missiles; and freight on pallets size 5 ft 7 in × 11 ft 6 in (1·7 × 3·5 m). Freight can be air-dropped through open rear doors. Cabin fitted with roller-conveyors, guide rails and winch for freight loading. Air-stair door on port side of cabin at front. Loading ramp which forms undersurface of rear fuselage can be lowered to ground or held horizontal at truck-bed height. Fuselage undersurface aft of ramp hinges up inside fuselage, and each adjacent side panel hinges outward, to provide maximum accessibility for tall vehicles.

SYSTEMS:
Two fully-independent hydraulic systems and emergency system, pressure 3,000 lb/sq in (210 kg/cm^2). First main system supplies one section of tandem or twin jacks of flying control system, landing gear, flaps, ramp, loading and side doors, nose-wheel steering system, brakes and lift-jet pod doors. Other main system supplies only second section of control jacks. Emergency system supplies flaps, landing gear, ramp loading and side doors when the first main hydraulic system or the electrical system has failed. AC electrical system supplied by four 9KVA three-phase 200/115V 400 c/s generators (two driven by each propulsion engine). DC power supplied by two 3KW 28V transformer/rectifiers. Standby battery fitted.

The vectored-thrust propulsion engines are under the wings, the lift-jet pods at the tips

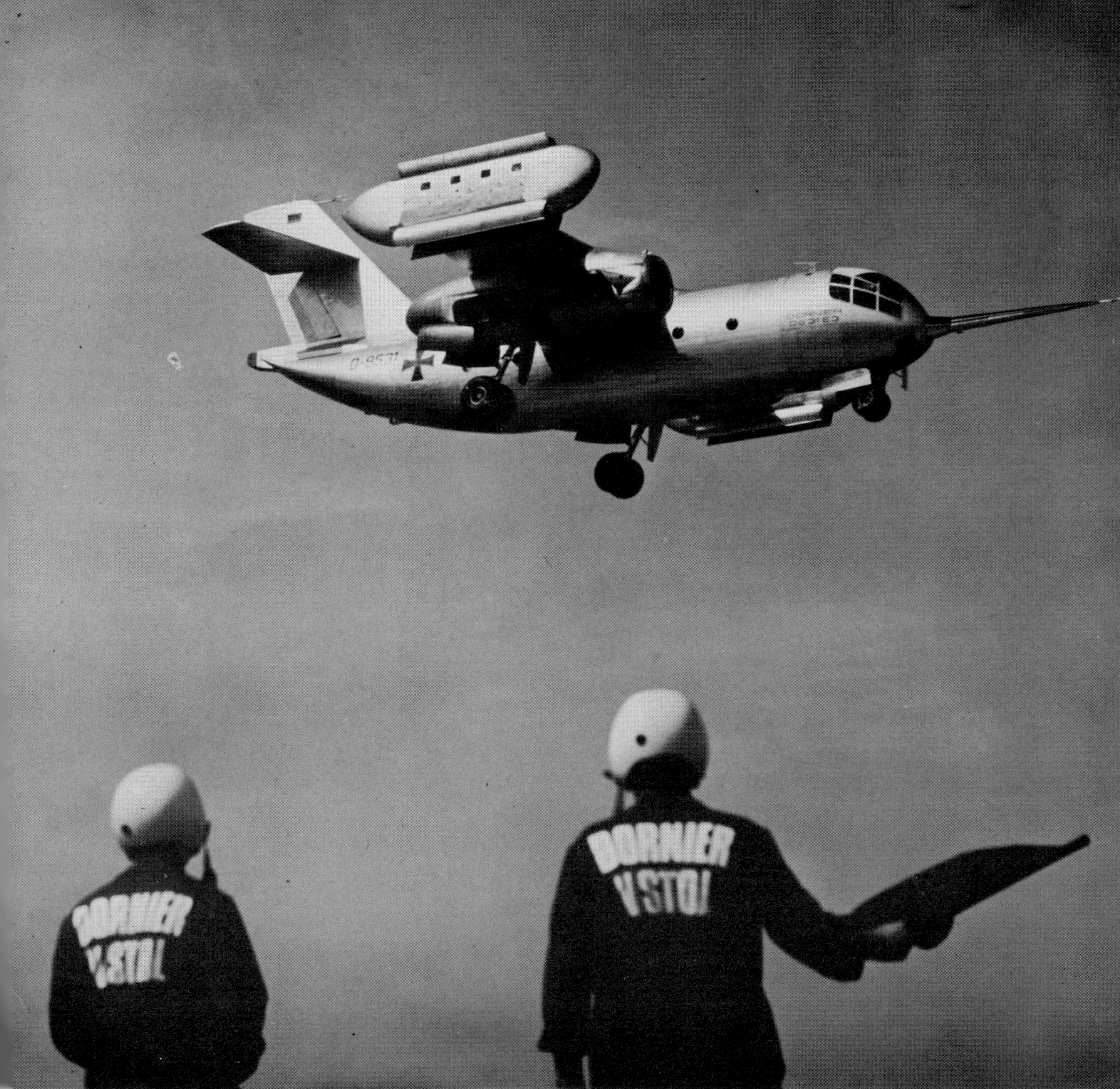

The wingtip location of the lift engines compensates roll moment if an inboard engine fails in vertical flight

ELECTRONICS AND EQUIPMENT:
Full range of radio and navigation aids, including VOR/ILS and TACAN. Three-axis autostabilisation system by Fluggerätewerk Bodensee GmbH.

DIMENSIONS, external:
Wing span 59 *ft* 3 *in* (18·06 *m*)
Length overall 68 *ft* 6 *in* (20·88 *m*)
Height overall 28 *ft* 0 *in* (8·53 *m*)
Wheel track 24 *ft* 7¼ *in* (7·50 *m*)
Wheelbase 28 *ft* 2½ *in* (8·60 *m*)

DIMENSIONS, internal:
Cabin:
Length, with ramp 43 *ft* 3½ *in* (13·20 *m*)
Length, excluding ramp 30 *ft* 2½ *in* (9·20 *m*)
Max height 7 *ft* 2½ *in* (2·20 *m*)
Width at floor 6 *ft* 11½ *in* (2·12 *m*)
Floor area, without ramp 210 *sq ft* (19·5 m^2)
Volume 1,765 *cu ft* (50 m^3)

AREAS:
Wings, gross 613 *sq ft* (57 m^2)
Horizontal tail surfaces (total) 176·3 *sq ft* (16·4 m^2)
Vertical tail surfaces (total) 165·7 *sq ft* (15·4 m^2)

WEIGHTS:
Basic design weight 49,500 *lb* (22,500 *kg*)
Payload 6,600–11,000 *lb* (3,000–5,000 *kg*)
Max T-O weight 60,500 *lb* (27,500 *kg*)

PERFORMANCE (estimated):
Cruising speed at 20,000 *ft* (6,000 *m*) 400 *mph* (650 *kmh*)
Rate of climb at S/L 5,250 *ft* (1,600 *m*) *min*
Service ceiling 34,500 *ft* (10,500 *m*)

The pressurised Beechcraft Duke

The fifteen-seater Beechcraft 99 Airliner is an outstanding example of the increasingly popular "third level" transport aircraft

BEECHCRAFT 99 AIRLINER

That Walter H. Beech was a pioneer in American light-aircraft production was noted in the context of the Cessna 150. In 1932, with Olive his wife as co-founder, Mr Beech established the Beech Aircraft Corporation, achieving a notable success with the Beech biplane still famed in the USA as the "Staggerwing", by reason of its backwardly staggered mainplanes. The first Model 18 monoplane flew on 15 January 1937, and in developed forms continues in production today—a record unmatched by any other aircraft. Mrs Beech likewise remains in office, though her husband died in 1950. For many years the Beech corporation has specialised in corporate and private aircraft, and no fewer than nineteen civilian types are now in production. The function of the aircraft now under review is evident from its newly bestowed name Beechcraft 99 Airliner; but it is an airliner in the relatively new "third level" category and matched also to the scheduled air taxi and executive markets. The demand for aircraft of this class is mounting dramatically throughout the world, and characteristics are being largely dictated by American requirements.

The prototype 99 Airliner flew for the first time in July 1966 and the first delivery of a production aircraft was made on 2 May 1968. Production was scheduled to attain a rate of 100 units per annum by mid-1968 to meet world-wide orders for $30 million worth of the Beech 99. These came from 15 US regional and scheduled commuter airlines and from 10 airlines in nine foreign countries. First US deliveries were to Commuter Airlines, Inc, with initial foreign deliveries going to Australia, Canada and Mexico, and by February 1969 a total of 70 of these aircraft were in service with 30 airlines.

Installation of an optional forward-hinged cargo door forward of the standard air-stair door permits the 99 Airliner to be used for all cargo or combined cargo-passenger operations, with a movable bulkhead separating freight and passengers in the latter configuration. In addition, a version known as the Beechcraft 99 Executive is available, which offers optional layouts for eight to 17 seats and various corporate interiors.

An optional "extra" on the 99 Airliner is a baggage/cargo pod, capacity 800 lb

TYPE:

Twin-turboprop light passenger and freight transport.

WINGS:

Cantilever low-wing monoplane. Dihedral 7°. Two-spar all-metal aluminium alloy structure. All-metal ailerons of magnesium. Single-slotted aluminium alloy flaps. Optional automatic pneumatic de-icing boots.

FUSELAGE:

All-metal semi-monocoque structure.

TAIL UNIT:

Cantilever all-metal structure, with sweptback vertical surfaces and a ventral stabilising fin. Trim-tabs in elevators and rudder. Pneumatic de-icing boots optional.

LANDING GEAR:

Retractable tricycle type with single steerable nose-wheel and twin wheels on each main unit. Electrical retraction, nose-wheel rearward, main units forward into engine nacelles. Beech oleo-pneumatic shock-absorbers. Goodrich wheels, tyres and multiple disc brakes. Shimmy damper on nose-wheel.

POWER PLANT:

Two 550 shp Pratt & Whitney (UAC) PT6A-20 turboprop engines, each driving a Hartzell three-blade fully-feathering and reversible-pitch constant-speed propeller, diameter 6 ft 7½ in (2·02 m). Automatic feathering system standard. Rubber fuel tanks in wings, with total capacity of 374 US gallons (1,415 litres).

ACCOMMODATION:

Crew of two side-by-side on flight deck, with full dual controls and instruments. Half-curtain or bulkhead between flight deck and cabin. Standard version has 15 removable high-density cabin chairs, two-abreast with centre aisle (single chair opposite door). Executive version has six standard seats in cabin, the two forward seats facing rearwards. Baggage space aft of rear seats, with external door. Nose baggage compartment with two external doors. Air-stair door on port side of cabin at rear. Optional forward-hinged cargo door forward of passenger door, to give wide unobstructed opening for cargo loading. A wide selection of corporate interiors and removable chemical or electric flushing toilet optional.

SYSTEMS:

Automatic 80,000 BTU heating system and high-capacity ventilation system, with individual fresh air outlets, standard. Hydraulic system for brakes only. 28V DC electrical system, with two 200A generators, 40Ah nickle-cadmium battery and dual solid-state inverters.

ELECTRONICS AND EQUIPMENT:

Standard electronics include dual 360-channel nav/com systems, dual VOR/ILS converter-indicators, three-light marker beacon with Beechcraft B-16 slope receiver, DME and transponder, with dual blind-flying instrumentation. Optional export electronics package comprises dual 360-channel nav/com systems with Beechcraft B-2 and B-3 antennae, dual VOR/LOC converter-indicators, marker beacon with Beechcraft B-16 antenna, dual ADF with amplifier and HF transceiver with fixed antenna. Standard equipment includes electric propeller anti-icing, landing and taxi lights, wing ice lights, cabin, instrument and map lights, dual rotating beacons, and fire detector system. Optional equipment includes high-pressure oxygen system, air-conditioning system with Freon compressor, engine fire extinguishing system, weather radar, propeller synchronisers, high-intensity anti-collision lights, autopilot and electrical windscreen anti-icing system.

DIMENSIONS:

Wing span 45 *ft* 10½ *in* (14·00 *m*)
Length overall 44 *ft* 6¾ *in* (13·58 *m*)

WEIGHTS:

Weight empty, equipped 5,780 *lb* (2,621 *kg*)
Max T-O weight 10,400 *lb* (4,717 *kg*)

PERFORMANCE:

Max cruising speed at 10,000 *ft* (3,050 *m*) *at AUW of* 10,000 *lb* (4,535 *kg*) 242 *mph* (409 *kmh*)
Normal cruising speed at 12,000 *ft* (3,650 *m*) 252 *mph* (406 *kmh*)
Rate of climb at S/L 1,700 *ft* (518 *m*) *min*
Service ceiling 23,650 *ft* (7,510 *m*)
T-O run 1,800 *ft* (549 *m*)
Range with 16 *passengers and* 480 *lb* (218 *kg*) *baggage,* 45 *min reserve,* 375 *miles* (603 *km*)

Another aspect of the Duke. The Lycoming engines are turbo-supercharged

CONCORDE

Anglo-French agreements were signed in November 1962 whereby the Concorde supersonic transport aircraft was to be constructed under a joint programme by British Aircraft Corporation Ltd and Sud-Aviation, Société Nationale de Constructions Aéronautiques. Prime contractors for the power plant were to be Rolls-Royce Ltd, Bristol Engine Division and Société Nationale d'Etude et de Construction de Moteurs d'Aviation. The agreements provided for a fair division of work, responsibility and development costs among the partners and covered the manufacture of two prototypes, followed by two pre-production aircraft and two complete airframes for static and fatigue testing. There will be two final assembly lines, at Toulouse and Filton. Construction of the two prototypes began in February 1965 and the first, assembled by Sud-Aviation, was rolled out in December 1967. The first flight by this aircraft took place at Toulouse on 2 March 1969 and the second

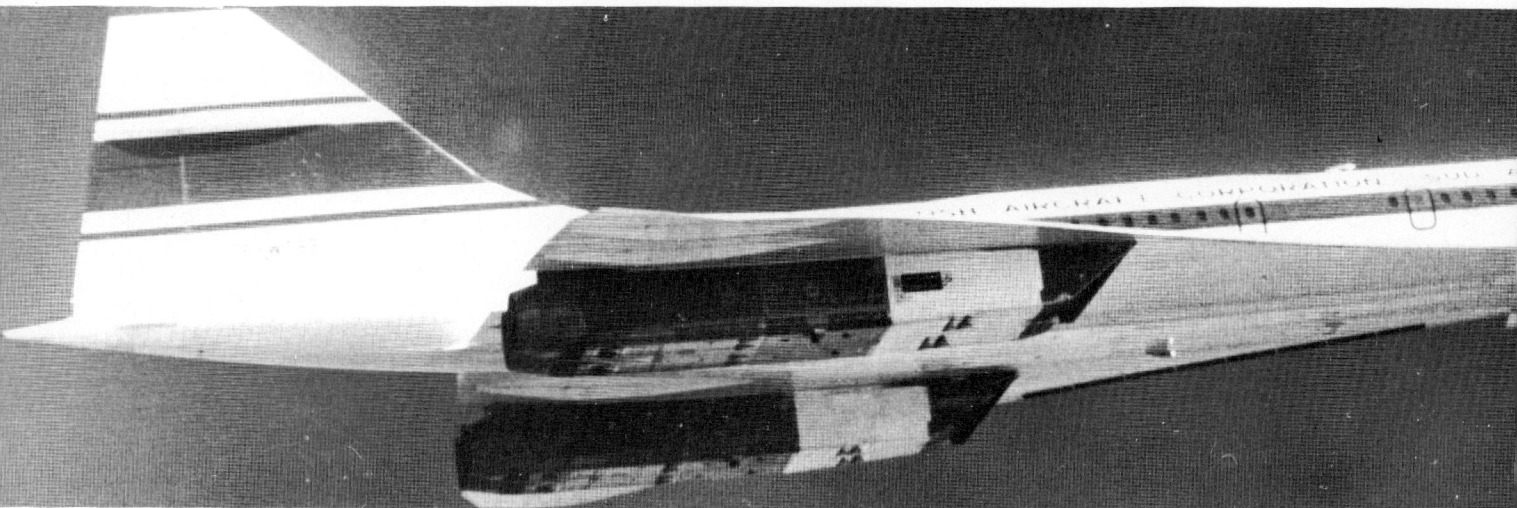

Depicted is first Concorde to fly (2 March 1969). This was assembled by Sud-Aviation at Toulouse. The second was assembled by British Aircraft Corporation at Filton and flew on 9 April 1969

prototype was initially flown at Filton on 9 April 1969. The Concorde, however, was not the first supersonic airliner to fly, this distinction having been gained by the Soviet Tu-144 on 31 December 1968. The Tu-144 bears a very strong resemblance to the Concorde and was designed not by Andrei Tupolev, who was responsible for many of the finest Soviet aircraft, including the record-breaking ANT-25 already described, but by his son Alexei.

The ogival wing plan-form which is the principal aerodynamic feature of the Concorde and the Tu-144 was flight-tested on the BAC 221 research aircraft. This form of wing may be compared with the plain delta as earlier described in the context of the Convair XF-92 A. The ogival wing is based on the discovery that the best shape for optimum cruise performance at Mach 2 is a straight-edged slender delta twice as long as its span, the modifications made to this basic shape resulting from the need to obtain optimum qualities at low speeds, particularly on approach and landing. Structurally, the chief material used in the Concorde is the British RR58 aluminium alloy or its French equivalent AU2GN. Steel and titanium alloys are used only locally. The following details apply to the pre-production aircraft.

TYPE:

Four-jet supersonic transport.

WINGS:

Cantilever low-wing monoplane of ogival slender delta plan-form. Aspect ratio 1·7. Thickness/chord ratio 3% at root, 2·15% from nacelle outboard. Slight anhedral. Continuous camber. Multi-spar torsion box structure. In centre-wing, spars are continuous across fuselage. Three stainless-steel elevons on trailing edge of each wing, each independently operated. Hydraulic artificial feel units protect the aircraft against excessive aerodynamic loads induced by the pilot through over-control. Auto-stabilisation is provided. Leading edges electrically de-iced.

FUSELAGE:

Pressurised aluminium alloy semi-monocoque structure of constant cross-section with unpressurised nose and tail cones. Skin panel/stringer attachments are by spot-welding. Nose can be drooped hydraulically to improve forward view during take-off, initial climb, approach and landing. Retractable visor is raised hydraulically to fair in windscreen for cruising flight.

TAIL UNIT:

Vertical fin and rudder only. Two-section steel rudder controlled in same way as elevons.

LANDING GEAR:

Hydraulically retracted tricycle type. Twin-wheel

On the Concorde prototypes a tail parachute is provided for emergency in-flight use and to augment wheel braking

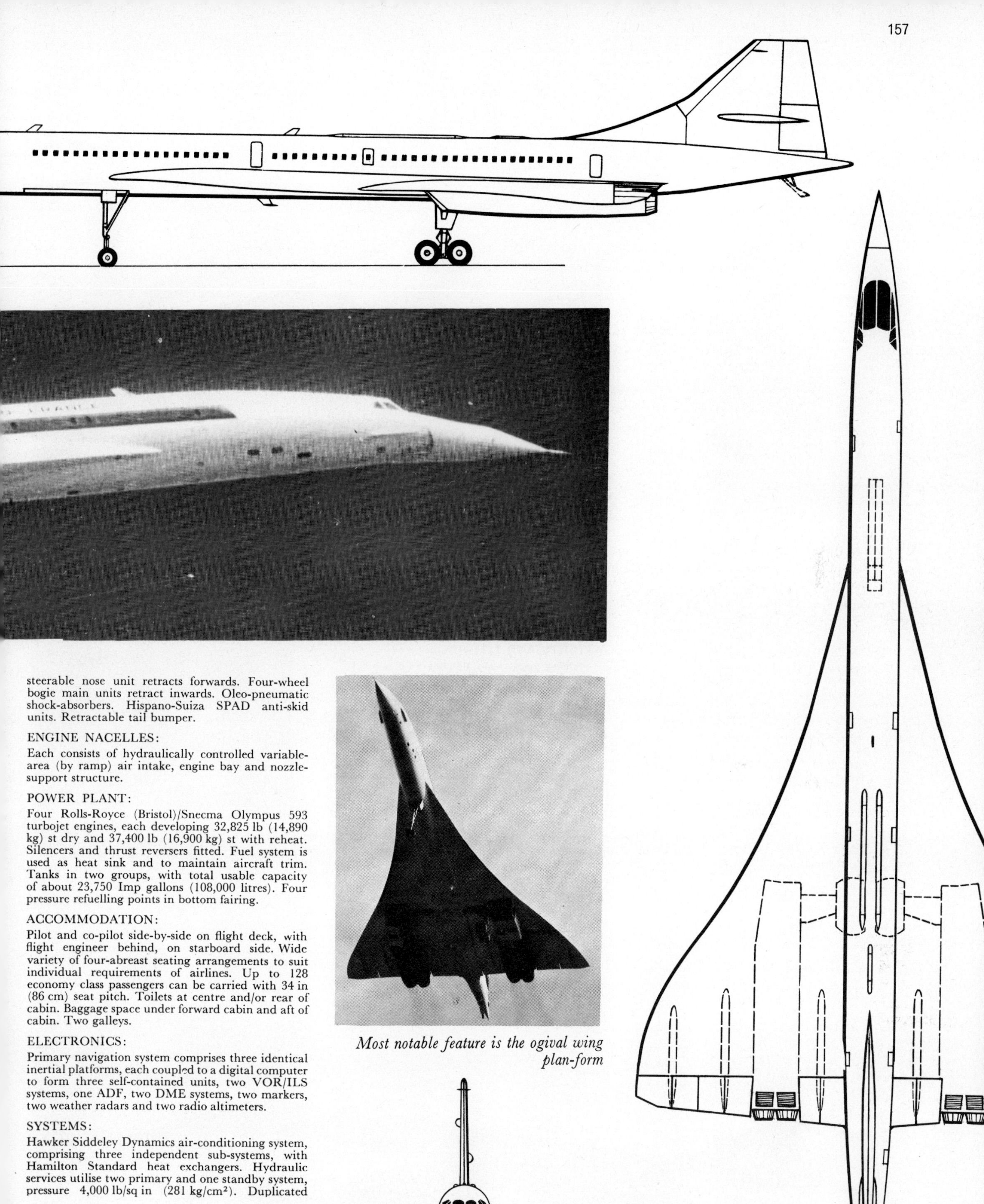

Most notable feature is the ogival wing plan-form

steerable nose unit retracts forwards. Four-wheel bogie main units retract inwards. Oleo-pneumatic shock-absorbers. Hispano-Suiza SPAD anti-skid units. Retractable tail bumper.

ENGINE NACELLES:

Each consists of hydraulically controlled variable-area (by ramp) air intake, engine bay and nozzle-support structure.

POWER PLANT:

Four Rolls-Royce (Bristol)/Snecma Olympus 593 turbojet engines, each developing 32,825 lb (14,890 kg) st dry and 37,400 lb (16,900 kg) st with reheat. Silencers and thrust reversers fitted. Fuel system is used as heat sink and to maintain aircraft trim. Tanks in two groups, with total usable capacity of about 23,750 Imp gallons (108,000 litres). Four pressure refuelling points in bottom fairing.

ACCOMMODATION:

Pilot and co-pilot side-by-side on flight deck, with flight engineer behind, on starboard side. Wide variety of four-abreast seating arrangements to suit individual requirements of airlines. Up to 128 economy class passengers can be carried with 34 in (86 cm) seat pitch. Toilets at centre and/or rear of cabin. Baggage space under forward cabin and aft of cabin. Two galleys.

ELECTRONICS:

Primary navigation system comprises three identical inertial platforms, each coupled to a digital computer to form three self-contained units, two VOR/ILS systems, one ADF, two DME systems, two markers, two weather radars and two radio altimeters.

SYSTEMS:

Hawker Siddeley Dynamics air-conditioning system, comprising three independent sub-systems, with Hamilton Standard heat exchangers. Hydraulic services utilise two primary and one standby system, pressure 4,000 lb/sq in (281 kg/cm²). Duplicated

The nose section is dropped hydraulically to improve forward view during take-off, initial climb, approach and landing. Nose-high attitudes are characteristic of delta wings

electrical systems, powered by four 50RVA brushless alternators. Four transformer-rectifiers and two 25Ah batteries provide 28V DC supply.

DIMENSIONS, external:
Wing span 83 *ft* 11⅞ *in* (25·60 *m*)
Length overall 193 *ft* 0½ *in* (58·84 *m*)
Height overall 38 *ft* 0⅝ *in* (11·60 *m*)
Wheel track 25 *ft* 4 *in* (7·72 *m*)
Wheelbase 59 *ft* 8¼ *in* (18·19 *m*)

DIMENSIONS, internal:
Cabin:
Length, flight deck door to rear pressure bulkhead, including galley and toilets 129 *ft* 0 *in* (39·32 *m*)
Width 8 *ft* 7½ *in* (2·63 *in*)
Height 6 *ft* 5 *in* (1·96 *m*)
Volume 8,500 *cu ft* (240·7 m^3)

AREAS:
Wings, gross 3,856 *sq ft* (358·25 m^2)
Elevons (total) 344·4 *sq ft* (32·00 m^2)

WEIGHTS AND LOADINGS:
Operating weight, empty 169,000 *lb* (76,650 *kg*)
Design payload 28,000 *lb* (12,700 *kg*)
Max T-O weight 385,000 *lb* (175,000 *kg*)
Max landing weight 240,000 *lb* (108,860 *kg*)
Max wing loading approx 95 *lb/sq ft* (465 *kg/m*²)

PERFORMANCE (estimated at max T-O weight):
Max cruising speed at 54,500 *ft* (16,600 *m*)
Mach 2·2 *or* 530 *knots CAS, whichever is the lesser, equivalent to TAS of* 1,450 *mph* (2,333 *kmh*)
Rate of climb at S/L 5,000 *ft* (1,525 *m*) *min*
Service ceiling approx 65,000 *ft* (19,800 *m*)
Range with max payload, FAA reserves: at Mach 0·93 *at* 30,000 *ft* (9,100 *m*) 3,600 *miles* (5,790 *km*)

The Olympus engines introduce reheat and variable-area intakes to civil flying

The Soviet Tu 144 resembles the Concorde in all design essentials. It was shown in model form at the 1965 Paris Show and was first flown on 31 December 1968